TRADING FOR BEGINNERS

4 Books in One:

Day Trading + Forex Trading + Options Trading

The Complete Guide to Start Creating Your Passive Income Step by Step, Using The Best Proven Strategies Out There

Matthew Swing

THIS BOOK INCLUDES:

BOOK 1:
FOREX TRADING INVESTING FOR BEGINNERS

BOOK 2:
OPTIONS TRADING FOR BEGINNERS

BOOK 3:
DAY TRADING FOR BEGINNERS

BOOK 4:
DAY TRADING OPTIONS

FOREX TRADING INVESTING FOR BEGINNERS

TABLE OF CONTENTS

OPTIONS TRADING FOR BEGINNERS

TABLE OF CONTENTS

DAY TRADING FOR BEGINNERS

TABLE OF CONTENTS

DAY TRADING OPTIONS

TABLE OF CONTENTS

FOREX TRADING INVESTING FOR BEGINNERS

Pen Name:

(Matthew Swing)

Introduction

The first thing you need to understand about the Forex market is that it is purely speculative which means that when a Forex transaction is completed, there is nothing that is actually changing hands. Instead, the entire market, such as it is, exists as little more than numbers in a database that are then tallied to determine if your total is in the black or in the red. This is because the Forex market only came into being as a way for major corporations with offices all around the world and other global powers to take care of various expenditures without having to worry about trading currencies in the traditional sense.

Instead, they make their transactions via the forex market and everyone else speculates on how their moves are going to affect the market. In general, about 20 percent of forex transactions are made by these major entities while the rest are all investors who are hoping to make a little profit in the interim. Of this 80 percent, 80 percent are professional traders while the rest are just individuals like you.

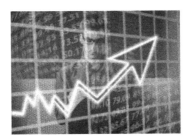

Unlike in other markets, when a forex trader commits to a trade, they are trading a pair of currencies rather than shares of a single asset. As such, due to its very nature every forex transaction involves buying a certain amount of one currency while also selling a certain amount of a second currency. Currencies are typically trade in a few different amounts. First of all, a micro lot is 1,000 units of a currency so $1,000 is a micro lot of dollars. Finally, a standard lot is the name given to 100,000 units of currencies which means that $100,000 is a standard lot of dollars.

Additionally, the smallest amount that a currency can move on the forex market is referred to as a pip. 1 pip equals a single percent of the total amount of the currency. When you are first getting started as a forex trader it is important to start with micro lots as when they move a pip your investment only moves 10 cents. This means that you don't necessarily need to be at the top of your game all the time at first and builds you in some natural resistance to failure. If you purchase a mini lot, then you stand to lose a dollar per every pip of negative moment and with a lot you will lose $10. Remember, currencies can often move 100 pips or more in a single day and never invest more than you can afford to lose.

While it might sound dramatically different than the more commonly seen markets available, the forex market is driven by the same primary forces as the stock market, namely supply and demand. This can be seen every time the world decides that it needs more of one specific type of currency; when this occurs, prices of that currency rise. This will continue up until the point that the market once again becomes oversaturated with that type of currency and the prices starts to move back in the other direction. The best way to keep tabs on this sort of thing Is by reading reports from world powers, rumors of geopolitical strife and the current interest rate.

What further separates it from other types of investment markets is the fact that rather than reopen and close every single day, is the fact that the forex market is only ever closed from Friday night until Monday morning. While this means the market as a whole never sleeps, it doesn't mean that all of the types of currencies are traded at a single time, rather, the market is broken up into three chunks, the United States, Europe and Asia. While there is some overlap at the edges, a majority of the trading during those hours is going to be focused around pairs of currency that feature one of the currency pairs of the region in question.

As an example, if you were interested in trading the US dollar then you would want to ensure you were available to do so during the American part of the day.

While there are numerous different currency pairs from all around the world, there are just 18 that are considered by most to be of the greatest importance. While this doesn't mean that you should try and trade all of the pairs at once, it does mean that you will need to be aware of them and what they are doing so you have a better forecast of the market as a whole. Even better, the 18 pairs are all from just 8 countries. While this doesn't make successful forex trading any easier, it will make it easier when it comes to knowing where to put your focus.

CHAPTER 1:

Technical And Fundamental Analysis

Fundamental Analysis

Fundamental analysis is a financial market analysis method to know the price movements and predict the future outcome of the prices of the asset in the market. Fundamental analysis in forex trading has its focus centered overly on the economy.

The analysis also researches on a variety of factors that affect the forex trade as well as how the elements affect the national currency value. Various factors influence the economy, and these include interest rates, employment, unemployment, GDP, international trade, and manufacturing industries.

In fundamental forex analysis, the price of the may differ from the value of the same asset in the market. Prices may vary because of various factors, and because of the difference in the price and the value of the asset, different markets underprice or overprice the demands for a short period. However, the fundamental analysists believe that despite the value of the assets being underpriced, mispriced, or overpriced in the short period, and it always goes back to its original correct price after some time. The main objective of any fundamental forex analyst is to get the right price and value of the asset, compare the two, and finally come up with an opportunity to trade.

Fundamental analysis is very different from technical analysis. Fundamental analysis does not pay a lot of attention to the current price like the technical analysis. The fact is that fundamental analysis is not an excellent analysis tool for intraday traders in forex trading. Forex fundamental analysis has many different theories that try to explain it and make it a suitable analysis tool for forex trading. The most common approach is economic theory. This theory attempts to explain that the price conditions should be exchanged when they are adjusted. It summarizes that this exchange should be done according to the local economic factors.

Major Economic Indicators

The economic data in the market shows the movement of the economy of different countries. A trader who wants to invest should be very keen on commercial change. The major economic indicators show the price movements, comparing it to their values giving the traders opportunities of finding new trading chances to invest and profit.

Inflation

Inflation is the balance between the circulation of money in economic growth and distribution. Each country or market has a set level of which the rise can reach. There is a healthy inflation level and unhealthy inflation level. When inflation is high in any economy, supply and demand are disturbed. Supply gets an advantage because there is more than what is demanded. This high inflation affects the currency negatively. The currency drops. Oppositely, when inflation is low-deflation, there is more demand than supply. During this deflation period, money value rises, and the cost of goods go down in the market. It is a strategy that most economies employ but on a short-term basis. If deflation strategy is used long term, it will have adverse effects on the economy. The responsible party will get a hard time stabilizing their economy again.

Gross Domestic Product (GDP)

Gross Domestic Product of a country is the sum of all the monetary value of all goods and services of a given country within a specific time frame. This monetary value of the goods and services must be produced within the borders of that same country. A country's Gross Domestic

Product is calculated annually, although there is a possibility of calculating it quarterly depending on the countries policy concerning the GDP calculation.

Gross Domestic Product is the best economic indicator among other economic indicators. Most people think GDP can never be an indicator because it only measures the market value of the goods and services, but they are wrong. From forex fundamental analysis view, when there is an increase in a gross domestic product without an increase in the demand of the products, this constitutes to a weak economy.

Interest Rates

There are different types of interest rates, but the main focus of fundamental forex analysis falls on the nominal and the base interest rates. The central banks of different states set these interest rates. The central bank has to lend money to private banks after creating money. Therefore, the interest amount paid by the private banks on the loans they have acquired from the central bank is called the nominal interest. The nominal interest rate is also known as the base interest rate.

Advantages of Fundamental Analysis

Show the trend of the market price.

Can be an excellent and reliable indicator, especially when it is combined with the technical analysis. It can work out for long term trades.

Technical Analysis of Forex Trading

When price patterns change from one to another, causing a change of prices in the market, these patterns have a specific way of doing so. When changes in price patterns in markets are studied and mastered to help in the prediction of future price patterns, this is now called the technical analysis. Most traders prefer using technical analysis over fundamental analysis. However, some traders use both the analysis techniques. Technical analysts use a different method to analyze the price patterns in markets. The techniques used include:

Chart Patterns

These are patterns where the prices are drawn on charts inform of graphs. When data is drawn on the graph, there is always a repetitive pattern. This pattern shows the movement of the prices in the forex markets. It shows the strength and the weakness of the trade. Some forex traders use the chart patterns as continuation signals or the reversal signals. The technical analysts using this chart patterns use horizontal lines, trend lines, and the Fibonacci retracement level to find the signals of the chart patterns. The chart patterns show the strengths and weaknesses of the forex market.

Horizontal Lines

These lines are also called sideways trends. These lines connect the lows and the highs in the variables. In this case the prices on the charts. These lines show the price that is below the support level and above the resistance level.

Trend lines

Trend lines are lines drawn on the chart or the graph to show support or resistance. These trend lines are dependent on the direction in which the prices are going in the forex trade. They are also known as horizontal support and resistance. When analysts are using trend lines in the chart patterns, they can see the increase or decrease in supply and demand.

The traders make up their mind whether to invest or not when this increase or decrease occur. When the prices are going up, it is called an upward trend, and the forex traders can sell. When the prices are going down, it is called a downward trend, and buyers can make their entry in the trade.

Fibonacci Levels

These levels in chart patterns exhume the hidden support and resistance. The support and resistance can be hidden due to the golden ratios. The origin pf Fibonacci is from the mathematical proportion, but it acts like the old support and resistance in the chart patterns when the price levels are laid out.

Candlestick Patterns

Forex technical analysts use to find the open, high, and low-price levels in the markets (OHL). The prices sought must be of a specific period in the trading session so that a comparison of the trader's behavior during the trade is made against the prices at that particular time. This analysis will help in predicting the future price movement in the forex trade market.

Technical Analysis Indicators

The technical forex analysts use the price action indicator. These indicators include;

The moving average

The moving average indicator shows the averages of prices in a given period. The moving averages display the direction of the market. The moving average helps balance the prices in the market by removing the unwanted prices. This removal helps the trader focus on the trend of the prices in the market. There are four types of the moving averages, namely the exponential moving averages (EMA), simple moving averages (SMA), linear weighted average (LWA), and the smoothed averages.

Bollinger Bands

This indicator is a tool used in technical analysis that comprises of three lines. These lines are plotted positively and negatively but away from the simple moving average of the currency price. These lines are adjustable to the trader's preference. The Bollinger bands help measure the variation degree of prices during the trade. In simpler terms, it measures the volatility of the market in a given period.   The Moving Average Convergence Divergence (MACD)

This price indicator shows the momentum of the market. It shows when the market is doing well or not and the force behind this action. While using this indicator, a signal will always be evident is a market is moving in one direction. The Moving Average Convergence Divergence indicator belongs to a class of oscillators. Oscillators are technical indicators too and shown separately, below the prices in the charts.

Technical analysis has principles that should be followed

Principle of Technical analysis

Price Moves according to trends

Technical analyses assume that the prices in the trend move according to the trend patterns. The prices move in a bullish trend, bearish trend, and the sideways trend.

All price movements repeat themselves

The theory in this principle called the Dow Theory assumes that the price of a commodity represents its actual value, and it does not have to look at other factors. The principle claims that the prices in the patterns are repetitive and any future price is likely to be the same as the current price.

Advantages of Technical Analysis

Shows the Trend of the Market

Technical analysis shows the traders direction of the market. They can know the time the downward movement of prices and the upward movement, hence enabling them to make to sell or buy at the appropriate time.

Shows the trader Both Entry and Exit points

Timing is essential to a person trading in the forex. Poor timing will cause significant losses, and which will cause the trade to fail. The technical analysis predicts the time for investment for traders. It gives traders the upper hand to know when entering the trade or exit that trade.

Different indicators in technical analysis aids traders get the advantage of knowing investment time early. The candlesticks, moving averages, chart patterns, trend lines, and other indicators help in the calculation of the entry and the exit time in the trade.

Technical Analysis is fast

Technical analysis is fast in giving information about a specific trade. This action makes it quick and reliable to short term traders like the intraday traders who trade in one minute to thirty minutes. In this trade, candlestick patterns are used.

Technical Analysis Gives Adequate Information

Short term traders use technical analysis, swing traders, and long-term traders. Enough information is found in the chart patterns, and forex traders can use this information to their advantage. The traders can pursue their trades utilizing this information and get satisfying returns. More details like the trading psychology, market momentum, volatility, support, and resistance are a portion of the vital information that the technical analysis provides.

Technical Analysis is Cheap

Technical analysis of software's is cheap. Some software's are free offers from different charting software companies, and they can even be downloaded on mobile apps.

CHAPTER 2:

Forex Trading Strategies

When you are trading a financial asset, you are going to have some wins, and you are going to have some losses. When you are a beginner, you might have more losses than wins if you don't put any time in to study how the markets work. Many beginners simply trade on the fly, going with their gut feelings. This is not a productive way to go about trading, and it can end up wiping out your account. When this happens, many traders simply give up and stop trading.

The goal of a trading strategy is to use proven methods to help you get more wins than losses. This can be combined with your knowledge of candlestick charts and what the indicators are telling you. It can also be combined with fundamental analysis. This is a term most frequently used in the stock markets, where fundamental analysis means studying the fundamentals of the company.

In the case of Forex markets, fundamental analysis is probably going to mean examining macro-economic factors. You are going to be checking how healthy a given economy is. You'll look at the GDP growth rates, the trends, and job creation numbers, for example. You are also going to want to look at the central bank policy, and what the current interest rates are. Trade and other factors are going to be important. Fundamental analysis will give you an overall idea of how strong a currency is relative to other currencies. However, fundamental analysis isn't really a strategy; it's more like another tool. So you can put it in the same category as candlesticks and indicators.

There are many different trading strategies. One of the things that you will need to consider before trading is the time frame over which you want to operate. Many traders want to trade over very short time frames, taking smaller profits over short-term and usually smaller price moves. Others prefer to go long term, holding positions for days or even weeks (beware of interest rate risk).

There is no right or wrong answer to this question. So you have to try it, and possibly research it to determine what the best time frames are for you to use. This is a matter of personal style, and it's possible to make profits using any time frame. Some people find a longer time frame to be something that can generate a large amount of anxiety.

Day trading or holding a position for a few hours is not something that appeals to everyone either. If you are following a short-term trading strategy, one of the consequences of this is that you must pay close attention to the markets. You will have to be constantly checking to see how your investment is performing and look to the right time to exit the trade. And you will have to exit your trades very quickly. This can put a lot of stress on people, some are well-suited for it, but others may not be. In addition, it simply requires a commitment of time. Some people simply don't have the time to stare at their computer screens for hours on end. Of course, one advantage of the Forex market is that it runs 24 hours a day. This has major practical implications, and if you are too busy in the daytime because of a commitment to a job, you can do short-term trading strategies in the evening.

With that in mind, let's consider some of the main trading strategies that are used in the Forex markets.

Swing Trading

Swing trading is a simple idea to describe. If you are a swing trader, you will buy positions at the bottom of a downtrend. Then you will sell positions at the top of an uptrend. Of course, the trick is actually recognizing when the bottom of a downtrend or top of an uptrend actually occurs. This will require a solid knowledge of charting. You will watch a downtrend, and during this process be looking out for signals indicating a coming price reversal. When you see the signals, then you buy the currency pair.

Note that if you are talking about a currency pair A/B, you might have "sold" the currency pair in a bet on currency B rising against currency A. That means that in this case when you buy, you are actually exiting or closing your position.

But if you are betting on currency A, this is the point at which you enter the position.

Then you will ride the trend as long as you can. You can have an automatic order placed to exit when the price rises to a pre-determined level, or you can watch the charts for signals of a new trend reversal, that would take the currency pair A/B into a trend that is heading back down. If you would prefer trading over a longer time period, swing trading is a trading style or strategy that might be to your liking. The idea behind swing trading is relatively simple. You look for price swings that take place over the course of days or weeks. Many Forex traders tend to be impatient, and if that is you, then you might not be suited for swing trading. As a swing trader, you are going to be required to hold your positions at least overnight. Some swing trades may involve holding a position for several weeks. In some ways, swing trading is a more relaxed style of trading. You aren't sitting in front of your computer screen sweating bullets, waiting for the exact moment to exit the trade and take your profits. Instead, you might be checking the position only periodically. However, swing trading cuts both ways. The Forex markets are highly volatile, and so this means that there are going to be a lot of short-term ups and downs. It requires a great deal of fortitude to wait these short-term price movements out. Some people actually find swing trading to be more stressful. For example, you might have bought the currency pair A/B, and so you are betting on A rising against B over a longer time frame. But you might see the price of the A/B pair drop considerably on its way to the higher price point. This is something that is important to be aware of because some people simply don't have the willpower to stick out a trade, when it appears to be going badly. But keep in mind that prices fluctuate all the time on Forex. It's unlikely that a price decline is going to be something that can be said to be a permanent thing. For the swing trader, it's a matter of simply waiting it out.

Intraday Trading

Intraday trading is another day trading style, but it's more relaxed than scalping. So you are looking to enter and exit a position on the same trading day. However, rather than getting out of the position quickly, you're going to be doing fewer trades and looking for a larger amount of profit per trade. This will give you some flexibility to trade with smaller lot sizes, but you will probably have to trade multiple lots at a time. While a scalper is probably going to do 10 or 20 trades per day, you're going to be looking for larger profits in the 3-10 trade per day range.

Position Trading

If you are a position trader, you are willing to hold a position for a very long time (in Forex terms). That means you will hold the position at least for weeks, and you are willing to hold it for months, or even more than a year. Think of position trading as longer-term swing trading. The techniques are going to be about the same, but you are willing to wait long term in order to take the kind of profits that you are looking for. Position traders are not people who frequently trade, and they may spend a long time on the sidelines waiting for the right time to enter a position.

News Traders

Items in the news, including political, economic, and trade news, can have a big impact on currency prices. The impact is probably not going to be very long-lived in most cases, but while it's working, it can cause big price moves. These days with the 24-hour news cycle, there are always new controversies coming up that are going to increase volatility and send the markets going one way or another. A news trader seeks to follow the news and enter trades when this happens, and then ride the wave of the trend that gets created from the result. For example, the president may remark (or issue a tweet) that would cause the U.S. dollar to either rise in value or fall by a large amount. As soon as the tweet was issued, the news trader would enter positions that they think are going to move a large amount as a result of the remark. So if the remark were one that would probably lead to a rise in the dollar against the Euro, the news trader would sell Euro/USD currency pairs. Then they would use the techniques of chart analysis to look for a reversal after the trend takes on momentum, and exit the trade when the trend shows signs of beginning to reverse.

Trend trading

Many traders simply trade with the trend, when a long-term trend one way or the other can be identified. This is also a technique that can be used in conjunction with swing trading or position trading. The trick is accurately identifying trends that appear to be set up for a long ride upward or downward. This is called trading with the trend, or some traders say the trend is your friend. If you are trend trading, you have the luxury of being able to trade less liquid currency pairs, provided that the trend is stable.

Of course, no trend is going to be stable forever, but it should be stable enough, so that you can ride the trend for a long period to earn profits and then remain in the trend for a time, when you try and exit the position. If you are looking at currency pairs that are not as liquid, getting out of the position is not going to be as easy, but you should be able to do it while still making good profits. Trend trading works with any lot size, and you can do fewer numbers of trades and seek larger profits per trade.

End of Day Trading

If you are an end of day trader, you are taking a more relaxed approach to trading, looking at the markets at the end of your day, and doing your technical analysis to enter or exit trades. This type of trading can be used within the context of other trading styles like swing trading and position trading, but of course, it's not going to be used with scalping or intraday trading. People who will retain a full-time commitment and don't have time to follow the markets all day long may use end of day trading. End of day is a figurative phrase, since Forex markets are open 24 hours, so it's a time of day that you pick in order to do your trades. You can do your analysis at this time, and determine which trades to enter or exit. The low-key aspect of this trading style makes it suitable for all lot sizes, and it does require some patience. You will have more flexibility and be able to wait for the size of profits you are hoping to take, and so you don't necessarily have to enter a large number of trades.

CHAPTER 3:

Currencies Explained

The Major Currency Pairs

The U.S. Dollar is involved in some 89% of currency trades, and currency pairs that included the U.S. Dollar and some other currency from a large, developed economy are called the majors. There are seven major currency pairs. Let's take a look at each one so that you will be familiar with what people are talking about when they mention the majors. A significant currency pair can be any of the following.

EUR/USD

The Euro and U.S. Dollar currency pair is the most popular and widely traded of the majors. The Euro was introduced in 1999, and it's a relatively stable currency that represents all the major countries in Europe that are part of the European Union. Although Brexit is dominating recent headlines, even with Britain as a part of the European Union, it has maintained its currency, the Great British Pound. Hence, the Euro is the currency used by members of the EU on the continent.

When it comes to this currency pair, you are going to want to watch moves by the European Central Bank or ECB, and also the U.S. Federal Reserve. Of course, in any of the majors, you are going to be looking at moves by the U.S. Federal Reserve.

The biggest strength of this currency pair from the perspective of a small retail trader is that it is a highly liquid financial asset that often has substantial volatility. In recent years, the volatility and the magnitude of moves (on average) have decreased somewhat, but it's still a rather strong average pip movement of 200 pips. The currency pair is so liquid, getting in and out of trades fast is not going to be an issue. This currency pair is undoubtedly the right choice for beginners or a trader of any level.

USD/JPY

This is the U.S. Dollar and Japanese Yen currency pair. Japan isn't quite the monolith that it was in the 1980s when everyone thought that Japan would take over the entire world economically. However, Japan still maintains a large and powerful economy dominated by well-known companies like Toyota, Subaru, and Sony, among others. One factor that is important when considering this currency pair is the fact that Japan remains one of the world's largest exporting nations. This means that it's a frequently traded and highly liquid currency because all that exporting means that people have to convert dollars into Yens and vice versa all the time. The interest rate is low, which also makes this currency pair more attractive for holding over more extended periods.

GBP/USD

As we mentioned above, despite being a long-time member of the European Union, Great Britain held onto its currency rather than adopt the Euro in 1999.

Now that Britain may exit the European Union, for good or for worse, this probably means that the Great British Pound is here to stay for the foreseeable future. We noted earlier in the book that this was once (and sometimes still is) referred to as the cable, as currency trading between the United States and Great Britain went on via electronic cable under the Atlantic Ocean starting in the late 19th century. Brexit may introduce a lot of volatility in this currency pair, and, in any currency pair involving GBP, and so traders may want to pay attention to it at least for the near future.

Even after Brexit is finalized, if it ever actually is, then there is likely to be some extra volatility introduced into the price movements of GBP currency pairs. You are not favoring one currency over another because you like it, you are picking currencies based on what works in a given trade.

USD/CHF

CHF is the ticker symbol (to use a stock analogy) for the Swiss Franc. Switzerland is another country maintaining its currency, and given Switzerland's strong banking presence, it's a vital currency despite the relatively small size of the country and its economy. Traders consider the Swiss Franc to be an essential currency during times of economic trouble, or when there is an international crisis. When there are global problems, in most cases, the Swiss Franc can be expected to increase against the U.S. Dollar because the demand for the Franc rises as people look for a relatively safe place to put their money. So, if there is an economic crisis that you happen to experience, remember this and bet on the Swiss Franc against the Dollar. In times of uncertainty, economic downturn, or emergency, the Swiss Franc may also do well against several other currencies such as the Japanese Yen. The USD/CHF pair sometimes goes by the nickname "Swissie."

USD/CAD

Although Canada has a relatively small population compared to the European Union, Japan, and the United States, its economy enjoys outsized importance because it shares a border with the United States, and a large amount of trade goes on between the two countries. Canada has a lot of natural resources that it exports, such as oil, natural gas, and timber, which again helps it to maintain an outsized level of importance in the world of economics and currency trading. Due to its direct relationship with the United States, the USD/CAD currency pair can be a good trade, even though it doesn't play as significant a role in the markets as the EUR/USD currency pair does. When relations between Canada and the United States are good, volatility can decrease for this currency pair. When there are some difficulties, this can lead to increased volatility making it more attractive to trade. Canada has significant exports of coal, raw aluminum, iron ore, gold, and copper ore. So to get a feel for how the movement of the Canadian Dollar may be trending concerning other currencies, you might want to see if the prices of these commodities are rising or falling. Since Canada is exporting these materials, this generally means that rising commodity prices are good for Canadian currency.

AUD/USD

Australia is a diverse and highly modern economy, but like Canada, it's economic fortunes are often influenced very heavily by the export of natural resources. When it comes to Australia, you will want to pay attention to iron ore and rare earth metals, along with coal. When commodity prices are rising, the fortunes of Australia are often rising with it, but when they are declining, the wealth of Australia is probably going down as well.

When you are trading any currency pair involving the Australian Dollar, you will want to look at the prices of various commodities. Still, especially coal and iron ore, to see how they are going. Australia also exports large amounts of gold, petroleum, and wheat. So favorable pricing moves for these commodities may put the Australian Dollar in a position to rise against other currencies.

NZD/USD

The last of the majors is the currency pair between the New Zealand Dollar and the U.S. Dollar. The New Zealand economy isn't as large as the others we've considered, and it's highly dependent on tourism and the export of agricultural products. It is a leading exporter of dairy products as well as lamb and other meats. If dairy prices are rising on commodities markets, this can bode well for any currency pair involving the NZD.

Crosses

If the USD is not in the currency pair, these are called crosses. There are crosses for each of the currencies from major economies, such as the Euro or the Japanese Yen. The majors enjoy the highest trading volume and are therefore the most liquid currency pairs that you can trade, but several crosses also have high trading volume, and so can be useful to trade as well.

First, let's look at some of the Euro crosses.

EUR/JPY: As you might imagine, there is a lot of trade that goes on between these two major economies. As a result, this can be a useful currency pair to trade. When exports are in favor, Japan might have an edge, in particular when electronic components are considered.

EUR/CHF: This is the Euro and Swiss Franc cross pair. The thing to look for here is the overall economic situation and whether there are any international tensions. Generally speaking, if people are looking for a safe refuge for their money, the Swiss Franc is going to be it. So when times are tough, you might look for increased volatility with this currency pair, and you might also look for the Swiss Franc to be rising in value against the Euro.

EUR/GBP: This is undoubtedly a currency pair to watch with the pending Brexit move, no matter how it turns out. If the situation is viewed favorably in terms of the European Union, then the Euro is going to rise in value against the Great British Pound. Shortly, at least, the Great British Pound is probably going to be declining in value against several major currencies, although over time, this will likely stabilize. Once things settle down, the Great British Pound is perhaps going to be rising in value. But for now, look for it to be the weaker member of a currency pair with another major country.

AUD: The Australian Dollar is also an excellent cross to look at when trading with the Japanese Yen, New Zealand Dollar, Euro, Canadian Dollar, and even against the Chinese Yuan. When commodity prices are rising, this is something that is going to favor the Australian Dollar against the currencies of those countries that are importing large amounts of raw materials from Australia. China is a significant consideration here.

Japanese Yen: Any cross pair involving JPY is going to be necessary. The essential data point for Japan is to remember that Japan has few (if any) natural resources. Still, it's going to be importing a large number of commodities since it has a thriving export business of primary manufactured goods like automobiles.

Exotic Currency Pairs

These are currencies that are not traded nearly as much, but many exotic currencies are going to be associated with developing countries. Examples can include countries like Mexico, Thailand, and Brazil. Some currencies that fall in the exotic category have manipulated or fixed exchange rates, making trading them problematic. The biggest weakness with exotic currencies is that they tend to have small trading volumes. Professional Forex traders are generally not spending their time focusing on exotic currency pairs.

Some exotics like the Mexican Peso are more stable than others, such as the Iraqi dinar. But the biggest weakness for any exotic currency is that traders do not highly desire them, and as a result, you might find yourself stuck in trade far longer than you want to be.

CHAPTER 4:

How To Concrete Start With Forex Trading With Practical Example – Step By Step

The first thing to get started besides educating yourself on how to trade is to open a trading or brokerage account. In many ways, this isn't too different from opening a stock trading account, and so it will be somewhat familiar to many readers. Some of the most leading brokerages also allow you to open a Forex trading account.

Step 1: Things to Look for When Selecting an FX Dealer

The first thing that I would consider if I were opening a new account is how experienced the dealer was. I would be less interested in opening an account with a brand-new dealer. The dealer may be legitimate, but you are taking a chance to open an account with someone who does not have a proven history. That was worth the gamble in the early days of Forex trading, but after 20 years, the market is in a more mature phase, and so there isn't any reason to be taking chances.

So, the first thing to consider is the length of time that the dealer has been in business. I would opt for at least five years of history, but you can shop around and find varying amounts of time in business. A longer time frame that the company has been in business means that the company is established and therefore is generally speaking, more trustworthy.

If a long time, the established brokerage has recently entered the Forex arena, that might be an exception. If the company is a well-known and experienced stock brokerage, then you know that this is a well-established and reliable business. They can be trusted to conduct honest trades, they are going to be upfront about their fees, and they are going to be trustworthy handling your financials.

Step 2: How to Open a Forex Trading Account

In some ways, opening a Forex trading account can be a little bit more complicated than opening a stock market account. The main reason is that Forex offers some opportunities for money laundering and other activities. As a result, a legitimate broker is going to be putting a little more effort into verifying your identity. Let's take a look at some of the steps involved in this process. Typically, when you open a stock trading account in your home country, all you have to do is link a bank account and provide some necessary information. When you open an account with an FX dealer, this is going to involve a few extra steps. It might take a little bit of time, but in the end, it will be no big deal. In a nutshell, legitimate FX dealers are required to verify that you are who you say you are and that you are a citizen and so forth. So what are the steps involved in the verification process?

The first is that you have to apply to open a trading account. This is a simple process that is done online. So, it will be familiar to anyone who has used for a credit card or anything else online. You will have to answer some simple questions about your identity, place of residence, and other necessary information. Then you are going to be required to provide documentation that the dealer uses to prove your identity to fight money laundering. You are going to have to prove that you are a citizen of the country, and you will also need to provide some proof of residence. In the United States, sending a copy of your driver's license is probably going to be adequate to verify your citizenship. I live in the United States so cannot give details on proving citizenship in other countries, please check with your local brokerage for more information.

Step 3: When Can You Begin Trading

Once the FX dealer has credited your account, you are ready to begin trading. This is done directly through the dealer's platform and often happens relatively quickly after you have initiated funding. You can trade 24 hours a day on business days. The beginning of the trading week starts in the late afternoon on Sunday, US Eastern time, when the markets in New Zealand open. These are going to be quickly followed by the market in Sydney, Australia, and Singapore, and then a little bit later, you will have Tokyo, Japan, and Hong Kong opening. London will be opening around 2 AM Eastern US time. You will be able to trade until the markets in New York close on Fridays, ending the trading week. So you have six days a week, 24 hours a day on most days to trade. This means that it's always active, and you can trade at hours that are the most convenient for your purposes.

Step 4: Some Well-Known FX dealers

In this section, we will take a look at a few of the well-known FX dealers that operate inside the United States. Some of them are also stock brokerages. I have to be honest that while there are many good options, I tend to favor the stock brokerages because these are dependable companies that have been around for a long time. Also, if you are also trading stocks or options, it can save you a little bit of hassle, since you can have one brokerage to handle everything that you are doing. That said, some people like to keep their Forex activities separate from other trading activities. The way you set this up is entirely personal, and so there are no rules to follow, other than selecting a well-respected and legitimate dealer.

Forex dealers are regulated in the United States. This is done by the National Futures Association, and also by the Commodity Futures Trading Commission. The regulation of these dealers helps to ensure that there are some protections in place for individual traders. Not to pick on the Bahamas, and I am sure many legitimate companies are operating in the Bahamas. Still, when you put your money in an overseas outfit that is not as tightly regulated, you put yourself at risk for being victimized, loss of capital, and lack of the kinds of protections that you get in the United States.

Step 5: Spreads

We will discuss spreads, but this is the way that brokerage dealers charge commissions on Forex. So when looking for a reputable dealer, you are also going to be wanting to take a look at the spreads they charge and compare them in between your options.

No matter what happens, as long as you have selected the right brokerage, this should not be too much of an issue.

CHAPTER 5:

How To Trade Without Emotions

With a correct attitude towards forex trading, you can be sure to achieve your goals. Here are a few suggestions that can help you develop the proper manner and mindset for forex trading and trading in general.

Be Patient

This is a virtue when it comes to forex trading, as it helps one cover everything at the right time and with the right state of mind. Patience can get you out of trouble as sometimes you might be forced to enter into a market hastily without understanding how it works. For beginners, Patience is a crucial aspect as you get to understand the pros and cons of forex trading. Patience also keeps you away from reacting out of a bad day in business and even making wrong choices and decisions that can cause significant losses. As the adage goes, Patience pays, so take your time off a hectic day and trust the process.

Be Objective

In forex trading, one is required to be objective and not trade with emotions. As stated earlier, a forex trader should keep the eyes on the final product, that is, his financial goals. Being subjective or acting on emotions is disastrous for any business, and learning to work by the book is key to a successful forex trading career. This means that you should not also listen to people who claim to be Pros in the game and trust your trading patterns instead of sheepishly following the crowd.

This doesn't, however, mean that you should not trade on mass thinking, but if you do, always keep in mind that the masses are not still right.

Be Disciplined

This ought to be a significant aspect in every business, and as earlier pointed out, discipline keeps one out of overreacting for a loss or a win. This cuts across happy and sad moments in business as both sides can affect the outcome if not subjected to some discipline. Being able to control yourself, to not overtrade or under trade, and take just enough risks is a skill that can be learned by following procedures and sticking to the game-plan. Remember, you should never, ever, stake half your capital, risk all your profits or worse, trade with money you don't have or money you can't afford to lose.

Be Realistic

Just like any other business, one should be real and expect a particular profit according to the capital traded-in. Always remember that forex trading is not like Lotto or betting where one can win a jackpot of a million dollars by staking just a little money. It takes time to build up your skills, your knowledge, and your confidence and secure good profits with forex trading. Therefore, one should expect the right amount of returns on investment and what comes with it. By not giving up, being disciplined and patient, and doing your research, you might end up achieving your goals and reaching top-level in the forex world. This mentality helps one to limit the number and types of transactions on a daily or weekly basis and to stay in the game even after losing a small percentage of the initial investment. This is a business opportunity, just like any other.

There are rules to abide by to reach your potential and, most importantly, realize your potential in terms of profit. Below are 12 rules that can help you achieve your goals in Forex Trading.

1 Trust the Process

Forex trading is a business and needs time and effort to grow and consolidate, which means that there is more than just waiting for profits. Profit oriented businesses can end if the thresholds one has set are not met, and the overall approach is not thoroughly planned. Any business is not only buying and selling as it involves huddles and logistics to make the whole institution work and doable. Some profit-oriented forex traders tend to give up easily if they don't meet their target after a few operations or a short period. However, one can set a timeline and work towards meeting the set target without having to achieve a specific point, which might turn to be the opposite. some points are process-oriented and help in reaching the high note in forex trading and are outlined.

2 Outline Daily Activities

Day to day activities can only be achieved when put down on paper for a specific task in forex trading. Having in mind the right thing to do on a specific day is good as it helps to avoid distractions and other things that may get in the way on a business day. This means that the more you know what you are doing on a busy day, you will not waste time doing other things that do not help achieve your goal and the needs you want to build your forex trading skills.

3 Analyze the Market

As pointed out earlier, trading with emotions is bad for business as it does not go by the plans and strategy, but with the reaction of business gone wrong or even a big win. Being greedy is so bad in forex trading, and it is advisable to analyze the market first before trying out forex trading and giving a shot on the most promising patterns. When you play by the rules, you train the mind to follow the right procedures and even helps in becoming more discipline in forex trading. Training the mind helps in a vulnerable situation, which will make you hold on when there is a crisis.

4 Be Defensive

This is another important rule to follow in forex trading, for it is the core purpose of joining the business and what will keep you survive storms that will come your way in one way or the other. This simply means that you should not trade everything, including your capital, defend your initial capital, and aim at making profits. When you make a target and do not meet it, then at least you tried, but trading profusely just to meet the target with limited time is not good at all, as it is an offensive approach. You should always protect your capital as it is the only thing keeping you in the business, and one mistake can send you to factory reset, i.e., going back to the drawing board wondering when the rain started beating you.

5 Have A Trading Plan

Just like any other venture, Forex trading needs a business plan that has been tested to be working and giving impressive results. The plan involves things that you need to do from A-Z; this may include the rules of engagement, trading pattern, market analysis, and other key aspects that make the business run well. After making the trading plan, you can test it virtually to see if it will go well with the market and if it is good, then give it the green light and start the forex trading. But make sure that you outline the plan as it is the backbone of the whole venture.

6 Know That Trading Is A Business

Forex trading is like a business and should be treated as such for one to get the best out of it by giving the attention it deserves. Other researches have talked about not comparing trading with job opportunities or hobby to be done in leisure time. This means that one should not expect a salary and works on getting profits and paying attention and not only focusing on it when you are free. With this, a forex trader will learn to prioritize forex trading just like any other business.

7 Outline Risk

Make sure that you point out the risk you intend to get yourself into and do not give it too much until you are out of business. Do not risk an amount that you cannot afford; risking is only for the amount you are capable of and not anywhere near initial capital. Remember, as said earlier, if you lose capital, that means that you are out of business, and you will not want that to happen to you. Only risk an amount that you know if they go, then you will not struggle with bringing back the business into living.

8 Use Technology

The modern era of inventions and innovations can be a plus in forex trading as it helps improve the outcome of a venture. Technology has played a big role in forex trading, thanks to innovators who come with new things every day to enhance the world in bringing people closer. With technology, one can trade anywhere in the world monitor charts using a computer or even mobile phones. This means that one can travel all over the world as well as working at the same time. This has been evident for bloggers and travel entrepreneurs who blog for a living and promote products online while they travel. This can be the same for forex traders, and it helps in even having a good time and relaxing the mind while working.

9 Have A Stop Loss

This is somehow similar to outlining risk but specifies the amount that one should be willing to lose in particular trading.

In Forex trading, you should only lose what you afford, and it is essential to outline the amount or percentage that one should only lose in trading. This also acts as a disciplined mode as it helps in controlling the mind and emotions not to surpass the limited amount of possible risk.

10 Focus on The Bigger Picture

What is the purpose of starting forex trading? Can you do the business to be aligned in that direction? Are you getting some profits and losing sometimes? then you are on the right track heading to greatness in forex trading.

Business is not about just making profits but making impacts on a personal level and getting more skills. So what is your bigger picture? To have gained at least 10 percent in the financial year 2020-2021? Having this in mind, then you can be sure of aiming in the right way as compared to only focusing on maximizing profits.

11 Keep Learning Markets

Forex trading is an ongoing process even after mastering markets and getting out of an amateur venture. One does not stop learning at anything, and things keep changing in the forex world; this is important to keep an open mind in everything to do with business. Some of the skilled forex traders can fall prey to crowd psychology, and some markets are unpredictable, making forex trading a learning experience every time one is trading.

12 Be A Progressive Trader

Every forex trader wants to earn profit as it is the main reason for venturing in forex trading in the first place, but are you only profit-oriented the first day in the market, or are you moving forward? Learning also can be huge progress as it helps one avoid making similar mistakes and open ways for more profit in the future. A progressive trade is the one that celebrates every win, either small or big, as long as it is a victory. Just like a child, you learn to sit then start crawling and in no time you start taking a few steps and eventually running. The same applies to forex trading, you gradually move from one stage to the other, and you cannot jump directly to only making profits. You either win or learn. After making a trading plan and testing it, one can join the trading business and encounter ups and downs as it shapes the ultimate goal of forex trading. With this progress, one can be sure of securing a future in forex trading full of experiences and lots of encounters that can prepare you for any hard hurdles that one might come across during your trading experience.

CHAPTER 6:

How To "Win" Forex Market and Create Passive Income – Step By Step Guide

Making Passive Income in The Forex Market

We do two things in the forex market; we either peddle or acquiring currencies. It is easy to place trades in the market and works similarly to that of the stock market. Anyone with experience in the stock market can perform trade actions in the forex.

Understanding Forex Quotes

When buying a particular currency, the exchange rate tells you the amount to compensate in terms of the quote currency to purchase an entity of the base currency. For instance, in our illustration, you have to wage 1.51258 for you to buy a single British pound

However, if you were to sell, you will get 1.51258 U.S. dollars for each 1 British pound you sell. The basis for buying or selling is the "base currency." You should not forget this because, without this understanding, your knowledge of forex will be distorted. This means that if you want to buy GBP/USD, it implies you are purchasing the base currency while trading the quote currency simultaneously. In a nonprofessional language, you buy GBP while selling USD.

If you anticipate the base currency to acknowledge proportionate to the quote currency, then you have to buy the currency. However, if you expect depreciation in the base currency, then the best option is to sell.

Determining to Buy Or Sell

Before going further, you have to establish to buy or sell a particular currency. Remember, buying and selling are not the same. A simple way to differentiate them is as follows:

Buying factors, you are acquiring the base currency while trading the quote currency. This connotes that you want a rise in the value of the base currency and peddle it back at a higher price. In forex, we use terminology such as taking a "long position" or "going long. To make it easier long is equivalent to buy

Bid and Ask Price

Now you know the difference between buying and selling the base currency in forex, it is essential to talk about the bid and ask price. Do not be confused when you see currency pairs quoted at two different rates. This indicates the proposal and asks the price, and in a better situation, the bid price is always lower in comparison to the asking price.

The bid price is the price your intermediary decides to purchase the base currency against the quote currency. It is the best price convenient at that time at which the trader is inclined to sell. Alternatively, the asking price is that a broker is willing to sell the base currency in exchange for the quote currency.

Time to Make Money

I know you are fired up to understand how to make money in the market. Well, in the examples below, I will teach you how you can use essential analysis to select to either buy or sell a particular currency pair. If you did economics while in school, then this section will be attractive to you. Notwithstanding, just act like you know everything I am going to talk about. Even if you do not understand, do not worry because the light is at the end of the tunnel, and you will surely reach there.

EUR/USD Pair

By now, I am convinced you now know the base and quote currency. Well, the euro is our base currency in this example and the basis for which we buy/sell. This is how traders make a profit – when they anticipate that the U.S. economy will fall, which is terrible news for the dollars; they will trigger a buy option of the EUR/USD pair. By doing so, the trader has purchased the euros in anticipation that it will rise against the U.S. dollar.

Alternatively, if the trader believes the U.S. economy will is strong. In contrast, the euro will fall adjacent to the dollar, and he will trigger the sell option, which allows him to sell the euros in anticipation that the price will fall.

USD/JPY

Always remember, the base currency is on the left while the quote currency is on the right-hand side. Our base currency, in this example, is the U.S. dollar and is the basis for our buy/sell. You will execute a buy option if you think the Japanese government will weaken its currency to boost its export industry. By this option, you have purchased the U.S. dollar in anticipation that the dollar will rise against the Yen.

However, if your hunch tells you that Japanese investors will pull their money from the U.S. financial market and exchange their dollars to yen, this will affect the U.S. dollar, and the best option is to execute the sell order. In this situation, you have sold the dollar while anticipating that it will depreciate when compared with the Japanese yen.

USD/CHF

This will be the last example of this session. The base currency is the U.S. dollar. If, as a trader, you consider the CHF overvalued, then you can trigger the buy order. In doing so, you have anticipated that the dollar will inflate over the Swiss Franc.

However, if you consider the opposite, then you could execute the sell order. This means you anticipate a depreciation in the value of the U.S. dollar over the Swiss Franc.

Pips and Pipettes

A pip is the unit of measurement to represent a change in terms of value that exists between two different currencies. Let us assume the following pair GBP/USD moves from 1.3250 to 1.3251. In this situation, the currency moves a pip. You will observe that the pip is the last decimal place of a particular pair. It is usually the fourth decimal place of any currency. However, if such a couple contains the Yen, then it is two decimal places.

For example, the pair GBP/USD moves from 1.35421 to 1.35422, and it has driven a single pipette. Because every currency has its unique value, it is essential to evaluate the cost of a pip for each currency.

The examples below we are using quotes that have four decimal places. In the cases below, the USD is the base currency.

USD/CAD at 1.5890

To get the pip value, that will be

Pip value = 0.0001/exchange rate

Therefore, in our example, that will be 0.0001/1.5890, which is equivalent to 0.00006293.

USD/CHF at 1.4898

Pip values = 0.0001/1.4898

=0.00006712

USD/JPY at 118.45

Did you notice anything different? Of course, the quote currency has two decimal points, whereas most currencies have four decimal places.

In this situation, a single pip movement will be .01, which will be divided by the exchange rate to get the value of the pip. Therefore, that will be:

.01/118.45

Pip value =0.0008442

In the examples above, the USD is the base currency. In the following examples, I will explain situations where the USD is not quoted first.

EUR/USD at 1.2120

Pip value = 0.0001 divided by exchange rate

0.0001/1.2120

EUR value = 0.00008250

However, we do not have to stop at the EUR; we have to go back to the U.S. dollar. To do that, it will be EUR x exchange rate.

0.00008250 x 1.2120

Rounding up the value, that will be 0.00001

I believe you understood what we did here because of the following examples; I will do the calculation without any explanation.

AUD/USD at 0.6752

.0001/0.6752

AUD = 0.0001418

To get the USD = 0.0001418*0.6752

=0.0001

Well, you do not have to border yourself with the calculations because your forex broker will help you sort this out. However, it is important to understand how your broker arrives at those figures. You can save yourself the stress if your broker does not do the calculation by using an online pip value calculator.

What is a lot?

We trade spot forex in specific amounts known as lots. We have mini, micro, and Nano lot sizes in the forex. However, the ideal lot size is 100,000 units.

Lot Size	Lot Unit
Nano	100
Micro	1,000
Mini	10,000
Standard	100,000

You have to trade a large amount of a currency pair to see any consequential loss or profit while trading. In the following example, I am using a standard lot size, which is equivalent to a 100,000 unit. The calculation will show how the pip value is affected.

USD/JPY at 118.45 = (0.1/118.45)*100,000 = $8.44 per pip

GBP/USD at 1.7030 = (0.0001/1.7030)*100,000 = $5.87 per pip

EUR/USD at 1.2500 = (0.0001/1.2500)*100000 = $8 per pip

What Is Leverage?

Remember, in the beginning, when I told you how you could use a small amount to trade big. Yes, that is what call leverage in forex. You can consider your forex broker as a bank, who gives you upfront investment funds of $100,000 to trade in the market. All the bank is asking is for you to come up with a thousand dollars. In other words, a deposit of $1,000 gives you $100,000 to trade in the market. Does that sound too correct for such hard times? Well, that is what leverage is when we talk about forex.

Notwithstanding, the total leverage you can on your forex broker. Usually, your broker will request a trade deposit, which is also the "initial margin" or "account margin." Immediately after the deposit, you can start trading currencies.

Market Order in Forex

A market order is simply an order placed by the trader to either sell or buy a currency pair at the best price available. For instance, let us assume that the bid price for USD/CAD presently stood at 1.3450, whereas the asking price is 1.3453. If you intended to buy USD/CAD at the market, then the seller will sell it to you using the asking price of 1.3453. Then you have to execute the buy option to purchase it at that price.

Types of Orders

This is similar to what major eCommerce stores do. You saw a beautiful pair of shoes and checked the price, you are satisfied with it, and you clicked the buy option, which indicates the current amount of the shoe. Notwithstanding, in the foreign exchange market, you either sell or buy currencies pairs. Nevertheless, in the eCommerce stores, you have the option of only buying things.

Limit Entry Order

This particular market order is placed when the buyer wants to sell above or buy below the market at a specific price. Let us assume USD/CAD is currently trading at 1.1290, and your objective is to go short peradventure the price gets to the 1.1300 marks. You are faced with two options. To sit and watch your trade for it to hit your target or you place a sell limit order at the targeted price (1.1300).

I will tell you the disadvantage of the first one; you have to abandon everything you are doing to wait for it to reach your target. Are you going to sit with your monitor for hours? Well, with a sell limit order, you can shut your computer and work on other projects.

Once the price reaches the 1.1300 marks, the trading platform you are using will automatically perform the sell order using the best price available.

When to use this order, type is when you anticipate a price reversal once it got to the price you detailed.

Stop-Entry Order

This order is required when you want to place a trade to buy above or sell below the current market. This is usually at a specific price, which must be indicated in the trading platform. For instance, EUR/USD is currently trading at 1.9080 and is moving in an upward direction. You anticipate the price will go higher in that direction if it gets to the 1.9090 mark. I know you will not want to sit in front of your computer pending when the price reaches the 1.9090 mark. However, with the stop-entry order, the platform will automatically close the trade once it gets to that point.

CHAPTER 7:

Money Mistake to Avoid

Now we'll turn our attention to giving some tips, tricks, and advice on errors to avoid ensuring as much as possible that you have a successful time trading.

Avoid the Get Rich Quick Mentality

Any time that people get involved with trading or investing, the hope is always there that there's a possibility of the big winning trade. It does happen now and then. But quite frankly, it's a rare event. On many occasions, even experienced traders are guessing wrong and taking losses. It's essential to approach Forex for what it is. It's a business. It is not a gambling casino even though a lot of people treated that way, so you need to come to your Forex business—and it is a business no matter if you do it part-time or quit your job and devote your entire life to it— with the utmost seriousness. You wouldn't open a restaurant and recklessly buy 1 thousand pounds of lobster without seeing if customers were coming first. So, why would you approach Forex as if you were playing slots at the casino? Take it seriously and act as if it's a business because it is.

Trade Small

You should always trade small and set small achievable goals for your trading. The first benefit of purchasing small is that this approach will help you avoid a margin call. Second, it will also help you set profit goals that are small and achievable. That will help you stay in business longer.

Simply put, you will start gaining confidence and learning how to trade if you get some trades that make $50 profits, rather than shooting for a couple of deals that would create thousands of dollars in one shot, but and up making you broke. Again, treat your trading like a real business. If you were opening a business, chances are you would start looking for slow and steady improvements, and you certainly would not hope to get rich quick.

Let's get specific. You are trading small means, never trading standard lots. Even if you have enough cash to open an account such that you could trade standard lots, I highly recommend that you stay away from them. A large amount of capital involved and margin that would be used could just get you into a lot of financial trouble.

Be Careful With Leverage

It's incredibly beneficial. It allows you to enter and trades that would otherwise not be possible. On the other hand, the temptation is there to use all your leverage in the hopes of making it big on one or two trades. You need to avoid using up all your advantage. Remember that you can have a margin call and get yourself into big trouble if your trades go wrong. And it's important to remember there's a high probability that some of your trades are going to go wrong no matter how carefully you do all your analysis.

Not Using A Demo Account

A big mistake the beginners make is jumping in too quickly. There is a reason that most broker-dealers provide demos or simulated accounts. If you don't have a clue what that reason is, let's go ahead and stated here. Brokers offer demo accounts because Forex is a high-risk trading activity. It can be something that offers a lot of rewards, and it does for large numbers of traders. But there is a substantial risk of losing your capital. Many beginners are impatient, hoping to make money right away. That's certainly understandable, but you don't want to fall into that trap. Take 30 days to practice with a demo account. This will provide several advantages. Trading on Forex is different than trading on the stock market. Using the demo account, you can become familiar with all the nuances of Forex trading. This includes everything from studying the charts, to placing your orders and, most importantly, understanding both pips and margin. The fact that there is so much leverage available means you need to learn how to use it responsibly.

Failing To Check Multiple Indicators

There is also a temptation to get into trades quickly just on a gut level hunch. You need to avoid this approach at all costs. Some beginners will start learning about candlesticks, and then when they first start trading, they will recognize a pattern on a chart. Later amid the excitement, they will enter a large trade based on what they saw. And then they will end up on the losing end of a trade. Some people are even worse, and they don't also look at the candlesticks. Instead, they just look at the trend and think they better get in on it, and they got all anxious about doing so. That means first checking the candlesticks and then confirming at least with the moving average before entering or exiting a position. You should also have the RSI handy, and you may or may not want to use Bollinger bands.

Use Stop Loss and Take Profit Orders

Well, I hate to repeat myself yet again, but this point is significant. I am emphasizing it over and over because it's one of the tools that you can use to protect yourself from heavy losses. One of the ways that you can get out of having to worry about margin calls and running out of money is to put stop-loss orders every time you trade. This will require studying the charts more carefully. You need to have an obvious idea where you want to get out of the trade if it doesn't go in the direction you hoped. But if you have a stop-loss order in place, then you can avoid the problem of having your account just go down the toilet. Secondly, although the temptation is always there to look for as many profits as possible, in most cases, you should opt to set a take profit order when you make your trade.

Remember Price Changes Are In Pips

Beginners often make the mistake of forgetting about pips. If you have trouble with pips and converting them to actual money, go back and review the examples we provided. Remember that pips play a central role in price changes; you need to know your dollar value per pip to keep tabs on your profit and losses. This is also important for understanding the right stop loss and take profit orders to execute.

Don't Try Too Many Strategies or Trading Styles At Once

When you are a beginning Forex trader, it can be tempting to try everything under the sun. That can be too much for a lot of people. The most advisable thing to do is to stick with one strategy, so don't try scalping and being a position trader at the same time. The shorter the time frame for your trades, the more time and energy you have to put into each trade. Scalping and day trading are activities that would require full-time devotion. They are also high-pressure, and that can help enhance emotions involved in the trades. For that reason, I don't recommend those styles or strategies for beginners. In my opinion, and to be honest, it's mine alone, I think position trading is also too much for a beginner. It requires too much patience.

Perhaps the best strategy to use when you're beginning Forex trading is to become a swing trader. It's an excellent middle ground between the most extremely active trading styles and something that is going to try people's patience, such as position trading. When you do swing trading, you can do periods more extended than a day indeed, but as long or short as you need to meet your goals otherwise.

Market Expectations

Life as a forex trader can sometimes get lonely. After all, this is the kind of career where you are entirely on your own. You enjoy your profits alone, but you also suffer losses on your own. There is no one in the forex market whom you can depend on to comfort you. Therefore, it is also useful if you connect with like-minded people. Feel free to make friends with other traders. After all, you are all players in the market who want the same thing. The good thing is that you are not competing with one another. You can even help one another by sharing information, insights, and strategies.

Have Fun

Forex trading is fun. This is a fact. Many traders get to enjoy this kind of life that they continue to learn despite their losses. It is also not uncommon to find traders, especially beginners, who spend their whole day just learning about forex trading. Like gambling in a casino, trading currencies can also be very addicting, especially if you are making a nice profit from it.

Learn to have fun and enjoy the journey. Sometimes taking things too seriously can ruin the experience and even make you less productive. In your life as a trader, you will make some mistakes from time to time. You would experience losing money from what otherwise would have been a profitable trade if only you knew better. Do not get too stressed. The important thing is for you to learn as much as you can from every mistake. Take it easy, but remember to learn from the experience. Making mistakes is part of the learning process. Of course, you should try to minimize them as much as possible. Learn and have fun.

CHAPTER 8:

Personal Recommendation

Tips For Success

Take advantage of volatility: Over time, the general baseline of the forex market has only grown more volatile. This means that if you want to compete in the forex market successfully, you are going to need to use this fact to your advantage. Generally speaking, there are two types of volatility that you will need to keep an eye out for, implied volatility and historical volatility. Historical fluctuations will help you determine how a specific currency has acted over a set period while implied volatility measures the current level of volatility a currency has at the moment and what it is more likely to look like in the future.

Diversify: While you will want to stick to a few different currency pairs when you are first getting started in the forex market, over time, you are going to want to diversify to find real success. Not only will this make it possible for you to ensure that a single wrong turn won't wipe out your trading capital, but it will also ensure that there is always something to focus on when your favored currency pairs aren't giving you much to work.

Never forget that, regardless of how thorough your research is, you can never trust a specific trade to go your way completely, especially if the market is currently in the midst of a period of high volatility. Spreading your trading capital around will thus provide you with a way to somewhat standardize profits, even in the middle of the unexpected. If trading in the forex market were gambling, then diversifying your holdings would be hedging your bets.

In this instance, a significant player is any entity that is massive enough to ensure that their trades are enough to cause ripples throughout the market as a whole.

One of the most commonly watched major players is national banks. Necessarily, they are the ones who set the bid price because they are the ones buying up currency most frequently. Even better, they often telegraph their moves to a significant degree, which means you can often learn what their movements are going to be if you take the time to look for them.

Read more economic reports: For every frequently traded currency, there are likely to be dozens, if not hundreds of relevant financial statements released each year.

This means that you are going to want to always be up to date on the latest economic reports on the currency pairs you favor as well as keeping an actively updated calendar with any relevant dates well-marked. If these early reports become widespread enough, they can even start their trends as they push the market in one direction or another.

Don't stick with your first broker or dealer forever: When getting started in forex, it makes sense to pick a cheap broker who doesn't require all that much trading capital to be present and accounted for before you start trading. There are far more relevant concerns for a more experienced trader to consider, which means that once you have a firm grasp of the basics, you are going to want to reevaluate your choice and look into brokers or dealers that offer more competitive benefits.

While many forex dealers refer to themselves brokers or brokerages, the difference between the two can generally be summed up in whether the company you are working with is willing to trading with or against you (dealer) or if they are setting up trades against other amiable parties (broker). Brokerages also often offer training courses and other extras that may appeal to new traders, while dealers usually provide a more bare-bones experience.

While many new traders will benefit from the oversight that a broker brings to the process, as you gain more experience, you may find that the flexibility and lower cost of a dealer make them a natural choice for your purposes. You are going to want to focus on more than which dealer has the lowest fees; however, as oversight is essential. After all, if you choose a dealer who has no official control, then you will mostly have no recourse if they end up taking your money and then disappearing.

Practice your patience: Another crucial part of money management when it comes to trading in the forex market is patience. While it is easy for new traders to feel the need to be continually trading, the fact of the matter is that there are always going to be times when the best option is to sit things out for a little while until your possibilities improve. This will come along with an understanding that the market is prone to moving in a wide variety of ways, only a few are going to result in the types of trends that are well defined enough to make it worth to at least attempt to make a profit from it.

Avoid anger and fear: When it comes to emotions that cloud your mind and kill your successful trade percentage, there is nothing less productive to active trading than rage. Anger is an insidious problem as it can often cloud your judgment slowly over time, making it difficult to see what is happening until it is too late. Rather than letting your anger influence the decision-making process, you will instead need to focus on keeping your losses to a minimum by working quickly to expel any angry feelings before they start to affect your successful trade percentage.

Besides anger, the emotion that you are going to need to deal with most frequently are going to fear. Whether it is the fear of missing out or the fear of committing to a trade, if you start listening to fear rather than the facts that you have available to you, your trading capital will suffer. While it is perfectly natural to be a little fearful when it comes to making significant trades, especially if they have the potential for high risk and great rewards, if you let it take over, then you will never reach your full potential.

There are two primary ways of getting over your fear, the first of which is by never starting a trade that you can't afford to lose. Investing is never a sure thing, which is why the potential for profit is so great, and the sooner you learn to live with that fact, the better. The only other way to mitigate fear is with practice. Remember, the more you trade, the more comfortable the entire process will feel.

CHAPTER 9:

Risk and Money Management

This focuses on how to budget for profit when trading forex and expounds on how you can manage risk and use leverage to your advantage. Addresses how the timeframe affects operations in forex.

Budgeting for Profit

Budgeting for profit means that you have to understand how the forex market works.

If you want to make profits when forex trading, there are a few tips you can use. For instance, ensure that you start small. This advice applies mainly to those who are new to forex trading; you can only be successful at trading millions when you have learned how to handle a few dollars as you can be successful in trading dollars when you have learned how to trade pennies. If you are lucky enough to buy many small stocks, there is a probability that they could tremendously increase in value, earning you profits. Luckily, there are traders today who can allow you to open an account with just a few dollars. If you constantly use the account, over time, your profits will begin to grow, and you will begin to experience success.

Additionally, if you want to succeed, you should be a regular investor. This does not mean you have to put in huge chunks of money for trading each time. It simply means that you could add manageable amounts to your investment every week — for instance, $10 or $20 per week. Being a regular investor not only refines your craft but also grows a sizeable account when the profits are compounded over time. When you invest small amounts, you will not feel the pinch, but the rewards will be great regardless.

Another tip when budgeting for profit is to be patient. As has been highlighted above, starting small is a good move. However, many people get frustrated because of the slow process. To enhance your tolerance, trade small, but do not view these small amounts as dollars. Instead, view them as percentages. If you get a profit of, let us say $1 when you have a $10 dollar account, then you have made a 10% profit.

On the other hand, if you lose a dollar, then you have lost 10%. You will then have learned a valuable lesson about forex trading at a low cost of just a dollar. Also, when you trade in bits, you learn to deal with the hurdles associated with learning how to trade forex.

Risk management

Risk management involves reducing the size of potential losses while getting the most benefit out of a single trade. Risk management is highly debated as a topic in forex trading and, yet, it remains important as an aspect of trading because of the volatile nature of the forex market. To understand risk management in detail, read on.

One of the fundamental rules of managing risk when trading forex is to ensure that you only risk what you can afford to lose. Interestingly, many traders make the mistake of investing more than they can afford to lose, especially when they are learning the trade. As a forex trader, however, you can avoid some of the fundamental mistakes made by traders and become an outstanding trader yourself. You should know when to cut your losses. Cutting of losses can be done in two ways. The first is when you impose a mental stop and decide that the right thing to do would be to limit the drawdown, you can take on a trade. Another way through which you can control losses is by using a trading platform that has technology that allows you to lock in stops when your losses reach a particular level.

To control risks, you can also use the correct lot sizes. When brokers advertise accounts, they make it seem like a good idea to open an account with, let us say, $300 and use leverage to enhance mini-lot trades. They make it look like this technique will help double your money in just a single trade. This kind of thinking can sometimes deviate so far from the reality. When starting as a new trader, it is important to start small so that you have many options for managing the trade.

Another risk management strategy that you can employ in your trading is to understand the nature of the currency pairs you have decided to trade. Understand the events scheduled to take place in the day and even week ahead and how the data looks. Look at your trade plan's time horizon and consider liquidity conditions. Have a clear view of what the market has priced in and out because anticipating market events can alert you of the possible disruptive circumstances even if it is not a complete indicator of how you can win a trade. By understanding that risk varies across currency pairs, based on different factors such as liquidity, data sensitivity, and volatility, you will be better placed at understanding the analytical tools and strategies that are best for you.

Also, you can trade with an edge. This means that you do not have to be in the market all the time despite the fact that the currency market operates round the clock. Block the noise and do not let it pull you in. You can do this, for instance, by picking a spot and timing yourself. Also, look for setups in which there is a clear risk/reward scenario to avoid an unnecessary headache. Being an opportunist in the real world can be a problem, but that does not mean this strategy cannot work in the digital world of forex trading. You can take your time looking at the coming trade opportunities and use these chances instead of getting caught up in the market moves of a single moment.

Look forward to future opportunities because there will be more opportunities and it pays to be ready.

It is also important that as a trader, you take your profits regularly. When you take your profits, you are, in essence, reducing your exposure to risks in the market. You may find that your trade plan has an aggressive profit target but imagine what would happen if events do not play in your favor. It is, therefore, a better idea to protect what you have already worked for instead. After all, nobody has ever gone broke while taking profit. This is a tactic that can be referred to as taking money off the table. If you keep your profits in your margin account, you are likely to be subject to future trading decisions and are susceptible to unknown risks. Taking money out of your account keeps you in a position where you can trade in comfortable sizes. As you trade, remember that trading is not purely a game of profits, you can as well use the profits you make to do other things. You can invest the profits into another venture once you withdraw them. Additionally, you should ensure accuracy by double-checking. By now, you must have understood that currency trading takes place in a fairly fast-paced environment. It is even faster, thanks to electronic trading. There is, therefore, a risk in human error when inputting orders and trades, and this may have serious implications for you as a trader. For instance, what would be the benefit of putting in place a stop-loss order if it not entered for the right amount of currency? As a result, it would pay to make it a part of your routine to double-check your order and trade entries to avoid unnecessary mistakes that may prove costly to your forex trading venture. Ideally, it would be good to double-check figures immediately you input them and just before submission. Mistakes happen, but this does not mean you let minor errors become the source of your downfall.

Leverage

By now, you must have an idea of what leverage is and what it can do for you in forex trading.

In forex, leverage can be described as the ratio of the trader's funds that you are allowed to use to the size of the broker's available funds. In essence, leverage is whatever capital you borrow to increase your returns potentially. In reality, the leverage size usually exceeds invested capital to a large extent. Leverage is not fixed in all companies and may largely depend on the trading conditions provided by the forex brokers. Using leverage can sometimes be a risky affair because just like a double-edged sword, it may work to your favor or not. Below, we highlight how leverage works and how it can affect your bottom-line.

How leverage works

When you take leverage, it essentially means that you have borrowed from a broker. To calculate the margin-based average, you should divide your total transaction value by the amount of margin required.

The formula is thus:

Margin-Based Leverage = Total Value of Transaction / Margin Required

If therefore, you are required to top up 2% of the transaction's total value as margin, and you intend to trade a standard lot of USD/CHF equivalent to $200,000, the required margin would be 4,000 dollars. The margin-based leverage, in this case, would be 200,000/4,000, which equates to 50:1.

Interestingly, margin-based leverage does not affect risk. Whether a trader is required to top up a percentage of the transaction, therefore, does not influence the profits and losses they make. An investor always has the chance to attribute more than the required margin when trading. Real leverages rather than margin-based leverages have a stronger influence on profit and loss.

Calculating the real average would require you to divide the total face value of open positions by the capital you have for trading. As such:

Real Leverage = Total Value of Transaction / Total Trading Capital

For instance, let us say you have $20,000 in your our account and the position you open is worth $200,000 (one lot). Your leverage will be 200,000/20,000. If you traded two lots with the same amount in your account, then the leverage on your account would be 400,000/20,000, which is 20 times.

The margin-based leverage is, therefore, equal to the real leverage you can use to trade. Most traders, however, do not make use of their entire accounts as margin, and this is why their real and margin-based leverages tend to differ. It is generally advised that you do not use all your available margin. You should only use your leverage if you clearly have an advantage on your side.

You should first establish the extent of risk in terms of pips numbers so that you determine the potential capital loss you are likely to incur. The general rule states that the loss should be less than 3% of your capital, if you leverage a position and the potential loss comes to approximately 30% of the capital, then you should reduce your leverage by an equal 30%. As an experienced trader, you may deviate from the standard 3%.

You may also calculate the margin level that you should use, to determine the level of risk a trade poses. Let us say you have $ 10,000 in your account and you decide that you are trading ten mini USD/JPY lots. A move in one pip in a mini account is around a dollar, but when trading minis, the amount rises to approximately $10 each. If you trade 100 minis, then a pip move will be worth approximately $100. If therefore, you take a stop-loss of 30 pips, you have a representation of a potential $30 in a mini lot and $3,000 for 100 mini lots. With $10,000, you should leverage 30 mini lots at most, even when you can possibly trade more.

CHAPTER 10:

How to Set-up Your Forex Trading Account and Begin Trading

At this point, you may feel that you can now begin to trade in the foreign exchange market.

We have also included other important considerations that you must understand before you open up your forex trading account.

Gearing Up With a Forex Practice Account

For beginners in the forex market, the best way to gear up in this new opportunity is to use a practice account.

Many online forex brokers provide free trials so you can sign up with a trading account and immediately experience real-time price action without spending your own real money first.

In most practice accounts, you will be provided with a virtual cash that you can make trades. The risk will be zero and you can take advantage of the experience as you learn how forex trading works.

With a practice account, you will actually see how prices fluctuate at different times of the day and you can see how currency pairs may vary from each other.

While trading in a practice account, you should alongside monitor the news relevant to the currencies you are trading. This will provide you an insight on how the forex market will react to news releases.

Aside from evaluating the market movement, you may also start trading in real-time conditions in the market without the risk of losing your money and you can also try various trading strategies to see if they work in your condition.

You can also improve your own understanding on how margin trading and leverage works and you can experience managing opening positions and you'll get a chance using various orders.

Most forex brokers will allow 30-day trials when you can also access charts and other technical supplements.

Before you sign up for a full membership, try to open practice accounts first with different forex brokers. Explore different features and capacities of these platforms. Also take note that different forex brokers have different trading policies.

Setting Up a Forex Trading Account

Forex trading is quite similar to stock market trading because you have first to open your own trading account. Similar to the stock market, every forex account as well as the services you can take advantage of can be different. Hence, it is crucial that you look for the most suitable platform for you.

Trading Leverage

When we speak of leverage, we refer to the opportunity to take control of bigger amounts of cash with minimal capital from your own pocket. The leverage level is directly proportional to the risk level. Take note that the leverage amount on a platform could be different according to the features of the account on its own. However, the most popular one is the 50:1 leverage. Some accounts could offer a maximum leverage of 250:1.

For example, a maximum leverage of 100:1 signifies that in each dollar that you hold in the brokerage account, you can use up to $100. For instance, if you have an account balance of $100, the brokerage can allow you to trade as much as $10,000 in the fx. This leverage could also define the total amount that you can hold in your account or your margin for trading a specific amount. In the stock market, the margin is often at 50 per cent and the leverage could be 50:1, which can be at least 2 per cent.

In general, leverage is regarded as a primary advantage of trading in the foreign exchange market, because this will allow you to create substantial gains with minimal capital. But leverage could also have extreme downsides when a trade is moving in the opposite direction, because the losses could also be big.

With this leverage type, there is always the actual probability that your losses are higher than what you have invested, even though most accounts have safeguard stops to prevent the account from hitting negative. As such, it is crucial that you take note of this when you open a brokerage account, and once you identify your preferred leverage, you could understand the involved risks.

Fees and Commissions

Another major advantage of forex platforms is that investing through them could be done through a commission, which is unlike stock market accounts where you need to pay a broker a certain fee for every trade. You are now directly dealing with market players and you don't have to pass through another layer such as brokers.

Every time that you enter a trade, it is the market makers, which can seize the spread. Hence, when the ask/bid for a forex market is 1.5300/50, the market maker can capture between the difference between the points. In setting up your own forex account, be sure to take note that every firm has various spreads on currency pairs that you trade. Even though they are usually different by only several pips, this could be substantial when you are planning to do a lot of trading. Hence, in setting up an account, be certain that you are aware of the pip and spread of specific currency pairs that you are interested in trading.

Other Factors

You must take note that there are several differences between every forex platform and the programs or software that they are offering. Every forex trading company may offer various levels of programs and services including the fees beyond and above the actual costs of trading. Moreover, because of the less strict conditions in the foreign exchange market, you should find a reliable firm. When you are also not completely confident to trade with real cash, you can also try trading in practice accounts or demos.

How to Start Trading in the Forex Market

After understanding the most crucial factors in opening your own forex account, it is time to look into what specifically you could trade within the platform. The two primary methods in trading in the forex market includes the actual trading (selling and buying) of forex pairs, in which you short a currency and long another.

Another method is via buying the derivatives that monitor the fluctuations of particular currency pair. These strategies are quite similar to the common techniques used in the stock market. Basically, buying and selling the currency pair is the most popular method, much in a similar manner that many traders are buying and selling currency units.

In this setting, a trader may hope that the currency pair's value will change in a profitable way. If you choose to short a pair, it signifies that you are betting on the possibility that the pair's value will fall. For instance, let's assume that you want a short position for the USD/JPY pair.

You can make profits when the value of the fx pair goes down, and you will lose your investment if it rises. This pair will rise if USD increases its price against the JPY, therefore it is actually a trust on the JPY.

Another alternative is to use futures and options, which are derivative products, so you can make money from the currency value changes. If you purchase a currency pair option, you can gain the privilege to buy a pair on a specific rate prior to a setting of point.

Meanwhile, a futures forex contract could build the agreement to purchase the currency pair at a specific point. These trading strategies are often employed by more experienced traders, but as a beginner, you should be aware of them.

Order Types

In looking for a new trading position, you may have to use a market order or a limit order, which are actually similar when you are placing a new position in the stock market. A market order can provide you the capacity to acquire the currency at specific exchange rate that it is presently trading in the foreign exchange market. On the other hand, the limit order will allow you to identify a specific entry price.

If you are already holding an open position in the market, you may have to consider employing a take profit order, so you could lock in your gains. For instance, let us assume that you are already sure that the USD/GBP will react at 1.8700, but you are not completely certain that the price will rise any higher. You can use a take-profit order that will immediately close your position if the price hits 1.8700, which will lock in your profits.

The stop loss order is also a tool that you can use when you want to hold the open positions. This will allow you to figure out if the price could decline prior to the closing of the position and more losses could be accumulated. Hence, if the USD/GBP rate starts to drop, the investor may put a stop-loss, which could halt the position to avoid any further loss. When you are also trading in the stock market, you will realize that the order types that you could enter in the forex trading accounts are quite similar. It is crucial to be familiar with these orders before you actually place your very first trade in the foreign exchange market.

CHAPTER 11:

Tools for Forex Trading

N ow we will get into talking about the different platforms and techniques you can use in regards to starting your Forex Trading business. Keep in mind that there are many ways to begin trading using different platforms. We will recommend you some. However, it is your choice which platform you're going to be using for your Forex Trading. Overall, all of them work, and they will yield you the results that you're looking for when it comes to Forex Trading.

Nonetheless, there are over nine platforms what you can use for your Forex Trading needs. With that being said, we're going to go through all those nine trading platforms that will give you a better idea on which one to pick and our opinion on them. The first one we're going to talk about is going to be IG.

IG

This platform has known by many people to be one of the most trusted and well-planned out trading platforms to use for Forex Traders. Many of the top Forex Traders, use this platform for their Forex needs. They have a big list of tradable products and also provide you with excellent rating tools. They are known to be the top in the industry, with both trading tools and education. This is perhaps known to be the best trading platform for Forex traders to use, lowest price, and the most reliable.

Saxo Bank

This bank is also one of the top Forex Trading platforms in the market, not only does have competitive prices, but it comes with excellent trading platforms. It has excellent quality research and has reliable customer service. Meaning of the word traitor swears by this platform, Saxo bank offers the complete package which is worth being a customer for. Many Forex Traders will say that these are the most trustworthy platforms to work with when it comes to Forex Trading.

CMC Markets

Even though this platform has been office regulated, CMC Markets offers Traders one of the most comprehensive ranges of offerings with excellent pricing. It also has the next Generation trading platform, which is very Innovative and attracts a lot of younger Forex Traders into the platform.

If you're looking for something that is futuristic and you can have fun with, then most definitely go for a CMC Markets. It has been known to be trustworthy amongst many Forex Traders, so this would be the right choice for you when it comes to starting your Forex Trading.

TD Ameritrade

This is perhaps one of the favorite platforms to trade in. Unfortunately, this is only available in the United States. However, what's nearly 80 currency pairs to trade alongside, and comes with a tremendous amount of trading tools this is no slouch. Moreover, the tools that provide you with the help you to succeed in Forex Trading.

One of the safest platforms to work in and comes with excellent customer service. Highly recommended by many top Forex traders who are living in the United States, if you are living in the United States than we would highly recommend that you use this platform for your Forex needs.

Forex.com

This website has plenty of options for Forex Trading and many other Traders. Known to be beginner-friendly many people offer this platform when they're first starting, although we don't recommend that much if you're a beginner then you can most definitely start with this. But remember once you get a little bit better at four trading, you will eventually have to learn more about it and therefore this one be so useful anymore. Nonetheless, this is a great platform to start with when you're starting your forex trading.

CityIndex

This platform is a multi-asset Forex broker, mostly regulated in the UK and Singapore. This offers competitive spreads across multiple trading platforms. The good thing is this broker caters to the client's needs. So, if you do decide to work with them, he will feel more welcomed, and you will be able to manage it a little bit better as compared to another Forex Trading platform. This would be great for beginners as well, as it will help you with the tools you need to succeed in Forex Trading. They also offer many programs for Forex Traders, including a high-volume investor.

XTB

This platform has been trusted by many, and several major Financial Centers have regulated it. Known to be one of the most excellent platform's trades in, it has competitive fitting experience and has fantastic customer service. If you're someone looking to be on top of your game, this platform would be an excellent idea for you. It offers fantastic tools that will help you to succeed in your forex trading needs.

Dukascopy

If you're looking for tools, under this platform offers many of them. More than any of the Forex Trading platforms that will be mentioned, not only that it has incredible market research and therefore can help you to succeed even more in Forex Trading. This would be our second option when it comes to starting your Forex Trading and to pick out a platform, and it is a mobile app that helps you to Forex trade. But also comes the desktop platform, the only problem with this platform is that they don't have too much to offer. Nonetheless, it is a great platform to get started with.

FXCM

If you're looking for a wide range of trading options, then this would be the best platform to go with. But this platform caters to more high-volume Traders, algorithmic raiders overall traders that appreciate tools and quality market research. If you're a beginner, then we would recommend that you stay away from this trading platform, however, once you've gotten your feet wet in Forex Trading then make sure to try the part for me as you will see great results from it.

As you can see, there are many tools which you can use to follow Forex Trading, and overall, these platforms will work for you regardless of which one you pick. Keep in mind that we can recommend specific platforms as we did; however, whichever one fits your need will be the best platform for you. There is no wrong or good platform, and it is merely a preference. However, don't test a lot of platforms too much as It can cause you to lose money. Keep in mind that moving money. A lot can add up with the fees, which is something you don't want to do in the long run. The best thing you can do, like to figure out your needs and find out which platform works best for you. We would still recommend that you start with either IG or TD if you live in the USA. Also, make sure that you find out all the policies that come with these platforms. However, you must understand what platform offers you with more specifically what kind of policies they have. Some systems might not work for you and certain type forms, so make sure, but you understand a strategy before you get into any of these platforms. In regards to technique, the platform you disable dictated what kind of methods you can and cannot use. The great news is that when you're using specific platforms, they will help you to understand and utilize the techniques which will help you to make more money with your Forex

Trading. Overall, understand that picking out the right platform for your Forex Trading needs is very important, so make sure you take your time with it and understand what platform you're getting yourself into.

CHAPTER 12:

Sector Analysis and Strategy

There are several types of forex strategies; however, it is important to choose the right one based preferred trading style to trade successfully. Some strategies work on short-term trades as well as long-term trades. The type of Forex strategies you choose depends on a few factors like:

- Entry points - traders need to determine the appropriate time to enter the market

- Exit point-trader need to develop rules on when to exit the market as well as how to get out a losing position

- Time availability

- If you have a full-time job, then you cannot use day trading or scalping styles

- Personal choices

People who prefer lower winning rates but larger gains should go for position trading while those who prefer higher winning rate but smaller gains can choose the swing trading

Common Forex Trading strategies include:

Range trading strategy

Range trading is one of the many viable trading strategies. This strategy is where a trader identifies the support and resistance levels and buys at the support level and sells at the resistance level.

This strategy works when there is a lack of market direction or the absence of a trend. Range trading strategies can be broken down into three steps:

Finding the Range

Finding the range uses the support and resistance zones. The support zone is the buying price of the security while the resistance zone price is the selling price of a security. A breakout happens in the event that the price goes beyond the trading range, whereas a breakdown occurs in the event that the price goes below the trading range.

Time Your Entry

Traders use a variety of indicators like price action and volume to enter and exit the trading range. They can also use oscillators like CCI, RSI, and stochastics to time their entry. The oscillators track prices using mathematical calculations. Then the traders wait for the prices to reach the support or resistance zones. They often strike when the momentum turns price in the opposing direction.

Managing Risk

The last step is risk management. When the level of support or resistance breaks, traders will want to exit any range-based positions. They can either use a stop loss above the previous high or invert the process with a stop below the current low.

Pros

- There are ranges that can last even for years producing multiple winning trades.

Cons

- Long-lasting ranges are not easy to come by, and when they do, every range trader wants to use it.

- Not all ranges are worth trading

Trend Trading Strategy

Another popular and common Forex Trading strategy is the trend trading strategy. This strategy attempts to make profits by analyzing trends. The process involves identifying an upward or downward trend in a currency price movement and choosing trade entry and exit points based on the currency price within the trend.

Trend traders use these four common indicators to evaluate trends; moving averages, relative strength index (RSI), On-Balance-Volume (OBV), and Moving Average Convergence Divergence (MACD). These indicators provide trend trade signals, warn of reversals, and simplify price information. A trader can combine several indicators to trade.

Pros

- Offers a better risk to reward

- Can be used across any markets

Cons

- Learning to trade on indicators can be challenging.

Pairs Trade

This is a neutral trading strategy, which allows pair traders to gain profits in any market conditions. This strategy uses two key strategies:

- Convergence trading - this strategy focuses on two historically correlated securities, where the trader buys one asset forward and sells a similar asset forward for a higher price anticipating that prices will become equal. Profits are made when the underperforming position gains value, and the outperforming position's price deflates

- Statistical trading - this is a short-term strategy that uses the mean reversion models involving broadly diversified Security Portfolios. This strategy uses data mining and statistical methods.

Pros

- If pair trades go as expected investors can make profits

Cons

- This strategy relies on a high statistical correlation between two securities, which can be a challenge.

- Pairs trade relies a lot on historical trends, which do not depict future trends accurately.

Price Action Trading

This Forex Trading strategy involves analyzing the historical prices of securities to come up with a trading strategy. Price action trading can be used in short, medium, and long periods. The most commonly used price action indicator is the price bar, which shows detailed information like high and low-price levels during a specific period. However, most traders use more than one strategy to recognize trading patterns, stop-losses, and entry, and exit levels. Technical analysis tools also help price action traders make decisions.

Pros

- No two traders will interpret certain price action the same way

Cons

- Past price history cannot predict future prices accurately

Carry Trade Strategy

Carry trade strategy involves borrowing a low-interest currency to buy a currency that has a high rate; the goal is to make a profit with the interest rate difference. For example, one can buy currency pairs like the Japanese yen (low interest) and the Australian dollar (high interest) because the interest rate spreads are very high. Initially, carry trade was used as a one-way trade that moved upwards without reversals, but carry traders soon discovered that everything went downhill once the trade collapsed.

With the carry trade strategy:

- You need to first identify which currencies offer high rates and which ones have low rates.

- Then match two currencies with a high-interest differential

- Check whether the pair has been in an upward tendency favoring the higher-interest rate currency

Pros

- The strategy works in a low volatility environment.

- Suitable for a long-term strategy

Cons

- Currency rates can change anytime

- Ricky because they are highly leveraged

- Used by many traders therefore overcrowded

Momentum Trading

This strategy involves buying and selling assets according to the strength of recent price trends. The basis for this strategy is that an asset price that is moving strongly in a given direction will continue to move in the same direction until the trend loses strength.

When assets reach a higher price, they tend to attract many investors and traders who push the market price even higher.

This continues until large pools of sellers enter the market and force the asset price down. Momentum traders identify how strong trends are in a given direction. They open positions to take advantage of the expected price change and close positions when the prices go down.

There are two kinds of momentum:

1. Relative momentum - different securities within the same class are compared against each other, and then traders and investors buy strong performing ones and sell the weak ones.

2. Absolute momentum - an asset's price is compared against its previous performance.

Pros

- Traders can capitalize on volatile market trends

- Traders can gain high profit over a short period

- This strategy can take advantage of changes in stock prices caused by emotional investors.

Cons

- A momentum investor is always at a risk of timing a buy incorrectly.

- This strategy works best in a bull market; therefore, it is market sensitive

- This strategy is time-intensive; investors need to keep monitoring the market daily.

- Prices can shift in a different direction anytime

Pivot Points

This strategy determines resistance and support levels using the average of the previous trading sessions, which predict the next prices. They take the average of the high, low, and closing prices. A pivot point is a price level used to indicate market movements. Bullish sentiment occurs when one trades above the pivot point while bearish sentiment occurs when one trades below the pivot point.

Pros

- Traders can use the levels to plan out their trading in advance because prices remain the same throughout the day

- Works well with other strategies

Cons

- Some traders do not find pivot points useful

- There is no guarantee that price will stop or reverse at the levels created on the chart

CHAPTER 13:

What a Beginner Needs to Know About Forex Trading

Forex trading is an avenue that is making people earn a more significant income. There are many platforms where you can put that little penny in the trading and amerce that profits. However, it needs you to be that wise speculator who knows who reads the indicator promptly and knows the point to make that trading.

Remember that Forex trading is all about the trading of currencies. Therefore, you have to be knowledgeable about how the different currencies perform. The following are the basics where a beginner should know.

You should first be interested in knowing how the currencies behave in the market. That is where one ought to recognize the values of different currencies. The major currencies traded across the globe shows significant value in the market. Some of these currencies include the Us Dollar, Sterling Pound, Swiss Franc, Japanese Yen and the Euro.

That is not to say that other currencies are not traded but this one has the commanding value in the Forex trade. Therefore, it requires the broker and the trader to be updated on the value of the stated monies. This is because at some instances the currencies may deteriorate and increase their worth significantly. Another thing to contemplate is how the paired currencies behave with each other. For example, in the Forex chart you may see the Us Dollar combined with the Euro or any other pair.

Another thing you ought to know is the type of indicators available and how one can make trading. These indicators follow specific movement criteria. First and foremost, before knowing that indicator thinks of the scales used in the chart. The chart represents a graphical diagram with both the independent and the depend scales.

The independent scales are normally plotted on the horizontal axis and the dependent scale on the vertical axis. Therefore, you have to know the different variables in the trading. Some of these variables are the price movement, the volume, and many others. Check on this chart's ad test the movement of these variables appropriately.

Concerning the indicators, you should be aware of how these indicators behave. They are of different types and are influenced by the variables you use. For a beginner it is essential to have that knowledge of how they behave is crucial. You have to know the different types of these indicators so that you can follow their trend.

Think of the indicators like the Moving Average Convergence and Divergence. This indicator measures the two exponential moving averages. There is the Bollinger band indicator that measures the standard deviation those currencies of the currencies. Some terms like the volatility market you also need to know them. Remember that the volatility of the currency is its behavior to have either a sharp increase or decrease in the market. That is where you can either gain a sizable profit or loss.

That is not to forget the relative strength index which is beneficial for ascertaining the overbought and the oversold. These indicators are very many in particular, but when you have their information is nothing that should stop you from earning.

Even the types of charts like the candlesticks, line charts and bar charts should be at your fingertips. There are different charts for every level of your trading. For example, in your case as the beginner, you can use the candlestick or the basic charts.

Another thing is the trend analysis. You should analyze the direction which the indicator flows whenever you make a trade. That should help you in analyzing the peak times and recession periods of a paired currency. You also can anticipate the next performance of the paired currency if you are experienced in reading the behaviors of the indicators.

You still use this information to know the right point of the market entry and the exits of the point. Those brokers who analyze the trend accordingly and are in a position of obtaining a sizeable return.

Which Qualities Make You as The Beginner Successful in The Trading

After knowing the basic you do not just start trading when you have the minimal qualities required in this business. You will realize how you will get frustrated when you stake a lot of cash then the trading fails. At other junctures you need to apply essential speculation tactics. That is the knowledge of probability and analyzing the statistics for you to stand a chance in trading. Some of these qualities are.

Be that guy who is good in decision making. Remember that the facility needs intelligence and critical thinking. You may find yourself succeeding a lot in particular segment of trading. However not to realize that it may be a trap where even after making sublime returns you will eventually gain a hefty loss.

Some other times you need not consider only short-term profit but fight for long-term returns. You may identify a promising venture but where whose returns are realized in long-term basis. However, if you are that person who needs quick money you will not be patient on that venture, but look for short-term profits. Moreover, those who take time in making a decision realizes a pattern trend and makes the right move.

Be that risk-taker who do not fear to make a loss. If all people were risk-averse, then there would no Forex trading. Hey, remember that this business is like a gamble. Am sure many people do not like hearing this term, but whenever you are dealing with uncertainties you are gambling. No matter what you do you have to sacrifice that penny expecting two possibilities which are either a win or a loss? Even other renowned investors cite that 'you have to stake big to win big'. Therefore, be a risk-taker who stakes big and hopes for massive earnings of returns. Even if you fail seldom, do not give up, as eventually you will win.

Persistent is another quality required for you beginners in the Forex trading. When you are persistent you normally are tolerant. You never give up hope even after failing many times. Why your needs are learning from mistakes. Do not repeat the same strategy that you did which failed you. Be that person who sees the failure as a lesson to improve their ways of staking.

Adopt a trial and error strategy which will eventually give you a winning edge. You do not expect keep winning all the time, you will undoubtedly lose in some instances. You will realize you will keep developing tactics of trading with this trial and error strategy. You will too familiarize yourself with the trend analysis. Therefore, what is stopping you from knowing how to make that currencies trade.

Timing is also operational in the business. You have to flexible enough to identify a profitable opportunity. The way the currencies behave is like a pendulum that goes in every direction. You can use a stopwatch and identify the specific time the trading signals a return and risks or an entry point or an exit point.

Those seconds or minutes you waste may be the advent of your failure. Do a demo trade which you do not have to input some cash? Look at the behavior of the currency and how they react in any substantial change. You may identify the correct timing when you need to stake. Therefore, you will have that confidence to stake your money in the trading.

What are the steps for a beginner in trading?

First, you have to have good preparations. Trading does not fall on the moon, however you need to have the proper tools for trading. You need to have an electronic device, it can be your phone, laptop, iPad or any other gadget that can connect to the Internet. Make sure you have the best source for Internet connection because you need to make many references to the currencies from the network. Make sure you are comfortably seated and good to go.

Choose the best agency company in Forex trading. Remember there are many companies online that broker those currencies. Before choosing a firms one should conduct an extensive study of them. You also need to consider if they are registered and licensed. Moreover, consider their brokerage fee and their essential features. It should have the necessary charts, variables and indicators that satisfy the trader. Consult other traders to recommend the best brokerage firm. When you are satisfied with this you can create an account with them. Find out if they provide a demo account which is necessary for trading practice.

The demo account is very vital for you to practice trading. Remember, you cannot put your money into a venture that you do not know, therefore you must understand it first. If you are satisfied with it then start the trading program. The good thing with a demo account is that you are not afraid of any risks since you have not staked any cash. Check with the trading platform and its charts.

Open the chart or the diagram and try to choose a currency pair. Most of the times the currencies are found in the top of the graph, on its sides or the below the graph. Look at the available currencies and think about them. You have to be keen in choosing the pair. You can even do research on the values of different currencies and how they behave with each other. Do not forget to check their volatility and how they fair when traded. Choose those pairs and fix them at the graph.

Then choose the indicators you like. Indicators are of different types and it is upon you the trader to examine which you will understand. You can use the Moving Average Convergence and Divergence which measure the exponential averages. You may think of the Bollinger band in the standard deviation or the RSI which identifies the overbought or the oversold. If you don't understand them ask an expert to teach you.

Place the order if you feel you are ready for that trade. Prioritize price as the main element in harnessing a profit from the currencies. With the currencies, pairs evaluate how the indicators move. They may move in different directions or together. You have to know the peak time and the recession times.

When the waves are on a higher point that is the peak period and when they are low then that is the lower period. Select your value and see the behavior and you will realize whether it is a return or a loss. If the pair disappoints you, then choose another and repeat the same action. That is until you are convinced of the best pair of trading currencies.

Doing a lot of practice with a demo and will help you realize a trend. Therefore, conduct an effective trend analysis that should help you to predict the exact behavior of the pair currency. You will also know the point to amerce greater profit and big losses. Also, the trend analysis will help you to identify the specific points where you can exit the trade with a profit.

When you are satisfied with the demo you can stake the amount and follow the same procedures. Be accurate and persistent and try many times even if you fail.

CHAPTER 14:

What Do You Do If the Market Is Going In The Wrong Direction?

Pay Attention to Daily Pivot Points

Forex traders should watch daily pivot points closely. This is especially important for day traders. However, it is also important for swing traders, position traders, and even traders who focus on long-term positions. It is important to do so because tons of other forex traders do the same. In a certain way, pivot trading is like a self-fulfilling prophecy. Essentially, markets often find resistance or support at pivot points since thousands of pivot traders place orders at those points. Consequently, when a large volume of trading moves happens at these points or levels, there is no other reason for the move except that many traders placed orders expecting such a move. However, pivot points should not be the only basis of a Forex Trading strategy. Rather, regardless of one's strategy, one should watch these points for signs of either potential market or continuation of a trend. Forex traders should look at pivot levels and the trading activities that take place around them as a confirming indicator to use in conjunction with their chosen strategy.

Define Trading Style and Goals

Before setting out on any journey, travelers need to have a clear idea of where they are going and how to get to their destination. In the same way, forex traders need to have clear goals, in addition to ensuring that their trading strategies will help them achieve those goals.

Each Forex Trading style or strategy comes with a different risk profile. Therefore, traders who want to win in Forex Trading need to find and adopt the right approach and attitude to trade profitably. Those who cannot imagine going to sleep with an open market position, for example, should consider focusing on day trading.

Forex traders with funds they believe will benefit from a trade appreciation over several months; on the other hand, they should think about position trading. Essentially, it is important for a forex trader to determine whether his/her personality will fit any particular trading strategy. Any mismatch will probably lead to certain losses and stress.

Trade with an Edge

Successful forex traders only risk their hard-earned money when a market opportunity provides them with an edge. In other words, they do so when the opportunity presents them with something that will boost the chances of their trades being successful. This edge can be various things, even a simple thing, such as selling at a price level that one identifies as strong resistance.

Forex traders can also increase their probability of success and their edge by having several technical factors in their favor. If the 100-period, 50-period, and 10-period moving averages all meet at the same price level, for example, it will likely offer significant resistance or support for a market because many traders will be acting together by trading off any of those averages. Converging technical indicators also provide a similar edge. This happens when different indicators on many periods converge to provide resistance or support. Having the price hit an identified resistance or support level, in addition to having price movement at that level, is an indication of a potential market reversal.

The Trading Platform and Broker

Forex traders should spend adequate time researching a suitable trading platform and a reputable broker. It is important to identify and understand the difference between brokers and determine how each of them goes about making a market, as well as their policies. Trading the exchange-driven market, for example, is different from trading in the spot market or OTC market.

Traders should also choose the trading platform that fits the analysis they want to do. Traders who want to use Fibonacci numbers to trade, for example, should ensure the trading platform they choose has the ability to draw Fibonacci lives. A good platform with a bad broker is just as bad as a poor trading platform with a good broker. Therefore, forex traders need to find the best of both.

Preserve Capital

It is more important for traders to avoid huge losses than to make huge profits. For people who are new to Forex Trading, this concept may not sound quite right. However, it is important to understand that winning in Forex Trading means knowing how to preserve or protect one's capital.

According to the founder of Tudor Corporation, Paul Tudor Jones, playing great defense is the most important rule of trading. Actually, he is a great trader to learn from and study. In addition to building a hugely successful hedge fund, Tudor Jones has an excellent record of profitable trading.

He also played an important role in creating the ethics-training program needed to gain membership in all futures exchanges in the United States. Protecting the trading capital, or playing great defense, is very important in Forex Trading because many people who venture into Forex Trading are unable to continue trading as a result of running out of money.

Many forex traders drain their accounts soon after they make a few trades. Having strict risk management practices is important for people who want to win in Forex Trading. Traders who manage to preserve their trading capital are able to continue trading for as long as they want to, and might eventually become huge winners.

One great trade can fall into a trader's lap and significantly increase his/her profits and account size. One does not need to be the smartest trader in the world to make money in the forex market. If nothing else, the luck of the draw can have traders who manage to protect their capital stumble into trades that generate enough profits to make their trading careers a huge success.

Small Losses and Focus

After forex traders fund their trading accounts, they need to understand that their capital is at risk. Therefore, they should not depend on that money for their daily living expenses. Actually, it is better to think of those funds as vacation funds. Once their vacation is over, their money is gone.

Having this trading attitude will help prepare them to accept and learn from small losses, which will also help them manage their risk better. Forex traders should focus on their trades and accept small losses, which are normal in any type of business, rather than constantly and obsessively focusing on their equity.

Simple Technical Analysis

Consider this example of two forex traders in extremely different situations. The first trader has a specially designed trading computer with several monitors, a large office, swanky furnishings, trading charts, and market news feeds. He also has several moving averages, technical indicators, momentum indicators, and much more.

The other trader, on the other hand, works from a relatively simple office space and uses a regular desktop or laptop computer. His charts reveal just one or two technical indicators on the price action of the market.

Most people would consider the first trader to be more professional and extremely successful, and they would probably be wrong in their assumption. Actually, the second trader is closer to the image of a forex trader who wins consistently. Traders can apply numerous forms of technical analysis to a chart. Having more, however, does not necessarily mean having better.

Using a huge number of indicators might actually make things more complicated and confusing for a forex trader. They amplify indecision and doubt, causing him/her to miss many potentially profitable trades. Therefore, it is better to have a simple trading strategy with just a few rules, as well as a minimum of indicators to consider.

A few very successful forex traders make money from the forex market almost every day without using any technical indicators overlaid on their charts. They achieve this impressive feat without taking advantage of a relative strength indicator, trend lines, trading robots, moving averages, or expert advisors. Their market analysis involves a simple candlestick chart.

Weekend Analysis

The forex market ceases operation on the weekend. Therefore, forex traders should use this time to study their weekly charts to identify news or patterns that could affect their trades in either a positive or a negative way. This will give the objectivity, which will help them make smarter trading plans.

Placing Stop-Loss Orders at the Right Price Levels

In addition to protecting one's capital in case of a losing trade, this strategy is also an important aspect of smart Forex Trading. Many newcomers to the forex market assume that risk management simply means placing stop-loss orders close to the entry point of their trades. This is partly accurate; however, habitually placing stop-loss orders too close to their trade entry points is something that might contribute to their lack of success.

Sometimes, stop-loss orders can stop a trade, only to see the market make a reversal in favor of the trade. It is common for novice traders to endure watching this happen. Sometimes, this reversal proceeds to a level that would have seen them gain a sizable profit if the stop-loss order had not terminated the trade.

Obviously, traders should enter trades that allow them to place stop-loss orders close enough to their trade entry points to avoid making huge losses. However, they should place them at a reasonable price level, based on their analysis of the market. When it comes to reasonable placement of stop-loss orders, the general rule of thumb is to place them a bit further than the price the market should not trade at, based on market analysis.

Use a Consistent Methodology

Before a prospective trader enters the forex market, he/she needs to have a good idea of how he/she will make trading decisions. Essentially, forex traders should know the information they will need to make smart decisions on entering a trade or exiting one. Some traders choose to analyze a chart and the fundamental of the economy to decide the best time to trade. Others, however, prefer to perform technical analysis to determine the ideal time to execute a trade. Whichever methodology or strategy a trader chooses to employ, he/she needs to be consistent and ensure the chosen methodology is adequately adaptive. In other words, it should be flexible enough to handle the forex market's changing dynamics.

Choosing the Right Entry and Exit Points

Most inexperienced forex traders do not know how to judge conflicting information that often presents when analyzing charts in various timeframes. Certain information, for example, might indicate a sell signal on a weekly chart, but show up as a purchasing opportunity in an intraday chart. Therefore, if a trader is using a weekly chart to determine his/her basic trading direction and a daily chart to tie his/her entry, then he/she should try to synchronize the two charts. If the weekly chart is providing a buy signal, for example, he/she should wait for the daily chart to confirm this signal. In other words, keeping signal timing in sync is a good tip for winning in Forex Trading.

CHAPTER 15:

The Right Approach

In order to be successful in currency trading, you definitely need to make sure that you are approaching things the right way. First is understanding that you are in this for the long haul. That means that you understand that you are not going to turn your $10,000 to $100,000 in two or three weeks by engaging in three or four trades every day. Sure, you could try that, but if that strategy worked then the internet would be littered with tales of how this unemployed dad or that soccer mom made $100,000 in two weeks trading currency and there haven't been any stories like that—at least none that we have heard of. Currency trading is a long-term investment. You make a trade today based on an informed decision on a particular currency and perhaps you hold onto that currency for three weeks, patiently waiting as it slowly rises in value: three pips, four pips, 12 pips. Meanwhile, as you did not invest all of your capital on that trade, perhaps later in the week you engage in a second trade with a plan of holding onto that currency for a little while, too. Perhaps as soon as you purchase this second currency you see that it begins to fall. As you have established a threshold at which you will sell your currency (as part of a trading plan), you end up selling that currency for a slight loss. That's three trades in a week's time. Not three trades in a single day, but in a week.

Being successful at currency trading requires this sort of approach. You have to be patient. Just as a president or other government official has to be patient in order to see the changes that he or she has instituted take effect over time, so too will you have to be patient as the currency you traded for rises in value, falls, and then rises again We mentioned briefly the importance of having a trading plan. Many professional traders have a trading plan (if not most of them), in part because they have a superior that they are answering to and that superior wants to know that they are actually using that money wisely. Having a trading plan has been shown to work for professional traders and it will certainly work for you, an independent retail trader. Think about it this way: you are not investing your company's money; you are investing your own. Shouldn't you be doing at least what the professional traders are doing, if not more? If they are investing in a real-time news source and coming up with a trading plan then you should be doing at least that much.

A trading plan does not have to be something extremely elaborate. You will have to decide what's important for you to know down the line when you are trying to figure out why you bought so much Thai baht when the news reports from the day prior suggested that actually, you should have bought South Korean won. Your plan should explain why you are buying this currency vs that based on concrete information that you have (like the resolution of a political crisis, foreign investment, revised economic forecasts, etc.). Your plan should also go into how long you plan to hold onto that currency and why. Perhaps your plan will also explain the conditions under which you might sell. For example, perhaps you planned to hold on to those Japanese yen for two weeks, but the value has increased so rapidly that you feel you need to sell after only one week as it is likely that the value will have fallen if you wait to reach the two-week mark. Your trading plan could easily take the format of explaining where the yen is today, when you plan to purchase yen, when you plan to sell, and at what threshold you will sell early if the yen rises or falls quicker than you imagined.

The purpose of a trading plan isn't to waste your time or to bore you with the intricacies of an endeavor that you expected to be quick, easy, and fun. Currency trading, like the stock market, is subject to vicissitudes. It is not enough to have capital, a broker, and a news source. You may have all that and still lose money. You need to have a trading plan. Again, this is for no one's benefit, but your own. This plan will not only guide you on making informed, well-thought-out decisions on the foreign exchange market, it may also prevent you from making stupid ones, like engaging in more trades than you need to. Once you have a solid plan, and once you understand the idea that you are in this game for the long haul, then you have embarked on the first step towards success in currency trading.

The Importance of a Trading Plan

It is important first to settle your trading style before you start developing your forex trading plan. Various trading styles basically call for variations on trading plans, even though there are a lot of overarching rules in trading that are applicable to all styles.

Time Frame
You need to determine how long you would hold your position. Some forex traders look at short-term trade opportunities. This is known as day trading. Meanwhile, some traders are trying to capture more significant movements in forex prices over days, weeks or even months.

Currency Pair
Are you looking to trade in different currency pairs or are you more interested to focus your energy into few pairs?

Risk Appetite
How much money are you willing to risk and what is your level of expectations for your trading profits?

Rationale
Are you technically or fundamentally inclined? Are you looking to develop a systematic trading model? What strategies are you looking to follow? Are you comfortable in following forex trends? Or are you more inclined to become a breakout forex trader?

Don't worry if you still don't have answers to these questions. Hopefully as you read this book, you can choose the forex trading approach you are interested to pursue.

You can try different strategies and styles by using demo accounts. But don't forget that your goal is to zero in your trading style that you feel comfortable with and that you can pursue regularly.

In addition, you also need to consider other factors such as your individual circumstances such as personal discipline, temperament, finances, free time, family, and work obligations. These are essential variables and you are the only one who knows how they impact your forex trading.

Regardless of the trading style you choose to pursue, achieving success can be challenging if you don't set your trade plan then follow it. Remember, trade plans will help you avoid losing a lot of money from bad trades and can also help you win big in the market.

Moreover, your trading plan serves as your guide, which helps you explore the trades after the emotions and adrenaline begin pumping regardless of what the market presents to you. But this doesn't mean that forex trading is any easier compared to other financial markets.

However, it is proven that trading with a plan will significantly improve the probability of your success in the forex market over time. Also, you need to understand that trading without a plan is a guaranteed way to lose money in the forex market.

Sure, you may make money from a few trades, but a day of reckoning will eventually come to any trader who is only guided by his guts. This is always the trend in any financial markets.

The starting line of any trading plan is to determine an opportunity for trading. Do not wait for any writing on the wall that will tell you what and when to trade. You must devote your effort and energy in looking for lucrative opportunities for trading.

CHAPTER 16:

Choosing a Broker

A broker refers to a firm or an individual who charges a certain fee or rather a commission for executing the buying and the selling process. In other words, they play the role of connecting the customer and the seller of the product. Thus, they are generally paid for acting as a link between the two parties.

For instance, a client might be willing to buy shares from a particular organization. However, he might be lacking enough information about the places that he can purchase these shares. Thus, he will be forced to seek a person who understands the stock trade markets well. The broker will, therefore, educate the client as well as link them with the right sellers. The broker will thus earn by offering such a connection.

List of Common Brokers

IG

It is rated as one of the best Forex brokers in the world. It was one of the pioneers in offering contracts for difference as well as spread beating. The organization was founded in the year 1974 and had been growing as a leader in online trading as well as the marketing industry.

One of the features that have boosted its growth is the fact that it has linked a lot of customers, hence gaining more trust. In other words, a duet to its large customer base, a lot of clients prefers selling and buying their services.

The other feature worth noting is that this organization is London based, and it is among one of the companies that are listed on the

London Stock Trade market for more than 250 times. The feature is due to the fact that it offers more than 15,000 products across several asset classes.

Such classes include CFDs on shares, Forex, commodities, bonds, crypto currencies as well as indices. Another feature worth noting is that the 2019 May report, the firm is serving more than 120,000 active clients around the globe. Also, there are more than 350,000 clients that are served on a daily basis. The feature has been critical in boosting its expansion as this group of individuals does more advertisements.

Some of the benefits that one gains by working in this industry are the fact that it allows comprehensive trading and the utilization of tools that enhance the real trade of data. The other feature worth noting is that it has a public traded license that allows a regular jurisdiction across the entire globe. In other words, one can acquire the services of this organization across the whole world with ease without the fear of acting against the laws of the nation.

Also, the premises offer some of the competitive based commission that enhances pricing as spreading of Forex. There is also a broad range of markets that are associated with the premises too, there several currencies and multi assets CFDs that are offered by the organization. The feature has been critical in the sense that it allows the perfect utilization of all the services as well as the resources available across the globe. Some of the services that are offered by the organization are permitted globally, such that even after traveling from one nation to the other, one can still access their services. Since the year 1974, the organization has joined more than 195,000 traders across the entire globe. The feature has allowed the selling of its shares as well as services, hence its fame.

Saxo Bank

The Forex broker was established in 1992and has then been among the leading organization in offering Forex services as well as the multi-asset brokerages across more than 15 nations. Some of these nations include the UK, Denmark, and Singapore, among others. One of the features of the organization is that it offers services to both retailers as well as institutional clients in the globe. The appeal has allowed the premises to provide more than one million transactions each day. Thus, it holds over $ 16 billion in asset management.

The Saxo bank also offers more services to all of her clients. Such services include Spot FX, Non-deliverable Forwards (NDFs), contract difference as well as all the stock trade options. The feature has been critical in increasing its customer base across the globe. Some of the services such as crypto and bond services offered in the premises has allowed its expansion in the sense that they are sensitive and essentials.

Some of the benefits that one gain by assessing the services of the premises are that it enhances diverse selection of quality, it increases competitive commissions and Forex spread as well as an improved multiple financial jurisdiction function that is allowed across the entire globe. In other words, the premises offer services allowed worldwide, and that considers the rules and policies provided in each nation. The feature has enhanced its continued growth despite the increased competition.

One must pay a minimum deposit of about $2,000 and have an automated trading solution for all the traders. There are times when the premises offer bonuses of 182 trade Forex pairs to all its clients. This feature has also been the key reason behind its increased expansion. In other words, there are various services offered at a relatively low price, hence the widening of its customer base.

CMC Markets

The premises were founded in 1989 and since then, it has grown to be one of the leading retail Forex, as well as a CFD brokerage. The premises thus serve more than 10,000 CFD instruments that cut across all the classes such as Forex, commodities as well as security markets. The feature has allowed the premises to spread its services to more than 60,000 clients across the entire globe.

The premises have more than 15 offices that are well distributed in the nation; it offers the services. Most of its actions are thus related in UK, Australia as well as Canada. The feature is due to the fact that the premises have customer bases in some of these nations. In other words, its services are well accepted in Canada and the UK.

There are various benefits one gains by joining the premises. One, the premise offers some of the best competitive spread to all her customers. In other words, there are a variety of services that one can choose from. Also, the premises offer some of the largest selection of currency pairs in the entire industry. There are more than one hundred and eighty currencies that one can access by joining the premises.

The other feature worth noting is that the premises offer some of the best regulated financial agents in the entire globe. In other words, there are policies as well as rules that govern the provision of services in the world. Also, it is easy to identify the premises as there are potent charts as well as patterns that are used as recognition tools.

City Index

This Forex broker was founded in 1983 in the UK. Since then, the premises have gained popularity and has turned out to be one of the leading brokers in London. It is worth noting that in 2015, the premises acquired GAIN Capital Holding Company that enhanced its increased customer base. Since 2015, the premises have been providing traders with services such as CFDs and spreading-betting derivatives. The premises have been further expanding the Forex services with the acquisition of markets as well as FX solutions before gaining the capital market. Nowadays, the City Index has been operating as an independent brand under GAIN Capital in Asia as well as the UK. The feature has allowed a multi-asset solution hence offering traders access to over 12,000 products across the global markets.

Some of the benefits that one gains part of the capital holding, a large selection of CFDs as well as regulated in several jurisdictions. The organization has tight spreads as well as low margins and fast execution.

In others, the premises have been time from time, offering average ranges to all the clients; hence its increased customer base.

XTB Review

The organization was founded in Poland in the year 2002. Since then the organization has been well known for its Forex and CFDs brokerage. Since then, the organization has maintained its offices in several nations; it offers its services. The premise has been working as a multi-asset broker that is regulated in several centers, hence increasing their competitive advantage. The premises have been trading as multiple financial centers offering a lot of services to all her traders.

Signs of Illegitimate Brokers

Although numerous brokers have been working in the Forex industry, the feature of legitimacy has been an issue affecting the progress of some these premises. One of the elements that are considered is the vulnerability of the clients. In most cases illegitimate brokers tend to rob their customers. Most of them are self-reliant and optimistic. Most of them operate above their financial knowledge, hence making numerous mistakes. Most of these organization record big loses as they are relatively weak in term of management. The organization offers a lot of transactions that tend to be cumbersome in terms of management. It is worth noting that most of their operations aren't legitimate and never approved by the necessary authorities.

Thus, when deciding on the kind of Forex premises to seek services from, it is essential to consider some factors. Avoid assumptions that are exaggerative in terms of offering services that are above their knowledge. The feature is harmful in the sense that they provide services that are not well planned, hence recording a number of loses that befalls many clients in the long run. In other words, the drops recorded in the organization.

CHAPTER 17:

Benefits of Forex Trading

There are many benefits to trading in forex markets. Let us look at some of them.

Liquidity

The first and most important benefit of forex trading is its liquidity. As you know, the forex market is extremely liquid meaning you can sell your currency at any time. There will be a lot of takers for it, as they will be looking to buy the particular currency. The highly liquid market can help you avoid any loss as you don't have to wait on your currency to be sold. And all of it is automatic. You only have to give the sell order, and within no time your entire order will be sold.

Timing

The forex market is open 24 hours a day, which makes it a great place to invest at. You can keep trading during the day and also during the night if you are dealing with a country's currency whose day timings coincide with your night timings. You can come up with a schedule that will allow you to conveniently trade with all of the different countries that lie in the different time zones. You can also quickly sell off a bad currency without having to wait the whole night or day.

Returns

The rate of returns in foreign currency trade is quite high. You will see that it is possible for you to invest just $10 and control as much as $1000 with it. All you have to do is look for the best currency pairs and start buying and selling them

The leverage that these investments provide is always on the higher side, which makes them an ideal investment avenue for both beginners and old hands.

Costs

The transaction costs of this type of trade are very low. You don't have to worry about big fees when you buy and sell foreign currencies. That is the one big concern that most stock traders have, as they will worry about having to shell out a lot of money towards transaction costs. But that worry is eliminated in currency exchanges, and you can save on quite a lot of money just by choosing to invest in currency.

Non-Directional Trade

The forex market follows a non-directional trade. This means that it does not matter if the difference in the currencies is going upwards or downwards, you will always have the chance to remain with a profit. This is mostly because there is scope for you to short a deal or go long on it depending on the situation and rate of difference. You will understand how this works as and when you partake in it. The main aim of investing in forex is to remain with a steady profit, which is only possible if you know when to hold on to an investment and when to sell it off. This very aspect is seen as being a buffer by traders and is the main reason for them choosing to invest in forex.

Middlemen Eliminated

With forex trade, it is possible for you to eliminate any middlemen. These middlemen will unnecessarily charge you a fee and your costs with keeping piling up. So, you can easily avoid these unnecessary costs and increase your profit margin. These middlemen need not always be brokers and can also be other people who will simply get in the way of your trade just to make a quick buck out of it. You have to be careful and stave such people off in order to avoid any unnecessary costs that they will bring about. Education is key here and the more you know, the better your chances of avoiding any such frauds.

No Unfair Trade

There is no possibility of anyone rich investor controlling the market. This is quite common in the stock market where a single big investor will end up investing a lot of money in a particular stock and then withdraw from it quickly and affect the market negatively. This is not a possibility in the foreign currency market as there is no scope for a single large trader to dominate the market. These traders will all belong to different countries, and it will not be possible for them to control the entire market as a whole. There will be free trade, and you can make the most use of it.

No Entry Barrier

There is no entry barrier, and you can enter and exit the market at any time you like. There is also no limit on the investment amount that you can enter with. You have to try and diversify your currency investments in a way that you minimize your risk potential and increase your profit potential. You can start out with a small sum and then gradually increase it as you go.

Certainty

There is a certain security attached to foreign currencies. You will have the chance to avail guaranteed profits if you invest in currency pairs that are doing well. These can be surmised by going through all the different currency pairs that are doing well in the market. With experience, you will be able to cut down on your losses with ease and also increase your profits. You have to learn from your experience and ensure that you know exactly what you are doing.

Easy Information

Information on the topic of foreign currencies is easily available on the internet and from other sources. This information can be utilized to invest in the best currency pairs. You have to do a quick search of which two pairs are doing well and invest in them without wasting too much time. If you need any other information on the topic, then this book will guide you through it. You can directly go to the topic that you seek and look at the details to provide there.

Apart from these, there are certain other benefits like minimal commission charged by the OTC agent and instant execution of your market orders. No agency will be able to control the foreign exchange market.

These form the different benefits of trading in the forex market but are not limited to just these. You will be acquainted with the others as and when you start investing in it.

CHAPTER 18:

Time Management and Money Management

Time Management

Time management, a key aspect in forex trading, is one of the determinants of the gains and losses a trader is to make from the opening and the close of a trading period. It is therefore paramount that a trader has a solid plan in his or her time management in trading to reap off gains. A trader has to know when to enter and exit the market when to get the necessary information on trading patterns, these and many more being among the aspects of time management of a forex trader.

Match your personality and your trading pattern with the time you have

It is suicidal for a trader to operate on the basis of a trading pattern that does not suit their personality and goes against them in all odds. The personality type being referred to in this case is major whether the trader is patient or not. An impatient trader will want to have instant results and gains for trades made and will therefore not tarry around for trading systems that are long term. Such traders do not find the trade analysis tools that are long term to be useful to their course. Impatient traders are mostly associated with swing traders who get antsy and do not stay put to trade for the long term. Analysis tools that evaluate for long term trade may not be suitable for such traders. Short term analysis tools are mostly preferred for such traders and will work perfectly to their trading plan.

Analysis tools and trading patterns that work for the long term are applicable to those whose personality is being patient. Long term strategies work for these kinds of people. They should, however, take caution not to be blind to current events that may drastically and completely change the trading pattern in existence and therefore results in losses for them. Their strategy also has to be within a time frame that they are comfortable trading in.

Consider the important trading analysis

Irrespective of the type of a trader that you are, critical and important analysis on trading patterns and factors affecting trading of forexes is not to be ignored. Just a small bit of information may change the trading scales to either make profits or losses.

Even when a trader is pressed for time, never make a trade on a pair of currencies without thoroughly evaluating them to avoid regretting later. For the long-term traders, an important analysis is to trigger you to make a change in the currency pairs for a profitable trade. Make use of the little time, if you are a swing trader, and do a proper analysis on the currencies before putting your money at stake for a loss. Many traders have failed to do so where their efforts to pairing profitable currencies came to naught.

Unplug from distractions when analyzing trading patterns

Distractions such as social media, the TV, background noise and many others are to be avoided when making an analysis. They tend to eat up a lot of time when it could have been spent wisely in analyzing and not miss out on an opportunity to make a trade that could have resulted in profits.

Unplug from social media for a while trading and shout out all the noise in your surrounding and fully concentrate on evaluating the currencies and making wise decisions on pairing them.

This saves a lot of time that otherwise could have been used in multitasking trading and other activities all the while not fully concentrating on each activity.

Come up with an information sorting strategy

There could be information overload on forex exchange and a lot of unnecessary news regarding the same that waste time for a trader goes through all that in a bid to make a successful pairing of currencies. There are also a lot of sites online that offer updates on forex trading and if a trader could subscribe to all of them, then all they could be doing is analyzing trading forexes and doing zero trading at all. Sort out the relevant information that only has effect on your currency pairs. It is also advisable to have reliable sites to get information from and not a lot of them or some bogus ones. This could have done by looking at the reviews that the sites have to prove whether that is useful or not. This is a strategy that could save a lot of time, especially to the new traders who jump into every forex trading bandwagon.

Sync your preferred trading time with profitable trading widows

In forex trading, timing goes a long way. It is everything. A trader should, therefore, come up with a strategy that ensures that their available time is also a profitable window to trade-in. It is not always that the free time you get and available to trade in will result in profits. Choose the most appropriate window and execute a trade. However, a trader should also be able to enjoy his or her free time and also at the same time make money through forex trading. This cannot be reiterated enough, sync your 'available time' with profitable trading windows.

Money Management

Money management strategies are important to a forex trader to ensure that the trades made are profitable and reduce the chance of a loss happening to the bare minimum. Forex can be a game of chance to the traders who are not so keen on learning about managing their money in this type of trade. New traders lose their money when pairing the wrong currencies, and even made the correct currencies by the trading patterns but at the wrong time. The rules on money management reduce the chances of having a negative account balance when it could have been avoided. Below are some of the important money management tips to consider when trading currencies to maximize profits.

Avoid overexcitement of the forex market

This I mainly applicable to the new traders who get overexcited on the trading patterns and tend to trade currencies in a rush with no proper analyzation of the currencies and the market, thereby leading to huge losses.

This should be avoided where the habit can turn out to be more of a game of chance or betting rather than wise trading. You don't have to make a new trade when an opening presents itself every hour. It can prove to a fateful and a damning idea where the profits made and accumulated may be lost in an attempt to reach for more. Don't be afraid to lie low for days when waiting for an opportune time to make a good trade that may have huge profits. Being antsy for quick money and chasing the forex market will most of the times result in losses.

Most assuredly it will. Analyze the market, an opening for a profitable trade will surely come. A trade made in an overexcitement of the market will not equate that made after a careful analysis of the trading patterns. Very few trades will be lost when this strategy is put into employ, especially to the new traders. No opportunities to trade and make profits, then no trade at all, a philosophy that should be a guide in making decisions in the forex market.

Overexcitement for the market can also be displayed by opening a lot of trades in a short period of time, which may work against you should the tables turned. This habit, coupled with other equally poor money management strategies in forex trading, has left traders' accounts on the negative balance, wiping off a lot of profits. Let several necessary trades work for you.

Take caution to trade on leverage

Leverage might be a great way to make money, double money, as is the thought of many new traders. This is however not the way leverage tends to work. It may turn against your trade wiping all your profits. While on one hand, large leverage might increase your money when one pair of currency is making profits, it can also create losses in a very quick way. A trader has to look into ways how they can protect their startup capital before making huge profits on the same capital. Leverage can either work for the good or work for the worst where your money in trading forex is concerned. It is therefore advisable in choosing the level of leverage to trade in, putting in mind that it may go either way and when it doesn't work, the losses are steep, especially on large levels of leverage. Being a cautious trader, you'll look into the balance that you have in your account before making the decision on the level of leverage you'll have on your capital. Other factors to put into consideration are such as the risk per trade and the stop loss distance. You have to look at how fast the system can respond to the cut of loss before running a lot of losses. When considering the risk per trade, carefully analyze whether the trade you are about to make will profitable and whether it is worth your money, or whether there is a change of a loss occurring, especially when you have a high level of leverage on your money.

Cut the trade when running a loss, keep the trade when gaining

Most of the new traders do not know when to cut the trade when they are on a streak of running losses. Not all trades making losses will reversibly start to make profits and the losses made will be converted to profits. In some cases, this is not what happens. It is advisable to keep the profits and let the cut loose of the losses by doing away with the trade that may wipe off your account. On the other hand, when your trade is making gains and profits, let it run. Let the profits accumulate. Some traders, in fear of the volatility of the market, often close trades that are making profits while fearing that there will be a reversal on the trade and losses will start to be made. This can happen when trades making profits have run for a long time and traders become skeptical. Traders who've been around for a long time have the philosophy of letting the winning trades run and not leaving losing trades open. This is a money management strategy that is very crucial. Traders who are mainly unprofessional and inexperienced fall mainly on leaving the losing trades open. The reason behind it may be because of greed for more money. This works against traders in many cases. Fear, on the other hand, motivates the traders who cut the trades that are making profits. They miss out on many opportunities to make a lot of money from the trades they closed. On this, it is also of great import to be cautious when making a decision on which trade to close and which trade to leave open. It is the forex market, after all, it is volatile as it is. Use the information available for proper analysis and make informed decisions.

CHAPTER 19:

How Is Forex Trading Beneficial to the Financial Market?

More than a hundred years ago, institutional traders and large banks were the only entities that had the means to access Forex markets. Today, the recent technological advancements and the wide use of IoT devices have enabled small traders to take advantage of the various benefits of the foreign exchange market. Similar to NASDAQ, online trading platforms allow small traders to buy and sell currencies on the market.

Forex and the World

Most of the currencies of the world are on a flexible exchange rate. This means that the value of a currency of a particular country fluctuates in response to the latest trends and events that are related to the foreign exchange market.

A floating currency is the exact opposite e of a fixed currency. The value of the latter depends on material goods, another currency, or a currency basket—a portfolio of selected currencies with different weightings. Commonly, governments used the currency basket to reduce the risk of currency fluctuation

In the modern world, the most widely used currencies are floating. These include the Swiss franc, the Indian rupee, the euro, the pound sterling, the Japanese yen, the Australian dollar, and the US dollar. Still. Even with floating currencies, central banks often participate in the foreign exchange market to influence the value of fluctuating exchange rates.

Worldwide, most nations have central banks. About seventy-five percent of the central bank assets are controlled by China, Japan, the US, and the countries in the Eurozone. A central bank is a national bank. It provides banking and financial services for its country's government and banking system. It also implements the government's monetary policy and currency issuance.

The Canadian dollar closely resembles an untainted floating currency. The central bank of Canada hasn't interfered with its value since 1998. The USD runs second to the CAD since the US made little change to its FX reserves. Forex reserves are assets and cash held by a central bank or similar monetary authority. The primary purposes of such organizations are to balance payments of the country, to maintain confidence in financial markets, and to influence the Forex rate of its currency.

Contrastingly, Japan and the United Kingdom intervene a lot. Japan is known for its systematic currency devaluation, and more recently, North Korea also devalued their won to curb inflation rates.

One of the largest and most influential macro-economic themes that affected automation suppliers was the devaluation of Japan's currency. Both Japan and China are manufacturing economies. As stated earlier, exports become cheaper when the currency of a country is devalued. This increases the number of local jobs since tourists and that country's citizens use the local currency pay for local products. This improves the economy, curbs inflation, and increases demand. When demand is high, more job opportunities are available for the people.

In 1973, the Smithsonian Agreement collapsed, and most of the currencies around the world followed suit. Yet, some countries, like the Gulf States, fixed their currency to another currency's value. This, however, is associated with a slower growth rate. With a floating currency, targets, except for the exchange rate, are utilized to implement monetary policy.

Today, it's considered that the currencies all over the world are on a floating rate of exchange. They're always traded in pairs, such as Dollar/Yen, Euro/Dollar, etc. Approximately eighty-five percent of worldwide daily transactions involve Forex trading of major currencies.

Four currency pairs are often utilized for investment purposes. They are the following: US dollar against Japanese yen, Euro against the US, US dollar against the Swiss franc, and British pound against the US dollar. In the trading market, they look like the following: USD/JPY, GBP/USD, USD/CHF, and EUR/USD.

If one currency will appreciate against another, it's recommended to exchange the quote currency for the base currency. By doing so, you can stay in it. In general terms, appreciation is the increase in an asset's value over time. In a floating rate exchange system, the changes in the value are based on demand and supply in the FX market. Appreciation is linked directly to demand. If the value goes up (appreciates), the demand for the currency rises as well.

If your predictions are right, you can initiate the opposite deal. This is done to exchange the first currency for the other and then collecting the profits from it.

Dealers at forex brokerage companies perform transactions on the FX market. Forex is integral to the world market. Hence, while you sleep in your bed, the dealers in the Eurozone are trading currencies with their American counterparts.

Clients can place stop-loss and take-profit orders with brokers. Brokers perform overnight executions. Price movements on the foreign exchange market are smooth. Unlike in the stock market, they don't have gaps every morning. New investors can exit and enter positions without encountering issues because the daily turnover on the Forex market is approximately USD 1.2 trillion.

In truth, the FX market never ceases to stop. The foreign exchange market is the oldest and largest financial market worldwide. When you compare the Forex market with others, you'll see that the market for currency futures only comprises one percent of all Forex transactions. Unlike the stock and futures market, currency trading is decentralized. This means that it isn't centered on any exchange. Currency trading moves from major financial centers of the United States to Europe, Australia, and New Zealand, to Europe, and back to the US. It's a sort of a cycling trading game. To reiterate, large financial institutions and major currency dealers were the only ones to take advantage of the Forex market's liquidity and the amazing trending nature of the world's primary currency pairs. However, today, Forex brokers can break down larger-sized inter-bank units. Because of this, they can offer total beginners and small traders' opportunities to trade in small increments.

Brokers and trading platforms offer small-to-medium companies and individual spectators' options for trading at the same rates and price movements. Two decades ago, only big players like banks dominated the Forex market.

How Can Banks Intervene with Forex Rates?

Central banks have the power to influence foreign exchange rates. The member countries of the European Union (EU) agreed to maintain a band around target exchange rates. When necessary, they will implement this monetary policy through intervention in Forex markets. Even without exchange rate commitments, Japan and the United States often intervene in global FX markets in order to stabilize the value of their domestic currency. Central banks can use a "foreign exchange intervention" as a monetary policy device. When a central bank influences a currency's funds transfer rate, they do so use their asset reserves or their authority to generate banknotes and coinage.

More often than not, central banks in developing countries intervene in Forex markets so that they could build reserves for themselves. Or, they provide for another country's national banks to stabilize exchange rates. Stabilization invites traders to place investments on a particular nation or Forex market. It makes them feel comfortable with the exchanges that are going to transpire on the marketplace. Currency stabilization requires both long-term and short-term interventions. Destabilizing effects may come from both non-market or market forces.

When a central financial institution increases the amount of money circulating within an economy, extra care is needed to reduce its inadvertent effects like hyperinflation.

The efficacy of a Forex intervention relies heavily on how the organization central to the policy mitigates the consequences of the intervention.

In implementing an intervention, central banks face three challenges:

1. The number of reserve assets of a country

2. The economic issues faced by the government

3. The volatile market conditions of the Forex exchanges associated with the nation

Often, after the execution of monetary policies, a corrective intervention may be required. This is done to fix and mitigate the consequences and issues that resulted from the initial intervention of the central bank.

Forex Intercessions Come in Two Types:

1. The government or central agency assesses its currency

When the financial organization determines that the value of the domestic currency is too high for the economies of other countries, especially those that import their products or goods, the central bank of the country in question or another nation will definitely intervene. Their fiat currency should be affordable for their major consumers.

Hence, even though the majority of the world's currencies are floating, there are instances wherein a central agency needs to control or bolster the value of their currency. The only currency that can be considered pure, in terms of being tarnished with repeated interventions, is the CAD. As stated before, the Canadian government had not intervened with the exchange rate of their legal tender in the last forty years.

For example, from the end of Q3 2011 to the start of Q1 2015, the Swiss National Bank (SNB) set a minimum exchange rate between the Euro and Swiss Franc. This prevented the Swiss franc from increasing beyond a level at which their major importers couldn't afford their Swiss goods.

For more than three years, this proved to be advantageous for Switzerland and its importers. However, the Swiss National Bank determined that it must let the Swiss Franc to freely float. Without warning other countries, they released the minimum exchange rate.

2. The intervention is a short-term response to an economic or political event

Often, an event can make a country's currency move in a specific direction over a short period. In this case, a central bank will try to reduce the market's volatility and provide liquidity through intervention.

After the SNB allowed their currency to stay afloat, the Swiss franc decreased in value by approximately twenty-five percent. After this, the SNB implemented a corrective intervention to mitigate the volatility.

On paper, Forex interventions can sometimes be risky. Set monetary policies can even undermine the credibility of a bank when it can't maintain stability.

Defending the domestic currency from speculators was the cause of the economic crisis in Mexico in 1994. A similar event also happened in Thailand, which sparked the 1997 Asian Financial Crisis.

CHAPTER 20:

Pips and What You Need to Know About Them

What Is A Pip?

When you get into the foreign exchange circle, chances are you will encounter the word pip countless times as you begin your journey through the currency trading market. So, what is a pip, and why is it so important in this trade?

In foreign exchange (Forex), pip is the 'point in percentage'. When a currency pair is traded, the pip is what is used to detect losses and gains.

A pip is seen as the basic unit in the Forex market and therefore, for you to be successful in this trade, you will need to understand it. In most currencies, it is represented by the last figure in four decimal places. 0.0003. The three here is the pip.

Therefore, if an exchange rate of the USD to say KSHS is 1 USD = 102.1675, the 5 at the end is the pip.

For example, the US Dollar, probably them the most stable currency in the world and therefore, the currency onto which others are held up against, is often measured on a pip of 0.0001.

There are notable exceptions though, with the Japanese Yen being the most common.

The USD pip point against the JPY is often to three decimal places; therefore, the pip is 0.001.

What is The Function of the Pip?

Now, we have stated above that the pip is a basic unit of foreign exchange and therefore, is one of the things you will need to be aware of as you enter the currency trading market. But right now, the question you ask 'Why is the pip and understanding it important?'

Due to fluctuations in the Forex market, the pip was developed to be able to handle the shifts in the exchange rates. Had it been a larger figure, say well into the ones and tens units of measurement, it would greatly affect not just prices in the Forex market, but it would have the potential to cause far-reaching effects, like changes in prices in commodities in the consumer market. if the pip was said, 1, an increase of two would be a huge shift, with the potential to shift economies.

Therefore, by having the pip value low in the decimal figure, they were able to develop a mechanism that would ensure more stability during fluctuations, even though, as we will discover further down the article, it still is a figure that can quickly grow into huge amounts. So, let's look at some of the terms we could encounter in this field.

Ask Price, Bid Price, and Spread: Term You Should Be Familiar With

Once you set foot in the Forex trading world, you will come across several terminologies, and today, right here, we look at some of the most important ones used.

Let's say you want to sell a currency pair. The price you put forth is what we will define as the 'ask' price as the price. The asking price is, then, the price that you would give when buying a currency pair. It is slightly higher than the market price.

The price that you can sell a currency pair is called the bid price. It is often the price put on display in banks and Forex halls. You will find that this bid price is lower than the market price, which will ensure that whoever buys from you sells it at the market price so as to get a profit.

Then, we have spread. If, say, the bid price is 1.9786 and the asking price is 1.9792, the difference of 6 pips (1.9792 - 1.9786) is the spread. So, we can look at spread as the pip difference between a bid and ask price.

In foreign exchange, it is important to note that Forex happens with two pairs of currencies, where one sells one to buy another. They are called currency pairs

For example, if you have the GBP (Great Britain Pound) and wants to change it with the USD, this will be called trading the USD/GBP pair. Therefore, when you give your GBP to get the USD, you will be selling the GBP and buying the USD.

Popular Currency Pairs in Trading

So, now you think, in order to make the right risks, what popular currency pairs do I need to be aware of?

Popular currency pairs will often be from more developed countries. This is because, since they have more stable economies, their currencies are subjected to less volatility and manipulation due to very small pip values between their exchange rates. They tend to also have more political stability, thus making their markets more certain, and thus, trading in their currencies less risky than others. You will then find that these currencies become the most traded and often, the pairing of one stable currency to another becomes more popular and less risky. But, as it is said, in the Forex business, the risk is the name of the game.

Examples of some of the most popular currency pairs are GBP/USD (British Pound and the US Dollar, USD/JPY (The US Dollar and the Japanese Yen), EUR/USD

As seen from above, the US Dollar is seen to be the most stable, occurring in most of the common currency pair. It is the most stable currency in the world, which is why you can conduct business using US Dollars in pretty much any country in the world. It often has a low spread when traded with others hence its popularity. However, other common pairs could include GBP/JPY, EUR/GBP. These are referred to as Cross currencies, so defined because they do not feature the USD.

Then, there are the so-called exotic pairs. This is the currency pairs between the developing world, as they are colloquially known. Because of their instability, they are more volatile and therefore, are often considered riskier to trade. This is also influenced by the political temperatures, which often has wide implications in the market certainty/uncertainty. An example of this pair could be the USD/KSHS

How Do I Calculate Pips?

Now to the math.

To get the value of the pip, you will need to divide 1/10,000 or 0.0001 (the pip is calculated to the fourth decimal) by the exchange rate. As noted earlier, this is an exception when you are trading the USD, or the EUR with the Japanese Yen, which registers pips with 2 decimal place, that is 0.01.

Pip Value

So, hypothetically speaking, let's say you have the USD/GBP currency pair and you get a quote 0.7754. This means 1 USD will get you 0.7754

GBP. A one pip increase - 0.7755 - would mean that 1 USD will then become more valuable as it will earn you a bit more GBPs.

If, say, you then decide to buy 2000 GBPs with US Dollars, you will then first divide the USD/GBP exchange rate then multiply by the number of Euros you want to buy.

So, it will be [1/0.7754] x 2000 = 2579.31. The price paid will be 2579.31.

If there is a one pip increase in the exchange rate - to 0.7755 - then the calculation would be

[1/0.7755] x 2000 = 2578.98.

Therefore, the pip value between the currencies would be 2579.31 - 2578.98 = USD 0.33.

The more one puts in the trading, the higher the pip value.

Pipettes; a Further Figure

Further down the figures, we get the pipette. Pipettes allow spreading to happen over an even wider area, meaning that it further reduces the risks that come with Forex trading. This is measured as 1/10th of a pip. In most normal pair currencies, it is measured as the fifth number after the decimal place, but when it comes to the Japanese Yen against the dollar, it is represented as third decimal place. Usually, it is displayed in superscript format.

For example, in 1 USD = 0.77576 GBP, the 6 at the end is the pipette.

Pips and Profits: What Affects Your Gains/Losses?

As stated above, the movement of the currency pair determines whether you make gains or losses.

So, for example, if you want to buy into the USD/EUR pair. If the prices of the Euro goes up when you sell, you profit from the increase.

So, say you bought Euros for 1.1843 and then, when you sell, the market price is at 1.1896, your profit will be the 53 pips on the trade.

Relatively speaking, the difference is small. But the Forex market is a big deal, often determining economies of entire countries and the market prices.

Gains and losses add up quickly, thus, meaning that the slightest change can have a high impact and have far-reaching consequences. Small changes will often result in small fluctuations which, when considered over time and consistently, will have bigger consequences. Thus, while it may be a small figure to the untrained eye, a seasoned trader knows the value of a pip. Therefore, so should you.

Why Is It Important To Understand Pip

Understanding pips and pip values are important before you put your money into Forex trading. Among the benefits are;

To Follow the Gains/losses

Seasoned traders often gain the advantage by knowing how the fluctuations of pip values will influence their profit/losses.

Understanding the change in pip value helps you as a trader strategies on which deals will be worth putting your stakes.

To Identify Strong Currency Pairs

When you understand the pip values, you will better be able to access the currency pairs in the market, follow through those that combine well and trade favorably and thus, know where to place your risks.

As we have learned above, a small pip change can have wide implications and this could quickly add up to either gains or losses. Therefore, you will have an understanding of this when you look at the currency pairs.

Leverage

Leverage provides you with the ability to trade with amounts of money that are more than you have on your deposits. If the leverage is, say 30, this will mean that, for every one dollar you have in your deposit, for example, you will control 30 in the Forex market, thus, increasing chances of a huge profit.

Therefore, understanding the pip values will allow you better gauge the risks that are involved in the trading you are about to undertake and choose reasonable leverage sizes that won't dent your pockets in the event of losses.

CHAPTER 21:

Mistakes and Tips for Beginners in Forex Trading

The forex market due to its low restriction makes the market one of the most available market in the world. With an internet connection, phone or computer, and some few dollars, you can begin trading in the market. However, because of its free accessibility does not mean it is easy to make huge returns.

Forex Mistakes

Mistakes in forex are unavoidable but there are always remedies to deal with such a situation. Before you consider plunging into trading, it is important to consider the following mistakes and do everything possible to avoid them in the future. Most people are persuaded to venture into forex trading with fantasies of getting rich overnight.

Undeniably, the opportunities in the forex market are innumerable for you to make money and live the lifestyle you want. Notwithstanding, the forex road is not an easy road to travel because it is full of bumps. If there is anything, I can assure you as a beginner is that you will struggle for various reasons including having a poor forex foundation, poor trading structure, and impatience.

Tips for Trading Forex

Learning to trade successfully in the forex market is quite problematical for new traders. Most traders have the mindset of getting rich overnight, which is not something realistic. Forex trading can be prodigious particularly if you are a beginner and do not know the rules guiding the market. These tips will help you in your trading journey as a beginner. It is always advisable not to forget the basics because without them you will struggle in the market.

Pick Your Broker Cleverly

If you can choose the right broker, then you are halfway done in the forex market. Before choosing any broker, it is important for you to review various brokers. Ensure to seek recommendations from professional traders and make your own research because some traders will recommend a particular broker because of their affiliate programs. Take your time as we have various fake brokers looking for traders like you to ripe off. Do not be moved by mouthwatering deals, rather look for an authorized broker with years of accomplishment.

Develop Your Strategy

A list of tips on forex trading is not complete without mentioning strategy. As a beginner, you need to create your own trading strategy that works for you. Every trader should know what to expect and get from the market. You should set a definite goal because it will help discipline yourself when trading.

Learn Slowly

Forex is not something you learn and stop over time. Every new skill requires consistent learning to grasp the basics. Additionally, you do not have to rush your learning process. Take your time slowly and begin by investing a little amount of money. Remember that slow and steady will win the race as a beginner.

Control Your Emotions

If you allow your emotions to guide you when trading, you will regret it later. I am not telling you that it is easy but you can control it. You need to stay rational in order to make wise choices during trading.

If you let your emotions to rule over you, you are bound to expose yourself to pointless risks. Forex trading is risky but you can control the level of risk that can happen.

Do Not Trade If You Are Under Stress

Hardly can you see someone who concentrates optimally when under stress. Traders who decide to do that will surely make an irrational decision, which will cost them money. Therefore, before thinking of trading, ensure to identify anything that will cause stress and eliminate them before it eliminates your forex account (do not mind me I am just joking but there is a sense to it). If you had a stressful day and still had to trade, consider taking a deep breath while allowing your mind to focus on what you are about to do. You can overcome stress in various ways such as exercising, sleeping, and listening to music, hanging out with friends. Whatever the situation is, find a solution to your stress and manage it effectively.

Never Stop Practicing

Do not neglect this tip because it is crucial to your success or failure as a forex trader. Hardly can you succeed on your first encounter in the forex market. Therefore, when you make your first mistake, do not relent because, with consistent practicing, you will be among the top traders. However, you have the adventure of using a demo account to perfect your skill.

Risk Is Part of The Game

If you are not ready to risk, you are not ready for the forex market. Most brokers will advise you that trading is risky and you should accept that fact. If you think that in forex you are going to have a sweet ride, then you need a reality check. Additionally, I have seen mouthwatering advertisements promising you the "unpromising." Well, you should be realistic about your goals and strategies.

Patience is Priceless

Do you remember the old adage? "True success is never instantaneous." That holds true in the forex market. It is the product of consistent planning and work, which many beginners tend to overlook. There is no easy path to making a profit in the market. Let patience have her way in you.

Upgrade Your Knowledge Continuously

The more you trade, the newer things you learn. Improve your knowledge by looking at trends, analyzing news, and financial processes. Furthermore, do not neglect the fundamental basis you have learned. Significantly, you should study, practice, and continue this routine. A knife gets dull when it is left idle. Sharpen your trading skill with continuous learning and practicing.

Take Breaks

All work and no play make Jack a dull student. You can take routine breaks especially when you are under stress. For those glued to multiple computer winds to analyze data from various source, it is important to take a break as you may feel pressured.

Understand the Charts

You will trade in various markets and these require different information to analyze each trade. We have numerous tools you can use to make your trading easier. However, charts are time efficient and serve as the best option for beginners. You should not know them only; you should learn how to read and use them to your advantage.

Incorporate stop-losses in your trades

Setting stop-loss for trade is an efficient strategy to use when trading. With stop-loss, you minimize your risk and escape any trade that goes haywire.

Additionally, avoid greediness by setting the maximum profit and loss range. Once you hit your target, you should avoid the trap of placing another trade.

CHAPTER 22:

How to Make Money with
Forex Trading to Create Passive Income

According to experts in the field of Forex Trading, it is possible to create a passive income through this form of financial trading. However, before jumping headlong into this type of financial trading, prospective traders need to ask themselves whether it is suitable for them, in addition to learning as much as possible about this line of business.

A passive income is the income stream traders or investors get at regular intervals and require little or no effort on their part to maintain it. Some of the common types of passive income include dividends from stock owned in a listed corporation, rental income, and interest income from bonds.

Other less common forms of passive income include royalties from a music record or publishing a book, or dividends from a non-listed company run by a family member or friend. Passive income may also arise from a new business model or income from a multi-level marketing network, where the income originates from other people's activities.

Some internet marketers, such as affiliate marketers, also receive passive income from internet traffic that continues to stream in from blogs they posted a long time ago. Nowadays, traders can make a passive income through the forex market.

In fact, one does not have to participate directly in the trading process or have tons of experience in this field of business. Forex traders can earn a passive income from this form of financial trading in several ways, with some requiring more work or input from the trader. Some of these include:

Forex Signals

These are short messages new traders can use to determine the best currency to trade and the right time to trade. Traders can receive important trading information through email, text messages, or any other type of communication, including social media platforms such as TX forums, Twitter, and other leading financial trading platforms.

These signals or messages are usually brief snippets of information, which instruct users to take specific actions, such as purchasing EUR/USD at a certain price. Sometimes, these signals feature various types of orders, such as a market order, pending order, or limit order. There are tons of sites that teach traders how to read and understand forex signals.

These signals can also be premium or free, with the former leading to better trades. Many providers of forex signals freely send important trading information to investors to boost their reputation in the financial trading industry. Forex signals are also great for people who want to earn a passive income trading options but do not have the time or opportunity to learn much about Forex Trading.

However, it is important to perform adequate research into providers of forex signals to avoid losing money. Forex traders, however, should approach these signals with utmost caution to make a good passive income.

Forex Robots

One of the best ways to make a passive income from the forex market is using a tool known as a forex robot, which performs automated trades on a trader's behalf. Once traders set up these forex robots, they do not have to do much else; however, they should keep an eye on the trades the forex robots are making for them.

To get started, traders need to perform adequate research into the software available for forex robots. They need to choose software that will meet their needs, in addition to being reliable when it comes to executing the right forex trades. After setting up this software, it will make forex trades based on preset signals.

In addition, it will use its acquired knowledge to purchase or sell at specific times, earning users a passive income in the process. However, it is important to understand that not all forex robots make passive income for investors as claimed. In the same way that a human can make a losing trade, a forex robot can also make the same mistake.

It is also important to understand that many so-called forex robots are frauds, which is why respected news platforms such as the Wall Street Journal and Forbes refuse to promote or advertise them. Unfortunately, this is particularly true when it comes to free forex robots. Therefore, new forex traders should analyze testimonials and reviews carefully before entrusting their investment to a forex robot.

Fortunately, several leading sites focus on reviewing different trading platforms. These sites try to give an honest opinion of different investment platforms and outline all the benefits and limitations of each platform. They also offer a detailed analysis of how these platforms work and how traders can get started on them, which is especially helpful to new traders.

Social Trading

The social trading network works in the same way as a social networking platform. Instead of sharing selfies or pictures of pets playing the piano, however, social traders share important information about forex or financial trades. This allows others to copy them and make passive income as well.

New forex traders simply need experienced traders they trust and copy their trading strategies to make money. In addition to making a passive income, they will also learn when, why, and how successful traders make their trading moves, which will give them more insight and understanding into the forex industry.

However, finding traders, they can trust and emulate is not as easy as it may sound. New traders need to set aside adequate time to perform thorough research into different social trading platforms, in addition to learning more about forex traders they want to work with and copy.

In certain situations, they might need to spend some money on the trader whose trading strategies they copy. However, this commission is negligible and not a big concern for new traders who want to make a passive income. Forex Trading is something that most people looking for ways to make some extra cash look into.

However, most of them do not know where to start. This discussion provides three great ideas for Forex Trading beginners to consider. Each of the options above requires a different investment in terms of time and effort. The most important thing to remember is that beginners should perform adequate research before picking a trading platform or strategy to use.

Nowadays, Forex Trading is one of the best ways for people to make a passive income working online. Millions of traders are earning a passive or active income every day through Forex Trading. This line of business is just like any other online money-making concept, but its profit potential is unrivaled. With modern technological advances and the availability of detailed information, anyone can make a passive income through Forex Trading.

CHAPTER 23:

Compound Interest And Forex

E arning more means being paid more. We usually think that others should pay us more if we want to make more money, but this is not always true. We can earn more even if we pay ourselves more, and not the others.

This is a fundamental principle underlying the financial success, first disclosed in 1926 by George Samuel Clason through his book entitled The Richest Man in Babylon, a great motivational classic.

The principle states that part of what you earn must be maintained. Putting aside at least 10% of what you earn—and making that money inaccessible to ordinary expenses and possibly even extraordinary expenses—you can increase this amount exponentially over time. Considering any investments, thanks to the power of the compound investment, the amount saved or invested over the years can become important. In fact, many people can earn more and build their assets by paying themselves first. It is a true and effective principle today as it was in 1926.

Yet, as this 10% formula is easy, people are unwilling to listen to it and apply it. This is because you are usually looking for tricks to get rich quickly, and you do not have a medium to long-term vision. On the other hand, having a long-term investment plan is a solid foundation for building one's own economic stability. And you can start earning more by paying yourself first from today. The earlier you start, the quicker you will build your financial success.

Using The Power Of Compound Interest

To earn more, you can take advantage of the compound interest. Here's how it works: if you invest €1,000 at a 5% interest, you will earn €50 of interest, and at the end of the first year, you will have a total investment of €1,050. If you leave both the initial investment and the interest earned on the current account, you will receive a 5% interest the following year over €1,050, or €52.50. In the third year, you will earn 5% out of 1,102.50, and so on. At this rate, within 15-30 years your money will turn into an amount well above the sum invested initially. But precisely how much does the invested capital grow? Luca Pacioli explained it in the 15th century: any capital doubles in some years equal to 72 divided by the interest rate. Returning to our example: if the interest is at 5% per year, we divide 72 by 5; which makes 14.4 (i.e., in 14 years and 4 months the initial capital doubles). The sooner you start, the bigger the result will be, as you will have more time for the interest you capitalize on produce its powerful magic. Start now to save and invest for your future, even if you do not have a large sum. You do not need to have an extra sum of money. You can start with any amount and grow it over time.

The Secret Of Paying Of Yourself First

If you want to earn more money by paying yourself first, you have to make savings and investment a central part of your financial management, just like the mortgage payment. Get accustomed to saving a fixed percentage (at least 10%) of your monthly income and investing it in special savings account that you decide not to touch. Ideally, this step would be automatic, such as a fixed monthly deduction on your paycheck. The automation will ensure that you will not have to rely on your self-discipline and your ability to save will not be affected by your mood from domestic emergencies or otherwise. Continue to increase that account until you have saved enough to invest the sum accumulated in bonds, in a mutual fund or real estate (spending money on rent without building any assets is really a waste). Let your investments build your assets over time and try to live with what remains after you have paid yourself. If you want to spend, try to earn more to afford it. But never put your hands on your savings to finance a more ambitious lifestyle. The ideal would be for your investments to grow to the point where you could live with interest, if necessary. Only then will you really be financially autonomous and free.

If you want to earn more, you need to create assets, not liabilities. Rather than spending all the money you earn by enriching someone else, invest in assets that produce other income (stocks, bonds, real estate, gold, etc.). When your money starts to grow, educate yourself further about the best way to invest your money. Stay informed about news about investment opportunities and remember to protect what is yours through a good insurance policy. Do not blindly trust who will manage your money, but always try to improve your financial education. This will make you a financially prepared person ready to get rich. Once you understand this, money will follow.

What is compound interest? Not everyone may know how to respond immediately to this question. If everyone knows what the simple interest is (i.e., the one that withdraws at the end of the agreed time unit), fewer are those who know what the compound interest is, how it works, and, most importantly, how to take advantage of it.

The example of a bank account is enlightening.

If on 1 January, I have a net rate of 1% on my account, at the end of the year I have €101. A euro more is added to the capital and, if the conditions do not change, at the end of the second year, I will not have €102, but €102 and a cent where the cent represents 1% of the euro accumulated after the first year.

So far, everything is clear, but most of us cannot calculate the compound interest of investment and tend to treat it as simple interest. This is due to its slow start, that, especially with small capital, tends to be treated as "irrelevant". However, there is nothing more wrong that an investor could do.

If, for example, after 5 years of investment, my capital of €100 is now €140, we are led to believe that the interest was 8% per year.

This is incorrect because, in doing so, we do not take into account that at the end of each period the interest accumulate has gone to increase capital. If the interest had really been 8%, composing the 5 years we would have had

Initial capital: €100

· 1st year: €108

· 2nd year: €116.64

· 3rd year: €125.97

· 4th year: €136.04

· 5th year: €146.93

The difference (€6.93) represents almost 7% of the total. As you can see, it is easy to take dazzle (and worse, even "suffer", if for some reason we are offered a simple interest for a compound interest).

The Maths Behind Compound Interest: An Easy Example

Suppose we have an initial capital of €1,000. The capital yields a Y% interest and this interest is calculated on an annual basis.

What will be the value of the investment after X years?

The calculation formula is as follows:

(1) IV = CP (1 + Y) ^ X

IV is the value of the investment after X years, while CP is the initial capital. Y is expressed as a percentage, i.e. 0.04 indicates 4%. The symbol ^ is the symbol of elevation to power.

The inverse calculation tends to find the Y interest of an investment that now (net of inflation) is worth IV against a CP capital invested X periods (years) ago. The formula is:

(2) Y = (IV / CP) ^ (1 / X) - 1

Suppose that, after inflation, €1,000 invested 5 years ago are now worth €1,400, you immediately have that the yield was 6.96%.

Let's take a look at another example:

Marie has just taken the salary and can finally buy the air conditioner she needs.

But her friend Julie calls her to tell her that she has an urgent need that she cannot cope with immediately and asks her to borrow €1,000.

Marie is undecided because this would mean waiting another month before she can make her purchase.

To resolve the issue, the two girls agree on the loan provided that Julie returns the money to Mary with a 5% interest (the numbers are purely random for the example).

In this way, Marie has a greater incentive to have to delay her purchase.

When Julie returns the sum loaned, she will receive €1,050 instead of €1,000.

The following month, Marie can buy the air conditioner and, to celebrate, use the accumulated interest (€50) to go out to dinner with her boyfriend.

In short, in the end, this recognition for the delayed use was not bad!

Now that we understand the concept behind the rate of interest, it is good to enter a little more in detail and make some distinctions.

In this regard, we can divide the interest rate into two broad categories:

1. The simple interest

2. The compound interest

Simple Interest:

Let's go back to the previous example.

At the end of the period, Julie returns the money plus the interest to Mary. Soon after, however, the girl asks the same amount again to buy a new refrigerator, as the old one suddenly broke.

Marie agrees to lend the money back to her friend.

The following month, Julie firmed up her debt plus new interests, again for a total of €1,050.

Now, Marie is with her initial capital, plus €100 in interest, for a total of €1,100.

Interest is defined as simple when, once it has matured on the underlying capital, it does not generate further interest.

In our example, we note that the first €50 was not added to the capital loaned the second time.

Compound Interest:

Change of scenery.

Julie asks Marie to lend her €1,000 with the promise to return them in two years.

Mary agrees, as long as Julie accepts a compound interest on the mature borrowed capital.

In this case, Julie will not have to pay the interest immediately at the end of the 1st year but will add the € 50 interest in the capital, which will accumulate 5% in the 2nd year.

At the end of the agreed period, Julie must therefore return:

1. €1,000 capital

2. €50 interest for the first year (€1,000 + 5%)

3. €52.50 interest for the second year (€1.050 + 5%)

The total capital to be returned to Mary is, therefore, € 1,102.50.

Here we have materialized € 2.50 more than the previous example, due to the compound interest.

The interest is defined as compound when, once it has matured on the underlying capital, it is added to the latter and contributes to generating further increased interest in the future.

Do you understand why the compound interest is your new best friend?

When you deposit your money in the bank account you are doing as Marie, that is, you are "lending" your money to the bank, which uses them to perform its credit function and lend it to people and businesses.

CHAPTER 24:

The Resistance Trading Strategy

The support and resistance that we talked about before can be used to help you come up with the perfect trading strategy as well. In fact, this can be a great way to help you do well with purchasing securities at the right time and to reduce your costs and increase your profits.

In these strategies, the support is going to be the price level you will purchase. This price level is going to be very strong, and it is about to reverse or interrupt the downtrend and will go back up soon. When the downward trend hits the support level, it is likely to bounce again, and the price will rise. If you purchase the security when it is almost to the support, you will receive the lowest price for the security at that time.

Then there is the resistance. This is going to be the opposite of the support. This is going to occur where the price level is so strong that it is going to reverse the uptrend and start going down. When the uptrends start to get near this level, the trend will likely stop, and then it will go down. You will want to sell the security as close to this resistance level to increase your profits as much as possible.

The resistance and the support are going to change daily. But sometimes it is difficult to find the line as clearly as others. The price movement of the security may be really volatile at some points of the day. And then there may be full days where you won't be able to create either the support line, the resistance line, or either of them. If you can't create the line, it may be better to pick out a different strategy. But if you can start your day looking at the charts and can draw some strong support or resistance lines, then this is the strategy that you should work with.

The good news is that there are various steps that you can work with on the charts that you gather for an asset. Bring those out, and use the steps below to help you draw your own support and resistance levels to help you work on your own trades:

- Often half dollars and whole dollars can be good support and resistance levels. This is especially true when you work on stocks under $10. If you can't find your support or your resistance lines, check here and see if your line would work there.

- When you make your own lines, you need to have the most recent data available. This ensures that you are getting the best information for that stock.

- The more that your line can touch the extreme price of the stock, the better option this line is for your support and resistance. If it is too far from this extreme point, then it is not going to have enough value to make it strong.

- Only look at any support or resistance lines that stay with the current price range. For example, if the stock's price is around $20 right now, you do not need to look at the region on the graph where the stock randomly jumped up to $40. This is not an area where the stock will probably go back to, so it doesn't make much sense to work from there.

- Many times, the support and resistance are not just one exact number. Often it is more of an area. If you come up with a support or resistance that is about $19.69, then you know that the movement is somewhere near that number, not exactly that number. You can usually estimate that the area will be somewhere between five to ten cents above or under that line.

- The price that you want to work from will need to have a clear bounce off that level. If you can't find that this price bounces at that level, then this is not a good support or resistance level for you to work with. Your levels need to be easy to notice and need to make sense for the charts you look at. If you have any questions about whether you picked the right one or not, it's not the right one.

As you are going through and creating these lines, you will find that it isn't always as simple as it seems. You want to take extra care to pick out the right spots for these lines, or you will make bad decisions with your trading. The good news is that the more you draw these lines and do the trades, the better you will get at doing it.

After you take the time to draw the lines on your charts, you can then make your own trading strategy, which is there to help you purchase or sell the securities you want, and the timing will be based on the lines you drew. The steps that you can take to make this kind of trading strategy to work after drawing your lines will include:

1. When you first get up in the morning, sit down and make a watchlist. Take a look at your charts and draw out the

resistance and the support lines that go with the information you have. Use the steps above to help draw these lines.

2. Now you need to create your five-minute chart. Then spend some time watching the action of the price, watching how it responds to those lines. If you find that near the line there is a type of indecision candle, then this is the exact confirmation you are looking for to determine you picked the right line. Now is the time to get into the trade. Your goal here is to purchase your security as near to that support level as you can to reduce the risks but realize that it's unlikely you will get right on the line.

3. Once you enter the trade, you need to consider when you would like to withdraw from the trade to profit.

4. Keep the trade open for a bit, even after you have withdrawn. This makes it easier to hit the target you set for profit, or until you see that the security is forming with a new resistance and support level compared to what you originally drew.

5. You may decide that trading at a half position near your profit target. This allows them to move the stop when they want closer to the entry point to at least reach a break-even point.

6. If you are looking through the charts that you have, and you see that the support and resistance level have gone away, or they aren't obvious any longer, then it is time to close the trade and move on.

This is a very effective trading method to work with as a beginner. If it is done properly, and after you have some time to experiment withdrawing support and resistance levels, it is a great way to learn when to enter and exit the market.

As long as you create the lines in the right places, and you know how to watch the market for the right entry and exit points, you will find that this strategy is really easy to work with.

Exchange Traded Funds (Etfs)

One of the most important trends of the financial world in the last two decades has been the rise of Exchange Traded Funds or ETFs. The first ETF like asset was introduced in 1989 and currently ETFs hold a total of more than 2.5 trillion dollars worldwide in over 1800 funds and the sector is still growing.

But what are they exactly? ETFs are "tracking" assets that follow certain groups (indices, sectors) of stocks bonds and other, mostly financial products. They are a bit like mutual funds but are traded like stocks on exchanges and also they are mostly passively managed—meaning that no fund manager is deciding on the allocation.

ETFs Versus Mutual Funds

According to numerous studies most fund managers fail to achieve the returns of stock indices that have a profound effect on asset allocation by money managers and individual investors alike. Whatever is the strategy or how sophisticated the manager is, 80% of funds underperform indices even without accounting for fees.

Passive investing is very cheap with ETFs, that's why a lot of investors choose index tracking ETFs and sector ETFs to get exposure to whole markets or particular sectors or industries rather than constructing a portfolio of individual stocks or buying a mutual fund.

And it is not just the direct costs that are lower— taxing of gains is much more attractive in ETFs, although the difference is not the same in every country.

Still, the mutual fund industry is a magnitude bigger than the ETF industry as many big investment pools (such as insurance companies and pension funds) are simply not allowed to buy them as they are technically individual stocks.

Global exchange-traded funds
Assets under management, $trn

Types Of ETFs

There is a wide variety of ETF choices that can help individual investors create a balanced portfolio throughout asset classes. To name a few, you can get exposure to the already mentioned

- Global stock indices

- Industry Sectors

And also

- Commodities

- Government Bonds

- Corporate Bonds

- Currencies

- Volatility

- Short exposure (inverse ETFs)

You can find comprehensive screeners for ETFs

Examples And Up-To-Date Tips

The biggest ETF, SPY, is naturally tracking the most traded stock index, the S&P 500. It's very low-cost structure (0.1%/year) and high liquidity makes it the top choice to get exposure to U.S. stocks for individuals and managers who are allowed to invest in or trade with it.

Bond and commodity ETFs might be very attractive in the current environment for several reasons. The market rout of the first few weeks of 2016 has been triggered by weakness in commodities that led to problems among high-yield ("junk") bonds. With ETFs, you can benefit from a possible rebound or more downside in those assets directly, and easily.

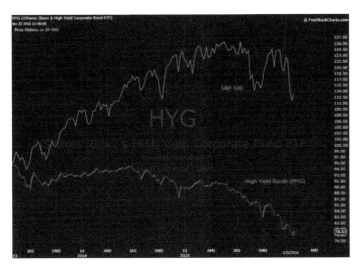

As you can see on the chart above, HYG, one of the biggest the high-yield bonds ETF, has been leading stocks lower lately and by buying or shorting it, you can play both sides of the current trend in a simple manner. The numerous commodity ETFs and inverse ETFs provide versatile ways of hedging, investing, or trading in these volatile times.

And whatever trends you think the future will bring these funds provide very effective choices to invest in your ideas and views without any middleman or extra commissions; so always kep ETFs in mind before deciding on asset allocation.

CHAPTER 25:

Practical Guide to the Trend-Line

To invest better in the financial markets, you must undoubtedly use the right indicators, so fortunately we can tell you that you have landed in the right place because here in our portal we want to offer professional advice and strategies for those who intend to take trading seriously and do it with technical analysis indicators.

We often hear that trading is simple, but this must not lead any trader to underestimate an activity that in all respects entrepreneurial and serious like trading, consequently you have to plan everything, have a solid foundation and do studies with dedication to achieve important results.

As you probably already know with trading you will not get results immediately especially if you do not perform a very detailed graphic analysis. We often see traders throwing their capital away for the simple fact of investing without any criteria and without using any tactics or strategy.

For completeness, we also say that many traders throw capital upside down because they choose the trading platform incorrectly.

The importance of the trend-line indicator

One of the simplest but effective ways to study the price movements on the markets and to use technical indicators and in particular the trend-lines, each indicator has its qualities but there are some more important and used than others all of them are used to read the past. The topicality of the market to foreshadow future price movements with the greatest possible precision, of course, this does not mean being able to predict the future of what will happen in the market. Still, the interesting thing is that you can reach an excellent degree of approximation.

This is why we strive to emphasize the importance of using indicators and that is why we choose to draw up such papers. By continuing to read, you can learn more about the use of trend-lines and how you can use them in investing on the markets, whether it is forex, stocks, indices or commodities, it makes no difference because trend-lines are a usable tool whenever you wish.

In addition to explaining how to use the trend-line indicator, we will provide you with some valid, proven strategic advice from industry experts, therefore by dedicating 5 minutes of your time to reading this strategy, you can achieve excellent results need is a little patience. .

How does the trend-line indicator work?

You will surely already be aware that we don't like to leave anything to chance especially when we explain the operation of a technical indicator. Clarifying is the best way so that once you have finished reading this article, you can go to the financial markets directly to start using the trend-lines and try to make some investments through them. To begin with, therefore, it is really necessary to give a clear and simple definition of the trend-line concept. This indicator has been used since time immemorial in trading and has always offered excellent results to its users.

If you are observing the price trend on a graph and you seem to be able to identify a real trend or a trend within the market, it will be precisely with the trend lines that you will be able to properly highlight the directionality of the market both it is bullish or bearish.

The Italian name of the indicator as we have already mentioned is "trend lines", they are precisely half-lines drawn on a graph when the price moves in a specific direction.

There are, to be precise, 2 distinct types of trend-lines:

Support trend-line: a support trend-line and bullish or bullish trend-line, it is a dynamic support line that joins two or more increasing lows reached by the price.

Resistance trend-line: on the contrary when we talk about a resistance trend-line we refer to a bearish trend line or a bearish trend-line. It is a dynamic resistance line drawn on a graph by joining two or more decreasing maximums reached by the price.

Not all trend-lines should be considered reliable in the same way, a trend line can be considered solid only when it has touched at least two or more points on the price, increasing or decreasing as we have highlighted above.

Opening positions with the trend-line indicator

So let's now find out the most interesting aspect of the use of the trend-lines this means that we are going to offer you some methods of use operating on the trend-line graphs for the opening of purchase or sale positions that are valid for any tool financial you decide to use with the particular expediency to always turn to those lively and highly directional markets, characterized by strong volatility, with particular reference to the Forex market of course and by the main pair of this market the EUR / USD.

The advantage of using this indicator certainly lies in allowing an effective investment both in the long term and in the medium term. Still, ultimately also the operators who prefer investments in intraday trading can benefit enormously from the use of the trend lines that however, they should always be used also with the help of other technical indicators that enrich and optimize the information already obtained through the trend-lines.

Long market entry: you can choose to enter a long market when the breakdown of a resistance trend line occurs, however it will be necessary for the new level of support to be tested by the price without a new breakdown occurring or, an unsuccessful side phase.

Short market entry: on the contrary you can decide to open a bearish position when the breakdown of a support trend-line occurs, in this case the new dominant market forces will be the sellers, but as always wait for the signal to be confirmed by the succession of the highest decreases touched by the price 2-3 times.

Use the trend-lines to invest and enjoy their ease of use like many other operators before you. Doing technical analysis and earning thanks to your reading skills of the graphs could be much simpler than you thought. By illustrating the functioning of the trendlines we have amply demonstrated it to you now it is up to you to apply these simple principles to get the most out of your performed.

Trading Strategy With The Use Of RSI

Many traders want to scalp but cannot find a valid way that allows them to put the technique into practice to its full potential. It is not easy to find a strategy that can give excellent results in most of the trades that take place. Still, today you have the opportunity to know a scalping strategy that is used a lot and by a large number of investors for the simple fact that everyone understood that it works, but above all nobody has difficulty in putting it into practice.

The RSI oscillator and its operation

In practice this indicator of the relative strength of the price is a useful tool for studying graphs similar to the stochastic. If you want to insert it on your price chart you can see that its standard value is set at 14 periods, but you can change it according to your preferences even if the advice is always to leave it as it is.

If what we have said so far seems complicated to you, just know that the RSI oscillator is nothing more than a line, very similar to a moving average that is lent below your price chart and oscillates between two values: 0 and 100. Between these two values it is possible to indicate two particularly significant areas that you must always keep under close control, the area above the value of 70 and the one below the value of 30.

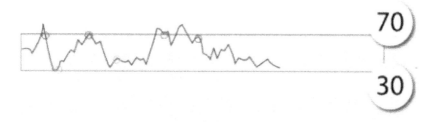

But why are these two areas so important to achieve results using this strategy?

Here we come to the point because it is the key concept of this strategy. In fact, when the RSI is below the value of 30, the security or asset on which you want to trade is in an oversold phase, while when it is above 30 you are in an overbought phase. As you will know in trading, reversals and price corrections are extremely important and very often they represent the only, if not the most important, opportunities to place an investment. This is why it is necessary to pay attention to the overbought and unsold items: when the price is in those areas there may be a reversal of the trend.

A 50 line is also shown in the indicator, which is very useful for identifying the prevailing direction of the market you are analyzing. Especially you have to notice if the line is oscillating from the bottom up or vice versa.

If you want to confirm the real formation of a new trend on the market, you just need to identify a divergence. Divergences are very important in trading because they can offer very reliable signals that lead to successful trading in most cases.

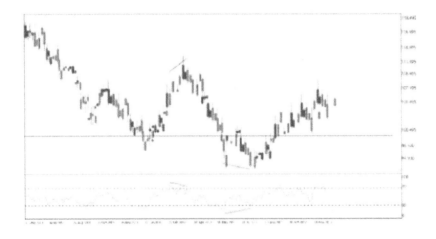

In the graph you can see 2 examples of divergences relating to the RSI oscillator. In the first case we have a rise in the price and a RSI in the descending phase, which indicates that a bearish reversal could occur in the short term, which we actually find in the graph. In the second case, however, we can observe the opposite case: a decrease in the price and a RSI in a bullish phase, here too the same rule applies and therefore the price shortly after begins to rise.

Trading signals with the scalping strategy with RSI

Now that you understand how the RSI indicator works, let us go into more detail to understand how to use the indicator by scalping...

First you need to select a suitable time frame of the chart. Obviously, if you intend to scalp the time frame of the be very narrow and in no case should it exceed 15 minutes.

Remember that with scalping then, and operating at such low time frames, your operation cannot last very long. Some performed remain open even for only a few seconds, up to a maximum of 4-5 minutes, only rarely longer, also because it is very difficult for new trends to last very long on such a short time frame.

Long market entry: a bullish position can be opened when the market is oversold. Therefore below the limit threshold of 30 indicates that the market is not strong enough to continue its bearish direction and a reversal of the trend. Thus, it is imminent and will be bullish.

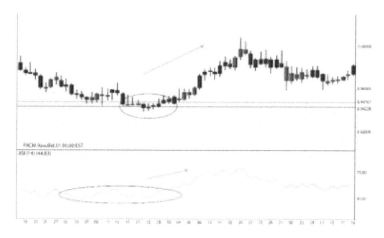

Entry to short market: instead you can earn by opening a short position when the market is in the overbought phase so you will notice that the RSI line moves too high up to exceed the value of 70, so here by force of things the market will change direction because there has been an excess of upward and you can get in and out quickly by taking advantage of the trend correction.

CHAPTER 26:

Currency Futures And Cryptocurrencies

WHAT ARE CURRENCY FUTURES?

Futures markets and easy access to the currency speculation they provide have been around for decades. In this book, I chose to put a little more emphasis on the relatively new and somewhat unknown world of FOREX. However, it is essential that traders fully understand the opportunities available to them in future currency markets. As you will see from this text, I am trying to be a champion of monetary speculation through centralized and regulated futures instead of ready-to-use products (FOREX).

Although the futures market is the most mature, many novice traders are unaware of the possibility of speculating on currencies through futures. Even worse, they are not aware of the benefits of doing so. This is likely because futures markets have been overshadowed by the widespread and aggressive marketing techniques used by foreign exchange dealers to acquire new customers and gain a speculative market share from futures brokers. Nevertheless, currency futures are traded in abundance on the CME Group's Globex Futures trading platform and may offer a more liquid trading environment than most credits.

Like foreign exchange contracts, futures contracts are electronic contracts that create or receive the underlying asset at a particular future date. In other words, the seller of a future contract agrees to deliver the declared goods on a predetermined delivery date; the buyer of a futures contract agrees to receive the goods declared on the stipulated delivery date. The only variable in a futures transaction is the price at which it is made - and buyers and sellers in the market determine it. Traders often underestimate the big difference between traded shares versus leveraged futures trades and FOREX environments. When an equity trader buys part of a particular business, he buys an asset. As the owner of these shares, he is entitled to any future cash flow generated by the share, such as dividends and capital gains (assuming the stock is sold at a profit). Traders and futures do not trade or sell an asset; instead, they negotiate a liability derived from the underlying asset's value; thus, they are known as derivatives.

Unlike foreign exchange contracts, currency futures are delivered only four times a year, according to the quarterly cycle. As you may recall, currency traders technically review deliveries to positions that have been occupied for more than two days but are forced to flip them daily to avoid making or receiving deliveries. Forex traders, on the other hand, only have to worry about rolling positions in March, June, September, and December. Scrolling is simply deleting a contract that expires and entering the next available contract month. For example, a trader bought a futures contract on the yen in December to deliver the underlying asset that was approaching. It would sell a yen in December to exit the position and buy a yen in March to restore a long position. Again, this process is called rollover and must be run manually by the merchant. This is different from FOREX, where the broker automatically launches the customer's positions.

Contract expiration

Now, you know that futures contracts are expiring agreements between buyers and sellers of these contracts to trade the underlying currency. You also know that most speculators have little interest in participating in the delivery process. However, it is a bit more complicated to avoid the delivery obligations inherent in the conclusion of a future contract than to spend the day before your official salary.

The expiry of the contract is the day and time when a given month of maturity of a future foreign exchange contract is no longer negotiated, and the final settlement price is determined. That's when the delivery process begins. Except for a few obscure contracts, CME-listed currency futures are delivered four times a year on the third Wednesday of March, June, September, and December. If there is no holiday or other holidays, the last trading day for the CME coins is the Monday before the expiry date. As a result, traders should be outside their positions well before they expire. Traders who are not interested in creating or receiving the underlying currency should leave their positions on the previous Friday, but preferably before.

The WEC publishes an official renewal date in which traders are advised to move from the due month to the month following the contract. The suggested date for doing this is exactly one week before the last trading day and probably does not prevent hitting the flock. You would not want to hold open positions until the last trading day because the market will likely have declined to this point. This will not only result in wider gaps between supply and demand but may also result in irrational volatility.

As a reminder, foreign exchange renewals occur daily, while renewals of futures contracts occur only four times a year. However, one of the advantages of FX trading is that your broker will automatically roll over your positions without you lifting a finger. A futures broker will not give you the same courtesy. Still, if you negotiate with a legitimate broker, you will do everything possible to inform you of the expiration of the contract and prevent the delivery process from occurring. While this may be among the most common fears among futures traders, accidental possession of positions during delivery is rare. If you make the mistake of triggering delivery, do not panic! It is repairable, but it can cost you a few hundred dollars to give up your obligation. This is something you would like to avoid.

Unlike currency transfers, which involve the inconvenience and potential cost of interest rate differentials, term traders should not be overburdened with credit and interest rates. The commission and the natural spread between the bid and ask minimal prices (usually a tick) are only the cost of a futures contract.

Futures markets have high standards

Without the standardization of contracts, buyers and sellers would be forced to negotiate the details of each transaction. As you can imagine, this would significantly slow down speculation and eliminate liquidity and market efficiency.

Despite significant differences in the size of contracts between futures and foreign exchange contracts, trading in both arenas uses standard contracts that can be easily purchased or sold in any order. In currency futures, there are three standard contract sizes. For example, futures traders have the opportunity to negotiate a full contract that varies in size (except for the yen and the pound sterling) from 100,000 to 125,000 units. A mini-contract is measured at half of the standard, and E-micro futures represent one-tenth of the size of the original futures contract.

How can a futures market guarantee every trade?

Once again, FOREX trades are subject to counterparty risk. If the person or entity that assumes the other part of your foreign exchange transaction cannot fulfill your obligation, you cannot be compensated by specific speculation especially if you trade through a trading desk where your brokerage acts as a market maker. As you can imagine, it is not always able to fulfill its financial obligations. This is especially true if you can accumulate significant profits, resulting in huge losses for the counterparty. Such events are rare in frequency, but I think we can all agree that once, it's too much! It is not because it was not a common problem in the past that this will not happen in the future - and it is difficult to justify taking unnecessary risks in negotiations. It is hard enough to make money in the markets based on controllable factors, not to mention the fate of your trading account for the finances of others. REFCO, the well-known US-based FOREX broker that collapsed in 2005, turns balances into customer accounts in cents after the bankruptcy courts split the remains.

One of the most interesting features of futures is the foreign exchange guarantee. Each transaction canceled by a futures exchange is guaranteed; Unfortunately, such a guarantee does not mean that you will earn money. Instead, it is the guarantee that, if you speculate correctly, you will be compensated for the deserved amount based on the price of entries and exits. Most traders believe that this will always be the case, regardless of the markets they trade and the broker they use, but this is not the case. FOREX traders do not have the same luxury of knowing that market integrity is always protected by applicable rules and regulations.

Although the NFA recently limited the leverage offered by currency brokers, they were free to provide clients with significant leverage. As wonderful as some traders thought it was, that's exactly why currency brokers could never guarantee business; excessive leverage is more risk to the counterparty and the trader. Futures markets stipulate and impose margin requirements for each foreign exchange contract at a rate generally greater than that of similar foreign exchange contracts. This allows them the risk management needed to provide operators with a performance guarantee.

Margin is a necessary nemesis; without ensuring that speculators have sufficient funds in hand to cover potential losses, stock exchanges and futures brokers run the risk that speculators move away from their trading losses to let them hold the purse. Even with the margin required on the deposit, traders can lose more than the funds in their trading account (yes, this is possible with leveraged speculation, and this happens). If this happens, it creates a negative balance on the customer's account, called the balance owing, and gives rise to a chargeable customer of his brokerage firm. As a result, the broker's role has been entrusted to the lender and not to the entity bringing together buyers and sellers. To strengthen the ability of futures markets to secure transactions, it is customary to keep the broker-dealer responsible for covering the client's obligations with the exchange until he can reconstitute the entire account. ... where appropriate.

Term exchanges act as a bank, giving traders access to products of substantial value in exchange for a "payment" or a minimum margin. Fortunately, the rules that are actively enforced concerning the appropriate margin and futures exchanges hold brokerages accountable for their clients' debit balances contribute to market liquidity and stability attempts - a feature that real estate, cannot always portray.

On the contrary, while foreign exchange traders seem less exposed to the risk of counterparty default in the current environment, thanks to NFA's new margin rules which limit leverage to 50 to 1, these gap trading platforms seem to make currency futures much more advantageous. more attractive for FX

Now that we have made it clear that FOREX traders are subject to counterparty risk and that futures traders are not, let's look at the process that allows futures exchanges to guarantee transactions executed with a little more detail. As you know, to establish a position in the US futures market, an operator must have a specific amount of margin on the deposit. If the trader's positions change unfavorably to trigger a margin call, an adjustment, settlement, or deposit of funds is required to continue the speculative game.

CHAPTER 27:

Easy Ways to Reduce Your Risks

Trading in the Forex market can be risky. There are a lot of different options to choose from since the market is open 24-hours a day, and you have to worry not only about the two currencies that you want to trade in but also about other countries that interact with your chosen countries. All of this can mean a lot of risk on your part. The good news is that there are some easy things that you can do to ensure that you reduce your risks and see great results in the end.

Research the Economies You Want to Invest In

Research is so important when it comes to picking out the right currency pairs. Not only do you need to worry about the two currencies that you want to work with, but you also have to worry about any countries that trade with those countries, and how changes in that country will affect your trade.

You should never just jump into a trade when you join the Forex market. Steady research, including before, during, and after the trade, can make a big difference in the results that you see. Pick out the newspapers, magazines, and other resources that you want to use and then read through them on a regular basis.

And always make sure that at least one of your sources gives you daily news so you can keep up with what is happening around you and if any big events will change the value of your currency pair.

Keep the Emotions at Home

Emotions are going to be a deal breaker with any investment. As soon as you allow the emotions to come into the game, things are going to head downhill for you. These emotions can get in the way of clear thinking and often cause you to lose a lot of extra money in the Forex market. Learning how to keep the emotions out of your trades is critical if you would like to make a profit in the process.

This is why it's so important to have a solid trading plan from the beginning. That way, when you enter the market, you know exactly what you will invest in, how long you plan to invest, what needs to happen for you to leave the market, and more. And as long as you stick with that plan, you should be able to limit any potential losses and even help yourself make more money in the Forex market overall.

If you are someone who often falls prey to their emotions, then it may be best to consider a different form of trading. Emotions will force you into revenge trading, staying in the market for too long, speculation, and other behaviors that are risky and can make you lose a lot of money. Sticking with a good trading plan and trading strategy can make the difference in how successful you are with this market though.

Work with a Broker

As a beginner, it is a good idea to work with a broker. The Forex market can be confusing sometimes and having a professional by your side, someone who can answer any of your questions and who will walk you through some of the steps can be a game saver. Add in that brokers often have the platforms that you need, at least the good and secure ones, and it makes sense that you would want to work with a good broker.

Before you pick a broker though, make sure to discuss their fees and any other information with them. Some brokers charge based on how much you trade in the market, and some will charge a flat fee. You will also be charged more or less depending on how much help you need from the broker in the process. Have a listing of all the fees ahead of time so you know how much of your profits will go to someone else.

Put Your Stop Losses in Place

Always make sure that you have your stop losses in place when you begin to trade. These will ensure that you keep your losses to a minimum and help you to keep any of your profits as well. These stop points tell the market when you want to exit, even if you are asleep and can't watch your computer all the time. The stop losses can do a great job of keeping you in the game, limiting your losses, and preventing more risk than is necessary.

First, you must step a stop loss for losing money. This needs to be placed at the point where you are comfortable losing that much money. When the market goes down and reaches that point, your trade will be closed, and you will just have to settle that loss. Even if the market continues to go down, your stop loss took you out and ensured you didn't lose more money.

If you had gotten into the market without the stop loss, you might have wanted to stay in the market and hoped that things got better. Or the downturn may have happened while you were asleep, and you wouldn't be able to fix the issue. Either way, this stop loss can help save you a bunch of money.

You should also put in a stop loss for your profits as well. This will be at the place where you are most comfortable with the profits that you make. Doing this ensures that if the stock reaches that certain point, you will be able to walk away with a profit. This way, if you are away from the computer for some reason, and the currency hits your profit point, but then takes a sharp turn down, you get to take the profit because the system took you out before the downturn occurred. This helps you to maintain your profits and can-do wonders for keeping your emotions out of the game.

Never Revenge Trade

Revenge trading can take all of your hard work and throws it down the drain. With revenge trading, the investor often loses money in a trade, and it is usually a significant amount. After losing that money, they panic and decide to try to earn it all back as quickly as possible. They make a succession of bad trading decisions, don't stick with their trading plan, and run into a lot more trouble. Since the investor is not really taking care of their money or the way that they spend it, they end up losing more money in the long run.

Never fall prey to revenge trading. Even after losing money, which is something that everyone runs into at some point or another, just restart and do your trading just like normal. If you find this too hard to accomplish because you got emotionally tied into a trade, this is fine. Just make sure you stop trading for at least a few days and take a break. Once you have regrouped and feel a bit better, and know that you can make good decisions, you can come back and trade the market again.

Find a Mentor to Work With

This can be your broker or someone else you trust and who has spent some time investing in the past. You may find that working with someone who has direct experience in the Forex market is the best but working with someone who has invested at all can make a big difference. This person is perfect to ask questions of, to test out strategies with, and to get some help when things seem tough with your trades.

Most people will be happy to help you with your trades. Just remember to be respectful of the time they are giving you. You may want to bring along some questions and concerns to the meeting and use those to keep the flow of the conversation going. This ensures that you get all of your questions done, without taking up too much time from the individual who agreed to be your mentor.

Of course, you are the trader in this market, and it is your money that is on the line. While your mentor is going to give you some good advice (if you pick the right mentor), you also have to think through the process ahead of time and make sure that any advice makes sense for what you want to do. If you feel that another trade would work better, or you are not comfortable taking that much risk, even if it is recommended by a good mentor, then you don't have to do it.

A good trader can think critically for themselves, and while they appreciate the advice and help, they get from others, it is still important to think through things on your own and consider whether they make sense for your investment or not.

Take a Break When Needed

It can be hard sometimes, but you need to know when it's time to take a break from trading. If you are making a series of bad trades in the market, if you happen to lose a lot of money on one trade, or you just can't seem to get really good results at all, then it may be time to take a break and try again after a few weeks or so have passed.

The problem with staying in the market during these situations is that your thinking is going to become clouded in many cases. The more that you lose, the more that you struggle, the harder it will be to make the decisions that are needed for trading. Taking a few weeks off to clear the head and then coming back fresh can be one of the best decisions that you can make.

Do Not Invest with More Than You Can Afford to Lose

Many traders fall into the trap of investing more than they can really afford to lose. This can be really tempting for those who want to use leverage to make their positions a bit stronger. Unless you have been in the market for some time, it is not a good idea to trade on leverage. This is just asking for the market to go the opposite way of your prediction and can make you lose out on a lot of money in the process.

It is always risky to invest more money than you can afford to lose. Often, the investor will make rash decisions or will decide not to do the right research, and this can result in a disaster. It is much better to figure out how much you can comfortably lose, in case the position is wrong, and then only invest that much. It may limit the amount of profit that you can earn, but it ensures that you aren't left without options and scrounging for the money at the end.

While there is always going to be a little bit of risk when it comes to trading on the Forex market, there are some ways that you can help to reduce the risk and ensure that you see some great results.

Conclusion

Thank you for making it to the end. If your forex targets are ambitious (such that it will come to represent an essential component of your income or even the lion's share), then you should treat forex as though it were a company. You'll need to adopt an organized approach, in other words. Forex shouldn't be something you seek to get in whenever you feel like it; instead, you should strive to set aside a specific amount of time and incorporate forex into your daily routine. It would help if you devoted your time solely to education and research, unlike when you trade and track your account. Ideally, you might want to leave this kind of homework for the weekends if you are not distracted by live markets and the possibility of doing business.

Always remember that multiple factors affect the forex market. That is the reason why forex traders usually rely on technical analysis. With so many factors that influence the prices of different currencies, it becomes almost impossible to predict the price movement of money. Of course, you can always apply an effective strategy, but it does not change the fact that the forex market is challenging, if not impossible, to predict.

A business also needs its own space. You might also consider getting a separate computer devoted exclusively to forex-related operations, depending on your forex regime's rigor. Forex isn't like your 9-to-5 job, which is probably interrupted by checking your Facebook account and espn.com frequently. It's Forex time when your laptop computer is powered on.

Ultimately, you'll have to control your forex company finances. All expenses should be reported with due care, and you should try to measure the return on investment for all costs, including this book! You will conduct an analysis of your account at monthly, quarterly, and yearly intervals. You will display the productivity and efficiency metrics in real-time if you maintain a trading log. Did the result fulfill your expectations? If so, consider withdrawing from your account a fraction of your profits so that your earnings become real, not just digital. If your performance has been unsatisfactory, what can you do to make it better?

Remember, it will take time for your forex business to develop, as is the case with any new business. Give yourself a reasonable time in which you hope to succeed. Profits won't come immediately, but your forex company will one day be able to stand on its own two feet with hard work!

Success in Forex trading needs not only research but also understanding, not only preparation but also execution, not only achieving profits but also minimizing losses. Luckily, now you're well on your way to being an expert or becoming a good currency trader.

Our main adjective in writing this book was to provide you with a robust framework and base of knowledge to interact with the forex trading. Then it is up to you to apply for your experience. Good luck and take things slowly. I hope you have learned something!

Bonus Chapter

Forex Robots

One of the best ways to make a passive income from the forex market is using a tool known as a forex robot, which performs automated trades on a trader's behalf. Once traders set up these forex robots, they do not have to do much else; however, they should keep an eye on the trades the forex robots are making for them. To get started, traders need to perform adequate research into the software available for forex robots. They need to choose software that will meet their needs, in addition to being reliable when it comes to executing the right forex trades. After setting up this software, it will make forex trades based on preset signals. In addition, it will use its acquired knowledge to purchase or sell at specific times, earning users a passive income in the process. However, it is important to understand that not all forex robots make passive income for investors as claimed. In the same way that a human can make a losing trade, a forex robot can also make the same mistake. It is also important to understand that many so-called forex robots are frauds, which is why respected news platforms such as the Wall Street Journal and Forbes refuse to promote or advertise them. Unfortunately, this is particularly true when it comes to free forex robots. Therefore, new forex traders should analyze testimonials and reviews carefully before entrusting their investment to a forex robot.

Fortunately, several leading sites focus on reviewing different trading platforms. These sites try to give an honest opinion of different investment platforms and outline all the benefits and limitations of each platform. They also offer a detailed analysis of how these platforms work and how traders can get started on them, which is especially helpful to new traders.

How To Program The Metatrader 4 To Automate The Management Of Operations With A Custom Trading Console

There are many benefits in an automated trading system and most of them are centered around saving time, reducing stress and so on. For example, when a trader knows that the system will be sending him/her an alert when a new trade signal is generated, he/she can go about doing something else such as spending time with the family or preparing for the next day's work. Other benefits include easy maintenance of your program or code, reduced space for errors and so on.

The Meta Trader 4 programming language has been around for a while and many expert programmers have come up with huge number of programs to suit various trading styles. However with time as we get more familiar with MQL4 , it becomes easier to write our own programs. One fantastic thing about MQL4 is that anything you type can be auto compiled into binary code and executed just like any other program even without compilation which we will see towards the end of this article. So if you are going to learn programming in Metatrader 4, then let us start by learning how to program GUI based indicators and then we can move on to advanced topics like algo trading.

MT4 GUI based indicators are a great way to start learning programming in MQL4. Most professionals will choose to start with a simple indicator such as the MACD. It is not necessary that you have to use the MACD as a jumping off point; you can create any sort of indicator using the GUI. Once you are comfortable with that, then it's time to move on and create our own indicators which will help us make money out of the market. These types of indicators (GUI based) have inbuilt alerts which send updates in real time and this gives us a great advantage over other traders who don't know how to program their own automation system at all.

If you are new to Metatrader 4 programming, then gaining proficiency in creating these types of indicators should be your first priority because they have a lot more features than those based on price bar charts.

MT4 can be made automated by writing in-built functions called MQL4 prog. So instead of using the GUI to build your indicators, you can use that available programming language using which you will write every piece of code for the indicator i.e. graphical representation, alerts and so on. To write a function using MT4 prog, all we have to do is create a file with extension "prog" and then name it accordingly (ex: "ADX" would be an example). Once we create the file, we have to right click on it from the Meta Trader's main menu bar and select "Properties". From here, select all tabs except 'Security' tab which needs confirmation before being changed as shown below: There are two types of programming languages in Meta Trader 4 graphical user interface (GUI) e-charting section: One is simple scripting language and other is advanced scripting language which also compiles into binary code making it operational. The simple scripting language allows programmers to code any parameter they wish but if you want to program advanced features like algo trading or exporting data into other platforms such as Excel or TradingStation etc.

some practical example include :

Simple scripting language:

Programmer can code any parameter they wish. Theoretically it can be used to program any indicator or strategy.

simple example: "if(state==1,price<1,0,"+")"

Advanced scripting language: this programming language also compiles into binary code which is operational and can be used directly in a trading account with no need for compilation.

some practical examples:

Note that the above two programming languages are the same as simple scripting language but are more advanced and compiled into binary code.

Actually all of MQL4 programming languages are the same type of programming language (simple scripting) except one which is compiled into binary code and is operational.

In simple scripting language, we use a combination of mainly two characters to create a program: "If" and "EndIf". For example: if price > range then put order in trade box else put order in profit box. These programmed scripts can be saved with different names like "MySignals1", "MySignals2", etc. A sample of the script would look like this :

if(state == 1,price < 1, 0,"+")

This will work as long as no other variables were added to this script after creating it or if another script was added with different names. This program is limited to what you can code it for and they can not be used for complicated algorithms or any advanced strategy trading because these require compilation into binary code which we will see later on how to do it using Metatrader4 prog. An example of un-compiled script for simple alert box is shown below:

if(state == 1,price > 1,0,"+")

In this case output will be "+" because price is greater than 1.

Advanced scripting language is more advanced and can be used to write any kind of indicator or strategy. It uses the same "If" and "EndIf", but the difference between simple programming language and advanced programming languages is that in advance languages are compiled into binary code to make it operational without any need for compilation.

A simple example of an advanced script with an ADX indicator can be seen below:

```
static void MA_ADX( int period1, double price1, int period2, double
price2, string name ) { double Adx1 = iMA( NULL , 0 ,period1,price1);
        double Adx2 = iMA( NULL , 0 ,period2,price2);  return Adx1 -
Adx2; }
```

Compiling MQL4 prog files : All .

Machine Learning For Algorithmic Trading

Trading now contributes significantly to the wealth of individuals and companies globally. It is not surprising that many people want to cash in on this opportunity for increased wealth. At the same time, algorithmic trading and machine learning has become a hot area in finance. The availability of open source machine learning libraries and access to cheap computational power has made it easier for an individual or a company to apply machine learning techniques to trading problems.

However, while applying machine learning methods to trading problems is becoming increasingly popular, there are many issues that need to be addressed, not least the fact that researchers and practitioners have yet to agree on what constitutes best practice in this area.

Machine learning is typically concerned with creating models that are based on historical data and that can be used to predict future outcomes. The accuracy of any model is dependent on the quality of the historical data set. When dealing with financial instruments, there are two main issues:

This poses a particular problem when dealing with longer time series of data, as problems such as these can be difficult to avoid.

This issue has recently been highlighted by research from TABB Group (Tabb Group 2015). They have noted that out-of-sample testing shows a risk to the performance of long-short stock trading strategies since February 2000, and that for the top ten firms in this study, out-of-sample forecasting increases from roughly 80% in 2012 to about 90% in 2014 (TABB Group 2015). While it is interesting that their results show what they claim are "decreasing returns" over time for these strategies (Zeiler 2013), it should not be assumed that this is necessarily due to a failure of machine learning methods; rather this is more likely an indication of significant changes in financial markets over the past few years.

The fact remains that, for most financial data sets, there are significant issues with the in-sample and out-of-sample data sets. Machine learning, however, is not limited to dealing with the historical aspect of financial data; it also has something to offer when it comes to capturing the complexity of financial time series.

While an important research area in its own right (Geman et al 2015, Dacorogna et al 2002), machine learning can be applied not only to predicting future values of securities but also to the identification of structural changes in these values – such as market crashes (Wüthrich 2004). For example, LeBaron et al (LeBaron et al 2008) applied machine learning methods to the identification of market crashes in several of the global stock markets. They found that by using machine learning approaches they could successfully detect market changes with a significant impact on specific stocks.

In addition, there is increasing interest in developing strategies that can automatically rebalance portfolios based on expected returns and risks (Reeve 2014). To do this, one needs to develop strategies that are able to make decisions based on both historical and real-time data. Since many stock exchanges do not have complete historical data sets, it is difficult to use purely historical data for making trading decisions. Therefore, it becomes useful to develop systems capable of making decisions based on both historical and real-time data – such as when dealing with tick data (i.e., high frequency financial time series).

Automatic trading systems can be developed using machine learning through the use of components such as artificial neural networks (ANNs), support vector machines (SVMs), random forests, or k-nearest neighbours.

DAY Trading diary

Day trading is a form of active trading of stocks, futures, options and other securities. It is the use of short-term price movements for profit where the goal is not long-term growth.

Trading can rarely be called "day" because "day traders" are typically in and out of positions within a few hours (when working from home or off-hours). Though most trades are completed in less than a day, it may take days or weeks for the resulting position to be realized by closing out the trade.

Light trading volume is considered to be less than 50% of a stock's average daily volume. A high trading volume suggests a strong interest in the stock and usually, therefore, a high price volatility. High trading volumes also suggest a greater liquidity of stocks.

The risk associated with day trading is substantial, like gambling, and day traders can and do lose all their capital in short periods of time or suffer large losses from price volatility.

Day traders may employ chart analysis or use computer programs that can assist in making buy/sell decisions. Many day traders also trade using technical analysis by downloading price quotes from a financial data service provider or an exchange, and use programs that display the resulting data in charts. The technical analysis can help the trader figure out optimal times for entering into positions as well as getting an idea about the overall trend of prices. Day traders will often have several positions open at once (commonly called "leverage" — on margin) which allows them to have greater exposure to the market while not having to put up as much capital as they otherwise would need to maintain their positions if they were not using leverage or maintaining such open positions for longer periods of time.

Stock exchanges and most futures exchanges operate on a principle of "last price/time traded" for reporting prices. Such price quotes will show up on the ticker tape or on data sites as bid and offer prices, which are the last price at which a trading bid was made or an offer made to buy, and the last price at which a bid was made at ask or an offer to sell. These prices are known as "inside market" or "spot" prices. The inside market is essentially determined by only one bid and ask: the highest bid and lowest ask. For active day traders this is critical information in determining price direction because it reflects the true supply and demand of securities at any given moment in time, and reveals how close buyers or sellers may be to the supply/demand level (also known as support and resistance levels).

In order to maintain a position over time, day traders are constantly monitoring current market activity by looking for changes in current opinion about value which would indicate new momentum in either direction based upon a continuing increase in buyer interest (demand) or continuing decrease in buyer interest (supply), respectively.

OPTIONS TRADING FOR BEGINNERS

Options Trading for Beginners: The Easiest Guide To Start Creating Your Passive Income Step By Step, Using The Best Proven Strategies Out There

Matthew Swing

Introduction

O ptions allow you the right, but not the obligation, to purchase something at a later date while paying today's prices. They can be based on many different assets and, there are many strategies that you will be able to use in order to see success with options that it makes sense why so many people would choose this as their investment.

This guidebook is going to take some time to talk about options trading and how it works. We will start with some of the basics that come with options, such as how they work, what they are all about and the benefits of trading these rather than working with some other investment types. We will then move on to some of the best strategies that you can go with when trading options, and how you can pick a good strategy that will help you to earn a profit, no matter how the market is doing.

When you are ready to start making some money with options and you want to learn the right way to do it to reduce your risks and actually make some money, then take the time to look through this guidebook to help you get started.

What Kind of Investor Are You?

Long or short-term investor?
While they are polar opposites, going long and going short both describe the state of ownership of the asset associated with the option. Going short is also known as having a short position. It describes the state of the seller, not owning the asset associated with the option. Going long is also described as having a long position. It means that the seller owns the asset associated with the option.

There is another application of long and short positions that is applied to both call and put options. Having a long call option means that the trader expects the price of the asset to go up so that he or she can benefit. The opposite is true for having a long-put option. The trader expects the price of the asset to depreciate so that he or she can exercise the right to sell the option at the strike price.

As you can see, neither of these options refer to the period associated with that option. Rather, the focus is on the ownership of the associated asset. As such, the person who owns the asset is called the long position holder. If this person expects the price of the asset to rise, then this is called having a bullish view. This applies to a trader holding a long call option.

If this person expects the price of the asset to fall, this is known as having a bearish view. This is the scenario where a trader has a long put option.

Plenty of advice exists for investing in retirement or other long term visions. There is also plenty of advice on savings accounts for goals in the shorter term, like saving for an upcoming vacation next summer. But what if your goals fall in between these two?

The difference between long and short term goals:
When your goals are over 10 years away, you are able to take on risk and invest in stocks to reach better potential for returns. You will have time to adjust accordingly, if needed, by saving more money or by shifting your goal a bit. People also opt for long term investing because the stock market has a tendency to go up over time periods. This is not possible with short term goals.

Long-term goal considerations:

Is the long term always a safer choice? If these benefits exist from the quality of the market in the past, does this mean that they always will? No, but you are more likely to receive at least a portion of a beneficial return from investing in long periods of time rather than opting for a shorter time.

Should you invest it all-in long-term goals?
Does this mean it's wise to place all of your savings into the market? Although some choose to do so, it isn't recommended.

The optimal balance: A smarter choice would be to pick an assortment of investments that allow you to benefit from the upsides of the market and give you protection when the market is falling. It doesn't need to be much more complicated.

A savings account may be better for some: When it comes to shorter periods of time, the money you end up saving is a lot more important than what you might earn in an interest rate. For one, the money is guaranteed. Plus, the amount you earn may not be much more than what you'd earn from the interest in the savings account.

A quality account with interest rates that are competitive:

The best choice is to find an account that gives you good interest rates, considering competition, or even a CD that goes along with your goals and their time frames.

Medium-term goal considerations:

A medium goal is considered to be less than 10 years but more than three. This gives you a variety of choices to make. You could choose to invest part of your savings, hoping that the return you get back will make your long-term goals more possible.

The risk of that idea: Investing money from your savings account might end up making your goal more difficult to accomplish if the market ends up going through something rough.

Less time to recover if something goes wrong:

Unlike longer-term goals, medium goals don't give you as much time to recover from unexpected issues in the market.

There is no objective answer for medium investing goals. It has more to do with your personality and specifics of your finances than anything else. So, how do you decide what to do?

How to play it safe with these uncertainties:

The uncertainties of the first type: When it comes to goals that involving you needing the capital specifically at some point, even with an undefined date, you should always be conservative with your money. In cases like this, it's better to know for sure that you have capital waiting when the need arises rather than attempting to earn a return that is slightly higher and not even a certain event.

The uncertainties of the second type: The goals of the second variety give you a bit more freedom with engaging in risk. Since you don't need the capital on a specific date, you will be able to strive for returns that are higher without the risk of it coming back to haunt you later. Obviously, being able to take this chance doesn't necessarily mean it's the wisest decision.

Are you in need of higher returns?
Considering the length of time that must elapse between right now and the time when your goal is reached; the capital you have put into savings, and the extra money you put into savings regularly, what type of return are you needing?

Perhaps you don't need more than what is possible from a CD or savings fund online. If this applies to you, is it worth the trouble of risking having a lower savings account that you will need in the future?

Is it worth watching the value of your account go down?

Even if you are capable of taking on a great deal of risk, this doesn't mean that you have to do it. Deciding to place money into stocks, even in small amounts, is deciding to subject your capital to the downs and ups that come along with that. Of course, we all enjoy the ups and dislike the downs, which can be quite substantial at times. A great rule to follow is to assume that during any period of 12 months, you could lose up to half of the capital you invested in stocks. You could also assume that you would be able to recover from that, but when it comes to short periods, it may be harder to do.

Whether you are interested in the long, medium, or short-term goals, you should ask yourself some questions and take time to answer them. Think about these for a while before giving your answer.

Remember why you are investing in the first place:

People are often bored with the idea of using a savings account, but even the most experienced of investors should have one since having guaranteed money is better than having no funds guaranteed.

Remember that people invest because they need extra money and risking it all on a chance of earning is not smart. Only you can decide what works best for you.

How Much Time Can You Learn It?

Don't expect yourself to do well just from the get-go. It can happen, but it is rare. There will be a steep learning curve where you will see some gains and losses. But do not be discouraged. Keep at it.

More importantly, you should be long-term focused. You should expect that it will take some time before you rule like a pro. Look, it's like learning guitar. You won't be playing the solo from Stairway to Heaven anytime soon, but with practice, you will surely improve. Think of trading like that. It is like learning

Do your homework daily

Get up early and study the financial environment before the market opens and look at the news. This allows you to develop a daily options trading plan. The process of analyzing the financial climate before the market opens is called pre-market preparation. It is a necessary task that needs to be performed every day to asset competition and to align your overall strategy with the short-term conditions of that day.

An easy way to do this is to develop a pre-market checklist. An example of a pre-market checklist includes but is not limited to:

- Checking the individual markets that you frequently trade options in or plan to trade options in to evaluate support and resistance.
- Checking the news to assess whether events that could affect the market developed overnight.
- Assessing what other options traders are doing to determined volume and competition.
- Determining what safe exits for losing positions are.
- Considering the seasonality of certain markets are some as affected by the day of the week, the month of the year, *etc.*

Options Trading Time Frames

Time frames are an integral part of trading options and need to be given careful consideration when initiating any investment. Essentially, time frames are represented with charts, such as those that will be outlined in the next chapter. There are countless time frames, as they can range from as short as one hour to several months long. It is up to the investor to analyze the time frames in order to predict how the market will move, and thus if the investor needs to sell or buy options.

So what exactly needs to be analyzed? That would be the trendline, which is detailed in the time frame chart. By looking at the chart, an investor will be able to tell if it is bearish or bullish in nature and, using the trade signals discussed in the next chapter, when the market is going to continue or reverse its trend. However, there is not just one trend that investors need to be concerned with. There are actually three trends: primary, intermediate, and short term.

Every underlying security can be represented with these trends, which are reliable depending on the length of their time frame. Having a longer time frame allows investors to track the trend of an underlying stock more accurately. Take, for example, a 3-month long time frame versus a 5-minute time frame. The 5-minute frame would only show a very small portion of the asset's trend, which may be an abnormality when taking a longer time frame trend into account or even may be plain inaccurate, depending on how much noise is occurring in regard to that particular asset. Thus, since a long-term trend is more reliable, it is the most accurate for locating the primary trend.

The primary trend should always be the investor's main concern. This is not because it is the only one worth paying attention to. On the contrary, different trends will be used by different types of investors, such as a day trader versus a position trader. In the case of the position trader, it would be wise to make the primary trend a priority because it focuses on long-term time frames and then makes smaller profits using the intermediate-and short-term frames. In juxtaposition to this, a day trader would mainly use the primary trend as an umbrella for the short-term time frame he or she would mostly work with as calls and puts are swiftly traded. It is, therefore, the best for a beginning investor to concentrate on the work he or she would most like to do and then find the appropriate time frame for it, always basing calculations off of the primary trend. This can be achieved by using the short-term trend in correlation with the faster time frame and the investor's preferred time frame for the intermediate trend, all while tracking the primary trend in the long-time frame.

In line with the idea of tailoring time frames and securities to an investor's personal preference, the two-time frames not chosen as the investor's primary concern should be used to complement the primary time frame. Depending upon how the investor chooses to utilize the time frames, the investor could potentially reap the rewards on three separate levels, enacting many of the strategies discussed in the previous chapter. For example, an investor may hold a long position on a stock using the primary trend to predict movements within the market for that particular underlying investment, also known as the underlying trend. Once this has been identified, the investor uses whatever time frame is most suited to his or her style of trading (short for day trading, long for position trading, etc.) in order to determine the intermediate trend pattern. The investor then brings in the short-term trend in order to implement strategies that may fulfill any number of purposes. These may include using the short-term trend and time frame to create insurance for the long position, to reap benefits with calls or puts as the trend fluctuates, or any other of the numerous uses of short-term trends and time frames. How the time frames are utilized is completely up to the individual investor and thus is a flexible way to generate and multiply income using the investor's natural trading strengths.

Because there are time frames containing trends representing all underlying assets, neophyte options traders can often become confused by the contradictory information. Say, for example, the primary trend for the stock of company XYZ in a long-time frame shows the stock is bullish. However, when the investor looks at a short-term trend on a 2-day time frame, the stock appears to be completely bearish with no obvious signs of a rally. The investor should not panic and, begin selling all of his or her shares. Instead, the investor must realize that the short-term trend is merely a small portion of the primary trend, which, if it is a continuation pattern, will keep its bullish outlook and continue climbing the chart. It is easy to see from this example why organization and a clear understanding of options trading before entering the business are priceless tools.

One of the keys to growing a portfolio is concentrating on the future trends of the market rather than the past. Many investors who are either beginners or overly scared of losing money rely purely on past data given by long time frames, rather than concentrating on how the trend may act in the future. Trends do reverse and fluctuate; it is up to the investor to decipher the patterns and make informed decisions on how to act on the trend.

How Realistic Is Getting Rich in Investing?

There are several ways that investors can maximize their investments. Of course, practicing proper business techniques will help you get the most out of it. However, there are several other ways that investors can do this, such as reducing investment costs, increasing diversification, rebalancing, among other techniques. It is important to know all the possible ways to maximize your own investments because you don't know what you don't know. Every bit counts. Just saving a little here and there will add up and your goal will be achieved quickly.

Investors may maximize their investments by decreasing the cost of investing. There are several ways that investing may cost one money, and that money is coming directly out of the investment. Investors may switch from hiring a financial advisor to doing the investing themselves, cutting the costs of the commission. Investors commonly forget about transaction costs. There is typically a flat fee for buying stock through a broker. Instead of making many small purchases, investors may save up and only buy stocks in certain increments (for example, perhaps the investor won't buy more stocks until they have saved $1000). By doing this, a much smaller percentage of the investment is being cut out and used to cover those fees. This may require more patience, but that money will add up. Lowering one's expenses will increase their return. Instead of being spent, that money may be growing and earning a return on it. Because of compound interest, this money will earn money on itself and multiply over the years. This is why it's crucial to save every bit possible.

Investors must also really pay attention to their portfolios. Diversification is crucial, and it can save the investor from losing all of their investment. Markets typically fall much more quickly than markets rise. This means that the investor must prepare for such occurrences. It is important to regularly rebalance one's portfolio to ensure that it is positioned correctly for the investor to make the largest possible gains.

Investors must also truly pay attention to what they want. Maximizing one's investments will depend on the person and what their goals are. Although it is wise to listen to the advice of experts and see what other ways that one may invest, it is crucial to follow the path that is best for the goals and preferences of the individual. This is why a plan is necessary and should be followed. Investors must not stop investing. This is another way to take advantage of compound interest. The investor's portfolio should never stop growing. This growth should be due to both growths in the investment and regular contributions by the investor themselves. Despite the great returns that may be experienced in a bull market, contributions are still necessary. Bear markets should also not discourage investors from continuing investing; this can be a great time to get a good deal on a stock!

How to Be a Winning Trader While Everyone Else Loses

When it comes to trading, there are some important personality traits that you need to possess if you would like to be successful. Not everyone will do well with day trading. It is a fast-paced world of investing, and you can quickly lose a lot of money in the process. And if you do not possess the right characteristics, you will find that you increase your risk of losing money more than before.

Before you decide to get into the world of day trading, you should consider whether you have the right personality to start this field. It can be tough for some people, but with the right personality traits, it will be a great option to help you make some money.

Some of the personality traits that you need to possess to do well with day trading include:

- Personal independence: This is a good work from home business. You need to enjoy the freedom of working on your own and not having someone looking over your shoulders all of the time. If you are not able to motivate yourself to get the work done or you thrive when you are in an office setting, you may find that it is difficult to get started in this kind of business.

- Decisiveness: When you are dealing with the market over the long term, you will notice that the market stays pretty steady. But when you work in the market on one day, there are a lot of ups and downs, and the market may change on you in just a few seconds. Because of this, a day trader needs to be able to make quick and decisive decisions to keep them in the market. As a good day trader, you will need to rely on some of your past experiences to read what is going on with a new situation and make your decisions. There isn't a ton of room for second-guessing when it comes to day trading.

- Discipline and persistence: Since you do not have a boss on your back when you work in day trading, you need to be able to keep yourself focused on the task at hand, to watch the market, do your research, and be prepared to make the right decisions to make more money. And you need to realize that there will be a time when you are learning the ropes, and it may not be going the way that you would like. However, once you find a strategy that works for you and helps you to make a profit, then you will stick with it.

- Interest in trading: Good traders will have some enthusiasm for the market for a long time before deciding to get into day trading. You should already have a natural inclination to follow commodities, bonds, stocks, and some of the other securities that are available. If you do not really have any interest in business or finances at all, then this will be a struggle to become a day trader.

- Personal support: You need to have your own discipline and to be self-motivated, it is still nice to have some personal support throughout the day. The daily life of a day trader can be stressful and having some friends and family who will help you to keep in touch with the world can make a big difference.

- Financial independence: It is not a requirement to have a ton of money to get started with day trading. With that being said, you need to have enough that you can do your chosen trades and then still have a little bit of a safety net in case the trades do not do that much. You should never trade with money that you cannot afford to lose. If you are someone who is living paycheck to paycheck, you need to take some time to build up savings before you even get started with day trading.

- Understand technology: All of your day trading will happen on your computer. If you do not have some familiarity with using a computer and with some of the platforms that are available, you will have a hard time working with day trading.

- Can keep your cool: there will be times, even with a good day trading strategy, when you make the wrong decisions, and your stocks will lose you money. If you are not able to keep your cool, you will end up making the situation a lot worse. You need to be able to look at the situation, whether you are earning or losing money, and make good decisions that will help you to turn things around or to at least limit your losses.

There are a lot of different parts that come with becoming a day trader, and if you are not in the right frame of mind or do not have the personality for this; you will be disappointed with the lack of results that you will get. It takes a specific person to do day trading, and for those who do not have the right personality, it is best to pick out different investing options.

The What, the When, the How
What are you going to trade?

When are you going to make those trades?

How are you going to make money on those trades? Thus, when are you
going to get out?

What's your expected risk? When do you reevaluate if things aren't going
as planned? How do you test a different approach so that you can find
the best way for you to make money in the markets?

What to do if the market gaps up, gaps down, trends up, trends down,
or trades sideways and bounces back and forth between the two?

You need to answer all of these questions. You need to examine what
you believe in the market and why.

You need to break down each market you're going to trade and explain
how you've come to believe what you believe of each of these markets,
and what your thoughts are on how to trade them.

Once that's done, you should be ready to start looking at your system as
a whole.

Manage Losses
Winners take care of themselves. Losers are the only thing you have to
know to manage. When you are trading and you are taking a risk with
your money, you need to know when you're getting into a trade and
when you're getting out of one. Most people spend all their time trying
to figure out the perfect system to get into winning trades. Most winners
spend all their time trying to figure out how to not have a losing trade.
There is a difference and a very big difference at that. If you don't think
so, you will by the end of this section.

For winning traders, they expect to spend money on trade sometimes,
but they never want to lose money. Which is to say, they never want to

lose more than they have to on a trade when they are wrong? It is the only time when they lose money. The market moves against them. They get out down 1% of their account, and they're fine. Ready to get back in when the next set-up announces itself. What a winning trader hates is when they abandon their own system, start doubling down on their bet, go on tilt, and suddenly, they are down to 5%, 10%, even 20% of their account, when at 1%, they could have known that they were wrong.

Losing traders think that is a normal process. They have excuses. The market just would not cooperate. The President made a tweet and it sent the markets into chaos; otherwise, I'd have been right. My broker cheats the market to get you kicked out of your position, and then the market turns around and does what it was supposed to do. On and on, it goes. Because, for the losing trader, it's easy to blame everyone and anyone else, except the person whose responsibility it is for them to come home with money each day–themselves!

The market doesn't care about you. It's not waiting for you to make the trade and then go in the exact opposite direction the moment your trade goes in. The market is nothing but an engine to make, lose, and spend money. Which one you do is always up to you?

So, how do you go about managing your losses?

Know Your Stop
Once you have defined your exit, you need to put a stop there, so that you're automatically closed out of the position the moment it goes against you. Why? Because when it's left up to you, that means you can start talking to yourself and saying, "I think I'm right, I'm just going to hold this position." You don't need that stress or that ability to mess yourself up like that. It's stressful when you have to decide whether or not to get out of a trade. It's easy when it's done for you and you can reevaluate the market without the need for it to go the way your position is going.

Traders who trade without a stop order are like people who ride motorcycles without a helmet. It feels good; you think you're safe, you know you're a great driver until your brains are all over the sidewalk. Stop orders make everything easier. And they're the number one tool to profitable traders.

CHAPTER 1:

Option Basics For Beginners

What Are Options?

By definition, an option is a financial derivative or contract that allows you to purchase or sell a financial asset within a predetermined cost and time frame. The predetermined date or time frame is also known as the exercise date. For options trading to take place, the seller must meet all the requirements of the trade.

Options trading differs from market to market, and from platform to platform. As a trader, you must be able to differentiate between the various categories of options, including ETF options, stock options, and futures options, among several others.

Options are considered a low-risk form of trade because you can terminate a contract before the exercise or expiry date. The value of an option only represents a percentage of a seller's underlying security or asset.

The price at which the buyer agrees to place for the option is called the strike price, while the fee used to purchase the option contract is called the premium.

How Do Options Work?

When it comes to looking at the worth of options contracts, this is determined by the probability of future price events occurring. If something is more likely to happen, its option will be more expensive.

If the value of a stock is increasing, the cost of the call will increase too. This is a great way to understand how the value of a call works.

If an option has lesser time for it to expire, the lower the value of such an option is. This occurs because the probability of a price moving in that stock reduces as the expiry date draws near. That's one reason an option is said to be a wasting asset.

Let's say you purchase an out of money one-month option, and its stock refuses to increase, the option loses its value as each day goes by.

Time is an important aspect of the option price, meaning that a one-month option will end up being less valuable than a choice of three months. Why this is so is the fact that there is a lot of time, meaning that there is a chance that the price can improve.

The same can be said for an option that expires in a year is more valuable than one that expires in a month even when they are derivatives of the same stock.

The reason it has this characteristic is because of time decay. That option that had a great worth the previous day would have its worth reducing the next day.

Another thing that is said to improve the worth of an option is volatility. This occurs because the uncertainty factor improves the odds of a result occurring. When an asset's volatility level increases, the greater price swings improve the chances of substantial moves going down and up.

When you notice more massive price swings, it means that there is a great chance that an event will happen, meaning that the higher the level of volatility, the higher the option's price.

Volatility and Options trading are related to each other.

In a lot of U.S. exchanges, a stock option contract is seen as the alternative to sell or purchase 100 shares. This is one reason a contract premium is multiplied by 100 to have access to the total amount that will be spent to purchase the call.

In a lot of cases, buyers decide to have their profits taken by trading out their position. What this means is that the option holders can decide to sell their options, while the writers purchase their positions again.

The alterations in the prices of options are explained by either extrinsic value or intrinsic value. This is also called time value.

The premium of an option is seen as mixing the time value and intrinsic value. The intrinsic value is that options contract's in-the-money amount. In the case of a call option, this is that amount that is higher than what the stock is currently trading for.

As for the time value, it shows the extra value a trader is expected to spend on an option, which is higher than the intrinsic value. This is what is called the time value or extrinsic value.

What Is an Option Contract?

An option contract is basically an agreement struck connecting two traders to trade an asset at an established date and price. Option contracts are common in the trade of commodities, securities as well as real estate investments.

Normally, an option contract comprises of the following:

The type of Option - This can either be a call or put option. A call option allows you to purchase a specific number of shares over time, while a put option is for buying shares of a certain commodity or security on specified terms.

The Unit of Trade refers to a single indivisible amount of any trade item. For options, the common unit of trade is a contract.

The Strike Price – as stated earlier, this is the price at which an options contract can be exercised (sold or bought). In the case of a call option, it is the cost where the shares are bought by the buyer before the expiration date. For the put option, it refers to the cost at which the shares can be sold by the buyer before the expiration date.

Underlying security is the commodity, bond, index, currency, or stock used to establish the worth of an option. This value is derived from the price or performance of the underlying security.

The expiration date is the last day for buying or selling an option.

Other Types of Options

Besides the call and put options, there are several other types of options you can trade in on the market. These are categorized using the methods used for trade, underlying securities, and the expiration cycle. You, however, have to bear in mind that not all of them are suitable for intraday trading. Some of these options include:

- Index options

- Options on futures

- Stock options

- Weekly SPY options

- Mini and Mini Index options

- ETF options

- IRA Accounts

- QQQ options

- Crude oil options

- OEX options

- ES Weekly options

- ITM options

- E-Mini options

- S & P options

Know the Lingo

When it comes to trading options effectively, one of the first things you are going to want to do is to familiarize yourself with the common terms that options traders are likely to use to ensure that even if you can't trade like a professional at least, you can speak like one.

Strike Price

The price of a given underlying asset at the moment the option is purchased is called its strike price.

Exercised

When the movement of an underlying asset makes the specifications of a given option favorable, then it is exercised or taken advantage of and the ownership of the underlying asset changes hands.

Trade out

If a holder exercises an option that the writer feels is not worth the current market value of the underlying asset, then they can trade out, which means they essentially buy back the holder's shares and relist them because they believe that a better deal is readily available even with the additional trouble taken into account. All told, some 50 percent of trades expire without any action being taken. Of the remaining 5o percent, only 10 percent is actually exercised, with the remaining 40 percent ending up getting traded out.

Listing

The process of creating a new call is referred to as listing an option. Listed options appear on national exchanges, and it is recommended that you only deal with listed options until you make it past your options trader novice phase. If you are dealing with vanilla options, then you can realistically expect all of the options you find to include 100 shares of the underlying stock in question.

In the money

If an option is currently in the money, then the underlying stock that it is tied to is currently sitting at a point that is above whatever it is you initially paid for it. If, however, it is out of the money instead, then this means that it previously was in the money but has now dropped back down to a point where it is no longer profitable. If the underlying stock is exactly at the price at which you originally purchased it, then the option can currently be thought of as at the money.

Value

The value of the underlying stock related to a given option can be broken into two parts, intrinsic and time. Intrinsic value is the difference between the current price and the strike price, assuming it is a positive difference. If the difference is negative, then the intrinsic value is said to be zero, as it cannot be a negative number. Time value is simply the amount of time that the option has until it expires, with options with a lower amount of time value having a lower overall value as a result.

Premium

The sum total of the intrinsic value, stock price, time value, strike price and the total amount of volatility is said to be an option's premium.

Understanding Pricing Influences

When it comes to being an effective options trader, one of the most important things that you will learn is how the various types of different options that you see come by the value that they are currently assigned. The price of a specific option is an amalgamation of its volatility, the price of the underlying asset, the amount of interest involved and the intrinsic and time value. As such, when it comes to deciding on which options to pursue, you are going to need to understand the different between what are known as premiums (guaranteed profits) and the theoretical maximum value (what the option should currently be worth based on the visible signs).

Price of the underlying asset

While they often will not move at the same speed or for the same amounts, an option is always going to follow the lead of its underlying asset. As such, you can always expect the price of related calls to increase along with rising asset prices, while puts will always decrease and vice versa.

Intrinsic value

The amount of value that an option is going to hold onto, even at the very end of its lifespan, is known as the intrinsic value. When working with a call option, you can find the intrinsic value by taking the current price of the underlying asset and dividing that by the difference between the strike price and the current price. When it comes to finding the intrinsic value of a put option, the process is mostly the same; to start, you subtract the amount the underlying asset is currently worth from its strike price before dividing that number by the current stock price.

The results of this equation will provide you with a clearer idea of the type of advantage that choosing to exercise the option at the moment would provide you with. This number can also be thought of as the minimum that the option will ever be worth, even at the moment of its expiration.

Time value

The amount of time that an option has until it expires is directly related to how likely that same option is going to ultimately end in a profit greater than the intrinsic value before things are said and done. To determine the amount of time value that the option you are considering currently offers you will want to find the current price of the option and subtract from it the amount of intrinsic value that the same option currently has. It is common for options to hold onto 70 percent of their total value, or more, during the first half of their lifetime before losing value much more rapidly after that point. It is also important to note that time value can change dramatically based on the volatility of the underlying asset both in the moment and based on its expectations in the future. As a general rule, the lower the time value, the more stable the option is likely to be.

Volatility

Compared to the other factors that most affect options pricing, volatility is much more subjective, though measuring it properly is still important as well. This can be easier said than done, however, especially for those traders who are still new to the process. Luckily, there are a wide variety of programs that track such things automatically online these days, so the problem is much less pronounced. The historical volatility of a specific option can be found by taking into account the overall volatility of its underlying asset in both the short and the long term. Volatility is especially important to be aware of if you expect a major shakeup in the near future as it will show you how the underlying asset responded the last time events unfolded this way, which makes it more likely that events will repeat themselves next time around.

Why You Should Trade Options

Let us look at some of the most notable reasons why one may need to trade options, besides making serious money.

Low prices
While trading options, you can create and close contracts faster and with minimal risk compared to other securities. The cost of purchasing an option is relatively cheaper than that of buying the underlying security, or shares in the case of stock trading. This means that you can make more profit using less capital.

High possibility of success
It is easier to make a profit from options since you do not need to close a contract to gain from it. Options are also highly volatile.

Diverse markets
There are numerous investment opportunities related to options trading. These opportunities are often cheaper than the purchase of actual stock. The more you increase your capital, the more your profit potential grows.

It can be combined with stock trade
To maximize profits, you can easily combine options with stock trading. Doing this allows you to increase your stock from the profits made in trading options.

Easy to access
Various online platforms give you the opportunity to trade options from all over the world. With some good capital, all you need is a good internet connection to get started.

Disadvantages

Despite the many benefits of options trading, there are a few drawbacks that come with it. However, these are less likely to impact your experience in the trade and can be overlooked. Some disadvantages that come to mind include:

An extensive spread
A bid-ask spread is a variation between the maximum price that the buyer is ready to place and the minimum price the seller is prepared to allow for the asset. The spread is quite wide when selling options as compared to stocks trade. This is due to the reduced liquidity associated with the options markets and has a great impact on the profit of any daily trade.

Reduced price movements
In trading options, the changes in the price are limited to the time value of the contract and premium. Although this value increases with the cost of the underlying instrument, the profit may be reduced significantly in case the time value diminishes.

These drawbacks are highly insignificant and should not prevent you from engaging in the trade of options. You can easily adjust your trading plans to minimize their impact.

Types of Options

The two main types of options are called call options and put options. We will address the specifics of each type below.

Call Options

Most commonly just simply called a call; this type of option allows the trader of the option the right to buy the associated asset on or before the expiration date.

The reason that anyone would be interested in buying the attached asset is because the price is expected to rise within the lifetime of the option.

As a result, the profit lies in the price of the asset going above the strike price.

The seller makes a profit from the trader paying him or her a premium for that option. In the event that the asset does rise in price, then the buyer of the option has the right to exercise the option to buy the asset or sell the option. Both strategies lead to a profit for the buyer. In this scenario, the buyer has the potential for unlimited income, while the seller's income is limited to the premium paid for that option.

The terms that describe whether or not a trader has made a profit include in the money, out of the money and at the money. In the money describes the situation whereby the asset price has gone above the strike price.

This is favorable and describes a profitable situation for the trader. Out of the money describes the situation whereby the asset price has fallen below the strike price resulting in a loss from the option.

At the money means that the asset price is equivalent to the strike price and so the trader does not profit or loss from the option.

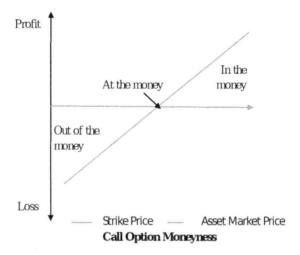

Call Option Moneyness

Put Options

Also commonly called a put, this type of option gives the trader the right to sell the asset attached to the contract at the strike price on or before the expiration date. Just like with a call option, the strike price is predetermined with this type of option.

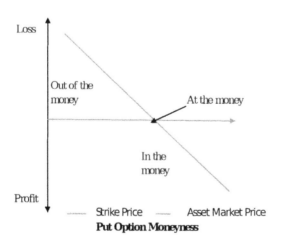

Put Option Moneyness

If the trader is in the money by the expiration date, he or she has the option to sell the asset associated with the option by a fixed time or sell the option to someone else.

Going Long vs. Going Short

While they are polar opposites, going long and going short both describe the state of ownership of the asset associated with the option. Going short is also known as having a short position. It describes the state of the seller not owning the asset associated with the option. Going long is also described as having a long position. It means that the seller owns the asset associated with the option.

As you can see, neither of these options refers to the time period associated with that option. Rather, the focus is on the ownership of the associated asset. As such, the person who owns the asset is called the long position holder. If this person expects the price of the asset to rise, then this is called having a bullish view. This applies to a trader holding a long call option.

If this person expects the price of the asset to fall, this is known as having a bearish view. This is the scenario where a trader has a long put option.

Financial Leverage

Leverage is a term that is, in most cases, made use in financial management. It comes up from borrowing capital as a way of funding as well as expanding an investment. It will then generate some returns on the risk capital. It is a strategy to invest in using money that is borrowed. It increases the profits of the investment made. Leverage can as well be the debt amount that a company puts in use to finance its assets. When the leverage is high, that means that the investor has more debt that has accumulated than the equity. Leverage is known to boost the returns and hence, an increase in the profit.

It multiplies the potential returns from a particular investment. It will bring down the likely to come up in case the investment you have made does not turn out as you had expected. The idea of leverage is put I use by investors as well as firms. An investor will use to make sure that there is an increase in returns on the investment. The investment will be levered using specific instruments, including margin accounts, options as well as futures. Companies will use leverage to finance their assets. Instead of issuing stock so that they can raise capital, they decide to use the debt to finance, aiming to increase the shareholder value.

Investors do not prefer to use leverage immediately. They have their means to access it indirectly. They opt to invest in a company that they know uses force to fund as well as expand their investments. The company does not have to increase the outlay necessarily. Leverage is an excellent approach anyone can put in use to multiply the buying power in the trade out there. However, you can decide to use margin as a way of creating leverage. There are several types of leverage, but they do not need to be combined with being productive. They instead form the entire process even though they are independent. They include;

Operating Leverage
Operating leverage is just concerned with the investment activities of an individual firm. It is about the incurrence of the fixed cost of operation in a company's income stream. The operating price can either be fixed, semi-fixed, variable as well as semi-variable. The fixed fee is contractual, and it is subject to time. It does not necessarily have to change when the sales change, and it is supposed to be paid despite the number of sales.

Variable cost t has a direct variation in the level of sales revenue. There will be no variable cost if there will be no any sales that are made in a certain period. Semi-variable, as well as semi-fixed, will vary partly with the number of purchases made, and it will remain partially fixed. The fixed operating cost can be subject to be put in a lever, and hence the decisions of investment will go in favor of using assets that have a fixed price.

When a firm decides to use the fixed cost, it will increase the effect that a change will have on the sales when EBIT changes. The ability that a firm will have to put the fixed operating cost in use to increase its earnings before the interest, as well as the taxes, is what is known as operating leverage. The leverage will be concerning the variation of the sales as well as profit. When the percentage of the operating cost is high, and then there will be a rise in the level of operating cost.

Financial Leverage

When there are financial charges in existence, the financial leverage will as well exist. The business costs should not depend on the operating profits in any way. The sources in which the funds that help to boost an investment come from can be put in categories. The funds can either be having a fixed charge, and some may not be having the fixed financial cost. Debentures, preference shares, bonds as well as long-term loans have a fixed financial burden. Equity shares are known to have no fixed charge at all.

The fixed financial charge is used as a lever, and hence, the business decisions will go in favor when you employ such funds. When there are fixed charges in a company's income stream, financial leverage will be an outcome. It is an excellent idea to make sure that the change that will be made in EBIT to affect EPS will be significant. The higher the level of fixed charges, the higher the probability that the degree of financial leverage will go up. When the fixed costs do down, the economic advantage will go down as well.

Combined Leverage

If you bring both the operating leverage and the financial leverage together, they will come up with the combined force. It is concerning the risk of one not being able to cover up for the total amount of the fixed charges when a firm can cover fully on the operating as well as the financial burdens, that is when the term combined leverage comes in. The higher the fixed operating cost as well as the financial charges, the higher the level of the combined force.

Working Capital Leverage

When there is a decrease in the investment of a particular asset, there will be an increase in profit. That means that risks, as well as returns, have direct relations. When the probability of risk goes up, there is a likely hood that the profit will increase as well. The ability of an individual firm to increase the effect of the change in the current stock on the firm's returns is working capital leverage. It is so when there is an assumption that the liabilities are constant.

How to Start Trading Options

Trading options is straightforward. Beginners can join the team of traders in a few steps as highlighted below:

Create a Brokerage Account

You need this account to liaise with your traders easily. Since options trading has become so much popular, the internet has a good number of brokers to select from. You must, however, ensure that you get one that suits your trading needs. When selecting an online broker, put the following factors into consideration.

Carry out some research on different brokers and compare their charges in terms of commission. This will ensure that you get the best competitive spreads. Be sure to check out whether there are hidden charges as well.

Develop a Strategy

Once you are done creating a brokerage account, you will need to create a winning strategy. Options trading strategies come in various designs. Some are straightforward, while others need a lot of time and resources. A good strategy is one that has several components in it. These include

Charts and patterns

Charts and patterns are a must for each trading engagement. They help you study and easily understand the history of an option. Each chart must have a good indicator for trading options. These indicators vary for each strategy and may include the Money Flow Index, Relative Strength Index, Bollinger Bands, Open Interest, and the Put-Call Ratio Indicator. You need more time to understand and practice pattern trading with options. However, you will need to try out a number of charts until you get one that is straightforward and easy to understand.

Timing

When it comes to trading options, time is of the essence. You must understand when to set up a trade, enter into contracts and when to make an exit. For a strategy to work there must be a trader who is willing to place contracts early enough. For instance, you may need to start as early as 6:00 am if you want to get the direction of the day's trade early enough.

Once you have determined the day's trend, you can use the information to come up with a strategy depending on how the market has been at night. You can take the E-mini option, for example, since up to 70% of stocks are entitled to move in the same direction during the day. It is good to note that the U.S stock market dictates the direction of trade in other countries. So, it is important to give the market an hour every morning for it to stabilize before sealing any contracts for the day

In and Out of the Money

The terms "in the money" and "out of the money" are slang used by options traders to indicate whether an option is really worth something or not. It turns out that even out of the money options are worth something, but before we get to that, let's learn what these terms mean and how different call options fit in with the definitions.

The first definition you need to know about is "in the money." A call option is in the money when the strike price of the call option is lower than the current share price. In other words, a call option is in the money when you can buy the shares at a discount price relative to the market price.

To really be worth it, however, you need to understand how the breakeven price fits in. If the stock is trading at $101 a share, technically speaking a call option with a strike price of $100 a share is in the money. However, if you paid $2 per share for that option, then it is not really in the money, because you'd lose $1 a share exercising the option.

So from a practical standpoint, an option has to be positioned such that the market share price has raised enough to account not only for the strike price, but also the price paid to buy the call option. So you need to pay more attention to the breakeven price rather than the in the money price – if you are interested in buying the shares of stock.

When Is an Option Liquid?

Liquidity is one of the most important concepts in finance and trading. Simply put, liquidity is a measure (vague, but real) of how quickly you can convert something into cash.

A cashier's check is very liquid. Cash is 100% liquid. A bar of gold is pretty liquid because you can take it to a gold or coin dealer and sell it immediately for cash. Stocks are liquid, but less liquid than these items because you can't immediately access the cash you get from selling stocks (most brokers will make you wait a few days).

You can compare liquidity between different types of assets. To explain what we mean, let's focus only on options. Some options are going to be more liquid than others. No matter what, your broker is going to have rules on being able to get the cash-out, but that isn't our concern when talking about the liquidity of options. Those rules are going to apply to all options.

Our concern here is how easy it is to buy and sell a particular option.

Options trading can move fast. In my own experience, I have seen options that I've purchased lose and gain $100 or more over a matter of 30-90 minutes. The rapid price movements of options coupled with the fact that they lose value through time decay every single day that passes means that when the time is right to get in and out of an options contract, you want to be able to do it right away.

So the concept of liquidity when it comes to trading options comes down to being able to buy and sell an option instantly. The market provides two important pieces of information that you can use in order to determine how liquid an option is.

Leverage and Options Trading

The reason why trading options strategy is so profitable compared to that of other securities is due to leverage. A small amount of money can leverage larger underlying security compared to the same amount placed in stocks or bonds, for instance.

With $100, you can probably buy 20 shares valued at $5 per share. However, this same amount of money can probably control 100 shares. This is what leverage is. When it comes to profits, the options trader will make a much larger profit compared to the stock trader. If you have trading capital, then you can make a much higher profit if you choose to trade options rather than stocks or any other security. The potential is huge and ranges in the 1000% possibility.

Options leverage is defined as the money equivalent in multiples of a single option position about the true cash value of an underlying asset. When these two are compared, then the difference becomes visibly noticeable. This is why options are considered so valuable. The potential they hold is astronomical.

Buying and Selling Options

If an options contract is "in the money," this means that the option can be exercised by a buyer to earn a profit, which means either buying or selling 100 shares of stock. On the other hand, if it is "out of the money," then it would not be profitable for the buyer to exercise the option. Sellers of options contracts generally hope that the option will be out of the money. If a contract was to expire and it was out of the money, it is said to "expire worthless." Since the contract has expired without any value, the seller of the option pockets any money they received selling it, and they don't have to worry about buying or selling shares of stock.

A buyer of an option is normally a trader. That means they are hoping to sell it at a higher price than they paid for it. As the price of the stock goes up and down, it can cause the market price of any options contract on that stock to move up or down. This provides traders with an opportunity to earn profits without actually investing in the stock. When the value of an option goes up, they can sell the option to another trader for a profit.

Keep in mind that if you buy an option to enter your investment position, you are not under any sort of obligation. In other words, if you later sell the option, you are not under the seller's obligation. Only the original seller of an option is required to either buy or sell shares of stock. So, you can buy an option, and if its value goes up, you can sell it off and take a profit and walk away from it. Many people trade options without having any intention to own the shares of stock or trade shares of stock whatsoever. But if you want to, you can definitely buy or sell the shares if it becomes advantageous and you can afford it.

CHAPTER 2:

Trading Fundamentals

Before you setup your options day trading business, there are a few things you need to have intimate knowledge of. They are your current financial circumstances, the time you are able to commit to day trading and your risk profile. Create a financial balance sheet that lists your expenses, and any other income that you obtain. This will allow you to assess your financial health and how much you can invest into options. This also allows you to know what risks you can take while trading options. Never invest capital or resources that you cannot afford to lose and never trade beyond your trading experience level. Becoming an options day trader requires a healthy time investment at the beginning because you need to learn your way around this arena as well as set up a strong foundation for your profile. Do not rush and squander your money in an overzealous move to get started.

Next, before you risk your hard-earned money, learn to trade options on paper. This is called paper trading and allows you to use real-life scenarios to assess your performance when it comes to trading options.

When you are ready to move forward to real-time practice, find a brokerage firm to represent you. Online brokerage firms are growing in popularity, but ensure that you properly research the firm to ensure reputability and that you are paying as little in commissions as possible. You may even be able to find a broken that does not charge commissions.

The brokerage firm will help you get set up as a qualified options trader at the level that is relevant for your experience as well as aid in setting up the appropriate accounts. You need to be able to process payments and other financial transfers online before you approach a broker.

Lastly, ensure that you have the tools for the trade. Ensure that your internet connection is fast and reliable. Also, ensure that your computer or laptop has a fast processor and adequate memory to prevent crashes as trading programs rely on a fast-moving computer. Most traders have a need for at least 2 monitors to keep abreast as to what is happing on the financial market.

Entry into the Options Trading Market

There are several different types of options that a day trader can pursue, but it makes no sense to try to pursue all of them as this will stretch you and your resources thin. The best thing to do is pinned down one or two niches that you will pursue at the beginning to find the ones that fit best with you and your trading style. Popular niches that day traders pursue include stocks, foreign exchange, and exchange-traded funds.

Planning for Success
Options day trading is a business. You need to treat it as such. You will not wake up one day and just start any other type of business with no plan. Therefore, you need to approach day trading options with the same foresight and planning. Just as you would create a business plan for any other type of business, you need to create a trading plan. This will serve as your guide with step-by-step details on how you will approach day trading options, how you will measure your success and how you will grow your business and income. As a result, here are a few vital categories that need to be developed in your trading plan:

Your Goals
Goal setting is a necessary life skill that everyone needs to learn and it will serve you well in this area. These need to be both long-term and short-term. You need to be very specific. Vague notions like "I want to be as successful as I can be," have no place in your trading plan. Your goals need to be quantifiable and trackable.

233 | P a g .

Setting your goals also allows you to outline what areas you need to improve your knowledge so that you become a better options day trader. You need to develop a system for rewarding yourself when you hit milestones on your goal's list.

An Efficient Workspace
You need to develop a plan for where you will work as well as the equipment that you will need. This does not have to be fancy. All you need is an adequate internet connection, a computer setup, and a working filing system. Ensure that you have plans to upgrade your equipment as needed.

Developing a Time Schedule
It is important to set regular trading hours to ensure that you do not become burnt out and that you maintain your perspective of your career and life. All work and no play leads to sickness. While you are setting working hours, also allocate time off, vacation and sick leave. Working yourself to the bone will remove the sense of fulfillment that you will find with this job. Therefore, finding balance is vital.

Personal Development
As you are your business, you need to ensure that you invest in yourself so that you continuously expand your knowledge of trading and develop yourself as an individual—schedule time for further reading, seminars and other learning tools.

Your trading plan is not set in stone. In fact, it is something that you should continuously evaluate and revise based on the conditions and circumstances that you experience as an options day trader. At the very least, your options trading plan should be re-evaluated once yearly.

Technical Indicators You Need to Know About

When it comes to technical indicators for trading options, there are three indicators that you need to know about to help you make your trades. These indicators are used to help you identify stock trends and patterns so that you can get a strong understanding as to what the stocks are doing and where your best positions are going to be.

You should always check technical indicators as a part of your technical analysis to ensure that the position you are taking is going to earn you the best income possible.

The three technical indicators that you need to know about include the relative strength index indicator (RSI), the moving average convergence divergence indicator (MACD), and the stochastic indicator. Each of these will let you know what is going on with any particular stock and whether or not that stock offers a good position for you to trade-in.

Relative Strength Index (RSI)

The relative strength index is a momentum indicator that sits on a separate scale from the candlestick chart that you will be looking at when you look at the stock market for any given stock value.

The indicator is shown as a single line that is scaled from 0 to 100 and it identifies any stocks that have been overbought or oversold, meaning that you will identify which stocks are due for a rebound in the coming days.

On the indicator, which is shown on the side of the screen, you will notice that there are two white "frames" on either side of it, each of which shows where the market is peaking at overbought or oversold. The top frame represents stocks that have risen over 70 on the indicator, which indicates the market has been overbought and people are about to start selling their shares in order to earn profits before the market switches in the opposite direction.

The bottom frame represents stocks that have dropped below 30 on the indicator, indicating that the market has been oversold and people are about to start buying those stocks. You can watch for trends in any given stock on the RSI to see how they tend to perform and where they are presently sitting based on the intensity of trades that have been happening with that particular stock.

Most stocks will not consistently swing back and forth between overbought and oversold, but instead will straddle one side of the indicator before taking a large swing in the opposite direction at any given point in the future.

With that being said, you should always take your time spotting trends on this indicator so that you can confirm the trend is actually happening. Although this will eat into some of your profits, it will still help you ensure that you are earning plenty from the trade that you are seeking to make.

Moving Average Convergence Divergence (MACD)
The MACD indicator shows a fast line, a slow line, and a histogram that is used to help identify what is taking place with any given stock. This particular indicator can be more challenging to understand, but it still offers a wealth of valuable knowledge that will help you identify how the stock is behaving.

You should take your time to understand the MACD and educate yourself by watching it on the active stock market screen so that you can get a feel for the information it provides you with. Once you understand how to read this indicator, you will find a great deal of information that helps reinforce your trade decisions going forward.

The MACD indicator shows the moving average of the "difference" between the fast line and the slow line on the indicator itself. This means that what you are reading is how quickly the market is moving back and forth, or how volatile the market is with any given stock at any given moment.

The MACD slow line actually shows you the moving average of the last line over a number of periods defined as "MA-periods."

The MACD indicator is shown by two lines with the last line being represented by the color blue and the slow line being represented by the color orange. The bigger the gap is between the two lines, the more volatile the market is. When the two lines cross, it shows that the market has switched in trend, resulting in it either turning bullish or bearish from a bearish or bullish trend, depending on what direction it moves into.

The histogram shows you the moving average of the stock so that you can get a feel for how volatile the stock has been in the past, allowing you to understand whether or not the current volatility of the stock is standard or unusual for that particular stock. If it is standard, you know that the patterns of the stock will more than likely follow patterns similar to the ones it has in the past.

In other words, this is considered a lower risk stock investment. If the indicator suggests that the stock is more volatile, this means that it is less likely to follow historical patterns and that it will likely perform in a more unpredictable manner.

In other words, the stock is riskier and could come with greater losses. With that being said, higher-risk stocks do generally offer higher rewards; too, meaning it may be worth the risk depending on how confident you are in your judgment of how the stock will truly behave.

In essence, a moving average works like any other average. It is the average of the high and low price of an asset over a given period of time.

The average price of an asset over a given period of time is a static measure that simply reflects the buy and sell price of the asset in a rather specific window of time. It is a snapshot, if you will, of what that asset's price has been over a longer period of time.

As such, a moving average becomes the calculation of the average price of an asset at given intervals, for instance, every hour. With this calculation on a recurring basis, the asset's price can be tracked to determine where the trend, if any, lies.

The various results of the moving average calculation can be plotted on a chart in which each point can be used to determine the overall trend of the asset's price. There are three possible types of trends:

Upward Trend

This type of trend indicates that the overall trend in the price of an asset is up, meaning, increase. It is very important to keep in mind that an upward trend is generally accompanied by higher demand though it is not always the case. Nevertheless, increased demand generally means an increase in price.

Downward Trend

This type of trend indicates that the overall trend in the price of an asset down, meaning a decrease. What this indicates is that the price is going down as a result of an increase of supply, or a decrease in demand. Both forces can converge, thus leading the asset's prices to spiral downward.

Sideways Trend

In this case, there is little to no change in the price of the asset. This means that the trend remains steady. When this happens, it is because investors are being cautious. Perhaps they are expecting a breakout. So, while the breakout happens, they are holding their positions in order to see that will transpire.

Additionally, moving averages use a statistical technique called "candlesticks" to track the high and low price of the asset at every interval the price is measured. In this regard, you can visualize the amount of volatility as reflected in the fluctuations of the asset's price. Consequently, you can gain a great deal of perspective as to what the sentiment of investors is with regard to the asset in question.

The main function of a moving average is to track the trend in the price of an asset.

It is the premier tool used by traders and analysts in order to gauge the sentiment of investors. If investors are piling on to an asset, you will see this reflected in the price of the asset. On the contrary, if investors are looking to dump an asset, the moving average will reflect this sentiment.

This is why you, as a day trader, need to recognize these trends. The most important thing to keep in mind is that depending on your overall trading approach, you will be able to figure out what the best play for you is.

Given the fact that the moving average reflects very short-term moves, in addition to longer-term moves, you can figure out if the asset in question is good for a short-term trade, or perhaps it might be better suited for a long-term approach.

Moving averages, when available, can serve to view the price of stocks over a very long period of time, such as several years. This is a powerful analytics tool as you can see what the performance of the stock has been over a much more extended period of time. Consequently, you can choose to hold on to it as part of a passive income strategy or as a means of hedging your portfolio against riskier propositions.

So, I would greatly encourage you to become familiar with moving averages as this will be the basic parameter by which you will be able to measure the performance of stocks, and any other asset, you wish to trade.

Stochastic Indicator
The stochastic indicator is a momentum indicator that can help you identify when a trend might end, letting you know when a stock has either been overbought or oversold. The information given by the stochastic indicator is similar to what you receive from an RSI, meaning

that it can help validate whether or not the trade position you are looking at is ideal.

The stochastic indicator is shown by two lines on a chart that is separate from the candlestick chart that represents the market itself. Typically, it is shown below the market chart and follows the exact same time stamps, meaning that the information you see in the stochastic indicator chart perfectly overlaps with the information you see in the market itself.

The stochastic indicator looks almost exactly like the RSI, with a frame on each the top and bottom of the chart itself, showing you the overbought and oversold portions of the market, respectively.

However, the stochastic indicator has two lines, a red and a blue line, moving through the chart to give you information about what is currently going on in the marketplace.

When the lines are above the "80" point, this means a downtrend is likely to follow, or the market is likely to go bearish. In this case, you would want to sell your call options or buy your put options, depending on what strategy you are using to earn your profits from the market.

If it drops below the "20" point, the market has been oversold and it is going to turn into an uptrend or a bullish market. This is where you would want to buy your call options, sell your put options, or otherwise position yourself with the best spread and strategy to earn profits from the incoming movement of the stock prices.

When reading the stochastic indicator, you want to see *both* lines rise above 80 or fall below 20 to indicate that there is a strong chance for the market to switch directions. If only one line crosses, this suggests that the market may be reaching overbought or oversold, but it has not reached it yet and therefore, it is not yet ready to swing back in the opposite direction.

Pay close attention to these stocks; however, as they will likely mature into their overbought or oversold position quickly, leading to an opportunity for you to secure an entry into the market.

Technical Analysis for Evaluating a Trade

Options trading requires less technical analysis than other trade styles, but you are still required to perform technical analysis to ensure that the market entry point you are looking at is going to be profitable. Entering any market at any time without having first completed proper technical analysis can lead to a greater risk of losses due to not clearly understanding what is likely going to happen with the market in its current state.

When you perform technical analysis, your goal is to identify possible positions that you can enter, validate the quality of those positions, choose the position(s) you will take, and then pick the perfect entry point. By following this exact system for entering the market, you can feel confident that you are entering the market at the best possible time, every single time. This way, you maximize your potential for profits and minimize your potential for losses.

Remember, the more educated you are on what you are doing and what position you are taking, the more likely you are going to be able to increase your profits with trading.

Conducting technical analysis for options trading should be completed as a routine every time you do it to ensure that you never miss out on a step. This way, you create a strong system that works for validating your positions, and you can always feel confident that you are taking on the best positions possible.

Creating Your Watch List for Possible Positions

The first thing you need to do when you are engaging in technical analysis is to create a watchlist that is complete with possible trade positions that you can take on that day. You can start identifying possible positions by looking at various stock news sites like the ones I mentioned earlier in this book to help you get a feel for what is going on in the market.

Using these news sites to identify possible positions simply helps by giving you the opportunity to narrow down your scope so that you are only looking at a few places in the market, rather than looking blankly at the market as a whole. This way, you are not spending hours every day scouring for the best possible places.

After you have gauged the market by looking at the news, you can start looking at the market itself to see which positions are looking most favorable. At this point, you can narrow down your listen even further just by getting a simple once over at the market itself. This should help you identify 3-5 positions, or possibly a few more, that may be ideal for you to take on for the day. If you have more than 3-5, start by picking the 3-5 that are most likely to be profitable and conduct your research on these positions, first. It is likely that you will find your best positions this way, however, if for some reason none of the ones you have looked at seem good, you can move on to the next 3-5 options to find a better position.

Validating the Quality of Your Possible Positions
Now that you have located a few possible positions that you could trade-in, you need to start the process of validating which ones are truly going to be a good position for you to hold and which ones are not.

You can find that out by conducting a deeper background analysis on the stocks through looking at the technical analysis indicators we talked about in the last section, as well as doing a deeper dive on any news relating to that stock.

If you are looking at a good position, everything you find out during the research phase should confirm what you already anticipated when you began to look into the position. If the information differs, this does not necessarily mean that it is a bad position, however, it does mean that you are going to have to consider the numbers to decide whether or not it has the capacity to earn you as many profits as you desire.

You also need to decide whether or not you are willing to endure the risk that is being

Choosing Which Position Will Earn Maximum Gains (And Minimize Losses)

Now that you have thoroughly researched how each position is likely to play out and what types of profits you are likely to incur with each one, as well as what risks you are exposed to, you can move into deciding what position you want to take on. Deciding what position, you are going to trade in the market is not entirely a science, although there are some things you are going to want to weigh into your consideration to help you make the best decision.

Picking Your Exact Entry Point

The last part of your analysis comes from deciding when your entry point is going to be. At this point, you have already designed your exit strategy during your research phase, so now you have to decide on when you are going to enter that position in order to maximize your gains.

This part cannot be broken down to a science, either, as there is never a way to truly guarantee what the market is going to do or when it is going to do it. Even if you are confident that the market is about to behave in a certain way, you cannot confidently guarantee the exact moment at which that shift is going to happen. For that reason, you truly just need to pay attention to your indicators, follow the pattern, and make your best-educated guess on when the best timing is for you to enter into a new options trader.

Candlestick Charts and Patterns

Candlestick charts weren't known in the West before the 1980s when they were introduced. However, Japan used this method for centuries, which at the same time makes Japan the place of origin of the candlestick method. As we have already seen before, these charts show the same information as the bar chart that was used in our country's way before we started using the Japanese system. The reason that the candlestick charts became so popular in such a short amount of time is the fact that it is easier to understand, and it uses simple yet innovative body illustration that helps the investor seeing every change at a glance.

Let's recap some of the basic characteristics of the candlestick as the general pattern. Firstly, the total length of the candle represents the trading range for the predetermined period. The body of the candle is connected to the distance between the prices known as the closing price and the opening price. The difference in color shows if the price went up or down for a certain period. The length of the candle also portrays the volatility of the price and the sum of the candle and the "body" of the candle can be viewed as the progress that was made for one day. If the chart shows that the candle's "body" is short, it means that the closing and the opening prices were close or similar. If that is the case, we can say that the buyers and the sellers were in balance.

When it comes to the candlestick chart, we can say that there are regular candles and then that there is Doji. Doji is a special candle which body is just a horizontal line. This line represents closing prices and opening prices, which in case you have Doji are equivalent.

If the candles have long bodies, which will indicate that the trend of the price is strong. If your chart has candles without any wicks, it means that you got Marubozu. Marumboza is an indicator that shows that the trades were only made in the range of the opening and closing prices, thus no trade was made outside of that range. This is a very strong indication, which means that the market was strongly pushing the price only in one direction.

Hammer

When it comes to ideal signals, in Hammer, that signal is represented with a small body. Its wick should be two times longer than the body regardless of the day being up or down for the price trend. Hammer sometimes signals that the trend of the price will reverse. The way to confirm such an assumption and make it actionable is to wait for the following day and see if the price is going to increase. If the price starts rising, it means that your interpretation of trend reversal has been confirmed. This pattern works because of many traders panic, and if the price is down for some time, they will sell at any price. If we try to express this situation in the candle chart, it means that the wick will be pushed down. However, smart investors come in, and they buy, which pushes the price up once again. These trend reversals can last through the whole day and even keep up happening the following day too.

Hanging Man

The Hanging Man is a pattern that looks the same as the Hammer; the only difference is that it comes in an uptrend. Just like before, we search for a change in the price trend on the following day so we could confirm our estimation of the trend's reversal. The psychology, in this case, is that traders mostly decide to take profits. That way, they push the prices down. Still, some of those who are new on the market see this as their chance to buy. That way, they push the price back up. In any case, this candle is considered to be weak. As a reflection of this pattern, it appears that traders have a hunch that this means that the trend is over, so the selling starts to rise again in the following few days.

Inverted Hammer

Once you see the diagrams for the first two candlestick patterns, you will realize that the inverted hammer also has similar characteristics. There is also certain psychology behind its signaling, and we will briefly explain it: Once the downtrend starts weakening and several traders have second thoughts, they start buying in which pushes the prices up. Sellers also come back in the game, which means that the price will close down. However, if the price starts increasing during the following day, than the conclusion is that the weakness of the trend made buyers buying even more while pushing up the prices, and that way, the uptrend started.

Shooting Star

Last but not least, in the set of four related candle signals is the pattern known as the Shooting Star comes, which comes in an uptrend. Everybody knows that beginners or novices if you prefer, tend to buy on the top. Shooting star demonstrates simply the exuberance that the future causes the traders to see the high wick that appears when novices enter the market. The traders who notice this are usually those who appeared thinking that it is time to sell. Just like in every other pattern above, the only way to confirm this is to wait up the following day and to determine if that was the signal that shows that the trend will reverse.

Bullish Engulfing

This is a pattern that consists of two candles, and it is graded as highly probable. When in a downtrend, the first candle pressures that the selling continues. The pressure is strong enough to allow the following candle to open up at an even lower price. But those investors who are smart see an opportunity here, and they start buying on the second candle in this case. This makes the price to grow and launches it above the limit of the preceding period. This is one of the numerous proofs that the real power is in the hands of the buyers and that there is a high possibility that the trend will reverse.

Bearish Engulfing

It has the same concept as bullish engulfing. The thing is that sometimes uptrend can stretch so badly that the opening price can even go higher than the current price in the earlier candle. Smart and experienced investors usually decide to sell on these occasions. The length of the candle, in this case, shows that the trend can be reversed from an uptrend to a downtrend due to the weight of an opinion.

Piercing Candle is a pattern that represents a strong bearish candle that is in a downtrend. This candle with another following candle, opens up at a price that is lower than the current one. However, the candle is rallying to have the finishing price, which has the same trading range as the earlier day. This pattern can be seen as a signal for the trend reversal and the reason for that is piercing candle as an indicator that sellers are feeling hopeless. When the low prices go even lower, it is an opportunity for those who consider themselves to be smart investors to start buying and to push prices strongly up.

Dark Cloud Cover is a pattern that has entirely the same characteristic as the piercing candle pattern. The only difference is that the dark cloud cover is in an uptrend.

Bullish Harami

This pattern has a name that originated from the Japanese word Harami that means "pregnant." As the name suggests, the reason for this is that according to them, these candlestick patterns have a resemblance to the pregnant women. If you happen to encounter the bullish harami, it means that the market had a lot of active sellers. However, the other candle indicates that the current price became higher. If the second candle finishes up and provides buying enough pressure, you can see it as a signal that there is going to be a change in the price trend. As usual, the following day is a confirmation checker.

Bearish Harami

When a pattern reaches an end of an uptrend, there can be a candle that demonstrates exuberance that some might see as naïve. When the other period opens up, and the price is lower, continuing to go lower as the day goes by, we can say that it indicates second thoughts in buyers. The most probable income of this situation is that the selling will continue regularly and that everything will be resolved once when the price goes into a downtrend.

Keep in mind that trading should never be done based on one strategy or just one resource, which is why we wouldn't recommend that you start trading relying only on the information you gather through the candlestick principle, for example. Remember, the validity of the pattern depends on the right trend in which the pattern needs to work in. Also, many other indicators have to be taken into consideration.

Rules for Successful Trading

Ensuring dependable profits in the financial markets is much more difficult than it seems at first glance. It is assessed that over 75% of all members in the end wash out and take up more secure side interests. Be that as it may, the financier business once in a while distributes customer disappointment rates, since they're concerned reality may drive away new records, so the washout rate could be a lot higher.

Disregard the Holy Grail

Losing brokers fantasize about the mystery recipe that will mysteriously improve their outcomes. As a general rule, there are no mysteries in light of the fact that the way to progress consistently goes through cautious decision, viable risk the executives, and gifted benefit taking.

Have Realistic Expectations

It is sad to say that many people who enter the options trading industry are doing so to make a quick buck. Options trading is not a get-rich-quick scheme. It is a reputable career that has made many people rich, but that is only because these people have put in the time, effort, study, and dedication to learning the craft and mastering it.

Start Small to Grow a Big Portfolio

Caution is the name of the game when you just get started with day trading options. Remember that you are still learning options trading and developing an understanding of the financial market. Do not jump the gun even if you are eager. After you have practiced paper trading, start with smaller options positions, and steadily grow your standing as you get a lay of the options day trading land. This strategy allows you to keep your losses to a minimum and to develop a systematic way of entering positions.

Know Your Limits

You may be tempted to trade as much as possible to develop a winning monthly average, but that strategy will have the opposite effect and land you with a losing average.

Remember that every options trader needs careful consideration before that contract is set up. Never overtrade and tie up your investment fund.

Be Mentally, Physically and Emotionally Prepared Every Day

This is a mentally, physically, and emotionally tasking career, and you need to be able to meet the demands of this career. That means keeping your body, mind and heart in good health at all times. Ensure that you schedule a time for self-care every day. That can be as simple as taking the time to read for recreation to having an elaborate self-care routine carved out in the evenings. Not keeping your mind, heart and head in optimum health means that they are more likely to fail you. Signs that you need to buckle up and care for yourself more diligently include being constantly tired, being short-tempered, feeling preoccupied and being easily distracted. To ensure you perform your best every day, here a few tasks that you need to perform:

- Get the recommended amount of sleep daily. This is between 7 and 9 hours for an adult.

- Practice a balanced diet. The brain and body need adequate nutrition to work their best. Include fruits, complex carbs and veggies in this diet and reduce the consumption of processed foods.

- Exercise regularly. Being inactive increases your risk of developing chronic diseases like heart disease, certain cancers and other terrible health consequences. Adding just a few minutes of exercise to your daily routine not only reduces those risks but also allows your brain to function better, which is a huge advantage for an options day trader.

- Drink alcohol in moderation or not at all.

- Stop smoking.

- Reduce stress contributors in your environment.

Do Your Homework Daily
Get up early and study the financial environment before the market opens and look at the news. This allows you to develop a daily options trading plan. The process of analyzing the financial climate before the market opens is called pre-market preparation. It is a necessary task that needs to be performed every day to asset competition and to align your overall strategy with the short-term conditions of that day.

An easy way to do this is to develop a pre-market checklist. An example of a pre-market checklist includes but is not limited to:

- Checking the individual markets that you frequently trade options in or plan to trade options in to evaluate support and resistance.

- Checking the news to assess whether events that could affect the market developed overnight.

- Assessing what other options traders are doing to determined volume and competition.

- Determining what safe exits for losing positions are.

- Considering the seasonality of certain markets are some as affected by the day of the week, the month of the year, *etc.*

Analyze Your Daily Performance
To determine if the options day trading style and strategies that you have adopted are working for you, you need to track your performance. At the most basic, this needs to be done on a daily basis by virtue of the fact that you are trading options daily. This will allow you to notice patterns in your profit and loss. This can lead to you determining the why and how of these gains and losses. These determinations lead to fine-tuning your daily processes for maximum returns. These daily performance reviews allow you to also make determinations on the long-term activity of your options day trading career.

Do Not Be Greedy

If you are fortunate enough to make a 100% return on your investment, do not be greedy and try to reap more benefit from the position. You might have the position turn on you and you can lose everything. When and if such a rare circumstance happens to you, sell your position and take the profits.

Pay Attention to Volatility

Volatility speaks to how likely a price change will occur over a specific amount of time on the financial market. Volatility can work for an options day trader or against the options day trader. It all depends on what the options day trader is trying to accomplish and what his or her current position is.

Use the Greeks

Greeks are a collection of measures that provide a gage of an option's price sensitivity in relation to other factors. Each Greek is represented by a letter from the Greek alphabet. These Greeks use complex formulas to be determined, but they are the system that option pricing is based on. Even though these calculations can be complex, they can be done quickly and efficiently so that options day traders can use them as a method of advancing their trades for the most profitable position.

The 5 Greeks that are used in options trading are:

Delta

This Greek defines the price relationship between an option and its associated asset. Delta is a direct translation of a change in the price of the associated asset into the changing of the price of an option. Call options deltas range from 1 to 0 while put options deltas range from 0 to -1. An example of delta as it relates to a call option is a call option with a delta of 0.5. If the price of the associated asset increases by $200, then the price of the call option will increase by $100.

Vega

This Greek is a measure of the sensitivity of the price of an option to the implied volatility of the associated asset. Option prices are greatly impacted by the volatility of the associated asset's prices because greater volatility translates in a higher chance that the price of the associated asset will reach or surpass the strike price on or before the expiration date of the option.

Theta

This Greek is a measure of the sensitivity of the price of an option to time decay of the value of the option. Time decay describes the rate of deterioration in the value of the contract because of the passage of time. The closer the expiration date becomes, the more time decay accelerates because the time left to gain a profit narrows. Therefore, the longer it takes to reach an options' expiration date, the more value this option has because it has a longer time period to gain the trader a profit. The theta is a negative figure because time is always a diminishing factor. This figure becomes increasingly negative the closer the expiration date becomes.

Gamma

This Greek measures the rate of change of the delta of an option. At its most basic, it tells the likelihood of an option reaching or surpassing the strike price.

Rho

This Greek is a measure of an option's value compared to changes in interest rate. Options with longer expiration dates are more likely to be affected by changes in interest rates.

Be Flexible

Many options day traders find it difficult to try trading styles and strategies that they are not familiar with. While the saying of, "Do not fix it if it is not broken," is quite true, you will never become more effective and efficient in this career if you do not step out of your comfort zone at least once in a while. Yes, stick with want work but allow room for the consideration that there may be better alternatives.

Have an Accountability Partner or Mentorship?
Day trading options can be a rather solitary career. That means it becomes easy to sleep in if the urge strikes or just not put in a day of work. While there is nothing wrong with doing that when you have established a solid career in day trading options, this is a slippery slope that can become a harmful habit to your career. Having an accountability partner is an easy way to keep you on track with your trading plan and goals. It keeps you consistent with your actions. This can be a fellow trader, your spouse or romantic partners, a friend or family member.

Connect with your trading plan
Update your trading plan week by week or month to month to incorporate new thoughts and kill awful ones. Return and read the arrangement at whatever point you fall in an opening and are searching for an approach to get out.

Be careful with reinforcement
Dynamic trading discharges adrenaline and endorphins. These synthetics can create sentiments of happiness, notwithstanding when you are losing cash. Thus, this urges addictive characters to take terrible positions, just to get a hurry.

Try not to cut corners
Your opposition burns through many hours consummating methodologies and you are in for a severe shock in the event that you hope to toss a couple of darts and leave with a benefit. It's far more terrible in the event that you cut corners in a mind-blowing remainder since that unfortunate propensity is a lot harder to break.

Grasp simplicity
Concentrate on value activity, understanding that everything else is optional. Feel free to assemble complex; specialized markers yet

remember their essential capacity is to affirm or disprove what you're prepared eye as of now observes.

Evade the obvious
Benefit infrequently pursues the greater part. When you see an ideal exchange arrangement, almost certainly, every other person sees it too, planting you in the group and setting you up for disappointment.

Arrange your personal life
Whatever is not right in your life will, in the end, persist into your trading execution. This is particularly risky on the off chance that you haven't profited, riches and the attractive extremity of plenitude and shortage.

Try not to break your rules
You make trading principles to get you out of inconvenience when positions go seriously. On the off chance that you don't enable them to carry out their responsibility, you have lost your order and opened the entryway to significantly more noteworthy misfortunes.

Tune in to your intuition
Trading utilizes the scientific and imaginative sides of your cerebrum, so you have to develop both to prevail over the long haul. When you are alright with math, you can upgrade results with reflection, a couple of yoga stances or a tranquil stroll in the recreation center.

Make peace with losses
Trading is one of only a handful couple of callings where losing cash each day is a characteristic way to progress. Each trading misfortune accompanies a significant market exercise in case you are available to the message.

Try not to believe in a company
In case you are excessively enamored with your trading vehicle, you offer an approach to defective basic leadership. You must gain by wastefulness, profiting while every other person is inclining the incorrect way.

Lose the crowd

Long haul productivity requires situating in front of or behind the group, yet never in the group since that is the place savage techniques target. Avoid stock sheets and visit rooms. This is not kidding business and everybody in those spots has an ulterior thought process.

Try not to get even

Drawdowns are a characteristic piece of the merchant's life cycle. Acknowledge them effortlessly and adhere to the reliable methodologies you realize will in the long run, recover your presentation on track.

Try not to count your chickens

Like an exchange that is going your direction, yet the cash is not yours until you closeout. Lock in what you can as ahead of schedule as possible, with trailing stops or fractional benefits, so concealed hands cannot pickpocket your prosperity ultimately.

Watch for early warnings

Huge misfortunes once in a while happen without various specialized admonitions. Dealers routinely overlook those signs and enable would like to supplant keen control, setting themselves up for torment.

Apparatuses don't think

Dealers compensate for deficient aptitudes with costly programming, prepackaged with a wide range of exclusive purchase and sell signals. These apparatuses meddle with important experience since you think the product is more brilliant than you are.

Play with your head

It's normal for dealers to copy their monetary saints, but at the same time, it's an ideal method to lose cash. Take in what you can from others; at that point, back off and set up your very own market personality, in light of your one of a kind abilities and risk resistance.

Things That Affect the Price of Options

There are a few factors that affect how options are priced. These are implied volatility, the price of the underlying asset, time until expiration, and it's in or out-of-the-money status.

Implied volatility is the forecast of how the price of a security will perform in the future. If the security is more volatile, it means that the price will move dramatically. Volatility is about market fluctuations. In bearish markets, the implied volatility increases because it is believed the price will fall; in a bullish market, the implied volatility decreases. The number can only tell you how much it is believed that the price will change, but it will not tell you in what direction.

The price of the underlying asset affects how premiums are set because they have to be in some vicinity of the asset's price. So an option for a stock which is expensive will be expensive, while for one that is cheap will be cheap. However, this has no bearing on whether or not the option will be profitable, and it makes sense for the option to be priced at a price that is close to the value of the underlying asset since, in the end, you will decide whether to buy or sell the underlying asset.

The time before expiration is also important in determining the price of the premium paid for an option. The more time until expiration, the more expensive the option will be. This is because there is more time for the price of the underlying asset to move into territory that may be profitable for the person who owns the option. The issuer of the option holds more risk, so they charge more for the option. The less time there is, the less the option will cost because there is less time for the underlying asset price to move in a vicinity that may be profitable to the person who holds the option.

The moneyness of the option pertains to whether or not the underlying option is in-the-money or out-of-the-money. An in-the-money option will be more expensive than one that isn't. This is because there is a perceived starting position that is favorable to the option holder. At the same time, it looks like the issuer is in a losing position already from the beginning. As we have seen, options work because the writer of the option and the holder are betting against each other.

Tips for Success

Most successful traders have tips and tricks that they employ to ensure they make some good profit trading options. Here are some of them.

Understand technical and fundamental analysis

Before you start trading, ensure that you carry out an analysis of the market. Technical analysis involves the study of how the price is expected to change. The idea behind this concept is that you can study historical patterns in price changes and determine how the price may change in the future.

Always be flexible when trading options

When you are working with stocks and some of the other securities out there, you will need to do it on the idea of buying low and selling high. But when you are working with options, this approach often doesn't meet all of your needs. With options, you can profit even if the market is going down.

Working with break-even points

Another thing to consider when it comes to options trading is the break-even points. As a trader, you must understand these break-even points, so you know the best time to get out of a trade, and you don't exit too early and take a loss without even realizing it. The break-even point is often going to be specific, whether it's high or low, that the stock needs to reach before you can start to earn a profit.

Always do your research

Before you enter into any trade with options, make sure that you do sufficient amounts of research. Charts are going to be crucial when you work on your technical analysis. But this isn't always enough on its own. When you begin, take some time to figure out what kinds of stocks and underlying assets interest you the most, and then do some further research into those particular assets. Take your time to learn about the markets that you want to enter. Watch the charts and find out how they work.

Start with enough capital

You should always leave a little bit of money in your trading account. This is going to help you out when you are in the middle of a trade and can make it easier for your broker to keep working on trades without having to worry about a delay while your fund's transfer. The most successful traders in options will always check their accounts and make sure that they keep enough capital there so that even if there are a few bad trades along the way, they still have that nice cushion to rely on to help them.

Avoid the really big risks

It is true in investing that the higher the risk, the higher the reward. This may be the way to invest for some people, but for the average trader, it is going to spell disaster. If you want to be able to say that you are profitable with options trading, then you need to make sure that you keep your risks to a minimum as much as possible.

Trade at the right times

Since you are going to learn how to avoid big risks when you are an options trader, you are going to learn how to be very careful about your timing when it comes to entering and exiting the market. You have to be able to read the market the right way so that you are able to learn the best time to do both of those tasks. These investors have spent their time doing some research and they know how to look at the big picture, rather than always calling up the broker and hoping that they can trust that person.

Come up with your own plan

You also need to make sure that you are picking out a plan that is unique to you and that has things that you are willing to follow. While there is nothing wrong with listening to some experts in the field and considering what they say, it is never a good idea to just follow exactly what they say without considering it or thinking it through. What works for someone else may not completely work for you, so think things through before you just jump right in.

Learn how to be focused

Some of the most successful traders on the market are the ones who are able to keep themselves focused on the task at hand. There are quite a few people who have an idea that options trading is super easy, and then they jump in and become overwhelmed by what they are dealing with. If you are not used to this kind of investment, it may seem a bit hard to deal with in the beginning.

Never follow the crowd

Following the crowd is one of the quickest ways to lose money on the market. If you are looking at some of the trends that come up with the market, you will notice that the crowd hits on when things are too late. Options trading can get you on at the ground floor, offering you a good discount on the item or asset that you want and can yield a good profit if you play your cards right. This is something that you are only able to do if you think for yourself and do not fall into the trap of following the crowd.

Your exit point, or your escape plan

As part of your trading plan, you must have a clearly defined exit strategy, one that you stick with no matter what. To keep this simple, that exit point is the place where you will close out the trade and walk away if the business starts to head south and you start to lose money. If you follow this, you can protect your investment, and it ensures that you don't stay in the market for too long.

Have enough capital

The reason why most beginners do not make it in options trading is not having enough capital. Most people get excited at how easy options trading can be and think that they can make an instant profit from their little capital in a matter of days. However, before they realize it, a few trades have swallowed their capital. They are then left with nothing to trade on. To be on the safe side, start with a good amount of cash that can sustain you for a number of trades.

Get a suitable trading style
What differentiate traders is their preferences, personalities, and trading styles. You need to understand the style that suits you best. For example, some traders prefer working at night, while others are more effective in day trading. Some of the traders will make several short sales during the day, while others will factor in the issue of time and volatility just to gain a large profit over periods that may last between few days and a month.

Create a risk management plan
Having a plan is vital for your success. You need to have it in place before you start trading. Remember, options are high-risk tools, and it is important to have strategies in place that can help you minimize the risks involved with each trade. Use your money wisely. Diversify the stocks you trade in to reduce the potential of losing all your capital. Most of the expert traders only seal a contract when there are low risk and high profits.

Be patient and disciplined
To succeed in options trading, you must develop a high sense of discipline. Carry out extensive research and set the right goals. Stick to these goals and have them in mind as you seize trading opportunities. Be careful that you do not follow the crowd and don't believe in some facts and opinions before doing some research.

Patience and discipline will help you stick to your capital and risk management plans. These attributes also assist you to avoid trades you are not successful in.

Understand the market cycle

The options trading market keeps changing every time. You need to remain updated on the market trends and make the necessary adjustments to your plan accordingly. Through constant learning, you will be able to learn new strategies and identify better trading opportunities that other traders bypass.

Understand when to trade and when to exit. Know when the market is taking an uptrend or declining. Follow and interpret Forex news to understand what to expect in the future and where the industry is heading.

Keep records

Having a record of your past trades can help you determine when to make a call or put an option successfully. Some of the successful traders keep records of all their transactions. Analyzing these records continuously can help you identify vital patterns in the options you are trading in. It can also help improve your odds in the trade.

Identifying a Reliable Broker

There are plenty of brokerage firms available online. These brokerage firms provide traders like you with a platform to trade safely. These firms charge you a fee to access the platform and carry out your trades. They also provide you with tools that you need to trade successfully and customer service.

Generally, the lower the fees or commission charged, the less the customer service and assistance you can expect. On average, you should expect to pay between $2 and $5 per options contract that you invest in.

Sometimes you will be asked if you prefer a cash or margin account when opening an account with a broker. A cash account means you will trade using your own money. On the other hand, a margin account allows you access to credit facilities where you borrow money from the broker to invest in certain securities. Keep in mind that you are only able to borrow money from your broker against certain securities like bonds, stocks, and mutual funds.

You will not be able to borrow to invest in stock options because they are strictly cash-only trades. Options also settle trades the very same day or one business day. Therefore, you will require substantial cash amounts to enter trades. When you enter complex trades, you will also need to set some cash aside just in case you are obliged to buy shares at a certain price.

When opening an account, ensure that you choose a broker that rates you:

At this level, you are able to trade in options, even as a beginner. Also, tick on the margin box rather than cash just so that you always have access to borrowing from the broker. There are generally four levels of traders. They range from level 0 to level 3.

At level 3, you are allowed to enter profitable but risky trades. For instance, you can participate in naked calls and naked puts. You can also participate in other more complex trades. However, risky trades will require much higher deposits, so keep this in mind. All in all, brokers are all different. However, they will all need you to have access to cash and stocks in your account. This way, you will be able to fulfill your obligations and trade as often as you need to. Therefore, you will access options markets via your broker. Your broker will usually have access to the major platforms where options are traded, such as the Chicago Board Options Exchange.

Types of Brokers

We have different kinds of brokers. There are two main types. These are discount brokers and full-service brokers. A full-service broker, also known as a traditional broker, provides a wide variety of services to clients. These services include personalized advice to clients about where to invest or place their money. These professionals serve mostly active traders who prefer to make their own financial decisions.

On the other hand, we have discount brokers who are more suited to traders who know what they are doing and wish to manage their affairs. As such, clients pay only a minimal amount and, in return, get to make most, if not all, their financial decisions. What they do mostly is to execute orders from clients like you. This means that when you enter a trade or a position, the broker will execute these on your behalf.

You are also likely to encounter brokerage firms that provide a combination of these services. They generally offer a bouquet of services from which clients get to choose the services they desire. A lot of options traders, including beginners and novices, prefer the discounted services. Any trader that is confident enough to trade on their own and implement options strategies is very likely to be successful.

Speed of trades execution and availability
A good platform should also be responsive. There is no need for spending so much time coming up with a strategy only for the platform to fail you. Ensure that you find a good platform that is sufficiently responsive, so that you do not lose any advantages based on your analysis. Also remember to ensure that you have an excellent system from your PC or laptop computer to system, applications, and connectivity. These are crucial for successful trading experience.

Ease of Use
Another crucial aspect of any trading platform or online brokerage is its ease of use. All too often, brokerage firms will present quite complex or oblique platforms that take a while to master. Some keys may be spread apart, while some functions are complex and hard to master. Such platforms are not ideal for traders.

Fees and Commissions

Also crucial are fees, including commissions, penalties, and so on. It is crucial to find an affordable broker whose costs and charges are minimal. If you are not careful, fees will eat into your profits. As it is, options brokerages are super careful to stand out from the competition.

CHAPTER 3:

Quick And Accurate Basics Option Trading Strategies

Long Calls

Options terminologies can seem confusing, but once you understand the basics, you will be good to go. Long simply means to buy, and short means to sell. A long call option gives you the right to buy an underlying stock at strike price A. It offers you the opportunity to get your game right without getting wiped out directly if you were to be trading directly in the stock market.

If you are feeling bullish about a stock (meaning that you hope that a specific stock will rise in value at a point in the future), you can choose to buy the stock outright or use a long call option. You will profit in a long call option when the stock rises according to your prediction. But if the opposite happens, you will only lose your premium paid.

Apart from that, long calls are less expensive as compared with buying the stock outright. If you were to be investing in the stock market, a failure for a stock to rise could just get you absolutely disappointed. You will encounter a lot of risks since you have already bought part ownership into the company.

If you consider entering the market through a bullish strategy, you need to ensure you thoroughly analyze the time horizon a chosen stock moves in a specific direction and the number of points required for that stock price movement. To minimize risks, what most people do is to buy more short term out of the money calls. This can be dangerous if all those calls have not moved successfully to indicate a gain.

The first place to enter the market is through long calls options. Most beginner options traders enter the market through this area due to its simplicity. Sometimes it might very be challenging to make a profit through long calls, but then it is still not complicated like the advance option trading strategies.

Risk/reward analysis for long call options strategy
The following entails the risks and rewards to have in mind while using this strategy:

It involves a little money, making it attractive for beginner options traders. It helps stock traders to manage their portfolio and avoid trading in stocks that are expensive to buy.

The loss made is only limited, that is if the underlying stock falls, instead of rising. It helps to risk a little money than to lose, all in an underlying stock trade.

There is no need for any complex calculations before executing the stock options plan.

It does not involve margin debt and it also has lower commissions as compared with other complex option trading strategies.

Avoid using all your money in a long call option. Buying many out of the money call options because it is cheap can make you lose your trading capital.

You need to understand that the call option is subject to time decay, which depreciates with the passing time towards expiration.

Simple calculations for Long Call Options
To minimize your losses and maximize your gains, you need to do a simple calculation to have an overview of how the entire long call

options work. A breakeven point is to realize if the underlying financial instrument has neither made a loss or a gain. The following example will help you understand this better.

Source: Schwab Center for Financial Research (Strategy at Expiration)

- Long 1 GYZ June 50 Call @ $ 4
- Maximum Loss =$ 400.00 (4.00 option premium paid x 100 shares per contract)
- Breakeven Point =$ 54 (4 option premium + 50 strike price)
- Maximum Gain = Unlimited

To calculate the profit potential before aspiration: Profit = [(Rise in underlying stock) x delta value] / price of call options

The problem with a long call option is that it has a limited life span. Therefore, the underlying stock must move upward very fast above the breakeven point in order to generate unlimited gains for the owner. The downside is that the owner of the options stands to lose premium when the underlying stock hasn't moved upward as expected.

Short Call Options Strategy

A short call options strategy is where an options trader is betting on the fact that a particular price of an asset is going to drop and therefore placing an option on it. In this case, an options trader is taking a bearish position (he or she is forecasting or predicting that a particular financial instrument) will drop in pricing rather than go down).

Instead of buying calls, an options trader will rather be selling calls, which gives the holder the right to buy the underlying security at a given price. This is how a short call option works. It operates by the mode that if underlying security falls, the short call option will generate a profit for the owner.

In the case where the underlying security falls, it will merely give unlimited exposure to the owner at the time value of the option, making the call naked. This happens when the short call trader does not particularly own the underlying security. To cut losses, experienced options trader ensures they own the underlying security while betting against the market, thus creating a covered call.

Simple calculations for short call options
- Long 100 GYZ June 50 Call @ $ 4
- Maximum Gain =$ 500.00 (5.00 option premium received x 100 shares per contract)
- Breakeven Point =$ 55 (5 option premium + 50 strike price)
- Maximum Loss = Unlimited

To calculate the loss potential before aspiration: Loss = [(Rise in underlying stock) x delta value] / price of call options

In this example, let's say that you own shares of GYZ Company. The stock is trading at $4 per share and you notice that the share price is likely to go down after your technical and fundamental analysis on the stock market. Since you are feeling bearish about the stock and betting that GYZ stock will go down, you decided to sell shares of the company to Daniel Electricals Inc.

You sold a call for $ 5 per share, which amounted to an amount of $500 premium, creating a portfolio income for that asset. You collected the upfront premium money. What happens next? After a few days, the shares become to take an upward movement on the stock market. The share per stock moved from $4 per share to $ 7 per share. In this case, your analysis has gone against you.

Daniel Electricals Inc. can decide to exercise a naked shorting call and buy the underlying stock at $ 5 per share, they will net $ 700, generating a profit of $ 200 on their trading activities. Whilst you will take a losing position. On the other way, if the stock price drops to $ 2 per share, you will make a profit of $ 2 per share, netting $200.00.

Long Puts/Buying Put Options Strategy

A long-put strategy works in the same way as a long call. But in this case, you are taking a bearish position on the stock price movement in the market. Instead of betting on the fact that a stock price will be going down, you notice an upward trend in the movement of stocks through fundamental or technical analysis of publicly traded stocks in the financial market.

Just as a short call option strategy, you have to be right about the stock price movement direction, the magnitude, and the time frame for that change for you to make a profit in the market. There are many reasons for a trader to buy a short put. One of such reasons is hedging against potential loses in stock value due to the high amount of volatility in the market.

If an underlying asset falls in value, you can choose to buy a put option, which increases in value to offset the underlying loss. A long put option works as a protective put or married put. This is the reason you should use a put option only when you are feeling bullish about a particular stock.

Example of Long Put Option
An investor has long (bought) shares of XYZ Company at $ 50 per share. After holding the shares for some time, the investor feels bullish about the stock after a fundamental and technical analysis of the market and then decided to buy a put to hedge against the potential losses in the shares.

The strike price of the underlying stock was at $ 40 for $ 2.00 premium, generating profits of $ 200.00 for 100 shares of stock. In this case, even if XYZ Company falls in stock price, the only thing they will lose is $ 1,200 shares. The shares of stock are said to be a hedge against losses in the marketplace.

The trading strategy used here is that the underlying stock will increase in value when the main stock price falls in value. However, if the stock option has been exercised by the buyer, it will put the seller short of the underlying stock. This will mean the trader will have to buy back more of the underlying to realize a profit from that stock.

Alternative repair strategy

In this strategy, rather than rolling down into a bull call spread, you would instead roll down into a butterfly spread. To continue with the previous example, this would be useful if Microsoft dropped to $90. If this occurs, you would then want to sell the July $90 calls at $4 a piece while retaining ownership of the original long call for July $95. This will also require that you purchase a July call at $85, which should sell for around $7.30 once you factor in time decay.

When it comes to the downside of this scenario, the total amount of risk actually drops as the sum total when it comes to the debit amount is only $230, and these are also less upside risks when the underlying asset begins to return towards the breakeven point. It is also important to keep in mind that if the stock stays the same, the options trade will still successfully generate a profit.

Combined Repair Strategy

This strategy is a variation of the common butterfly spread, which means, returning the earlier example once more, that in the previous example, the maximum amount of profit you could expect to see would be the result of the strike price of the two $90 July short calls that were generated. However, if the movement leads to prices dropping away from this point to the point that losses are generated instead, then you may also find success by combining the two previous repair strategies to create a multifaceted approach which can be used to help maintain the types of ideal odds that tend to come along with ensuring a profit from an almost certain loss.

Consider the Strike Price

If you want to use this strategy as effectively as possible, it is important to ensure you start with an accurate strike price when it comes to the options you are considering. This is extremely important as the price will always determine the true cost of the trade while also playing a large factor in your ultimate breakeven point. The best way to start in most cases will be by first looking at the magnitude of the potential unrealized loss you are ultimately recovering from. As an example, if you purchased an underlying asset for $40, which is now only worth $30, then your loss would be equal to $10 per share.

In this instance, you would then need to purchase a call that is already at the money while also writing a call that is out of the money aimed at a higher overall strike price that is higher above the initial strike price of the calls that were originally purchased. Keep in mind that you need to purchase the related calls at a strike price that is half of the anticipated loss in order to come out on top. As such, you would want to plan on working with three-month options for the best results. As a general rule, the greater the loss you are recovering from, the longer it will take you to repair the damage.

Likewise, you will also need to understand that you won't get out of all mistakes scot-free as some mistakes will require a debit of one type or another in order for the setup to work properly. Furthermore, if you end up experiencing losses of greater than 70 percent, then you will have to be very lucky, or very good, to recover completely.

Time to Unwind

While breaking even will be enough in some situations, other times, you will still be able to turn things around to the point that you can still turn a profit. As an example, assume that you purchased an underlying stock for $60, which dropped to $50 for a time before robustly bouncing back to $65, which means you now no longer want to sell when it hits $70.

In order to unwind this position successfully, and turn a profit in the interim, you will want to close out a positive that has been previously working to offset additional investments. Unwinding will increase liquidity in some instances, and if an asset is less liquid, it can then be difficult to move, which increase the related liquidity risk as well. It doesn't matter if this transaction was set up deliberately or occurred by chance; all risks associated with the security will still apply when it comes to unwinding it successfully.

Unwinding proves even more beneficial when the volatility of the underlying stock is on the rise, and you still want to hold the stock as well. You should then find that your options are in a much more attractive position as long as you work to maintain a positive position with the underlying stock as well.

Keep in mind that it is possible for issues to arise in this scenario, if you try and exit the strategy while the stock is still greater than or equal to the breakeven price, as this will surely cost you because the value of the option will continue to be negative in this instance. Thus, the best course of action is going to be unwinding cautiously when a given position has a price that is lower than the first breakeven price. This is only the case, however, if all of the related prospects are promising at the time. If this is not the case, then the best course of action will typically be cutting your losses and starting a new position with the same stock at the new market price.

Covered Call Strategy

In this strategy, a trader buys a stock, and then they write a call option for that stock. The strategy generally works well on a stock that the investor is going long on. This means this is not a stock that you wish to speculate, but you would still like to receive some income on it while you keep it. And if you do sell it, you will sell it at a higher cost.

Here is the strategy in action. Say you own 300 shares of Lemonade Inc. that are currently going at $1.50. Then you write a call option at the strike rate of $1.70 per share. The premium you charge for this is 15¢ per share. If the stock price rises past $1.70 before expiration, let's say it is $1.90, the person to who you sold the call option to, will exercise their call option.

You will be forced to sell 300 shares at the price of $1.70 per share, but since they will be paying a premium of 15¢ per share, you are selling your shares at $1.85 per share (strike price + premium), which is still high.

The 5¢ that is left over is not the money that you lose. It is just money you missed out on. If the price of Lemonade Inc. stock does not rise sufficiently for the call option to be exercised, you will collect on the premium and still keep your shares. Regardless of what happens, you will leave with more money than you started with.

It is a very good strategy to use if you intend to keep the stock for a long time, and you don't think the price will increase that much in the near future but still want to collect some money on that stock.

This strategy is also referred to as a buy-write strategy. This even sounds better.

Bull Call Strategy

A bull call strategy is when a trader uses two call options on the same underlying asset, one with a lower strike price and the other with a higher strike price. The trader buys a call option above the current market price.

Then they simultaneously sell a call option that has a higher strike price. These two call options share the same expiry date. What this does is that it reduces the price of the call option you have bought. Since you believe the underlying stock will not rise significantly, you collect on a premium that gets deducted from the amount you have spent on a call option.

This allows you to benefit from small price increases, but it also has the effect of capping the maximum price you can make on a trade. Let's look at our Lemonade Inc. example.

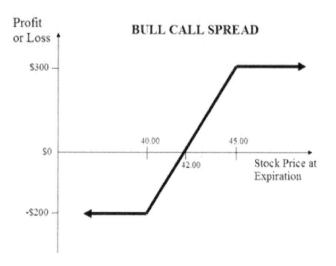

Mark looks at Lemonade Inc. stock currently trading at $1 per share, and he believes that the price of the stock will increase. There is a call option with a strike price of $1.20 per share that is currently selling at 50¢ per share. This means that for Mark to realize a profit, the stock price of Lemonade Inc. would have to rise above $1.70. This means the call option is very expensive. To limit the cost of the call option and also gain profit from the price movements, Mark buys the call option but simultaneously sells a call option for the same stock at 20¢ per share at a strike rate of $1.90. Now he can subtract the 20¢ he gets in premiums from the 50¢ he spent on the first call option. Meaning he has now spent 30¢ for the call option, the stock only has to rise above $1.50 for Mark to begin collecting a profit. This has another effect if the stock price rises above $1.90, Mark would have to sell his stock if the call option bought from him is exercised, which means that mark can only make a profit in the range between $1.50 between $1.90. This is where his profit is capped.

If the price of the stock does not rally, Mark has only spent 30¢ a contract for a call option that could have cost him 50¢ each ($30 instead of $50 in premiums), he does not lose that much. But if the stock rose, the maximum amount Mark could make per share is 40¢ (so $40 per call option since one call option bundles a hundred shares). The bull spread strategy is mainly bullish, as the name suggests. Investors using this strategy are confident that the price will go up and make trades that take advantage of upward movement at the lowest cost to them.

Bear Put Spread

To get started with this kind of strategy, you will want to pick out the right stock that will fit into the criteria that is needed for this strategy. Remember that for this strategy, you want to have a negative outlook on the chosen stock. You want a stock that is going to go down for some reason, whether you have heard some bad news about the stock or there is something else that is going to bring the value of your stock down.

After you have been able to pick out the right stock, you will need to purchase one slightly OTM put option. You will also want to sell one OTM put option, making sure that the strike price ends up being about one or two strikes lower than the option that you purchased in the first step. You also want to make sure that you are picking out ones that have the same stock and the same expiry date as what you did with the first step.

Once you are done with all of these trades, you want to make sure that you monitor your position and watch what is going on. You will then want to get out of both positions once they have helped you to receive significant profit, which is about 30 to 40 percent of the maximum potential profit.

This one is going to work similar to what you were able to do with the bull call spread. If you decide to increase the spread, you are going to increase how much potential profit you are able to make, but it also increases the risks that you are dealing with. In addition, you can choose to decrease the spread, the risk will also decrease, but you would also limit how much profit you could potentially make on the trade.

There are a few times when you will choose to trade using the bear put spread. You will want to go with this kind of strategy when the market has a pretty negative outlook on the stock that you want to use. This is usually going to happen when some development occurs, such as the company not making the earnings that it should, or the organization has made some new changes or decisions that the investors did not look at favorably.

Some people choose to trade with this kind of strategy when the company is part of or is selling under pressure. They do not want to sell, but there is something that is going on that will make them feel like they do need to sell. For example, there may be some environment or market conditions that are unfavorable to the company that surfaced and is changing the company.

Remember that since the bear put spread is considered a debit spread strategy, you will have to work with the time-decay, and it is going to go against your overall position, even though this kind of decay is considered a lot slower than what will happen with a naked long put position.

When it comes to the disadvantages and advantages, this spread is going to end up being pretty similar to the bull call spread. The primary advantage that comes with this trade is that the ratio for risk and reward is pretty good and even a moderate decrease on a stock can still help you to earn some good profits.

You will also be able to increase the amount of profit that you could potentially make by widening up the spread. To do this, you will want to increase the strike price that happens between your two options. You can also choose to reduce your risk in order to help you out as a beginner, and to do this, you will decrease the spread. In order to decrease the risk, you will want to decrease the number of strike prices that are going on between the two options.

The biggest disadvantage that comes with this strategy is dealing with the time decay that will work against the position. And while there is a limited amount of potential loss, if the stock ends up staying stagnant for a long period of time, the position is going to end up with a loss.

Let's take a look at how the bear put spread strategy is going to work. In this case study, the trade is entered on the 18th of May, and we are going to use Nifty 50 again, and we will have about seven days to expiry left for this kind of option. There are a number of reasons why you would want to use this for the bear put spread strategy. During the last month, the Nifty index has shown a good amount of rise, a rise that has been going in line with some of the positive global cues in the market. However, there is still a strong resistance at the 9500 mark, and while the market has let this stock stay around this mark for a bit of time now, it isn't showing any signs of being able to go above that mark. It is also trading on a narrow range, so this makes it perfect for this option.

Since there are less than seven days to go before the expiry of the May month options contract, it looks like some profit booking would take place, and there might be some corrections that happen in the near term. In addition, this stock has some premium options that are cheaper since there are only a few days to expiry, and a bull put spread can be entered into with a low amount of risk while still being pretty successful for you.

So, let's take a look at some of the steps that you need to take in order to finish this trade. The first thing that you need to do is to pick out the right option and stock that you want to trade with. For this strategy, there are a few conditions that need to be met to make sure you will see success, including: The overall risk of your position should never be more than three percent of the total amount of capital that you have to use. Since there are only seven days until expiry on this option, the prices for these options are going to be provided to you at a discount, so there is not really a reason to risk as much as you would with some of the other strategies that we have chosen.

Since we are only expecting a moderate correction of less than 100 points with this stock, the slightly OTM higher strike put option should not be more than 30 to 40 points below the market price of the chosen stock. At the time of the trade, the market price was 9460.

If you take the above criteria into consideration, the trader would decide to trade the 9450 put option, and the 9300 put option, with purchases of 40.75 and 13, respectively. The total risk to this one is going to be around 2081, which ends up being about 1.2 percent of the capital that is available for this trader. This is lower than the three percent that is recommended, so you are staying within the limits that you are given.

The second step that you should take is to purchase the OTM put option. For this one, the 9450 PE, with the May expiry, was bought at 40.75. You will also want to sell an OTM put option that has a lower strike price. The 9300 PE for Nifty, which is three strikes lower than that 9450 that we had talked about before. Here is a summary of the trade position that the trader used for this strategy below:

Summary Table		
Stock or Index Traded	Nifty	
Lot size for each option	75	
Option 1	Strike Price	9450
Higher-strike Put Option - Buy	Premium Paid	40.75
Option 2	Strike Price	9300
Lower-strike Put Option - Sell	Premium Received	13.00
Difference Between any 2 Consecutive Strikes-prices		50.00
Max Profit		9,169
Max Loss		2,081
Condition for maximum profit	Stock price at time of expiry < Strike Price of lower-Strike put option	
Condition for maximum loss	Stock Price at time of expiry > Strike Price of higher-strike put option	
Break-even	Stock Price at expiry =	₹ 9,422.25

Going off the information that is listed above, the maximum profit that you will be able to earn if this stock falls below 9300 at your time of expiry would be 9168.75. And then the maximum amount that the trader would lose if the stock goes or stays above the 9450 at the time of expiry would be 2081.25. The break-even point price that you need to reach in order to earn at least some sort of profit would be 9422.25.

Let's take a look at the profit and loss payoff diagram below in order to find the profit and loss of this kind of trade plotted against five different expiry prices for that particular stock.

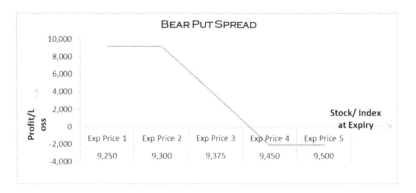

Let's see the results of the trade. After just being in the market or a day, this stock ends up going down by over sixty points, which means that the price of both of these put options went up. Since the trader did not think that the stock would go through and correct itself much further and that it may reverse its movement before too long, the position was closed by squaring of both legs on this trade and the profit was booked. The trader could have gone through and stayed in the trade, but it was becoming more likely that the position would go back up, and then the trader would end up losing money from their position, so it was much better to leave the trade early on. The return on investment was decent on this one. The ratio of the net loss or the net profit to the total sum that is invested in the trade will help you to learn the return on investment, or the profit percentage in this trade. Since the trader was able to put 40,000 into this trade and they were able to make a net profit that was 2,265. By dividing the profit by the total amount of investment that the trader did for the trade, the profit ratio is going to be about five percent. This is a decent amount of return on investment, considering you stayed in the market for only a day or two at most. You may have been able to make more profit in the long run, but it is possible that the position could have turned as well, making it so that the trader would lose all of their money in the process. It is much better to get out quickly, especially since the expiry date is near in the future to start with.

Calendar Put Spread

The calendar spread on puts works the same way as it does with the call calendar spread. Generally, the call spread is utilized more than the put, unless there is a greater than expected decline in the market or the put spread gives a greater return than the call spread.

This is a market-neutral strategy and is excellent for sideways markets. Like with the call spread, the aim of this strategy is to sell the shorter term put and earn the premium while going long on the longer-term put.

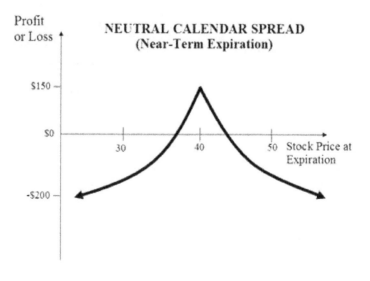

The trade has two legs to it: the short term put and the long term put. The first step is to identify a suitable short term put to write. Generally, if the price is near a support level and you're expecting it to meander a bit before declining in the longer term, you can choose an at the money or slightly out of the money option.

The exact strike price you choose depends on the distance between the current price and the support level ahead. If there is a gap, choose a strike price that is beyond the support level. Sticking with our example of AAPL, let's assume it is at a support level that is going to hold for the short term before folding in the medium term.

Currently, AAPL is trading at $181.30 so let's assume $180 is our support level for the short term. The current month $180 put is the most suitable to write, and doing this will fetch us a premium of $3.40. The near month $180 put will cost $5.95 to go long on, and thus, our entry cost of the trade works out to:

Cost of trade entry/ Maximum loss per share= Premium paid for near month put-Premium received for current month put= 5.95-3.4= $2.55 per share.

The maximum reward, just like the call calendar spread, is something that depends on whether or not the stock falls below the support level over the medium term. If it does, you could exercise your near month option and ride the stock as it declines. Alternatively, you could trade the option itself and save yourself the commissions that arise from exercising it.

The factors to take into account for this strategy are much the same as the call calendar spread, except this is a bearish version of that strategy. You want to identify a level that the price is likely to remain above for the short term, but will dip below during the medium term.

The reward risk profile of this trade is excellent, and under the right market conditions, the calendar spread is a great strategy to deploy.

It might seem on the surface that a lot of the strategies replicate one another, but their individual risk profiles are different. So, make sure you work out the numbers prior to entering them or deciding which one is better. Generally speaking, you can follow the below guidelines to help you decide.

When calls become expensive, as in the case of a bull market on its last legs, bull call spreads work best. This is to capture whatever moderate level of gains there might be left. Of course, this presumes that you can read the decreasing strength of a trend well enough to deploy it in the first place.

In the final stages of a bear market, when volatility spikes and there aren't too many downside gains to be had, a bear call spread works the best. Bear markets tend to be shorter than bullish ones since the general public doesn't indulge in the short side. Thus, bear markets don't suffer from the over-enthusiasm that tends to push bull markets for longer than expected.

The bull put spread works like a charm in a sideways market when you are certain that the overall trend is still bullish, but currently, the stock is moving sideways or suffering from a bout of counter-trend enthusiasm. This is a good way to earn some income in the meantime and is a far safer option than trying to time a directional entry.

When a bear trend is accelerating to the downside, a bear put spread works the best. You could use this to hedge your positions in a long market, but that's not a trading strategy per se. As it is, using it in the manner described previously is your best bet of making some money off it.

The term comes from the way in which option chains are displayed. The strike prices are listed vertically with the puts and calls arranged on either side of them. Thus, the lower strike price is above the current price and the higher ones below.

So, by employing two legs on the trade, you're creating a vertical spread, as per the option chain table. With a calendar spread, you're on the same strike price, but visualizing a calendar, you're moving sideways or horizontally to the next month. Hence, the term horizontal spread.

You also would have noticed how some strategies, upon entry, pay you and some require an upfront cost. The ones that pay you are called net credit strategies and the ones that have a cost are called net debit ones. Net credit strategies pay you your maximum reward upfront, while net debit ones require you to wait for the maximum reward.

Of course, the flip side is that net debit strategies have you experiencing your full loss upfront, as opposed to net credit ones, where you need to see how it plays out. Take care to not develop a mental bias towards either one. All that matters is the market condition, not which one pays you first or last.

Naked Call Shorting

When it comes to call options, there are two main practices investors engage in naked shorting and covered shorting. Naked shorting has been ban by the SEC after the 2008 and 2009 market crash; however, there are loopholes that allow people to still engage in naked shorting activities, one of such is options trading.

So what is naked shorting? It is simply the practice of short selling shares that have not been affirmed that they exist. This is to say that the trader borrows the stock or make arrangements to borrow the stock. Based on those agreements made to acquire the stock, the person exercises short selling activities, even though the stock has not been own yet.

Sometimes some shares become less than the required demand in the market. In order to meet supply needs, some people adopt naked short selling, which has been considered illegal in recent times.

Trading activities tend to fail at the supposed time when the invested short selling underlying shares have not yet own or possess the said number of shares for the transaction to be completed. This is the reason it is important to analyze your risks when you are using a naked short selling strategy in an options trading.

There are potentially high risks involve in naked call shorting. Therefore it is very important to consider several factors before engaging in this method of trading. To be on the safer side, some investors adopt a covered call shorting rather than a naked call.

The Bear Call Spread

Next on the list is the bear call spread. This is another directional strategy that will be used by a trader when they believe that their underlying stock has reached its upper resistance level, and they do not believe that the underlying stock is going to go up much more at this point. They usually believe that the price point of the stock is going to stay flat and not change or it is going to go back down. Basically, this is going to be the opposite strategy that we talked about earlier with the bull put spread.

Like the bull put spread, the bear call spread is also a credit spread. What this means is the premium that you end up receiving while selling one leg of this trade is going to be greater than any premium that you end up paying for the second leg of the trade. You will end up receiving a net credit to your account when you decide to go with this position.

The first step that you need to take to create your bear call spread is to select the right stock that fits this kind of strategy. You will find that there are a variety of stocks that you can choose from, but you will need to pick based on your outlook for this kind of index.

Next, you will need to sell an OTM call option of the stock that you selected. And third, you should purchase an OTM call option that has the same expiry date and the same underlying stock as your id with your ATM call option, but the second one needs to have a higher strike price.

Once you enter the market, you will want to constantly monitor your position each day. Once you have made a considerable profit, which is about fifty percent of your max profit, it is time to exit your position. Or, once you have started to recognize some of the signs of the market and you are sure that the stock is not going to end up reversing, you could wait until the stock reaches its expiry and then take the maximum amount of profit.

There are some time periods that are better for entering a bear call spread than others. You would want to choose the bear call spread any time that you believe that your chosen stock is not likely to rise in price in the near future and that this stock is probably going to decline from its current price rather than go up. This can happen when the stock from a particular company that had big market expectations posted their results, and these were way below the expectations of the market. In addition, the index option could hit a big resistance level and this could cause it to go down a bit.

This method is not going to work that well if the stock is really volatile and it has the potential to rise quite a bit over the short term. You want to pick out some options that are not likely to go up anymore. You would then be able to use the bear call spread and make some profit whether the stock stays stagnant or the price goes down.

The maximum profit that you will be able to make with the bear call spread is when at the time of expiry, the stock price is trading below the strike price of the call option that was sold. To get the maximum profit, you will need to take the premium received or selling the lower-strike call option and minus the premium paid for purchasing the higher-strike call option. Then you can multiply both of these by the lot size.

The biggest loss that you would incur with this kind of spread is when at the time of expiry, the stock price is trading above the strike price call option you bought with the higher-strike price. This is why you want to make sure that you are picking out stocks that are going to go down or remain steady. If the stock goes up with this option, you will end up losing money in the process. This is why this strategy is a good one to choose if you think that the market is about to go down or you want to work with a stock that is not really increasing at the time.

The biggest advantage of working with the bear call spread is that it is going to ensure that the time-decay is going to work in your favor. As long as you go with a stock that is able to stay below your lower strike-price when the expiry happens, you will get the benefit of keeping your entire credit that you received when you entered into this position, and you have the potential to make a good profit.

However, there is a disadvantage of working with this strategy. With this position, if you see that there is the possibility that the stock will make a big movement that goes against your expectations. This means that the stock starts rising in price quickly rather than remaining stagnant or going down like you had predicted. If this does happen, the maximum amount that you could lose can be a lot more than the maximum profit that you might have been able to gain with this strategy, so there is some risk.

Here we are going to look at a case study of a trade that was done in May of 2017 for this strategy. The stock that was used for this option trade is the Nifty 50, and the type of exchange that was used was the NSE in India. The Nifty 50 is a good option to go with because it is considered a benchmark index on the Indian NSA. It is a diversified 50 stock index and will account for 12 sectors of the economy in India. It has some good stability, and the volatility that occurs with it daily is not that high.

The market at this time had gone through a long bull run, and it was about to run out of steam. The Nifty stock was showing signs of meeting some resistance when it reached the 9500 mark and it wasn't likely to cross over that barrier any time soon. This made it the perfect stock to work with the bear call spread, making sure that your resistance point was 9500. The first step that you should take is to determine your options with the optimum strike-prices to trade. Since we found the resistance level to be bear the 9500 mark with this strategy, it was decided to sell an OTM option that was four strikes away from the spot price of Nifty. Since the spot price of this stock was at 9500 at the time of trading, the 9700 Nifty call options with a month expiry (so ending in June for this one) was picked to be written and to complete the second leg of the trade, the 9900 Nifty Call was selected.

With the help of a calculator in order to check the deltas, you would find that the delta of the lower-strike call is about 0.31. This implies that you are running the risk of 31 percent of the 9700 Nifty call reaching ITM at expiry time. This is a bit high for the risks than you should do, but since this index seems to have peaked, the risk was taken.

Now it is time to sell the OTM call option. The Nifty 9700 call option that was set to expire at the end of June was written for $46 to complete the first part of the trade. Then on the third step, the Nifty 9900 call option to expire at the end of June was bought for $9.80 to complete the second leg of the trade. Here is a chart to show what happened with this kind of trade:

Summary Table			
Stock or Index Traded	Nifty		
Lot size for each option	75		
Option 1	Strike Price		9700.00
Lower-strike Call Option : Sell	Premium Received		46.00
Option 2	Strike Price		9900.00
Higher-strike Call Option : Buy	Premium Paid		9.80
Difference Between any 2 Consecutive Strikes-prices			50.00
Max Profit			₹ 2,715
Max Loss			₹ -12,285
Condition for maximum profit	Stock/Index price at time of expiry <		9700
Condition for maximum loss	Stock/Index price at time of expiry >		9900
Break-even	Stock/Index at time of Expiry =		9,736.20

This table shows that the maximum profit you are able to make will be about $2,715 if the Nifty stock stays at or below the 9700 when the expiration occurs. However, the maximum loss that you could happen if the stock goes above the 9900 is 12,285. The break-even point that you would use here is the 9736.2, and as long as your index ends up over this point at the end of the trade, you would end up making a profit.

Here s a profit and loss payoff diagram that will show the profit and loss that you could earn plotted against five different prices for the index at expiration.

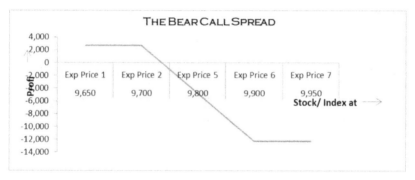

Results of the trade

With this case study, the Nifty stock did not go the way that the trader had hoped. Instead of moving down to 9500, it broke this resistance level and went up to 9700. Then the trading slowed down and it traded between the 9600 and 9700 range. Within a week, the 9700 call that sold for 46 had touched 80 before the premium came down to 70.

This trade position was left in a net loss for the following two weeks because of this development. However, this stock was not able to sustain itself over the 9700 level, and within three weeks, the time-decay brought in some erosion to your options. Three weeks into this four-week trend, the Nifty stock came down by about 25 points on its opening, and it was traded at the 9620. Because of this, the trader was able to exit the trade and make a profit.

With this one, the trader was able to earn a profit of 1087.50 if they exited at the three-week mark rather than waiting. There was some possibility of earning more profit by keeping the options for a bit longer and until the end of the month. But since the stock did go up unexpectedly, it is possible for this to happen again, and it is smart for the trader to choose to exit the market early and take some profit rather than running the risk of the stock going back up again and them losing all of their profit.

The return on investment in this option ends up being about 2.7 percent over the three weeks. This is not very high, but considering that the stock went against the expectations of the trader, it was better than the loss that they could have encountered. This still ended up being a profitable trade for the trader, despite things going up and against the wishes of the trader. In this one, the brokerages were not that high, so they have not been included into the calculations that we did to make things a little bit easier. You will have to pay a few fees for entering into these trades, but they are not too high and if you make good decisions with this trade, you will be able to cover them easily.

Short Put/Selling Put Options Strategy

A trader who writes a put option is referred to as the seller. In this case, an options trader will be required to buy the underlying stock and make sure everything is ready when the buyer is ready to exercise the option. A short put option is often referred to us naked or uncovered put since the seller is under obligation to purchase shares of the underlying stock before the buyer decides to exercise the right to the option.

Losses can be faced when the short put expires worthless without the underlying asset arising above the strike price of the put option. A short put should be used if you think that an underlying security will be able to rise up in price more than the strike price determined in the options contract.

To profit in options trading through a short put strategy, you need to ensure that the technical analysis conducted leads to a rise in stock price. When the price of the stock goes down in value over a period of the option, the option buyer can choose to exercise the right and hence making you incur potential losses.

However, you will make money through the premiums paid at the signing of the put options contract. Apart from making money through premiums by opening a put option, you can also be able to sell a stock at the underlying price in the financial market.

For example, say that a stock is currently selling at $ 100 in the financial market. You wish to buy the stock at $ 75. If you consider selling a put option at a strike price of $ 75 and receive a premium of let's say $ 2.00. If the price of the underlying stock drops to $ 75 as forecasted, then you will get to keep the premium while at the same time buying the underlying stock at the strike price.

The Importance of Volatility

While there are numerous reasons a person might want to start trading options on the regular, guaranteed returns are not one of them. There are a wide variety of different variables that can come into play when it comes to determining the premium for a given option, which means profits are never a sure thing. As such, if you are interested in trading options regularly, then you are going to need to do everything in your power to ensure you are aware of the implied volatility of a given asset to ensure you don't accidentally bite off more than you can chew.

Implied volatility can be thought of as the amount of volatility that you believe an underlying asset has, which means it will naturally be higher if the market is feeling bearish and as long as potential investors have a good reason to assume the asset is going to decrease in value at a point in the future. Meanwhile, if the market is feeling bullish, then you can anticipate the overall volatility to decrease as the market reacts to assumptions that the price of the asset is on the rise. This is due to the fact that most people naturally assume that bullish markets harbor less risk overall than markets that are bearish. This is what makes implied volatility so useful; it makes it possible for traders to reliably estimate the way the underly asset price is likely to move based on the overall state of the market and other types of predictive data.

Implied volatility is a factor in all types of asset trading but proves especially important when it comes to options trading as the greater the current level of implied volatility, the higher the related premium is going to do be. This is due to the fact that when an option is valued, implied volatility is already factored into the equation. Despite this fact, implied volatility is still just an estimate based on probability, which means it is more of a suggestion than a real indicator.

Despite this fact, many traders become overeager once they learn of it and treat it like the full-blown indicator it very much isn't. Thus if you can see the implied volatility for a given asset clearly you should feel safe in assuming that there are plenty of traders out there who can see the same thing and are already acting accordingly. Furthermore, implied volatility directly correlates to the current dominant opinion in the market, which is another pricing factor you will want to consider before making any serious moves.

When looking to implied volatility for answers, it is also important to understand that it does not actually predict the direction in which the price will be moving; only that change is coming. As an example, if the volatility of the asset is quite high, this typically means a price swing is on the horizon. However, the resulting swing could then be quite small, very large, or somewhere in between. If volatility is low, then this simply means that the price is likely to not make any changes that weren't clearly telegraphed.

Another common mistake that those who aren't familiar with implied volatility make is assuming it is similar to historical volatility when in fact the two are quite different. Historical volatility measures the previous changes the market has experienced and thus can have definitive results. As such, you are better off comparing the two types of volatility in order to understand the types of changes that the underlying asset in question is going to experience.

Key factors in determining implied volatility

The first factor you are going to want to be aware of in this instance is supply and demand, which affects implied volatility just as much as it does the market as a whole. While many traders rely on extremely complicated metrics to determine what trades to make and when it is important to keep in mind that the market still runs on the basic principles of supply and demand that it always did. As such, if you cut through the complicated theories and look for moments where supply and demand are extremely unbalanced, then you will always be able to make a profit no matter what. You will still need to learn as much as possible about the various strategies that you choose to move forward with, it is just important to keep in mind that the basics still apply.

In this case, if the demand for a security is especially high, then you can count on the implied volatility to be higher than normal as well. This, in turn, leads to higher than average premiums that come along with the added risk while the opposite remains true as well.

The next vital factor to consider is the time value that remains for the option in question as the shorter the remaining time for the option is the less implied volatility it will have left as well. This is due to the fact that the market assumes that with little time left, there isn't enough time for anything more to change for the underlying asset in the time left.

It is also important to understand that every option is going to have a different level of sensitivity when it comes to noticing changes in its implied volatility. As an example, the greater the amount of time value a given option has remaining, the lower its implied volatility will almost always be. Likewise, strike prices will always respond differently to implied volatility changes as strike prices that are closer to being in the money will naturally be more sensitive to volatility changes to those that are either in the money or very far out of the money. If you are unsure of how sensitive a given option is likely to be in the near future, the best way to double-check is to consider it's Vega (discussed in detail in the next chapter). Even still, it is important to not take the results as gospel as things could still change based on anything unexpected that hits the market between when you do your research and when you actually make your move.

Making the most of implied volatility

One of the best ways to figure out the implied volatility of any options you are working with is to take a closer look at the implied volatility chart that should already be a part of the trading platform you are currently using. Due to the fact that every stock is going to have its own range of implied volatility, it is important to analyze what you are working with regularly. When it comes to properly keeping tabs on these fluctuations, you will want to take a closer look at the various peaks and valleys the chart shows you like the points in-between tend to muddy the waters as opposed to actually clarifying things.

It is also important to understand that implied volatility is always going to move in cycles, which means that for every period of low implied volatility that you experience, you are guaranteed to see another period when implied volatility is high as long as you wait long enough for it to materialize. Thus, by keeping these ranges in mind and forecasting the implied volatility of the assets you frequent on the regular, you should have a firm template for choosing more reliable trades on the regular. When determining a suitable strategy, these concepts are critical in finding a high probability of success, helping you maximize returns and minimize risk.

If you are looking to forecast implied volatility, there are a few different things you should keep in mind. First, you need a way to accurately determine what the implied volatility is at the moment. The first thing you can do is to check the news to ensure you are up to date on anything that would explain the increase. As most movement is going to take place directly after these types of announcements, it is important to understand that anyone of the above is often enough to collapse the current level of implied volatility and zero it out.

CHAPTER 4:

Advanced Strategies

Married Put

Amarried put strategy is when a trader or investor is in a long position on a certain stock, and then they buy a put option that has a strike price that is equal to the current market price. They do this to protect against depreciation or downward movement in the price. This means that the investor can be confident that they will gain from the price increase of their stock, and they can also enjoy the benefits of owning the stock. The benefits of owning stock are things like voting and getting paid dividends when profits are made. The bad news is that it costs somewhat to pay the put premium of the stock. When an investor does this, they are saying that they don't want to sell their stock below a certain favorable price, so in the event that the stock falls, they want to be made whole. It is more like insurance; the cost to the investor is the premium, limiting how much they lose on any given trade. The married put options, unlike the bull call spread, have unlimited profit potential if the stock performs well.

Let's say you are long on 2o0 shares of Lemonade Inc. When you bought these shares, they were at $1.50 each. Now, after months, the price of the shares has appreciated to $2.00. This is great. You have been enjoying some benefits of owning a stock like dividends and voting rights in the company. But you are worried about an announcement that Lemonade Inc. is going to make that could negatively affect the price of your stock. However, you still think there is a chance that this new direction could work in the company's favor, and you could make more money. In a sense, you are married to this stock, you are in for the long haul, but you don't want to lose a lot of money either if things go south. To protect your profits, you buy two put options, which give you the right to sell 200 shares at $2.00 each. The put option costs you a premium of 30¢ per share. Meaning if you exercise the put option, you will collect a profit of 20¢ per share compared to where you got in at $1.50 per share. But you will only decide to sell your shares at this position if you think that the position the company finds itself in won't be resolved, meaning you think the stock price will not recover before the expiration date of your put option.

If the price of the stock continues to rise as a result of the company's new move and favorable market, you get to keep your stocks and receive all the profit and benefits, having only lost the $60 premium on insurance in case things went badly. Now, you see how this strategy limits your losses but open you up to unlimited benefits. Losses are capped while profits are virtually limitless. While insurance on stock can be costly, it is not as costly as a market fall that does not rebound.

The Straddle and the Strangle

Long Straddle

The straddle is a very profitable strategy when it is used in a market where high volatility is expected. So, you know that the price will move sharply, but you don't know which direction it will go. Regardless, you want to profit from that movement. To profit from an upswing, you buy a call option. To benefit from a fall, you buy a put option for the same asset for the same expiration date at the same strike price. You realize a profit when the money you make is more than the premium you have spent on both options. Now let's return to a Lemonade Inc. example to show this.

Let's say that Lemonade Inc. stock is trading at $100 per share. But you believe because of the pending company announcement, the price will move sharply in either direction. So you buy a call option for a $10 premium per share and a put option for a $10 premium a share, both at a strike price of $100. You have $10,000 dollars in your account. This will cost you a total of $2,000 in premiums. So you are left with $8,000. The announcement is made before the expiry date of both options. Lemonade Inc. has experienced losses in the last quarter. Its stock fell by 30%, meaning it is now trading at $70 a share. In this situation, you can buy 100 shares at $70, costing you $7,000 and exercise your put option, selling them for $10,000. You have just made $3,000 on that transaction. You now have $11,000 in your account.

If the announcement made by Lemonade Inc. reports increases in sales and the stock rises by a record 50%, you will be in a position to buy 100 shares at $100 and then sell them on the market for $150 each. Since you have $8,000 leftover, you can't afford to exercise your call option. But you use your margin account to borrow $2,000 and buy the shares at $10,000. You make $15,000 on the transaction. You pay your debt, plus interest, it costs you $2,300. You are left with $12,700. You have made a profit of $4,700.

As you can see, no matter the direction the stock moves, as long as it is beyond the premium you spent on the options, you made a profit. But if the market price moves only slightly, you will have lost $2,000, and you will be left with $8,000 in your account.

Long Strangle

The strangle is similar to the straddle strategy, but instead of buying options that share the same strike price, asset, and expiry date, they buy two options that only share an expiry date and asset. So the strike prices are different from each other. It is also a strategy often used in situations that are similar to that of a straddle. In both cases, the trader believes that the price of the underlying stock will move in some direction, but they do not know which. They might have a slight bias about where it might go, but they exercise the strangle to catch profits if they're mistaken. Just like the straddle, if the price does not move enough, the money will be lost on premiums—time for that lemonade example.

The situation is much like before. Lemonade Inc. will make an announcement, but the rumors around the report are positive, but investors are somewhat skeptical. For now, the stock price is stable, but once the announcement is made, the price might move sharply. Thinking the news might be positive, you buy a call option with a strike price at the current stock price. The stock is going at $100 per share. The premium costs you $10 a share. You think it is unlikely that the price will fall, but if it falls, you want some money for yourself. You buy a put option at a $98 strike price for $8 a share. You have spent a total of $1,800 on the premiums. Already, this strategy is cheaper than the straddle. If the price of the stock falls by 20%, you will collect a profit of $1,800, meaning you break even. If it rises sharply by 50%, you will rake in a profit of $5,000 from the transaction, that minus the premium paid is $3,200. If your bias was correct, you stand to make a few extra bucks that you would miss if using a straddle strategy. If your bias was wrong and the price falls sharply, you would still make money, but you will miss out on some of the action, although this doesn't translate to money lost. In both strategies, the price movement has to be sharp enough to overcome the premium spent. For instance, in a situation where Lemonade Inc.'s announcement doesn't sway the markets way, and they remain relatively stable, you will have lost $1,800, which is $200 less than you would have in a straddle strategy.

Here we are going to take a look at a case study using the long strangle in order to make a profit in options. This one was entered on the 8th of November in 2016 and the trader used the Nifty 50 stock.

During this time, there was a big political change around the world, and it was estimated that this would make some sort of impact over the global markets, at least for the short-term. This was the US election and many people were unsure about who would win. A win by the Democrats could add in some positive sentiment to the market, and it was expected that having the Republican candidate win would do the opposite. Either way, at the time it was looking as if the markets around the world would make a big change, either going up or down sharply.

Because of the conditions, it looked like the perfect time to work with the long straddle and strangle strategy. The first step that you want to do with this is to pick out a good option to trade in. For this case, the traded decided to use the Nifty index and use the long strangle strategy. At the time, the Nifty index was trading at 8530, which meant that the closest OTM call option was going to be 8550 and the closest OTM put option would be the 8500. These two were the ones selected for the trade and the trader decided to pick an expiry date of the 24th of November because this was the earliest expiring monthly service.

At the time, the volatility of this index was much higher than it usually was at 14.9, the trader decided that it was worth taking the risk because the volatility of the whole market was supposed to rise even further before the big changes occurred, which would make the options more expensive overall. So, the second step that you need to do is purchase your slightly OTM call option, which would be the Nifty 8550. This was bought for 130. Then you can purchase the slightly OTM put option. This was the Nifty 8500 and it was purchased or 90. Let's take a look at the table below to see a little summary of the options that the trader used in this trade.

Summary Table		
Stock or Index Traded	Nifty	
Lot size for each option	75	
Option 1 ATM Call Option - Buy	Strike Price	8550
	Premium Paid	130.00
Option 2 ATM Put Option - Buy	Strike Price	8500
	Premium Paid	90.00
Difference Between 2 Consecutive Strikes		50
Max Profit		No Limit
Max Loss		16,500
Condition for maximum profit	No Upper Limit for Profits	
Condition for maximum loss	For Straddle: Stock Price at expiry = Strike Price of Options	
	For Strangle: Stock Price at expiry lies between Strike Prices of Option 1 & Option 2	
Break-even Points	Upper	Stock price at Expiry = 8,770.00
	Lower	Stock price at Expiry = 8,280.00

For this trade, the trader is able to make a maximum profit that is unlimited, but they do have a maximum loss. Here, the trader would potential would be 16,500 if they end up being wrong. This amount is going to be the premium amount that they paid in order to purchase the two options. You will also know that for this trade, there are two break-even points because it is possible for the trade to earn profits no matter which way the market goes. The upper break-even point will be 8770 and the lower break-even point was 8280. Below is the profit loss payoff diagram. It is going to show the profit and the loss that is plotted against the various expiry prices for the stock that you choose.

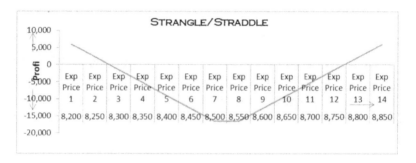

Now let's take a look at the results that the trader was able to get from these trades. This trade was held for three days. Then on the 11th of November, once the election votes were counted in the United States and the Republicans won, the stock market in India reacted negatively and the chosen index fell by more than 300 points. Because of this sharp fall, the Nifty index, thanks to the long straddle, feel into high profits. Both of your positions ended up squaring off back to back before the trading day closed and the profits were booked. However, it is important to know exactly when to get out of the market with this kind of trade. While the market quickly went down right after the election results were posted, this negative sentiment only lasted for a day and it did not take long for the market to swing back up the next day. If the trader had stayed in the market for another day, the upswing in the market would have meant they would have lost all of their money. The volatility drop ad the time decay issue would have made it so that the trader would lose out. But they got out of the market at the right time and they made a good amount of profit. The total amount that the trader decided to spend on this investment for both of the positions ended up being 16,500. In the end, they made a net profit of 11,250. This means that they made a return on investment of 68 percent in just three days. While this one had a big return on investment, you have to be careful with the volatility and you have to know when to get out of the market. If the trader had stayed in the market for a little bit longer, they would have lost a lot of their money instead of getting a profit in the process. These markets are hard to work with because they go up and down so quickly, but if you are able to guess the right time to get out and you pick the right strike prices, you can make unlimited profits in the process.

Protective Collar

The protective collar strategy is when an investor buys a put option that is out-of-the-money and then writes an out-of-the-money call option on the same asset with the same expiration date. The strategy can be conceived primarily as an exit strategy because it is usually written by traders who have been with a stock for a long while. The stock has performed well, and they are looking to protect their investment in case the price falls or rises surprisingly. So take the Lemonade Inc. shares. There has been an announcement on an exciting new product called the sugar-free lemonade slushy. The company is convinced that with the growing movement in society towards healthy habits, the new product will pick up and might even find its way into state schools without much resistance. So big sales are expected from this. You own Lemonade Inc. stock, a hundred shares now valued at $100 per share. The announcement causes a spike in the price. Over the next few months, the company is doing well, especially over the summer months and autumn. But with winter approaching, they might start to see sales dwindle. Your shares have appreciated by a tremendous amount to $170 per share. You can hop off now, and you would have made a profit of $7,000 from your starting point. The thing is, you hear rumors of Lemonade Inc. launching a new product that might do well in the winter. But this very product might hurt them and see those facing fierce competitors on the market. So you are in a position where if there is some gain, despite how weak that rise is, you want to profit off it, but if the plan backfires, you would like to exit with the profit you have already made. To achieve this, you would implement a protective collar. You would write a call option at a $175 strike price at $2 per share. Then you would go on and purchase a put option at the strike price of $168 at $2 per share. In this situation, if the price of Lemonade Inc. drops below $168, you would be in a position to cash out by selling your stock at $168 per share. If Lemonade Inc.'s price rises above $175, you would sell that stock at $175 and earn a profit from the rise in stock price. Since you have paid $2 per contract on your put options and received the same amount for the call option you sold, you now have paid virtually nothing for the protection you get from using this move because the two transactions cancel each other out. However, this is not always the case. All protective collar strategies will be different depending on the options prices, but showing it is possible is encouraging enough.

The Iron Condor

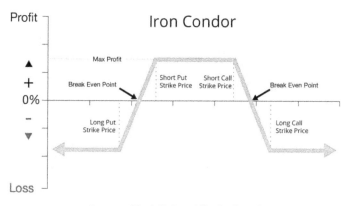

The other strategy that we talked about was directional strategies, but the iron condor is going to be a non-directional strategy. This one is going to limit your profit a bit but its probability of success is pretty high for the traders that are able to trade it well. When you are working with an Iron Condor trade, no matter which way the stock or the index ends up moving, the trader is going to become profitable as long as the movement stays inside the boundaries that the trader sets, at the time of expiry. Out of all the strategies that we are going to discuss in this guidebook, this one has the highest potential to give you profits and it has the least amount of risk as well.

You will use the iron condor to trade on stocks with very low volatility. It is not a good idea to go with a stock that moves around quite a bit and has big highs and lows that go all over the place. You will find that this is a credit spread strategy that will be viewed as a combination of the bear call spread (which we talk about in the following chapter) and the bull put spread.

You can consider the iron condor as a type of evergreen strategy, one that a lot of traders are going to use when they find a stable stock. As a trader, if you are able to choose any strategy and you want to go with one that is pretty easy to follow and will give you a higher probability of doing well, then the iron condor is the best option for you to choose.

The iron condor is going to be a little bit more difficult to work with because there are four legs to go with it, rather than the two legs on the other trading strategy. For the first step, you need to go through and find the stock that you would like to work with. Remember that for the iron condor to work, you need to have a stock that is pretty stable and is not going to go up or down too much in the process.

The next step is to sell one deep OTM put option of the stock that you selected. Then buy one OTM put options with the same expiry date and with the same stock that you sold in the first step, but make sure that this one has a lower strike price.

After those steps are done, it is time to sell again. This time you are going to sell a deep OTM, but it needs to be a call option. You want this to use the same stock and have the same expiry date as what you used in the last part. And finally, you can buy an OTM call option that has the same stock and the same expiry date as all the other steps, but this one needs to have a slightly higher strike-price. One thing to note is that there is going to be a difference between the strike prices the two put options need to be the same as the difference between the strikes of the two call options if you want to create this strategy accurately. Throughout the time until the expiry, you will want to monitor how your position is doing. Unless you are certain that your stock is going to keep within the limits that you have placed, you will want to consider exiting out of the trade when the position is making 50% or more of the maximum profit that you want out of this trade. If you find that the market goes against your expectations and there is a big directional movement of your stock, it is time to close out all of the positions and wait until that stock has time to stabilize before entering again. You would choose to go with this strategy any time that your stock is showing a really low amount of volatility. This means that the stock is not moving much or if it is moving within a range that you are able to define easily. For the most part, index options are going to be the best for executing this strategy compared to stock-based options since these indexes are often less volatile. If you are working with a market that is pretty stable, you will find that iron condors are the safest option for winning. The biggest advantage of using the iron condor is that it is considered a neutral position and you are likely to get some kind of profit as long as you execute this strategy the right way, no matter which way your chosen stock or index ends up moving. And since this is a net credit strategy, it will be able to help you work against the issues with time decay. The biggest disadvantage that you are going to find with the iron condor is that the returns that you will get out of it are quite a bit less than what you can get from a directional strategy. In addition, the maximum loss that you can incur is going to be quite a bit more than the maximum profit that you would be able to gain in this position if you are not careful with the stocks that you are using. However, when looking at the statistics for success with the iron condor, you will notice that the probability of a win is going to be much higher than that of a loss, which helps to make this a great strategy to work with.

Now it is time to take a look at an example of when the iron condor trade can be successful. For this one, we are going to enter into the trade on the 17th of April and the underlying index that is used is the Nifty 50. This is considered a benchmark index of the National Stock Exchange in India. This is a good one to use with the iron condor because it has a history of stability and doesn't usually move up and down too much. The reason that we are entering with this strategy is because the Nifty index has just reached a 52-week high and there has been some profit booking. Since that time, it has been trading in a narrow range showing that there is some support for it staying around 9100 and when it reaches 9300, there seems to be some strong resistance. When looking at the near future, it isn't expected that there are going to be some big triggers that would cause a big rise or drop in the price and when looking at the history of the index, it usually doesn't go up or down more than three percent on average through the money.

This means over the next month, it is not likely that the index is not going to go higher than the 9500, and it is not likely that it will fall below 8900 within the next month. This helps them to make the conditions perfect to work with the iron condor. The first step that you need to take when working on an iron condor trade is to pick out your stock. You want one that doesn't have a lot of movement or at least one that has predictable movement between the same two points. Some of the things that you should also consider when it comes to using the iron condor strategy includes: All of the options that you pick should have a minimum of 30 days to expiry so that enough premium can be collected. Because of this, this case study picked an expiry date that was 38 days in the future, so the 25th of May.

The trade needs to have a high probability of success, at least 70 percent. To make sure that this happens, the 8900 Nifty put option and then the 9500-call option were the points that are chosen. Since this stock has only recently fixed itself and was currency near the 9150 mark, the strikes that were chosen for the call gave some extra room because it was more likely that the index would increase rather than decrease.

The second thing that you should do is sell one deep OTM put option. The 8900 Nifty put option that expired in May was sold for 42.25. You need to buy an OTM put option that has a lower strike price than your sold option. For this example, we used the 8700 put option, gave it a May expiry, and then bought it for 19.70.

Now you need to work on the next leg. This one is going to ask you to sell a deep OTM call option. In this example, we bought a 9500-call option that would expire in May and we sold it for 23. And finally, you also need to purchase an OTM call option. We bought a 9700-call option for 4.85. Based on the prices that were present on the individual legs of the positions we chose, the maximum potential profit that can be made will be 3278 and the maximum potential loss that you could get if the stock doesn't go the way that you would like, would be 11,723.

Summary Table		
Stock or Index Traded	Nifty	
Lot size for each option	75	
Option 1 Lower-strike Put Option - Buy	Strike Price	8,700.00
	Premium Paid	19.70
Option 2 Higher-strike Put Option - Sell	Strike Price	8,900.00
	Premium Received	45.25
Option 3 Lower-strike Call Option - Sell	Strike Price	9,500.00
	Premium Received	23.00
Option 4 Higher-strike Call Option - Buy	Strike Price	9,700.00
	Premium Paid	4.85
Difference Between any 2 Consecutive Strikes-prices		50.00
Max Profit		₹ 3,278
Max Loss		₹ -11,723
Condition for meeting max profit	Stock price at expiry lies between Strike-Prices of Option 2 and Option 3	
Condition for meeting max loss	Stock Price at expiry > Strike-price of Option4 -OR- Stock Price at expiry < Strike-price of Option 1	
Upper Break-even Price at Expiry	Stock/Index at time of expiry =	9,543.70
Lower Break-even Price at Expiry	Stock/Index at time of expiry =	8,856.30

Remember that with the iron condor strategy, there are going to be two points that are the break-even point. The upper one is going to be at 9543.7, and the lower one is going to be 8856.2. The profit and loss diagram below are going to show the profit and loss that you can get based on the different expiry prices for this stock during this trade.

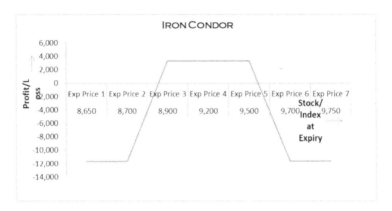

With this example, the position was held for three weeks before the trader closed it. The trader technically had two weeks in order to keep the stocks going before they hit their expiry, but in this case, the trader wanted to be able to exit the trade and free up their capital to work on another trade. In addition, this stock had started to climb up to a new high, and there was the possibility that this momentum was going to keep going up, and the trader may have lost all of their profit.

During these three weeks, the stock ended up gaining 250 points. Despite this, this trade still provided a profit of thirty percent of the maximum potential profit thanks to the time-day, and because of the time exit. The trader was still about to earn 1024 from this trade.

The return of investment on this option was lower. The trader was about to earn about 1.25 percent on their return on investment. Usually, the iron condor strategy is going to be more effective than this when it comes to a good return on investment, but during the time of the trade, the stock ended up moving more than was expected. A similar trade using this stock usually will give at least three percent return on investment, but the market was not as steady as it usually is. But the trader decided to get out of the market ahead of time to make sure that the market didn't go outside of their limits and make them lose money in the process.

Iron Butterfly

An iron butterfly is another strategy to use if you think the stock price will stay within a certain range. It will use four options, like the iron condor, but there will be three different strike prices.

In this case, you will sell a put option and a call option with the same strike price. The strategy is to get as close to at the money as possible. We will call the strike priced used the central strike. Then you set a differential price we will call x. Now you buy a put option with a strike price of (central strike $- x$), and you buy a call option with a strike price of (central strike $+ x$).

Like an iron condor, the profit from an iron butterfly is fixed at the net credit when you sell to open. This is given by the sum of the premiums earned from selling the at the money call and put, minus the prices paid for the out of the money options.

The maximum loss is the strike price of the purchased call – strike price of the sold put – total premium.

CHAPTER 5:

Option Trading And Stock Trading

Why use stock market strategies?

Here is a good question. Why is it worth using stock market strategies? You need to know that the financial instruments you are trading on, such as CFDs (contracts for difference), are already designed to be simplified and accessible for investment.

Even the platforms where you will find yourself performing from a practical point of view, your trading operations are very intuitive and can, therefore, be exploited both by industry experts who demand the possibility of trading professionally, via beginners who may never have put to this kind of tools but still want to create a monthly income by investing in the stock market.

One of the right reasons why it is worth learning the stock market strategies lies in the fact that we are sure that you too have always dreamed of finding a job that would not force you to move for long stretches, perhaps remaining stuck in traffic and city chaos, a job that does not oblige you to say yes to the boss on duty who may not even deserve to occupy that place, a job where you should not be forced to work overtime to be able to reach the end of the month charging you with stress and fatigue.

This is why we believe that trading with stock market strategies is the best possible alternative, not only offline but also online. Being independent in this promising world guarantees you the possibility to shake off the problems linked to the crisis to earn your freedom, even before the money, to become the master of your own life.

A thousand good reasons to trade with the right strategy

If you find yourself somehow, you have heard about the possibility of trading on the stock exchange, and maybe you know there is no way to do it online. If you want to take this path, we ask you not to feel intimidated or frightened by your possible future as a financial operator.

The stock exchange trading online has become a beginner or beginner's measure that it is. If, until today, you have only played lowly professions and do not have a higher degree, perhaps you think that you are not up to this kind of activity.

Perhaps you believe that the Stock Exchange and Markets, as well as the strategies to earn money, are beyond your means! Enough of this loser mentality.

The truth is that you are second to none, and you have the potential to be on a par with others and, why not, also to excel, especially in a world where meritocracy reigns like that of the stock market and financial markets on the internet.

Millions of people around the world have chosen the path of investment of their online capital, albeit very small. Now you can do it yourself by putting into practice the stock market strategies that we will propose to you during this guide.

Anyone who makes money from online trading does so from little to useful knowledge. It is, therefore, not a question of quantity; it is only a question of quality.

Few but good stock market strategies will allow you to become an established and successful trader who can afford to buy whatever he wants, in total independence, and without having to ask anyone for anything.

It is necessary to know as well as to apply the right bag technique. Learn it first through theory, then put it into practice in the field of trading, testing it continuously and optimizing it based on your trading methodology.

Do not miss the topics to come and immediately discover the best stock exchange strategies, the path that will lead you to become a real trader may be extended and tortuous, but in the end it will be worth it, and you will finally feel satisfied in an occupation free from conditioning and the harassment of the world of work as it has always known it.

If you start trading today, your old life will already be in the past because you're about to be immersed in a virtuous circle of real opportunities to become an ace of stock trading. Cheers!

Modern stock exchange strategies have been devised to permanently change the old canons of traditional investment that made everything too slow and stiff, too challenging to apply, and this caused traders many problems and dissatisfactions, so much that many were eventually led to abandon this promising activity.

With the new strategies, the goal has been to make trading affordable and feasible for everyone, the doors are wide open, and anyone who wants it today can enter without suffering the typical problems of the past.

What it takes to make the most of the strategies that we propose to you in all respects is only basic knowledge of the subject of trading. Consequently, you are not called to know everything to start earning.

Therefore, trading does not mean having a degree in economics. After all, those who would be prepared today to face 5 years of studies to earn money, it is really too much time and too much sacrifice to put in place, so the techniques that you have to use to earn are simple but effective strategies that guarantee the success of the trades in most cases.

But because in stock trading, we talk about strategies and not tactics and because the former is much more successful and secure than the latter. The speech is very simple, and we want to clarify it with the following short definitions:

Investment Strategies

The strategy is the description of a long-term action plan used to set and subsequently coordinate all the actions that serve to achieve a particular, specific purpose. Strategies can be applied in all fields to reach the goal.

Therefore, they carry out the task of obtaining greater security by making a series of separate operations that help reach an end goal. In the case of trading, we are talking about profit, which is undoubtedly the only primary aim that drives people to enter this business.

The simple tactic, on the other hand, is a course of action adopted according to the achievement of specific objectives, but in this case, we speak of small achievements in the short-term.

Adopting tactics would not be effective or satisfactory in the field of trading because it is not a structured plan, but simple plans to achieve small temporary objectives. In short, with a tactic, you can also win a battle, but not war; winning a war requires a broader STRATEGY.

What all traders aim to achieve is a constant and lasting success over time that gives total security of a monthly income and specific collections on an annual basis. In stock exchange trading, it is possible to achieve all this by using strategies. Without strategies, you might perish as a trader very soon.

Applying stock exchange strategies requires attention and many precautions, especially at the beginning, when you are not much of an expert. In certain situations, when the markets become uncertain or careless, you do not know how to act, and you risk making mistakes.

At specific errors, however, the strategies cannot be remedied; in those cases, it will be the experience to act as a master and to suggest the right moves to make.

How much do you earn if you use the best strategy to invest?

With financial instruments available today, profit margins are simply impressive; operating in the right way, you can earn a lot of money even on a daily basis, but at that point, you have to take into account other factors such as the skill of the trader, the ability to avoid the losses, the amount of capital you have available, but also the small strokes of luck that from time to time can help to increase profits.

The amount of money that can be earned then also depends, above all, on the financial product you intend to use. There are not very marked differences but still tangible, depending on whether you prefer to trade forex, CFD, or investing in social trading.

Stock Market Strategies and Money Management

If you intend to trade on the stock exchange, there is no doubt that you will, sooner or later, have to come into contact with the rules of money management or all that concerns the management of money and your precious investment capital.

Money Management shows you the way to correct money management, so it is fundamental in trading, but its rules are also applied in other fields that are as varied as in the domestic or business economy. Ultimately, the rules it dictates are quite simple and due to pure and simple common sense, but in any case, it will be necessary to observe them religiously to avoid running into severe problems in your career as a trader.

The creators of the first money management techniques had a clear idea that it was necessary to produce a new awareness of the use of money in their investments, for the first time imposing the concept of diversification and differentiation of the investment portfolio to reduce the risks of trading and losses on investment capital drastically.

A strategic approach to stock exchange trading cannot, therefore, ignore the knowledge of the fundamental precepts of money management that require you to always establish the spending limit and the budget available at the beginning.

In the field of trading, this will mean establishing the risks that you are willing to run within certain limits that not even an "Indiana Jones" of trading could ever think of crossing; otherwise, it would face economic suicide at the speed of light! The principles of money management help you put both the risks and the potential profits on the scales to understand if a particular movement on the markets should be exploited or not; in other words, it helps you to know if the game is worth the candle.

If you learn to put the rules of money management into practice, your long-term success can be practically assured, but even the short and medium-term will be more probable and easily accessible. In short, all this talk turns to a need for investment efficiency.

The best traders are those who can minimize losses, which not even the guru of the economy could ever avoid and increase profits more and more.

The key to all this is precisely the fact that before learning to earn aspiring traders, the importance of learning to lose should be taught! Suffering losses and spilling money is a natural thing in trading, and you have to try to understand it and not give too much weight when a loss occurs.

The main rule of money management states that you should never, never, ever put at risk more than 5% of the total capital available in a single trading operation.

Doing so would be stupid because it means that in case of loss, you should lose a lot of time trying to recover the negative position if you succeed. Furthermore, it is necessary to avoid losing more than 30% of the total capital available in a single trading day.

You simply have to recognize that when a bad day happens, you have to have the courage to turn off the computer or the device that you used to use to go for a nice walk and not run any further risk because it is clear that that day or you are not able to operate correctly or things in some way always row against you. It is the case to abandon the current session as soon as possible.

Guide to Investing in Stocks

Without a proper guide, all that information you have gained from reading through this instructive book would be for nothing. In this chapter, we will compress and expand on all the investment guidelines hinted at in earlier topics and provide you with an authoritative and practical guide to investing in stocks—the things you need to keep in mind and the exact order of actions that any investor hoping to establish themselves in the stock market ought to follow.

What comes first? What follows that first action? The activities described here are ordered as they are for maximum efficiency. They comprise of a three-step process that starts with the preparations you need to make before starting your investment journey, followed by the actual investment procedure, and ending with the follow-up activities you need to do to ensure that your investment flourishes. Thus ordered, it makes up for a complete guide to investing in stocks aimed at setting you off on your investment journey with the proper skills and capabilities to ensure profitability in the long run.

Laying the Groundwork

Before you start investing, it is important that you define your objectives and investment goals based on your current capital endowment. From there, you will then decide what style of investing best suits you. To make both of these decisions, you will need to build your knowledge bank.

Build Your Knowledge Bank

A wise investor is a wealthy investor. Knowledge is the most important asset an investor accumulates before putting down the money for their first investment. Good investment strategizing comes from having a good grasp of not just financial markets and what sends prices rising and dropping; it also requires that you have a proper understanding of investment strategies and all assets available for you to invest in. Lack of knowledge in the ins and outs of the stock market can have a debilitating effect on an investor. On the other hand, sufficient information, even when it is just theoretical, is a huge boost of confidence. Investors who have a good idea of how people make money in the stock market are more likely to succeed in the stock market themselves because they are exposed to all the strategies that others before them have accumulated.

On the other hand, acquiring even a rudimentary cache of knowledge of investing is assured to put you way ahead of contemporary investors who just put their money in the so-called "hottest" stocks. And the good thing about knowledge acquisition is that it comes in handy whether you are starting your investment journey at the age of 26 or 62. The deeper you go in your learning of the ropes, the more chances you stand for becoming an outstanding investor.

To build your knowledge bank, you will need to gather information from research, reading financial books, observing the masters of the game, and following the market very keenly.

Learn Research Skills

The first rule of investing in stocks is to invest only in companies that you understand. You will need thorough research to understand the current state of the stock market, rising trends, and future projections. Research skills are crucial not just to the actions you will carry out in this practical guide but also later in your investment journey as you pick assets to buy and determine the best buying and selling points for each one of them.

By learning to research, you unlock every successful investor's catalog of investing stratagems and tricks. Research skills are very handy as you lay the groundwork for your investment journey, when you start the real process of investing, and afterward, as you keep your portfolio balanced. In the preliminary process, your research skills will help you to learn, among other things, what information is needed to become a good investor. As you select the stockbrokers with whom to open a brokerage account, research skills will also be very handy. You will also need to have polished research skills as you conduct the due diligence analysis of prospective stocks and other assets to put in your stock portfolio.

The good thing about having technology in our hands is that research skills often entail a simple Google search and bookmarking a few articles for later reference. But people often neglect even the simple act of reading the Wikipedia article of the company they are thinking about buying stocks in. As a tip for those exhaustive online searches, use a PC if one is handy. Some of the most informative articles you will find about a critical topic will never make it into the search results of your mobile phone browser.

Read

Reading investment books may be the hardest method of adding to your knowledge bank. But the information that you gather from investment books goes a long way in building your investment skills. Books written by investment legends (a biography, for example) would be especially indispensable because investors will usually share information about their own investment journey, including the mistakes they made along the way. You can then avoid these mistakes in your own investment career and possibly save yourself a fortune.

Books actually make up for a short course you take on whatever topic they are about, giving you comprehensive information on various subtopics. And neither should your readership be limited to books written about the financial markets specifically. Read up, too, on other skills that could come in handy in your portfolio management, such as accounting and bookkeeping. These skills come in handy in the investment process as well as out of it—other areas of your life.

Deciding on how to invest in stocks

There are numerous ways on how to invest in stocks. All of these ways have some advantages and disadvantages, but every individual's situation is different. What's good for you may lead to a problematic situation for another. Considering the period and market value, while looking for stocks to invest in, is highly recommended.

Sometimes, the market may be going through a smooth and steady path that your emotional aspects may get in the way. You may invest in expensive stocks due to the success of the market. On the other hand, in a poorly performing market during situations like inflation, you may start to sell off your stocks.

So how can you decide where to invest? First off, you need to analyze how much a certain method of investment would be affected by the level of risk and potential loses. If the risk is too high, but the gains from it would be more fruitful, you would know what step to take. Such decision making requires proper research of all the methods and a proper understanding of how much would be at stake, in different situations.

Methods of investment

We know that all methods would have certain effects, but in the end, the success relies on how much risk you are ready to take, as well as how much knowledge you have in stock marketing. If you're into a more modern and technological way of business, then you should know, online buying of stocks is a thing. However, it is only recommended if you are well aware of how the stock market operates, and can give useful advice to yourself, as this one doesn't involve any advices to be given, so you're on your own. Also, it is far more risky, as you are charged only a flat fee for each transaction. Also, to mention, it's time-consuming, as you would have to train yourself until you're confident enough to take the next step.

Investment Club

The next method which you can consider is through the investment clubs. You meet a lot of people who may be going through the same situation you are, and people who can give professional and financial advices. Other people's experiences can make you learn a lot too. It is affordable and can help you to understand and differentiate between different market situations. Increased involvement and investing in stocks through this can help you gain a new perspective and a sense of direction.

Full-Service Broker

Then we have a full-service broker. Know that this is an expensive method, as the fees paid to your broker I quite high, but the excess information makes up for it. The broker will help you with the recommendation and advice on how to take the next step, and the precaution measure to be taken while looking for a good financial advisor. This leads to increased business know-how, more knowledge about the stock market, and increased confidence in your decisions.

Investing in the stock markets

If you purchase some clothes and neglect the fact that trying it on would help you decide whether to purchase it or not and come home to only find out that the clothes don't fit, you'll be pretty disappointed unless there is an exchange or return policy at the outlet. If not, you're at a loss. Trust me, investing in a market is nothing close to purchasing clothes. Hence, neglecting can lead to the loss of a fortune. Louder for the people at the back, investing in stock markets is nothing close to your day to day spending. So, you got to go smart about it.

Investing in stocks for the first time has a much greater risk. However, these risks are to be taken, but there is always supposed to be a margin. The potential risk always needs to be managed. How do you ask? Research gets you a long way. You don't want to trust the company blindly. It is important to analyze and study how the company is doing in the market. Their marketing tactics, financial weaknesses, and productivity need to be kept in mind.

If the business doesn't have a good marketing department, it's likely to go crashing down as soon as the competition gets tough. The finance department needs to be checked and observed at every point, as they handle a major part of the business. Any fishy business being done, the greater is the effect on you. Whatever the business is selling, it needs to have a good production plan, method, and a skilled and efficient workforce.

The trends in the market should be considered at all points

Consumer taste and changes in choices should be properly analyzed, and the reasons behind them should be known. If the owners of the business have enough knowledge about this, and the managers are efficient enough to make this happen, it means your potential risk may be lower.

As a beginner, what is important to take into account, is how the country's economy is doing. Inflation would mean that there can be a sudden downfall in the trends and a greater risk of bankruptcy. The time of investing should be carefully chosen. However, it is proven that there never is the perfect time to invest in the market. Comparison of different timings is important. This also depends on the type of goods or services being offered. The price elasticity of demand and supply would help you find out how the market will do during inflation.

Moreover, for long term success, the growth of the company needs to be taken into consideration. Over time, how much the company has actually grown, and what is the difference between its earnings when it started fresh, and what is it now? This determines the stability of the company you plan to invest in. Many businesses go through ups and downs, but the major ones are what you should avoid at all cost. The strength of the industry and how well it does in the market will show how much potential the company has for long-term success.

Coming on to the other important aspects, the debt and the equity ratio needs to be measured beforehand. If the company is in too much debt and isn't making enough profit to pay it off, it would call for the liquidation, which means selling off the assets of the company. You won't be left with anything in this case.

Learn to Follow the Market
When buying assets for your investment portfolio, timing the market is one of the most futile things you can ever do. But in building your knowledge bank, analyzing the market comes in very handy when analyzing how the stock market reacts to different stimuli. Following the market improves your understanding of it because, after all, observation is one of the most useful skills in building knowledge.

Financial news services, such as the Wall Street Journal, Bloomberg, Yahoo! Finance, and Morningstar, among numerous others, are practically indispensable for a new investor hoping to understand the stock market. You will be able to identify the most profitable sectors of the economy, making it easier for you to make the decision on what stocks to buy when it finally comes down to it. Following the market is the only way to identify trends as they form, stay updated on emerging business concepts, and learn more about general business practices and their impact on profitability.

Television is another great way to broaden your knowledge base. Apart from the jargon (which is also good to learn), analysts on TV teach you how to anticipate market reaction to geopolitical, economic, and public relations events. Of course, at some point, you will outgrow the rather shallow and junky analysis, but in the beginning, they could be a treasure trove of information.

Define Your Investment Style
After building your knowledge bank substantially and gaining a deeper understanding of the stock market in general, it is time now to narrow the focus down to your own investment. Everyone has the style of investing that best suits their needs and their personality. Risk-takers need an investment strategy quite different from risk-averse people, and those who treasure balance would like to combine aspects of both. In this step of your investment journey, you start thinking more about the exact ways that you are going to invest.

Vision Statement
A vision statement gives you the chance to define exactly what you are looking to achieve in monetary rewards. The rest of your investment journey is reliant on your ability to define your investment vision statement because this is the point where you factor in your goals (reasons for saving up through investment) and plot out the best route to follow to get there faster and with minimal risk. When defining your vision statement, establish exactly how much money you are looking to have at the end of your investment and how much time you have to raise it. From this assessment, you can determine the kind of investment strategy that will enable you to achieve your goal.

A popular vision for investing is the 25× goal, a dividend stock-investment strategy for people with visions of early retirement that stipulates that you should invest in stocks that pay you enough dividends to match your annual salary. So, assuming that the stocks in your investment portfolio give a dividend payout of about 4% and with $50,000 as your annual salary, you'd need to invest 25 times of that, which comes to $1.25 million to make exactly what you make now. All dividends and any additional savings go toward boosting your investment portfolio, buying more dividend stocks to increase the dividend payout, which is then reinvested for even greater yields.

Factoring in any possible future promotions (and the accompanying raise) and rising expenditures as you accumulate more responsibilities and develop more refined tastes, $50,000 a year will probably be too little twenty years from now. You will probably need $60,000–75,000 to maintain your current lifestyle, adjusting for inflation. You can solve for that discrepancy easily. Just factor in the desired annual dividend payout, calculate with the average yield and find out how much more you will need to have invested. The best thing about the 25× goal idea is that even when you finally start living off your investment, it will still leave your principal intact.

Investment Strategy
With the overarching determinant being your investment goals, your investment strategy is influenced by two main factors—the amount of risk you think you can shoulder and the kind of investor you would like to become in terms of active participation.

Based on risk tolerance, you can be a conservative investor, an aggressive one, or a moderate one. Aggressive investing produces massive profits very fast, and it is suitable for investors with huge goals and a short period of time to pursue them. The risks are rather massive, but then so are the rewards. Conservative investors opt for low-yield investments that are low in risk. Even though this strategy could be quite profitable over the long term, it could also make your investment a very unprofitable venture. Going for the most conservative investment opportunities also means that the chances of missing out on amazing investment opportunities also increase substantially. The balanced strategy is for those investors who want the best of both worlds—medium returns at average risk.

Based on participation, you can either be a passive investor or an active one. A passive investor invests and forgets all about the investment. They don't bother much with price fluctuations and such "trivial" matters. If you want to have the confidence to invest in a stock and forget about it (watch the money flow, as it were), then make *thorough background research* your friend. This way, you won't be worried that your portfolio is losing value because of a stock you picked. Active investors are a whole other breed altogether. More suited to day trading than long-term investments, active portfolio management nonetheless produces great profits.

Investment strategies ultimately come down to the choice of assets that an investor puts in their portfolio. Aggressive investment strategies call for massive growth stocks with high risks and price volatility, a balanced approach seeks out medium growth rate stocks, while conservative investors prefer the tried and tested stocks whose core business faces absolutely no risk of collapse. Active stock investing gravitates more toward the aggressive style, while conservative investing is often passive. Conservative stocks tend to belong to old companies that have established themselves. The opposite is true for aggressive stocks, whose companies are much younger and require a steady hand to halt any possible loss of investment from price volatility.

Having established your priorities and set your investment goals and strategies, it is high time you open an account and get down to the real investing. It is during this phase that you will pick the asset that will go into your investment portfolio. But first, you will need to open a brokerage account.

Open a Brokerage Account

To invest in the financial markets, you are going to need a broker to carry out your buy and sell orders. You should be very careful when picking out your brokerage because even though their only job is to facilitate your investments in stocks, bonds, investment trusts, and the money markets, not all brokers are created equal. There are those that facilitate your investment and do nothing more (discount brokers), and then you have the ones that throw in some sound investing advice into the deal (full-service brokers). A rising trend in brokerage account holding is the robo-advisor type of account where an automated system helps you set goals, buy stocks, and transact. Your choice of brokerage account will be determined by the amount of control you desire.

Discount Brokerage Accounts

Discount brokers carry out your buy/sell orders at a very low price. A discount brokerage account is the ultimate do-it-yourself investment account. Other than some basic information and price comparison tools, discount brokers offer investors virtually no guidance on investment strategizing, whether in the preliminary stages or later on as you manage your investment portfolio. The discount broker is a relatively recent development in the stock market. Previously, only the full-service broker existed, serving the rich because only they (with their deep pockets and huge investments) can afford their services. The discount broker opened up the stock market for people with less capital to participate.

One of the most outstanding discount brokerage accounts is TD Ameritrade. The firm offers great price comparison and analysis tools. Even though you will get no real investment guidance from a person sitting across the desk or on the other side of the phone, with TD Ameritrade, there will be enough information that you may not need an advisor anyways. If you created a good investment objective and came up with the correct strategy, then you probably won't miss these services anyway.

Full-Service Brokers

A full-service brokerage account entails more than the execution of just buy/sell orders. A wide variety of services, such as taxation advice, research tools, financial guidance, and retirement planning, are offered along with the usual execution of your buy and sell orders. The commission charged by full-service brokers eclipses that of discount ones a few times over. The advantage is that you need not get tied up with research, stock selection, and portfolio management.

Because full-service brokers tend to be more traditional and well-established, they tend to have a few benefits that discount brokers don't. For one thing, a full-service brokerage firm is more likely to have a direct link to IPOs, preferred stocks, and other glamorous opportunities. In the same manner, they tend to put together their own investment products, such as ETFs and mutual funds, giving investors an even wider range of investment opportunities to take advantage of.

Robo-advisor Accounts

The robo-advisor brokerage account is the rave in discount stock trading right now. In a few short steps, robo-advisors allow you to create a portfolio of diverse investments and manage these investment opportunities. Robo-advisors use technology to bring together the best features from full-service and discount brokerage to create an outstanding investment vehicle for the average investor. With little more than your personal details, investment goal, and risk tolerance, a robo-advisor creates a portfolio for you and administers it, performing such mundane tasks as rebalancing with little input from you. Keep updating the details and objectives to ensure that the account still reflects your needs. Other than that, investing using a rob-advisor is a pretty hands-off approach to investing.

Even though robo-advisors do not offer the deep house services of full-service brokerage firms, such as special investment opportunities, the wealth management tools are right up there with the best. The three features that make a robo-advisor account such an attractive opportunity for an investor include (1) low upfront investment, (2) great options, and (3) inclusive portfolio management. Moreover, robo-advisors are completely unbiased, making recommendations based solely on your investment goals. The conflict of interest that comes from financial advisors pushing preferential investments to their clients is totally eliminated. The requirements to open a robo-advisor account are also pretty relaxed, which means that you can start investing with as low as $500. Numerous robo-advisor account providers have come up in the past one decade or so, including Betterment, Schwab Intelligent Portfolios, Wealthfront, and SigFig, among numerous others.

With a brokerage account open, the only thing left to do is pick your investments. The options available to you include the 401(k) plan, the individual retirement plan (IRA), and of course, the stocks, bonds, and other assets that you can invest through a brokerage account.

401(K) and IRA Plans
The 401(k) plan is every employee's birthright to the world of investment. It allows you to save for your employment in the most productive way possible—with incremental returns. The contributions to the investment portfolio are also automatic and tax-deductible. A clause stipulating exactly when you will receive full access to your funds is another advantage of 401(k) plans—it allows you to plan for your own investment.

Whatever amount you decide to contribute to your 401(k) plan is taken out of your pay slip before you get the money, which means that your taxable income reduces substantially. As an investment that matures upon retirement, a 401(k) comes in very handy in addition to any other personal investment plan you may have going if your goal is to retire early, like if your investment vision is based on the 25× goal.

An IRA plan allows you to save for huge future cash expenditures, such as retirement, house buying, a car, college fees, *etc.* There are a few versions of the IRA plan available, including the traditional, Roth, SIMPLE, and SEP versions.

CHAPTER 6:

Take Control Of Your Money

Money & Risk Management Techniques

For successful trading in the stock markets, money management and risk management are crucial steps. Stock markets can turn highly volatile at times, and if you are not careful about protecting your money and risk of open trades, you can suffer huge monetary losses.

Therefore, the first step in day trading should be; learn how to reduce trading risk and manage your capital investment so you can tolerate the normal losses in day trading. Money management is like strengthening your defenses so you can survive in the stock market to trade another day. Safe trading practices to protect your money can increase your profits. A lack of it can also double your losses. Money and risk management can be the difference between the success and failure of a day trader. Often, beginners are so focused on making profits in stock markets, they forget to protect their invested capital, and soon, their losses wipe out the whole trading capital.

Part of good money management is using just a fraction of your trading capital on one trade. In other words, never put all your money on a single trade. As they say, 90% of traders do not make profits in day trading. A big reason for this failure is not paying attention to money management. If you keep on betting on stock prices for rising of falling with no proper strategy and risk management, then it is pure gambling and not any intelligent business venture.

Take day trading as a business, do it with proper money management, learn how you can reduce the risk in your trades; you will reduce the number of potential losses, and increase potential profits. Keep your trading cost to a minimum. Before opening any trade, always decide how much loss you will allow for that trade and put a stop loss to cover that much amount. Markets will come back the next day, but you should be left with enough capital to trade when markets open for the next session.

Risk Management

Risk management is one of the most important parts of option trading. Like with any other kind of investment, trading is inherently risky. There will always be some amount of risk involved, but the key to trading successfully is to manage your capital and risk carefully.

Everyone has a different risk tolerance threshold, and that's completely fine. You should never stretch yourself too thin. Only trade with money you can afford to lose. Let's look at some ways you can control and manage your risk efficiently.

When people think of day trading, they only think of potential profits, not losses. Therefore, day trading attracts so many people that don't see the risk of losses. In stock markets, various events can trigger losses for investors and traders, which are beyond their control. These events can be economic conditions such as recession, geopolitical changes, also, changes in the central bank policies, natural disasters, or sometimes terror attacks.

This is the market risk; the potential of losing money due to unknown and sudden factors. These factors affect the overall performance of stock markets, and regardless of how careful one is while day trading, the possibility of market risk is always present, which can cause losses. The market risk is known as the systematic risk because it influences the entire stock market. There is also a nonsystematic risk, which affects only a specific industry or company. Long-term investors tackle this risk by diversification in their investment portfolio.

Unlike investors, day traders have no method to neutralize market risk, but they can avoid it by keeping track of financial and business events, news, and economic calendars. For example, stock markets are very sensitive to the central banks' rate policies and become highly volatile on those days. Nobody knows what kind of policy any central bank will adopt in its monetary meeting. But day traders can check the economic calendar and know which day these meetings will take place. They can avoid trading on those days and reduce the risk of loss in trading.

Therefore, knowledge of stock markets and being aware of what is happening in the financial world is essential for day traders. Many successful traders have a policy of staying away from trading on days when any major economic event will take place, or a major decision will be announced. For example, on the day when the result of an important election is declared, any big company's court case decision comes in, or a central banks' policy meeting takes place. On such days, speculative trading dominates stock markets and market risk is very high. Similarly, on a day when any company announces earnings results, its stock price fluctuates wildly, increasing the market risk in trading of that stock.

For inexperienced day traders, the best way to tackle market risk is to avoid trading on such days.

If you plan well, prepare your trading strategies before starting to trade; you increase the possibility of a stable trading practice, which can lead to profits. Therefore, it is essential to prepare your trading plans every day, create trading strategies, and follow your trading rules. These three things can make or break your day trading business. Professional day traders always plan their trades first and then trade their plans. This can be understood by an example of two imaginary traders. Suppose there are two traders, trading in the same stock market, trading the same stock. One of them has prepared his trading plan and knows when and how he will trade. The other trader has done no planning and is just sitting there, taking the on-the-spot decisions for buying or selling the stock. Who do you think will be more successful? The one who is well prepared, or the one who has no inkling of what he will do the next second?

The second risk management technique is using stop orders. Use these orders to decide to fix your stop -loss and profit booking points, which will take emotions out of your decision-making process and automatically cut the losses or book the profit for you.

Many a time, profitable trade turns into loss-making because markets change their trend, but traders do not exit their positions, hoping to increase profits. Therefore, it is necessary to keep a profit booking point and exit the profitable trades at that point. Keeping a fix profit booking point can also help you calculate your returns with every trade and help you avoid taking the unnecessary risk for further trades.

Taking emotions out of day trading is a very important requirement for profitable trading. Do not prejudge the trend in stock markets, which many day traders do and trade against markets, ending with losses.

Using Risk-Reward Ratio
Day trading is done for financial rewards, and the good thing is, you can always calculate how much risk you take on every trade and how much reward you can expect. The risk-reward ratio represents the expected reward and expected risk traders can earn on the investment of every dollar.

The risk-reward ratio can excellently indicate your potential profits and potential loss, which can help you in managing your investment capital. For example, a trade with the risk-reward ratio of 1:4 shows that at the risk of $1, the trade has the potential of returning $4. Professional traders advise not to take any trade, which has a risk-reward ratio lower than 1:3. This indicates, the trader can expect the investment to be $1, and the potential profit $3.

Expert traders use this method for planning, which trade will be more profitable and take only those trades. Technical charting is a good technique to decide the risk-reward ratio of any trade by plotting the price moment from support to resistance levels. For example, if a stock has a support level at $20, it will probably rise from that level because many traders are likely to buy it at support levels. After finding out a potential support level, traders try to spot the nearby resistance level where the rising price is expected to pause. Suppose a technical level is appearing at $60. So, the trader can buy at $20 and exit when the price reaches $60. If everything goes right, he can risk $20 to reap a reward of $60. In this trade, the risk-reward ratio will be 1:3.

By calculating the risk-reward ratio, traders can plan how much money they will need to invest, and how much reward they can expect to gain from any trade. This makes them cautious about money management and risk management.

Some traders have a flexible risk-reward ratio for trading, while others prefer to take trades only with a fixed risk-reward ratio. Keeping stop-loss in all trades also helps in managing the risk-reward ratio. Traders can calculate their trade entry point to stop-loss as the risk, and trade entry to profit as the reward. This way, they can find out if any trade has a bigger risk than the potential reward or a bigger reward than the potential risk. Choosing trades with bigger profits and smaller risks can increase the amount of profit over a period.

Using Your Trading Plan

Having a detailed trading plan is very important as it lays down some basic rules and guidelines, you're going to follow in your trading activities. This helps you manage your money and limit your exposure to risk. Your plan should include how much risk you're comfortable taking and how much capital you're going to invest. This way, you allocate a fixed amount to option trading and you never end up touching the money you can't afford to lose.

You can't eliminate emotions from trading, but what you can do is minimize the impact they have on your trades by putting rules in place.

If you stick to your plan and use only the allocated amount of capital for trading, you avoid behaving irrationally and taking risks you can't afford to.

If you're generally conservative with your trades and it's been working fine for you, there's no reason for you to take higher risks suddenly. This is especially important when you make a few losing trades in a row. You might want to take a risky trade to recover past losses, but that's not a good idea. Remind yourself you have a trading plan in place for a reason.

Using Options Spreads

We've covered various types of spreads in the book. This is because they're one of the most powerful tools to dissipate your risk. Spreads let you combine different positions using the same underlying stocks, thereby helping you create a more secure overall position. The upfront costs to enter a position can be daunting, but you can use spreads to reduce them and thereby minimize the amount you stand to lose. Yes, it also reduces the potential profits you could make, but that's just part of controlling risk. We've covered several types of spreads in the book all ready to help you take advantage of pretty much any market condition.

For example, if you use a bull call spread, you reduce your initial investment and hence, limit the amount of money you stand to lose. This is done by buying ITM calls on a stock and then writing OOTM calls on the same stock since they're cheaper.

Similarly, when entering short positions, you can reduce your risk by using a bull put spread. This is done by writing ITM puts on a particular stock and then buying cheaper OOTM puts on the same stock by using some of that upfront payment you received from writing the put options.

As you can see, spreads are excellent strategies for risk management.

Portfolio Diversification

The most popular technique of risk management is Diversification. Investors using the buy and hold strategy are generally the users of this technique. The essence of diversification is spreading investments over various companies and sectors, thus creating an equitable portfolio of stocks instead of concentrating all the investment at a single point. This makes it less subjected to risk than a portfolio, which is largely composed of a particular type of investment.

Diversification isn't meant in the same way for options, but it has its uses. Diversification is used in options trading in different ways by using a combination of various strategies and trading options that have a multitude of underlying assets. The options being used can be of different types too. For using diversification, you just don't rely on a single outcome but create several ways of creating profits.

Using Options Orders

There's a range of orders you can use to manage your risk in a simple way. Besides the four main orders (buy-to-open, sell-to-close, sell-to-open, buy-to-close), there are a host of other orders we can use to manage our risk.

Let's see an example. It's typical for a market order to be filled automatically at the best price available, but this might not be a good price for you if the market is volatile. You can use limit orders here to set a minimum and maximum price. This way, you avoid selling or buying at a price you don't want to.

Similarly, you can use stop orders like market stop order or the limit stop order to control how you exit a position. This can help you avoid unmitigated losses or lock in profits you're comfortable cashing out at.

I advise you to read more about option orders once you have gained some experience in option trading.

Money Management and Position Sizing

Money management and risk management are closely entangled with each other.an investor has a certain amount available to invest, and hence it is crucial to control your capital budget. To not run into a position of inability to make more trades, one should take into consideration the size of a single position.

Position sizing means specifying the amount of capital you're willing to invest in a certain position. It's quite a simple tool to use. One must calculate what percent of their total invested capital is in each individual trade proposition. It is also kind of like diversification.

CHAPTER 7:

Trading Psychology

An Options Trading Mindset

When it comes to making money trading options, it is important to remember that you must control your emotions at all times, which is easier said than done, especially if you are in the moment and have just taken an unexpected loss. Cultivating the proper mindset can be done with practice. However, and doing so will make it easier for you to face the early parts of your options trading career with the proper expectations in regards to what sort of results you can expect from options trading. Specifically, this means that you will need to understand that investing in options isn't a quick and easy path to success and, rather, is sure to take plenty of dedication and hard work if you hope to see reap the potential rewards.

The first step to finding success via options trading is to get your emotions in check. The best traders are robotic, they only rely on the facts and they follow their trading plan 100 percent of the time. If you find yourself getting extremely emotional as far as trading is concerned, then it is important that you start off by keeping a log of the emotions you have while trading and the results of those emotions on your trading outcome. While this might seem unnecessary at first, you will be surprised how helpful having a clear outline of your personal patterns is when it comes to improving your overall trade percentage in the long term.

The fact of the matter is that if you ever hope to successfully trade options, then you are going to need to know you can stick with your plan no matter what the emotional part of your mind is telling you to do. A good plan is one that remains successful, not 100 percent of the time, or even 95 percent of the time and instead manages to be successful roughly 60 percent of the time. While 60 percent is certainly enough to ensure you turn a profit, it is not enough that it allows for additional wiggle room in terms of letting your emotions talking you into going off the book at every turn. Remember, trading options is a numbers game and keeping your emotions in check is key to not working with skewed data.

Setting up a reasonable expectation

A trader who is staring up should always have the patience to wait to know a market and should not expect that he or she would a large and handsome profit from their trading options. A new trader should never high expectations when they are just into the market. Rather they should be mentally prepared for losing capital rather than gaining capital. A trader should always begin to expect at least a minimum market experience of a year or a half. This can be illustrated very simply in any field. A famous successful person always bears time and patience to be the greatest achiever in their field.

Proof concept

If a trader starts off with the small trade, he or she will not only gain experience but will also save time. Noises of the stock market do not affect the small traders, but if a trader starts with big trading options, he or she will react to these noises in the stock market. A new trader will be in a bad situation with such reactions and at the early time period. Starting with a small trade will teach a trader to manage capital, which is very much necessary. A trader remembers all trades are not the same in nature. A good trader will generate great ideas after the proper experience. A trader must always have records and check on them to see what idea works for them and what does not.

Proper sorting and record-keeping
A good successful trader should always keep a record of a few important things of the market like:

The trader should keep a record of orders placed and quantity involved in it and money-making out of it.

The trader should keep in mind implied volatility and its reference to the current condition.

The trader should keep in mind about his competitors in the market in that particular trade.

When the traders begin to keep a record and maintain records, they begin to move towards success and chances of being in an odd position is also reduced.

Good position of the trader
Once a trader has achieved his or her position in a trade or stock market, there are frequent ups and downs. A good position trader must know how to react to these situations. By small trade, he or she won't be much affected by the noise of the stock market.

The trader should keep in mind about buying stock exchange at the perfect time. When a trader does so, he or she can perfectly be in the market and understand well.

Proper evaluation of the position
A trader must decide very well that a few decisions like backing out on losses must be decided well according to the perfect time.

There are few other decisions like a plan suddenly executed and whether he or she should move on with the profit or go for more?

Even if the sudden plan does not work out then he or she must have a backup and move on forward ahead and not repent on his or her loss and look for a new fresh start.

Hard work is the only way to success

It's easy to advise and listen to it. But when it comes up to the execution of the advice it's not that easy as things do not turn up the way it's told.

The simple way is to start with small trade and have a lot of patience. A trader should do proper planning for execution. The trader should learn about the market and get into a good position and stick well to it and work very hard to achieve success and be a good disciplined successful trader.

At this point, it is time to move on to the next step. You already know some of the basics that come with working on options as well as some of their benefits.

If you want to become a successful trader who consistently earns a passive income time and again, you need to know how to navigate the psychology of trading. Anywhere you look, you will discover that the psychology of trading is as crucial to your success as virtually anything else and that a truly magnificent trader enforces this proper psychology.

Through fostering the right mindset and preparing your psychology for success, you can ensure that you are able to make the best trades possible, allowing you to maximize your profits.

The biggest reason why your mindset is so important when it comes to trading is that trading in and of itself can be incredibly stressful, and there is a lot at stake with each trade that you make. Although options trading is significantly less risky than other trading strategies, it is still risky and should be treated like any other form of trading to protect yourself against the risk.

When we become stressed during any life experience, our emotions have a tendency to hijack the experience and prevent us from being able to make logical rational decisions. Naturally, this would not be productive to you making the best decisions with your trades, which mean that this needs to be avoided at all costs.

Fostering the right mindset allows you to remain objective and logical in every trade decision that you make so that you are always making decisions that lead to your profits, rather than mistakes that lead to your losses.

It does take time to learn how to foster this particular mindset, especially with the amount of stress that you might face with trading. Ideally, however, if you practice at it every single day, you will find that it becomes a lot easier for you to see your trades objectively. As a result, you will find that your trades become more productive and your passive income stream grows exponentially.

While there are many things that you can do to help you manage your mindset and your emotions and keep yourself primed for the psychology of trading, there are five significant steps that you can take today to get started. Enforcing these mindset strategies right away can help you start your trades with the best mindset possible so that you can experience larger levels of success right from the very beginning.

Never take anything personally
In life, it can be challenging to separate yourself from your experiences, especially when high emotions such as stress and overwhelm come into play. Early on, you might feel like every trade you make reflects you personally and like any bad trade, you make means that you are a bad trader or that you are incapable of earning an income through trading. This type of response is fairly natural, but it is also unhelpful when it comes to learning how to trade to earn a profit.

Experiencing losses and trade deals gone wrong is a natural part of trading, and virtually everyone experiences it. While senior traders are not as likely to experience as *many* losses as new traders, they do still experience losses that cut into their bottom line. This is natural, especially when you are trading on something as volatile as the stock market. With day trading, in particular, you never know *exactly* how that day is going to go, nor do you know whether or not sudden shifts in news and rumors could completely change the direction of the stock. As such, you are certainly exposed to risks that can be completely beyond your control. While you can protect yourself against them as much as possible, there is no real way to completely avoid risks, and so they are always a possibility.

The alternative of feeling like a bad trader when you experience a loss is feeling like a great trader when you experience a win. It is common amongst new traders who are on a winning streak to develop a sense of indestructibility that suggests that maybe they are incapable of experiencing losses because they somehow have the system beat.

This arrogance can lead to new traders exposing themselves to massive risks and losses because they stop taking their trades as seriously and reduce the amount of researching and risk management they conduct before every trade. As a result, they may experience a massive setback due to this arrogance.

In either scenario, creating a personal attachment to what your trades "mean" about who you are as a person is not healthy. Both can lead to self-doubt or arrogance, which has the capacity to destroy your trade deals and reduce your effectiveness as a trader.

Instead, you need to go into every single trade deal, knowing that your level of results in the trades is not reflective of you as a person. You are neither good nor bad for participating in trades that earn profits or losses. You are just a trader, trading. Keeping your personal attachment out of the trades will help you stay objective and continually practice logic and rational reasoning in every single trade you make.

Always Stay Hungry for Knowledge
Trading is not a one and done skill that can be learned and then executed the same way over and over again without ever requiring further education on what you are doing. If you want to be a great trader and earn massive profits, you need to stay hungry for knowledge so that you can continually improve your trading skills over time. Despite the fact

that the general rules of trading have always remained the same throughout history, there are several different factors that influence the market and how trades are being made. Over time you will learn more about technical indicators, how certain types of news tend to affect the market, and where the best sources of information are for you to learn more about your specific trades.

Chances are you will take what you learn here in this book and apply them, and over time you will find new information that helps you improve your trades even further.

It is important to understand that you should always be hungry and on the lookout for new information. Keeping your eyes and ears open ensures that you are always refining your practice and increasing your profitability in the market, which will, in turn, maximize your passive income. Every single person will have a different way of understanding the market, identifying important pieces of information, and preparing themselves for trades.

The best way to create your own method for doing all of this is to keep practicing and applying new strategies that you learn about as you go and seeing how they fit for you. When you find ones you like and that work for you, continue using them and refining them so that they work even better over time.

Conclusion

I hope this book was able to fulfill its purpose and help you understand what options trading is all about. Make sure you take the time to understand all the concepts covered in this book and then actually implement them in real life. If you don't put this knowledge you've gained to practice, you will forget it, and it would've all been just a waste of time. Remember to be patient, manage your risk, and keep learning more as you gain experience in the market. That's what makes a good trader.

The next step is to stop reading already and to get ready to get started taking advantage of the benefits that are unique to the options market. While it may not be exciting, what this means in practical terms is that it is time for you to get down to business and start doing your homework.

There is so much potential for making a profit when you work in options, but you have to come up with a plan and stick with it if you want a chance for success. This guidebook will help you to reach that success so that you can limit your risks and make as much money as possible with options.

Thanks for reading!

DAY TRADING FOR BEGINNERS

How To Trade And Make Money With Day Strategy Through A Beginner Guide To Learn The Best Strategies For Creating Your Passive Income For A Living. Includes Tips And Tricks

Matthew Swing

Introduction

The in-depth understanding of day trading cannot be achieved only from its mere definition. There is still more that encompasses day trading that you would require to know and understand before regarding yourself as an expert in day trading. Especially for you as a beginner, the journey is still long, but with a clear mindset and focus, you will soon get to understand all that revolves around day trading and be fully proficient. With day trading, it is absolutely possible to earn good pay for very few hours within a day. However, individuals who get into the market without a clear understanding of day trading always end up getting enormous losses.

Having a strategy, you realize that for all the various methods of carrying out any trade, require a certain strategy. You ought to adopt or rather create one that best suits you. Failure to which you risk making huge losses in your trade. Day trading is not just like any other kind of trade, which you would just succeed in a whim without a clear strategy. You need to ask yourself various questions like how will you get into the trade, what do you need to have to get into the trade, or how much in terms of profits do you think you will get?, how many shares of stock would you purchase with the money that you have set aside for the day trade, how much would you stand to lose in case things go haywire? Having these questions in mind, they will act as driving forces towards the know-how of starting the trade. Implementing them once you are in the trade gives you a kind of a method that you can try out over and over, analyze your results, and find out whether it works in your favor. You can also develop a strategy from other people as well who have been in the trade and have tried it and have worked for them.

To be successful in day trade, you will require to do as much practice as possible, especially before you decide on using your own hard-earned money in the trade. As the old saying goes, "practice makes perfect". You do not necessarily have to have high educational qualifications to make it in day trading. Practice hard to find that one strategy that suits you. The practice here is using demo accounts. Here you are at liberty to try out even your most recently learned strategy and see whether it works out well for you. When you find yourself being profitable in a demo account, then from there, you can decide to get into real trading. Use the same strategy that you have been using in your demo account. The idea here of practicing as much as possible is to spot repeating patterns. However, the demo account, to some extent, may not be similar to real trading in terms of the pressures and associated risks, but it still plays a critical role in ensuring that you acquire the necessary confidence and understand better your best trading method. Due to this, at first, you may realize that your trade may fail to do well as it was when you were doing the demo. This should not worry you. It is so natural and is expected. The choice of the demo account would, to some extent, also matter considering that some do not expire; hence, they provide you with an opportunity to trade as much as you would wish to.

The issue of the amount of capital that you would require to get into the trade is also a key factor. This determines how much you get as returns in case of profits within a day of trading. The minimum amount to start with maybe specific with some markets, while others do not have a set minimum. The majority of the traders, on the other hand, only put in the capital that they can afford to lose. Somehow this helps eliminate emotions while in the trade hence enable them to make sound decisions. Moreover, having very low capital for you day trade may disadvantage you as you may end up paying extremely high commissions while at the same time receive poor order executions? You will realize that all markets usually offer good profit potential. Hence the only factor that stands out is the amount of capital you invest — putting these into consideration, having a large capital to trade with stands out as an added advantage in Day Trading. Nonetheless, do not be misguided into believing that day trading is one quick, easy way of making money overnight. This only applies when you are well aware of the trade; have defined clear strategies and a deep understanding of your market. Moreover, despite the many skills, luck in one way or another, as well as good timing skills, counts.

You also need to understand that for day trade, you will require to have a broker. Your choice of a broker is quite critical, as this is the person whom you in one way or the other trust with all of your capital. Here you may decide to settle with the online broker whom you opened the demo account with or choose another. The majority of the day traders usually prefer those brokers who base their charges per share instead of per trade. In the case where a broker charges high commissions, then he can negatively affect your profitability based on your day's strategy despite you wanting to save your profits by looking for low fee brokers. You have to ensure that they are quite reliable; otherwise, you may end up losing a lot of your dollars. It would also be advisable to seek the services of those brokers who provide you with the opportunity to place multiple orders.

You also need to know when it is that you should be carrying out your trade. The consistency in this not only works for the beginners but the pros as well. You will not have to spend the whole day trading necessarily. The best way to achieve this consistency is to trade for say two to three hours. Understanding the best time to focus on doing your trades based on market volatility is also of the essence. Try knowing when the price moves are quite sizable and offer the best profit potential.

It would be wise to understand how to manage your risks. This involves the day's risks as well as the trading risks. For trade risks, you can reduce them to as much as 1% for each trade. This can be achieved by setting a stop loss. This will remove you from the trade, in case you start losing significantly against you. For the day's risk, you understand that one single day has the capability to ruin your entire week or even month! Setting it at around 3% of your entire capital is quite manageable. This protects you from being emotional as you make decisions in the trade as well; no matter how strong you may think you are when faced with enormous losses, your psychology always starts making hopeless and fruitless decisions that end up ruining your trade completely. Being affected emotionally by your trade is a clear indication that you are trading too much money. Day trading is more of betting, making bets in a way that the probability of winning is to your advantage, then is your ultimate success in day trade. However, the magnitude of the percentage loss that you decide on taking can change depending on the number of wins that you get as compared to the losses.

CHAPTER 1:

Why Learning Day Trading Today Is An Opportunity?

T his begs the question, why learning day trading today is an opportunity? There are many advantages of day trading so let's take the time to look at some of them.

Higher ROI on Time Investment

ROI stands for return on investment and in this case, I'm referring to the amount of time you need to spend trading in order to achieve a good return on your money. Day traders do not hold positions (an active trade is called a position) for more than the length of the market session. This means that you open a trade in the morning and exit by the time the market closes. The rest of the day is open for you! In America, the market is open from 9A.M to 5 P.M. This sounds like holding a 9 to 5 job but to be honest, there are many variations. Some traders trade just the morning session while some trade just the post lunch session. Trading volumes ebb and flow throughout the day and you may find that your most profitable trades occur in the three hour window in the morning before the lunch session begins at 12 P.M. Good day traders can earn returns of over 50% on their money after commissions so for a three hour workday, this is a pretty good payment!

Zero Gap Risk

Most beginners don't take this into account but gaps are one of the biggest reasons traders lose money. So what is a gap? Let's say the market closes at level X on Monday. It is now closed and will reopen on

Tuesday morning. In the intervening time, despite there being no orders being transacted, supply and demand for stocks doesn't stop.

The effects of these afterhours supply and demand will manifest in the opening price on Tuesday. It might open at (X+1) or at (X-50.) The difference in the previous closing price and the next opening price is called a gap. In the FX market, volatility is so high that gaps occur within a market session.

The FX market runs for 24 hours and closes only on the weekend. This means that the nature of order flow changes throughout the day. What happened in the Asian session, when Japan and Australia are online, can be very different from when London and Europe comes online and even more different from when New York comes online. Thus, you will see gaps form during the day, despite the market always being open.

With day trading in stocks, you'll close your position at the end of the day and will see zero gap risk. In FX, you can close your position as a session ends and this will reduce your risk significantly as well.

Faster Feedback

Most beginners stay away from day trading because they feel that the market moves too fast. This is true. You'll be trading lower time frames and as a result, you'll find that prices will change on a much quicker basis. Every five minutes or so, you'll have to reevaluate your stance in the market and will need to make decisions.

This fast pace of trading is not for everyone. The flip side is that if you're learning to trade, you'll gain feedback a lot faster and will improve at a faster rate. The faster you incorporate market feedback into your trading, the sooner you'll become successful. Instead of waiting for weeks or months to see if your trade works out, you'll know within a few minutes if you're doing things correctly.

CHAPTER 2:

What Is Day Trading And How To Get Started?

What is day trading?

The stock market is a vast place and there are millions of trades that take place all over the world, within a single day. There are both buyers and sellers in the market and they will all have the same motive in mind; to increase their wealth potential.

Of all these trades, not everything will be of the same nature. Some will be long-term investments and some short. Long-term investments refer to those that are held for a long period of time. They are preferred by those who are not in a hurry to make money. Short-term investments on the other hand are those that are liquidated within a short period of time. They are not meant to be held for a long time, as the owners will be interested in disposing them off early.

Short-term investments can be of many types based on the time that they are held. Some can be held for a month, some for a week and some will be disposed off on the same day.

Better known as Intraday trading, day trading is one of the most preferred ways to trade in the stock market. Preferred mostly by those willing to part with their investment within a single day and realize a profit, or loss, from.

Intraday traders are interested in realizing a profit by capitalizing on the difference in the rates of these securities as opposed to long-term investors who will be in it for the Dividends.

Difference in opinions

There is a difference of opinion in the investing community on what exactly day trading is. Some believe that the shares have to be bought and sold on the same day in order for it to count as intraday trading. Others are of the opinion that people holding it for 5 days will also count for intraday trading. When you buy a stock, you don't have to pay for it for 5 days and will also have a grace period of 2 extra days. And if you dispose of your stock within that time then it will count as intraday trading. Whatever the case, intraday trading is a great choice for both beginners and old hands. There are tips and tricks for you to follow to reel in the best results through your intraday investments. Before we proceed to understanding each type, let us look at how you can get started with intraday trading.

Laptop

The very first thing to buy is a laptop for yourself. You have to dedicate an entire computer system to day trading, as you will have to keep an eye on the markets the whole time. If you are using the computer for some other purpose as well then you might end up missing a good deal. You have to set up a different workstation if possible and only then will you be able to take it up seriously. It is a good idea to invest in a desktop as that will help you stay put in one place instead of carrying your computer around. You can also set up a computer system. Start by picking a good spot at home where you can set up the computer system. It is best for you to pick a desktop system as opposed to a laptop as the desktop will help you stay put in a single place. You will also have to have a high-speed Internet connection, without which you will not be able to buy and sell stocks fast enough.

Internet

The next thing is to get a good Internet connection. As you know, intraday trading requires you to look at the prices of stocks on a minute-to-minute basis and that is only possible if you have a fast and reliable

Internet connection. You have to have a back-up system in place as well to remain prepared for any erratic Internet. You must also have a connection on your phone, which will help you access the Internet from anywhere and keep an eye on the different stock prices.

Account

The next step is to open a trading account with a company. The trading company should be well reputed and should help you trade comfortably. You will not have to go through a lengthy process to open one and if your banker provides the service then you can ask them to open up the account for you. Remember that you need an online account in particular so that you can trade by yourself. Next, you have to create a trading account. It is what you will be using to buy and sell your stocks. The trading account should be opened through a brokering firm who will act as a connection between you and the stock market. You have to pick a firm that is well reputed in order to have a pleasant work experience. Read up some reviews about them before deciding upon the company. The account is simple to open and operate. They will ask you for some key information about yourself, after which they will issue you an online login and password.

Software

The next step is to have the software installed. The software here refers to the one that you will be using for your intraday trading. The trading company that you sign up with will provide you with the software and will also send across personnel to install it on your computer. If it is freely available on the Internet, then you can download it yourself. Once done, you will have to create a login account and only then can you start using it.

Broker

The next step is to employ a broker. A broker is one who helps you buy and sell the shares. But you have a choice. If you are willing to do it by yourself then you can employ a part time broker or not employ one at all. If you don't have the time for it and need help then you can employ a full time broker who will do everything for you including researching, buying, selling etc. The former will charge you quite less for his service whereas the latter will charge you much more. Remember that you have to employ an intraday broker in particular, as they will have knowledge on how to conduct the trading activities in the intraday market. Brokers can be quite an important part of your investment strategy, as they will have access to all the important information about your stocks. You have to find a broker that is well experienced and can help you pick the right stocks. Before you hire a broker, ensure that you do a thorough background check to see if they are good candidates for you.

Knowledge

The next step is for you to equip yourself with the knowledge of carrying out day-to-day trades in the intraday market. You have to go through other information that is present online and equip yourself as much as possible with the right type of information and trade with ease.

Research

You have to do a small research on the market trends before investing. That will help you invest in the right places. You have to look at the best stocks to invest in, in the individual categories. Once you do your research, make a list of the 5 best companies to invest with in the different categories and then further narrow them down.

Budget

It is important for you to set yourself a budget if you wish to trade wisely. The budget should be such that it allows you to invest in a variety of stocks and still remain with spare money that you can divert towards a backup account. The budget should be based on your spending capacity and how much you have at your disposal. It is best to consult an expert first to know how much you must ideally hold.

Buy stocks

Next, you have to buy the stocks. These stocks are picked from the stock market and you have to have a good variety to start with. It is best to observe the stocks for some time before making your final decision. Once you have made your choice, you can buy the stocks.

Generate a Watch list

A watch list can come in handy when you wish to keep track of the different stocks you own. A watch list is meant to help you study the different stocks so that you know exactly when to sell them. If you think a particular stock is going the way you want it to, then you can generate another list with just that one stock in it.

Sell your stocks

The next logical step is for you to sell your stocks. You have to ring in a profit and the only way to do so is by selling whatever is in your possession. But you have to ensure that you sell it when the stock's price is high. Don't sell it just to get rid of it, you have to remain patient and sell it only when the right time comes.

Repeat the steps

The next step is for you to repeat all the above steps, again. So, start by buying stocks, hold them and then sell them. You have to do this on a daily basis if you plan on being an intraday trader.

Journal

You have to maintain a journal where you will have to write down your daily experiences. This journal should help you keep track of your investments and tell you as to where your money has gone. You can invest in a digital diary or buy a physical journal.

These form the different things that you must do in order to start with your intraday investments on the right foot.

CHAPTER 3:

Interest Rates

Exchange Rates and Interest Rates

Fluctuations in the interest rates of a nation also disturb its currency because of its effect on the Demand and supply of financial resources in the U.K. and abroad. For instance, high-interest rates compared to other countries make U.K. business-friendly to stakeholders, leading to higher Demand for U.K.'s financial resources and higher Demand for Pound Sterling.

On the other hand, lower interest duties in one country compared to other countries contribute to higher supply, as speculators sell currency to buy currencies connected with higher interest rates. Such hypothetical flows are called hot money and have an essential influence on exchange rates in the short run.

The Demand for Currency

The market for currencies is consequent from a country's Demand for exports, and from investors trying to benefit from currency value changes.

The Supply of Currency

The availability of a currency is determined by the domestic Demand for foreign imports. For instance, when the U.K. imports cars from Japan, they have to pay in yen and sell pounds to buy yen. The more it imports into the foreign exchange market, the larger the supply of pounds. A substantial proportion of short-term currency trading is by traders who work for financial institutes. The foreign exchange market of London is the single biggest currency exchange market in the whole world.

Supply and Demand

Supply and Demand run the foreign exchange (or Forex) market, much like every other market in the world. Indeed, knowing the idea of supply and Demand in the Forex market is so critical that we can take a step back into Economics 101 for a minute to make sure we're all on the same page. Having a firm knowledge of supply and Demand would make all the difference in your Forex investment career because it will give you the prospect to search through the daily news mountain and find the most exciting messages. And how does the Forex market is affected by both supply and Demand?

Supply is the indicator of how much of a given product at any particular time is accessible. The value of a product, in this case, a currency, is directly connected to its production. The currency would get less cost, with the currency supply rising. On the other hand, money becomes more valuable as the currency supply drops.

Think of diamonds and rocks. Since rocks are everywhere, they're not really useful. You can walk along a country path and pick from hundreds or even thousands of rocks. On the other side, diamonds are costly because many of them aren't on track. A limited volume of diamonds is available internationally, so if you like it, you have to offer a fee.

We find Demand, on the other hand, of the economic calculation. Demand is the indicator of how much customers desire to buy one particular product at any particular moment. Currency demand has the reverse impact on currency value than availability. The currency gets more expensive as the market for a currency rises. Alternatively, the currency is less competitive as Demand for a currency decline.

You just have to look at Tickle Me Elmo in order to get a clear sense of the impact demand may have on anything's price. Upon the first appearance of Tickle Me Elmo, the market for the product was insane. Parents trampled on each other so anyone else could wipe Elmo off their arms and make sure that they both got on their kid's list. To those not fast or competitive enough to bring Tickle Me, Elmo, from the market, it was their last resort to pay outrageously high rates on eBay. This giant red giggling doll had become a tremendous demand far more desirable than it would have been if it had been desired by no one's girl.

So, the trick to be effective in the currency market is to know about where the supply on the market is increasing and where Demand is rising. In this competitive industry, if you can choose that, you're well on your way to making a huge profit.

We consider utilizing the "seesaw of supply and demand" to show yourself a very good view of what is happening in the money market environment. And it is with one currency that influences each currency pair you are willing to exchange that is the best way to start this: U.S. dollar.

CHAPTER 4:

Retail Vs Institutional Traders

R etail traders are individuals who can be either part-time or full
traders but don't work for a firm, and are not managing funds
from other people. These traders hold a small percentage of the
volume in the trade market.

On the other hand, institutional traders are composed of hedge funds,
mutual funds, and investment banks who are often armed with
advanced software, and are usually engaged in high-frequency trading.

Nowadays, human involvement is quite minimal in the operations of
investment firms. Backed up by professional analysts and huge
investments, institutional investors can be quite aggressive.

So at this point, you might be wondering how a beginner like you can
compete against the big players?

Our advantage is the freedom and flexibility we enjoy. Institutional
traders have the legal obligation to trade. Meanwhile, individual traders
are free to trade or to take a break from trading if the market is currently
unstable.

Institutional traders should be active in the market and trade huge
volumes of stocks regardless of the stock price. Individual traders are
free to sit out and trade if there are possible opportunities in the market.

But sadly, most retail traders do not possess the know-how in
identifying the right time to be active and the best time to wait. If you
want to be profitable in day trading, you need to eliminate greed and
develop patience.

The biggest problem of losers in day trading is not the size of their accounts or the lack of access to technology, but their sheer lack of discipline. Many are prone to bad money management and over-trading.

Some retail traders are successful by following the guerilla strategy, which refers to the unconventional approach to trading derived from guerilla warfare. Guerilla combatants are skilled in using hit-and-run tactics like raids, sabotage, and ambushes to manipulate a bigger and less-mobile conventional opponent.

The US military is considered as one of the strongest armies in the modern world. But this mighty force suffered humiliation caused by the guerilla warfare used by North Vietnam during the Vietnam War.

Following this analogy, guerilla trading involves waiting or hiding until you are ready to grab an opportunity to win small battles in the financial warfare. This can help you gain fast revenue while minimizing your risk.

Remember, your mission is not to defeat institutional traders. Instead, you should focus on waiting for the right opportunity to earn your target income.

As a retail trader, you can make profits from market volatility. It can be impossible to make money if the markets are flat. Only institutional traders have the tools, expertise, and money to gamble in such circumstances.

You must learn how to choose stocks that can help you make fast decisions to the downside or upside in a predictable approach. On the other hand, institutional traders follow high frequency trading, which allows them to profit from very small price movements.

As a retail trader, you should only work in the retail domain The advantage of retail trading is that other retail traders also use them. The more traders use these strategies, the better they can work.

As more traders learn effective stock market strategies, more people will join the market so more stocks will move up faster. The more players in the market, the faster it will move. This is the reason why it is important for successful traders to share their strategies. This will not only help other traders to become more profitable, but it can also increase the number of traders who are using proven strategies.

There's no benefit in hiding these strategies or keeping them secret. In computer-aided trading, most of the stocks will follow the trend of the market, unless there's a good reason not to follow. Therefore, when the market is rising, most stocks will also move up. If the overall market is declining, the prices of the stocks will also decline.

But you should also bear in mind that there will be a handful of stocks that can go against the grain because they have a catalyst.

But for a brief overview, Alpha Predators are what retail traders are hunting for. These stocks usually tank when the markets are running, and they run when the markets are tanking.

It is generally okay if the market is running, and the stocks are running as well. Just be sure that you are trading stocks that are moving because they have a valid reason to move, and are not just moving with the general market conditions.

Probably, you are wondering what the basic catalyst for stocks is to make them ideal for day trading.

Here are some catalysts:

- Debt offerings

- Buybacks

- Stock splits

- Management changes

- Layoffs

- Restructuring

- Major contract wins / losses

- Partnerships / alliances

- Major product releases

- Mergers and / or acquisitions

- FDA approval / disapproval

- Earnings surprises

- Earnings reports

Retail traders who are engaged in reversal trades usually choose stocks that are selling off because there has been some bad press about the company. Whenever there's a fast sell-off because of bad press, many traders will notice and begin monitoring the stock for what is called a bottom reversal.

It can be difficult to perform a reversal trade if the stocks are trending down with the overall market like what happened to oil several years ago. The stock value increases by 20 cents and you may think it is a reversal. Then they are quickly sold off for another 60 cents. The sell-off is happening because the stocks are getting bad press.

For a while, oil was a weak sector and the majority of the energy and oil stocks were selling off. If a sector is weak, then it is not a good time for a reversal trade. This is where you need to identify the reason behind any significant movement in the market.

In order to do that, you need to remember the fourth rule in day trading:

Rule No. 4 - Always ask: is this stock moving because the general market is moving, or there's a unique catalyst behind this movement?

Research is crucial at this point. As you gain experience as a day trader, you will need to identify the difference between general market trends and catalyst-based movements. As a day trader, you need to be careful that you are not on the wrong side of the trade, and going against institutional traders.

How can you do that?

Stay away from trading stocks that are not getting enough attention. You will be in a sandbox doing your own thing. Go where everyone else is going. Concentrate on the stocks that are moving every day and are getting attention from retail traders.

Are blue-chip stocks like IBM, Coca-Cola, or Apple ideal for retail traders? You can try, but you need to remember that these are slow-paced stocks, which are heavily dominated by algorithmic traders and institutional traders. Plus, they are often very hard to trade.

How can you identify the stocks that are alluring retail traders? There are some proven ways to do this.

First, you can use day trading stock scanners. Basically, the stocks that are significantly moving up or down are the stocks that are being monitored by retail traders.

Second, find online community groups or social media groups where retail traders hang out. Twitter and Stock Twits are often good places to learn what is currently trending. If you regularly follow successful traders, then you may see for yourself what everyone is following. There's a big advantage to being part of a community of day traders.

You can read the insights of traders and the specific stocks they are considering. If you are a lone trader, then you may be out of touch in the market. You will just make it difficult for yourself because you will not know where the action is.

CHAPTER 5:

Advantage And Negatives Of Day Trading

The first time I told my friends that I started day trading, I got two types of reactions: those who did not know anything about it thought that I was one of those big shots at Wall Street, who could be earning thousands or even millions of dollars every year. Meanwhile, those who had some understanding about investing and trading, since they were doing similar things themselves, probably thought I was a nut case.

Day trading is controversial. Some traders believe that it is a get-rich-quick scheme, and you know how people feel and think about that: the faster you climb, the quicker and harder you fall. In other words, while you gain something faster than you think, you also lose a lot in return.

They were concerned that I was about to lose my money—let me correct that. I think they believed that I would go bankrupt. Of course, I lost capital, but I did not have to file for bankruptcy.

Perhaps these people also do not understand the simple fact that day trading is not for everyone.

Advantage Of Day Trading

You should probably consider day trading if:

• **You want to earn profits at the end of the day.** The idea that it is a "get rich quick" scheme may be part truth since you do get to earn a profit after the market closes. For example, let us pretend that you invested $100 for 100 shares. The market fluctuation is in your favor so when you sell it you double your money, which means you now have revenue of $2 per share—not too shabby, right?

•   **You want to think less about your investments.** This is because once the market closes, your trading also ends. Whether you win or lose, that is left to your skill and fate. The main point is that you will not have to think about whether your stock value will fall the next day or whether US dollar is going to be strong in the following week. You think day by day, moment by moment.

•   **You can build cash inflow and liquidity very quickly** – This can be related to the first point. Because you can earn revenues and profits by the end of the day, you can also boost your assets, which then means you can buy more securities and increase your chance of earning more money in a short period of time. I highly encourage that you diversify your portfolio even if they belong to the same class (e.g. class of stocks) to protect yourself in deep market fluctuations, which are not that common anyway.

•   **You are better protected against market fluctuations.** Okay, I mentioned just a while ago that diversification can help shield you from deep fluctuations in the market. But here is something to be happy about: the likelihood that it is going to dip extremely low is very small. As expected, market prices can change very fast in a blink of an eye, but the movements are often small.

•   **You can be your own boss.** As a retail trader, you call the shots. You decide how much to invest, where to put your money, when to buy or sell, how much you like to earn, the securities you like to trade, etc.

•   **You have help.** You may be a beginner, but the learning curve is not as difficult as it is with other securities or types of investing or trading. A variety of materials are available to make sure you do not have to trade blindly.

Negative Day Trading

If day trading is not as bad as others say, now why should I say it is not meant for everyone?

• **It requires a lot of time.** Okay, all types of work or endeavor needs it. I still have to find one that does not, and if it is legal and good, then I am definitely in. But when I say a lot, I truly mean it. You see, although there are specific hours of the day when you trade best, you still have to be alert as long as the market stays open because you will never really know what is going to happen. Stock prices could plunge, which gives you the perfect moment to buy blue chips or those that you can't afford before. If the European forex session is bad, there is a good chance US's session will suffer the same fate as well. It is almost the same scenario when we talk about other securities like bonds, hedge contracts, futures, or commodities.

Let us not forget too that you would have to do your research after or in between trading!

• **It is risky.** To be honest, life is all about and related to risk. You are surrounded by it. When you cross the road or drive the car, you run the risk of meeting an accident. When you sleep, there is still a good chance you will never wake up! Have you heard of the term idiopathic? In science, it means a disease or a condition happens with no known or determined cause. It is simply saying it occurred just because it can.

The levels of risks we face on a daily basis, however, can vary. In the world of day trading, it can be on opposite ends, depending on how you trade and how much you put in. The bigger the money, the bigger the possible loss. The higher the returns, the higher the chance of falling hard. Losing is all part of the game. The problem comes in if you lose everything—that is a possibility, you know.

• **It can make you emotional.** What has emotion got to do with day trading or any kind of trading for that matter? A whole lot than you can imagine. I remember the first time I earned a profit in day trading.

It was not much, for someone who is just beginning, it meant something. I was so ecstatic I tried to trade more. Sadly, I lost the next day what I gained and traded. On the other hand, I know of friends who turn into monsters—angry, bitter, resentful, and irritable—once they begin trading. You can blame it on pressure, sense of competition, pride, or whatever. Whether you like it or not, day trading can get to you, and in many days, it is not a pleasant activity to do.

The relationship between emotions and commerce is strong. Many studies have already shown that customers are more likely to buy items on impulse and buy products that capture their emotions. The theory or concept of scarcity to sell something is also based on emotion. By instilling fear—the idea that if they do not act fast they can no longer take advantage of the offer—is what has earned several businesspeople millions or even billions of dollars.

You can therefore not avoid being emotional, whether it is positive or negative, when you are trading. However, you should learn how to control it and/or decrease its influence and impact on your decisions.

• **It can make you complacent.** These days it is so easy to get confident or even cocky with day trading. After all, you have more tools and resources compared to many years ago. You even have auto programs who can do the trading for you just in case you want have some me time in the middle of the day. But complacency can be one of your biggest mistakes. As you relax, that is when you become least prepared for the uncertainties. Your software can bog down, the analyses it provides you can be wrong, markets go down quickly without you knowing it—these things you could have resolved to minimize effect on you only if you have paid attention and be more proactive or do your part.

• **There are fees.** A lot of people think that they can just trade for free. Of course, it does not work that way. You have different expenses and fees to pay including commissions for every execution (e.g. buying or selling). And there are tax implications! Yup, you still have to pay your taxes because you are getting some profit from the transaction. In fact, taxes are higher for short-term investments such as those of day trading than the ones held for a long time, which is at least a year. But the good news is there are caps set. Also, if you're having a loss, you can write it off up to the amount of your capital gains. In cases where you have more losses than gains in a year, you can go beyond the amount of your capital gains and carry it over the succeeding year. For instance, for last year, you have 10,000 capital gains and $15,000 loss. You can zero your capital gains liability, leaving you with $5,000 more loss. You can then further reduce your tax liability by $3,000 and offset the next capital gains this year with $2,000. If you declare $18,000 capital gains this year, then your total liability is only $16,000.

Can You Do It for a Living?

Now that you know the advantage and negative parts of day trading, it's time that you answer the question: Can you do it for a living? By this, I mean you trade not just as a hobby or a one-time thing or an occasional gig. I mean you do it every day for as long as you can.

To help you answer that question, I have some more questions to ask:

• **Are you willing to invest money?** I am not just talking about hundreds or a couple of dollars. I am talking about thousands of them. As you go along the way, or as you trade for many years, you'll realize that you may be trading already a million dollars!

• **Are you ready to lose?** Between winning and losing, we definitely know what's a lot harder to take and get over with.

• **Are you ready to win?** Surprising question, isn't it? Why is it important for you to be ready for it? The answer is simple: I don't want you to be complacent. Haven't you noticed that when everything in your life is going well, you tend to forget about what's happening around you? You pay less attention to them because you think your life is so good it doesn't matter what is occurring around you anymore.

• **Are you willing to learn?** Many of my friends can attest that one of the beauties of day trading is the huge opportunity to earn and learn at the same time. I for one believe that you can't put a price tag on education even if it means committing mistakes first before you learn your lessons. You also need to learn too as the market is dynamic, and you need to change and grow along with it.

• **Are you ready to take the risks?** If you don't, then the immediate answer to the main question is big NO.

• **Are you willing to sacrifice?** Day trading requires commitment of your skill, time, effort, knowledge, and expertise. If you can't give a hundred percent of any of these to it, then you're not ready to make this a living.

Think about it.

CHAPTER 6:

Types Of Trading

There are different reasons some traders love to use forex instead of the stock market. One of them is the forex leverage.

When it comes to forex trading, the entire system is totally different. Before you can trade using leverage, you need to have opened the forex trading account. That's the only requirement that is out there, nothing else. When you open a forex account, you can easily use the leverage feature.

If you are trading in the United States of America, you will be restricted to a leveraging of 50: 1 leveraging. Countries outside of the US are restricted to leverage of about 200: 1. It is better when you are outside the US, than in the US. Liquidity differences

When you decide to trade stocks, you end up purchasing the companies' shares that have a cost from a bit of dollars down to even hundreds of dollars. Usually, the price in the market tends to share with demand and supply.

Paired trades

When you trade with forex, you are facing another world, unseen in the stock market. Though the currency of a country tends to change, there will always be a great supply of currency that you can trade. What this means is that the main currencies in the world tend to be very liquid. When you are in forex trading, you will see that the currencies are normally quoted in pairs. They are not quoted alone. This means that you should be interested in the country's economic health that you have decided to trade in. The economic health of the country tends to affect the worth of the currency.

The basic considerations change from one forex market to the next. If you decide to purchase the Intel shares, the main aim is to see if the stock's value will improve. You aren't interested in how the prices of other stocks are.

On the other hand, if you have decided to sell or buy forex, you need to analyze the economies of those countries that are involved in the pairs.

You should find out if the country has better jobs, GDP, as well as political prospects.

To do a successful trade in the Forex market, you will be expected to analyze not only one financial entity, but two.

The forex market tends to show higher level of sensitivity in upcoming economic and political scenarios in many countries.

You should note that the U.S. stock market, unlike many other stock markets is not so sensitive to a lot of foreign matters.

Price sensitivity to trade activities

When we look at both markets, we have no choice but to notice that there is varying price sensitivity when it comes to trade activities done.

If a small company that has fewer shares has about ten thousand shares bought from it, it could go a long way to impact the price of the stock. For a big company such as Apple, such n number of shares when bought from it won't affect the stock price.

When you look at forex trades, you will realize that trades of a few hundreds of millions of dollars won't affect the major currency at all. If it affects, it would be minute.

Market accessibility

It is easy to access the currency market, unlike its counterpart, the stock market. Though you may be able to trade stocks every second of the day, five days weekly in the twenty first century, it is not easy.

A lot of retail investors end up trading via a United States brokerage that makes use of a single major trading period every day, which spans from 9: 30 AM to 4: 00 PM. They go ahead to have a minute trading hour past that time, and this period has price and volatility issues, which end up dissuading a lot of retail traders from making use of such time. Forex trading is different. One can carry out such trading every second of the day because there are a lot of forex exchanges in the world, and they are constantly trading in one time zone or the other.

Forex Trading Vs Options

A trader may believe the United States Dollar will become better when compared to the Euro, and if the results pan out, the person earns.

CHAPTER 7:

Platforms And Broker

Platforms

If you are an experienced trader and you want to take a chance at taking on the market, you probably know what you want in a brokerage like comprehensive trading platforms, innovative strategy tools, premium research, and low costs. We have chosen some of the best brokers that you can use only in several different categories, so you will be able to choose one that is based on your personal priorities.

These next brokers have great pricing over their competitors and they have great trading tools and platforms:

Interactive Brokers and Options House have a powerful combination that each trader wants: Advanced trading tools and platforms paired with low commissions. Interactive Brokers tend to be the choice of traders that like per share pricing and is able to meet a minimum account of $10,000 with a minimum monthly commission of $10. This slightly affects their rating. Options House, on the other hand, gives traders a flat rate, and they don't require a minimum balance. The downside is they don't have forex trading. Interactive Brokers gives you access to forex, futures, and precious metals.

These brokers offer the most powerful platforms that are available without any fees or minimums:

Options House and Interactive Brokers have powerful platforms. Charles Schwab and TD Ameritrade also surpass others. TD Ameritrade probably has the best platform out there, think or swim, as well as Trade Architect that is very simple to use. Charles Schwab also gives you two great platforms: Streetsamrt.com is a great platform for beginners. Street-smart Edge is a more advanced functionality in charting. Both of which can be used by traders and they don't require any balance or activity minimums. Remember that there is an avoidable account minimum account balance of $1,000.

These brokers offer powerful tools and competitive pricing for options traders:

Trade Station and Options press are two more great options for traders to use. Which one you like the best will depend on what you are looking for in trade activity and platform needs. Trade Station is aimed more towards the professional trader. This platform will cost $99.95 each month, which is waived if you trade at least 5,000 shares, ten futures options or round-turn futures contracts, 50 options contracts, or carried a $100,000 balance. Trade Station's pricing is favorable to bulk traders, which give per-contract, flat fees, or volume discounts. Options Xpress don't require trade or account balance minimums, carry the extra fees, or offers competitive commissions, and they don't have vigorous trading. Trades with Options Xpress only cost $1.25 for each contract for traders who are active, and they have a $12.95 minimum charge for ten or fewer contracts

Traders that utilize margin needs to prioritize broker's margin rates while they search. These online brokers have the lowest margin rates:

None of the others can even come close to Interactive Brokers when you look at their margin rates. If margin rates are your priority, then this is a good option for you. This broker will charge you a grouped rate that is based on the balance of your account but also has a calculator to help traders to perform their math quicker. Interactive Brokers do have a minimum of monthly trade. E-Option's deposit requirement is a lot lower, and they have a more reasonable trade requirement. They only charge a $50 inactivity fee when you don't trade at least two times a year or who has less than $100,000 in debit or credit balances. Both of these options have competitive commissions for their options and stock trades.

Who Is A Broker?

This is someone who buys and sells goods or things on behalf of someone else. They mostly are middle men in transactions, that often they make profit out of. They only have to organize and plan for transactions to take place between a purchaser/buyer and a vendor/seller. The broker ends up getting a commission out of the deal, either from the buyer or seller. Most of the time they represent the seller.

Brokers may be individuals or firms. When it is a firm, it still acts as a go between their customer and the vendor.

Brokers exist in many different industries. An example would be real estate brokers who advertise and sell properties on behalf of the owners. We also have insurance brokers who sell insurance on behalf of firms. We have stock market brokers who work on the stock market.

Why Use A Broker?

There are a few advantages of using brokers in any kind of business. As usual, before getting into any business with a broker, always do intensive research on what you are about to get into. There are a few bad crops in the market.

They know their market well

Most brokers are people or firms who have been in the field for quite a while and always know what is best for one client to the other. They also know who to talk to if you need anything specific and always do it well knowing they will benefit.

Brokers have been on the market for a long time and have seen what goes on and know too well what to expect. They have all the information you need right from the time you enter the market to the time you leave.

They are particularly important when you are entering a foreign market that you aren't familiar with. You need to take time and look for the perfect broker that will tell you what you need and how to do things the right way. However, you need to be wary of the brokers who are out to exploit you. Use referrals and other methods to try and get the right broker who understands your needs.

Wider representation

A client is able to reach more people or a wide marker when using a broker, compared to them doing it by themselves. Brokers are also quite affordable, and have a network they work with; hence there is limited cost incurrence with them. Because most of them are well known, they are able to reach a wider market ratio easily.

When you decide to work with a broker, you get to cast your net wider so that you can get better business. Coming up with a network takes time, which is why it is just right that you work with a person that already has a network which you can tap in. This saves you time and effort, as well as money. Take time to work with a broker that already has a network of established clients.

Special skills and knowledge

Brokers mostly have special knowledge of the field they are in and are good at the specific brokerage area. This is because they work in detail so as to know the needs of different types of clients. Because of this, they are an asset to anyone who is looking for their services.

The skills that a broker has vary from customer relationship management to money management. They will help you to grow your empire as you sit and wait for them to do the work you want. It takes experience and a lot of patience for you to learn the skills and be able to do the things that a broker can do. So, always make use of a broker when making trading decisions.

Customer choice

Brokers always work with the customer's choice. They will always want to know what one needs they will always endeavor to ensure the customer is satisfied and has what they originally wanted, or better.

Time saving

Because they mostly know their trade well, a broker would be able to achieve more within a shorter period of time for the customer. This is because of their great networking within their field of specialization. They always know where to find what, at what time and for what amount.

The time that you save when you work with a broker can be used to handle other tasks that you have. Take time to make sure the broker knows what they are doing otherwise you will end up wasting a lot of time.

Types of Brokers

- Stock broker
- Business broker
- Pawn Broker
- Information broker
- Insurance broker
- Investment broker

CHAPTER 8:

What Is An Option Contracts

An options contract sounds fancy but it's a pretty simple concept.

• It's a contract. That means it's a legal agreement between a buyer and a seller.

• It gives the purchaser of the contract the opportunity to purchase or dispose of an asset with a fixed amount.

• The purchase is optional – so the buyer of the contract does not have to buy or sell the asset.

• The contract has an expiration date, so the purchaser – if they choose to exercise their right – must make the trade on or before the expiration date.

• The purchaser of the contract pays a non-refundable fee for the contract.

Suppose you are itching to buy a BMW and you've decided the model you want must be silver. You drop by a local dealer and it turns out they don't have a silver model in stock. The dealer claims he can get you one by the end of the month. You say you'll take the car if the dealer can get it by the last day of the month and he'll sell it to you for $67,500. He agrees and requires you to put a $3,000 deposit on the car.

If the last day of the month arrives and the dealer hasn't produced the car, then you're freed from the contract and get your money back. In the event he does produce the car at any date before the end of the month, you have the option to buy it or not. If you really wanted the car you can buy it, but of course, you can't be forced to buy the car, and maybe you've changed your mind in the interim.

The right is there but not the obligation to purchase, in short, no pressure if you decided not to push through with the purchase of the car. If you decide to let the opportunity pass, however, since the dealer met his end of the bargain and produced the car, you lose the $3,000 deposit.

In this case, the dealer, who plays the role of the writer of the contract, has the obligation to follow through with the sale based upon the agreed upon price.

Suppose that when the car arrives at the dealership, BMW announces it will no longer make silver cars. As a result, prices of new silver BMW is that were the last ones to roll off the assembly line, skyrocket. Other dealers are selling their silver BMW is for $100,000. However, since this dealer entered into an options contract with you, he must sell the car to you for the pre-agreed price of $67,500. You decide to get the car and drive away smiling, knowing that you saved $32,500 and that you could sell it at a profit if you wanted to.

The situation here is capturing the essence of options contracts, even if you've never thought of haggling with a car dealer in those terms.

An option is in a sense a kind of bet. In the example of the car, the bet is that the dealer can produce the exact car you want within the specified time period and at the agreed upon price. The dealer is betting too. His bet is that the pre-agreed to price is a good one for him. Of course, if BMW stops making silver cars, then he's made the wrong bet.

It can work the other way too. Let's say that instead of BMW deciding not to make silver cars anymore when your car is being driven onto the lot, another car crashes into it. Now your silver BMW has a small dent on the rear bumper with some scratches. As a result, the car has immediately declined in value. But if you want the car, since you've agreed to the options contract, you must pay $67,500, even though with the dent it's only really worth $55,000. You can walk away and lose your $3,000 or pay what is now a premium price on a damaged car.

Another example that is commonly used to explain options contracts is the purchase of a home to be built by a developer under the agreement that certain conditions are met. The buyer will be required to put a non-refundable down payment or deposit on the home. Let's say that the developer agrees to build them the home for $300,000 provided that a new school is built within 5 miles of the development within one year. So, the contract expires within a year. At any time during the year, the buyer has the option to go forward with the construction of the home for $300,000 if the school is built. The developer has agreed to the price no matter what. So if the housing market in general and the construction of the school, in particular, drive up demand for housing in the area, and the developer is selling new homes that are now priced at $500,000, he has to sell this home for $300,000 because that was the price agreed to when the contract was signed. The home buyer got what they wanted, being within 5 miles of the new school with the home price fixed at $300,000. The developer was assured of the sale but missed out on the unknown, which was the skyrocketing price that occurred as a result of increased demand. On the other hand, if the school isn't built and the buyers don't exercise their option to buy the house before the contract expires at one year, the developer can pocket the $20,000 cash.

CHAPTER 9:

Call And Put Option On The Stock Market

Call Option

A call option comes with an expiration date. You can find options that expire in the current week, over the next few weeks to a month, out to several months to two year from the present date.

Why Invest in Call Options?

You buy a call option when you are bullish on a stock. In other words, you buy a call option when you are expecting the price of the underlying stock to rise. Theoretically, if you are buying a call option, you are hoping to buy shares of stock at the strike price, which you expect to be lower than the market price at some point.

So, let's say that a stock is trading at $99 a share. You could buy a call option with a strike price of $100 a share, if there is a consensus that the stock is going to see a significant rise in prices before the option expires. Say for the sake of example that the option costs you $1. Options prices are quoted on a per share basis, so that means you have to spend $100 to buy the option.

Now say that before the option expires, the share price goes up as expected, say to $103 a share. Now you have two possibilities. When the price of the underlying stock goes up, the value of the option contract goes up as well. Maybe the price of the option has risen to $1.50 per share, say. So, in that case, you can simply sell the option and take the $0.50 per share profit.

You can also choose to exercise the option. This means you can buy the stock at the strike price of $100 a share, even though the market price of the stock has risen to $103 a share. So, your total expense is now $101 a share since you paid $1 to buy the option (assuming zero commissions, which is reasonable these days). So now, you can turn around and sell the stock at $103 a share on the open market, earning yourself a profit of $2 a share. And in some cases, investors may decide to keep the stock that they have now been able to purchase at a discount.

Breakeven Price.

An important concept in options trading is the breakeven price. For a call option, the breakeven price is the strike price + the price paid to buy the option, on a per share basis. So, if you are buying an option with a strike price of $212 for $2.50, the breakeven price is simply $212 + $2.50 = $214.50. This means that the share price must rise to at least $214.50 before exercising the option even warrants consideration, otherwise you would be losing money as a buyer. For options sellers, the breakeven price is important to note as well. If you are selling to open call options, you don't have to worry if the market price of the stock stays at or below the breakeven price. In this example, a call options seller would be fine as long as the stock price stayed at or below $214.50.

The Call Seller.

An options contract goes on the market when a seller "writes" the contract. For retail traders (individual, small traders) you sell to open from a list of available options. So, you would find a call option with an expiration date and strike price that you like, and then you sell it using your brokerage software. There are three ways that you can sell a call option, the most basic way is to sell a covered call. To do this, you would need 100 shares of the underlying stock. Keep in mind that there is a risk you will lose ownership of the shares; in the event the option is exercised, and the shares are "called away" from you. But a carefully selected strike price and expiration date can lower your risk. The goal of selling a covered call option is to generate income from shares of stock that you own. Remember that the breakeven price is going to be something to keep your eye on in this case.

In those types of strategies, there is a single transaction involving multiple options that are bought and sold, and so using a strategy you are never going to be selling a single option.

Finally, you can sell a call option "naked", which means that you don't own the shares of stock. You must be a level four trader in order to sell naked options.

The call seller has a risk of assignment. That means, if the share price rises above the breakeven price, a buyer of an option may choose to exercise the option. As a seller you will be assigned and that means you will be forced to sell 100 shares of stock at the strike price. Many articles about options will assert that most options expire worthless, but the reality is if the option you have sold goes "in the money", there is a real risk that the option will be exercised. In fact, options that expire in the money are often automatically exercised by the broker. Check with your broker to find out their specific policies.

Profits from Call Options.

If you are buying call options, then you are hoping to make a profit from either exercising the option or simply selling it at a profit. Most beginning options traders are going to be working with smaller amounts of capital, and so you are probably not going to be interested in exercising the option. Rather, you are going to earn profits from the option itself. As the price of the underlying stock increases, the value of a call option increases as well.

There are several factors working in options pricing, and so you have to take more than just the underlying price of the stock into account. The most important of these is the expiration date. Simply put, the more time there is until an option expires, the more valuable it is. The value in the options price is referred to as time value, and it also makes up a part of "extrinsic" value of the option. With each passing day, the option will lose time value. At market open, that amount is automatically deducted from the options price. That doesn't mean you can't hold options overnight, because other factors will be operating to push up the price of the option as well, and this may overwhelm the decline in price from the loss of time value. This loss of time value is called "time decay".

The most important factor in the price of the option, therefore, is the underlying share price on the open market. For a call option, whenever the share price increases, the value of the option is going to increase. This happens most strongly for in the money options, but all call options will increase in value when there is a movement upward in the share price. So, you can even earn significant profits from out of the money options on a day when there are large upward movements in the price of the stock. These movements don't have to be particularly large; a single dollar rise in share price can mean anywhere from a $50 to $100 increase in the price of an option. So, you could buy an option in the morning and if the share price rises by a dollar during the day, you could sell it for a $50 to $100 profit. The more the share price rises, the more profit is possible. While out of the money options will often yield lower profit amounts for a given share price movement, the profits can still be substantial.

Put Option

Put options work in many ways in the same manner as call options. They have an expiration date, they have 100 shares of underlying stock, and their price depends on the price of the underlying stock. Meanwhile, they also suffer from time decay as the expiration date of the option approaches. However, put options actually gain value when the stock price drops, and they lose value when the stock price rises.

This means that put options can be used to "short" the stock. Shorting the stock is just jargon for earning a profit when the stock price declines. Normally, shorting a stock works like this. If you think that a stock is going to drop in value, you borrow shares from your broker – and you immediately sell them on the market at the current stock price. Then, assuming that your bet was the correct one, you buy the shares back when the price drops. Suppose for the sake of example that when you initially borrowed the shares, you sold them at $100 a share. Then the price drops to $80 a share – maybe the company had a bad earnings call, for example. When the price drops, you buy the shares back at $80 a share, and you return them to the broker (remember, you started the process by borrowing shares from the broker). This exercise leaves you with a $20 per share profit.

Of course, most small investors don't have $10,000 or more to chance on schemes like this, but put options enable you to earn profits if the price of a stock declines, using much smaller investments. The idea is basically the same, but when you suspect that the price of a stock is going to drop in the near future, you can buy put options on the stock. A put option has a strike price just like a call option, and when the share price is below the strike price, the put option is in the money. That's because you would be able to buy shares of stock at the market price, and then sell them at the strike price – earning a profit in the process.

Using the same example, we considered before, you could buy a put option with a $100 strike price. Then when the price of the shares dropped to $80, you could buy them on the market, and then sell them to the originator of the put option contract at the strike price - $100 a share. Buying a put option is something that doesn't require a large margin account to do.

When a put option is exercised, that is you sell the stock at the strike price, they say that the stock was "put to" the originator of the option contract. Of course, most options traders are not looking to exercise individual put options. If the stock price were really to drop $20 a share on a stock where you bought put options with a $100 strike price, the value of the put options would go up substantially, because you could exercise them and make solid profits. Since there are other traders who would be interested in selling the stock, you will be able to sell your put option to another trader for a profit. Remember that if you buy to open an options contract, you are not obligated to anything and are free and clear once you sell it to someone else.

Think of put options in the same way as call options, but with the price going up $100 every time the stock drops by $1. Like call options, the pricing of put options is impacted by many factors, and so this is an ideal relationship that we are thinking about here. But it gives you a rule of thumb to understand how put options work (the more in the money they are, the closer they are going to get to the ideal case). Likewise, if the price of the stock rises by $1, the value of a put option would move down by $100.

CHAPTER 10:

Volatily In The Markets

Volatility is something that long-term investors ignore. It's why you will hear people that promote conservative investment strategies suggesting that buyers use dollar cost averaging. What this does is it averages out the volatility in the market. That way you don't risk making the mistake of buying stocks when the price is a bit higher than it should be, because you'll average that out by buying shares when it's a bit lower than it should be.

In a sense, over the short term, the stock market can be considered as a chaotic system. So from one day to the next, unless there is something specific on offer, like Apple introducing a new gadget that investors are going to think will be a major hit, you can't be sure what the stock price is going to be tomorrow or the day after that. An increase on one day doesn't mean more increases are coming; it might be followed by a major dip the following day.

For example, at the time of writing, checking Apple's stock price, on the previous Friday it bottomed out at $196. Over the following days, it went up and down several times, and on the most recent close, it was $203. The movements over a short-term period appear random, and to a certain extent, they are. It's only over the long term that we see the actual direction that Apple is heading.

Of course, Apple is at the end of a ten-year run that began with the introduction of the iPhone and iPad. It's a reasonable bet that while it's a solid long-term investment, the stock probably isn't going to be moving enough for the purposes of making good profits over the short term from trades on call options (not too mention the per share price is relatively high).

The truth is volatility is actually a friend of the trader who buys call options. But it's a friend you have to be wary of because you can benefit from volatility while also getting in big trouble from it.

The reason stocks with more volatility are the friend of the options trader is that in part the options trader is playing a probability game. In other words, you're looking for stocks that have a chance of beating the strike price you need in order to make profits. A volatile stock that has large movements has a greater probability of not only passing your strike price but doing so in such a fashion that it far exceeds your strike price enabling you to make a large profit.

Of course, the alternative problem exists – that the stock price will suddenly drop. That is why care needs to be a part of your trader's toolkit. A stock with a high level of volatility is just as likely to suddenly drop in price as it is to skip right past your strike price.

Moreover, while you're a beginner and might get caught with your pants down, volatile stocks are going to attract experienced options traders. That means that the stock will be in high demand when it comes to options contracts. What happens when there is a high demand for something? The price shoots up. In the case of call options, that means the stock will come with a higher premium. You will need to take the higher premium into account when being able to exercise your options at the right time and make sure the price is high enough above your strike price that you don't end up losing money.

Traders take some time to examine the volatility of a given stock over the recent past, but they also look into what's known as implied volatility. This is a kind of weather forecast for stocks. It's an estimate of the future price movements of a stock, and it has a large influence on the pricing of options. Implied volatility is denoted by the Greek symbol σ, implied volatility increases in bear markets, and it actually decreases when investors are bullish. Implied volatility is a tool that can provide insight into the options future value.

For options traders, more volatility is a good thing. A stock that doesn't have much volatility is going to be a stable stock whose price isn't going to change very much over the lifetime of a contract. So while you may want to sell a covered call for a stock with low volatility, you're probably not going to want to buy one if you're buying call options because that means there will be a lower probability that the stock will change enough to exceed the strike price so you can earn a profit on a trade. Remember too that stocks that are very volatile will attract a lot of interest from options traders and command higher premiums. You will have to do some balancing in picking stocks that are of interest.

Being able to pick stocks that will have the right amount of volatility so that you can be sure of getting one that will earn profits on short term trades is something you're only going to get from experience. You should spend some time practicing before actually investing large amounts of money. That is, pick stocks you are interested in and make your bets but don't actually make the trades. Then follow them over the time period of the contract and see what happens. In the meantime, you can purchase safer call options, and so using this two-pronged approach gain experience that will lead to more surefire success down the road.

One thing that volatility means for everyone is that predicting the future is an impossible exercise. You're going to have some misses no matter how much knowledge and experience you gain. The only thing to aim for is to beat the market more often than you lose. The biggest mistake you can make is putting your life savings into a single stock that you think is a sure thing and then losing it all.

CHAPTER 11:

Day Trading And Swing Trading

The definition of day trading, which includes day traders keep their shares for the day. His posit they close their positions at the end of each day, and again the next day. On the other hand, they have a swing trader bonuses for days and sometimes even months; Investors are sometimes left for years. The short-term nature of the trading day reduced some risks because nothing can happen overnight, causing significant losses. At the same time, many other types of investors to go to bed thinking that his position is in perfect condition to wake up the next morning and discovered that the company announced huge profits or CEO is accused of fraud.

But there is another side (not always a disadvantage, right?): Select the values and positions that have to work a day trader or the day is done. Tomorrow does not exist for a given office. Meanwhile, swing trader or investor has the luxury of time, as it may take some time to get into the role they should. In the long run, markets are practical and efficient, and the prices reflect all information on the link.

Take a few days to realize efficiency.

Day traders are speculators, who work in a zero-sum market one day at a time. This makes the dynamics of various other types of financial activities that you can participate in. On the business rules, adoption day to help choose a good deed or to find significant investment funds in recent years are no longer used. Day Trading is a different game with different rules.

Hedgers and speculators. Speculators were looking to take advantage of price changes. Arbitrageurs try to protect themselves against price changes. They ensure that your choice of buying and selling are safe and cannot win. Therefore, select the elements that offset their exposure to another market.

For example, the cover should be considered as a food, a farmer who creates or increases the ingredients that the company needs. The Company may seek to hedge against the risk of rising prices of elemental components - like corn, oil and meat - purchase agreements with these ingredients. Therefore, if rates rise, corporate profits in contracts to help finance the rising costs will have to pay for these ingredients. If prices remain the same or fall, the company loses the contract price, which is the compensation for the company.

Secondly, it is beneficial if prices rise and suffer if they fall. To protect against falling prices, the farmer can sell futures contracts on these products. Their futures position to make money if the price dropped to compensate for a decrease in their products. And if rates rose, losing money on contracts, but the increase in its harvest offsets this loss.

The commodity markets were designed to help farmers manage risk and find buyers for their products. The equity and bond markets were created to encourage investors to finance businesses. Almost immediately, rumors ran in all these markets, but it was not his primary goal.

Day traders are speculators. They try to make money in the market as they are now. They manage risk by spreading wealth carefully, using stop orders and limit orders (positions predetermined price levels were reached as quickly as possible in the vicinity) and the sunset. They use other techniques to reduce losses, such as money management with caution and stop and limit orders.

Day Trading Strategies

Specify the number of things you need to become a reseller of the day is a good computer and Internet settings. They are necessary for the commercial success of the day. Most entrepreneurs have two or more monitors with integrated PC for managing a large number of data sources simultaneously. Windows XP or Vista is a popular form of day traders, as most trading platforms are written for these environments and can support multiple monitors.

Daily computer maintenance is essential for day traders. Computer problems are the last thing you want to live in the middle of the day, especially when long positions were opened. You can lose more money if you wait until the computer restarts and disappears store. Operators should delete cookies (files that websites send to your computer when used) Internet cache and defragment daily (change your data so that more effective teamwork).

Another critical step is to find an Internet provider that offers reliable service broadband (ISP). Many operators have more than one online service provider, so they have a backup in case the first serious.

The risk is high; Prices may be high.

A study of business models and wholesale volumes, you've probably already discovered for themselves that the risk is high. In minutes, enter and can be cumbersome for the shares in blocks of thousands of stocks quickly when the action moves in an unexpected direction.

The Senate of the United States considered the risk in trading the day after the shooting in a mall in Atlanta, Georgia, killing nine people in July 1999. Sniper Mark Barton was a chemist before engaging in day trading and only lose $ 105 000 per month. He committed suicide after injection.

Researchers found that the income of the Senate of the 15 largest companies trading in 1999 was $ 541.5 million, 276% more than their salary income in 1997 increased by more than 66 million in 2000, $ 15 businesses opened 12,000 new accounts. The researchers also found that the 4000 and 5000 most active traders have vast amounts of money and lose. Also, in 2000, buyers pay an average of $ 16 per transaction and an average of 29 sales per day. Using these statistics, the researchers concluded that the trader must win more than $ 111,000 per year for capital gains to offset the cost level.

The second study, published in May 2004 by university professors who analyzed the daily life of the Taiwan Stock Exchange, it was found that 82% of traders lost money.

You can do almost every day but ended up losing money after calculating operating costs.

Swing Trading

Swing trading is described as the art and science of making short term ranging from several days to several weeks or two months to get the most out of bond price movements. Swing traders may be individuals or institutions, such as hedge funds. Rarely 100% invested in the market at any time. Instead of waiting for low-risk opportunities and try to take the part of the significant lion movement up or down. When the demand is generally increasing, they buy more often they are short. When the market is usually low, which are shorter than buying. And if the market does keep away patiently.

Swing trading is different from the purchase and care or day trading. This approach of investors on the various frequencies trade market, and pay particular attention to the different data sources. You must understand that these differences do not focus on issues that have an impact on long-term investors.

One of the highlights of the action is the efficiency with which they are traded, in part because they provide exposure to other asset classes. For example, you can get exposure to the assets of gold products marketing funds trading gold. Guard things about yourself, because that is my area of expertise, and also recommended after exposure to other asset classes and a variety of items that you can select.

American Depositary receipts (ADR): ADR is increasingly essential in today's globalized world. In simple terms, we ADR allows investors to buy shares of foreign companies. Adverse reactions are denominated in US dollars and the payment of dividends in US dollars. Exchange ADR is much more cost-effective than creating accounts in various other countries to convert their dollar, etc. And as economic growth in developing countries is higher than in developed countries, ADR can be substantial profit opportunities. ADR markets-based companies (such as Brazil and China) emerging sometimes have a significant impact on a particular product, allowing them to benefit from high commodity prices.

Exchange-Traded Funds (ETFs):

Investments. Most courses ETF reflects the movement of the index (by famous ETF SPY following example the S & P 500) index or sub-sector. If you want to enjoy the technology of the future will be better able to negotiate the selection of specific techniques, Technology ETF that may or may not be in the area of global technology. If you travel, you will have a diversified technology ETF. However, only safety technology can resist the trend. ETFs also offer the ability to use indices and international products.

The closed funds: These funds are mainly traded funds on the secondary value of equity investments. Traditional investment funds and open-end are valued based on their net worth - or the amount left after deducting the liabilities of the fund's assets. Closed-end funds are different. Its price is determined by supply and demand of shares of the fund. Sometimes the lower closed change of the NAV; at other times, to negotiate less. Closed-end funds can be an effective way to tap international markets.

Debt markets: These markets include bonds issued by governments at the federal, state and local, as well as those issued by companies. The value of fixed income securities depends on interest rates, inflation, the creditworthiness of the issuer and other factors—the bond market generally less volatility than equities and other asset classes.

CHAPTER 12:

Candlestick

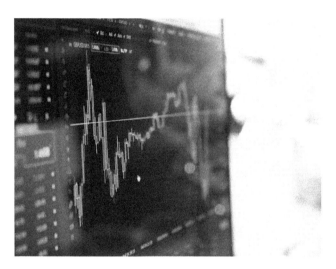

Price action

I t is no secret that the main thing involved in a stock market is "price fluctuation". It is the rise and fall of the stock prices that makes it possible for the trader to break into a profit, or suffer a loss. So to remain successful, the trader has to predict the price rise and fall successfully. This can be done through a method known as price action. Price action is conducted by taking into account the various prices that the stock has held over a period of time along with other data, statistics and mathematical formulas that are applied in order to arrive at the price fluctuation rate and range. This will help the trader make accurate speculations and realize profit whilst minimizing losses. However, as good as it sounds, the formulas that are used are extremely complex and the average person might not be able to do it easily.

Bullish candlesticks

Candles that have a larger body towards the top are considered bullish, and they mean that the buyers will be the ones who are in control of the price. When you see this kind of chart, realize that it is likely that the buyers will keep pushing so that the price goes higher. This kind of candlestick is not only going to tell you the price, but it is also able to tell you that the bulls are winning and that they have the power.

Bearish candlesticks

There are also the bearish candles. They will work a bit differently than you will find with the bullish candlesticks and can have you react in a different manner. When you see a bearish candle, it means that the sellers are the ones in control of the price action that goes on in the market and that buying would probably not be a good idea at this time.

When you see a candle that is filled and has a pretty long filled body, it means that your opening was high, but the closing was low. This is one way to tell that the market is bearish right now and it is probably not a good idea to get into the market at this time. You will probably not get a good price for the stocks because the market price is going down and there are not as many buyers interested right now.

Just by being able to read these candlesticks, you will be able to generate an opinion for how the stock will generally, or the price action. You need to understand which party (the buyer or the seller) is in charge of the price can help you determine whether now is a good time to purchase the stock or not.

When you have a bullish market, the price will keep going up, so it is a good idea to jump in and then sell the stock at a higher price. But if you are in a bearish market, the price is most likely going to go down, and it is not in your best interest to make a purchase.

Indecision candlesticks

There are also some candlesticks that are known as indecision candlesticks. There are two main types of indecision candlesticks including spinning tops and Dojis. Let's take a look at these and determine what they both mean for the market.

Spinning tops

The spinning tops are candles that have the high wicks that are similarly sized and then low wicks that happen to be larger than the bottom and look a bit indecisive. With these candlesticks, the sellers and the buyers have powers that are pretty close to even. No one is really in control over the price of the stock, but there is still a fight that is going on. The volume on these will be lower because the traders want to wait and see whether the buyers or the sellers will be the ones that wend.

You will notice that a trend in the price is often going to change right away after this kind of indecision candle, once the fight has been won by either the sellers or the buyers, so it is worth your time to recognize this kind of price action. You may want to wait a bit before jumping into the market to see which way the market will go. Sometimes it will go well, and the price will go up, but the market could also go the other way, and you could see the price drop.

Dojis

Another type of candlestick pattern that you should watch out for is the Doji. There are actually a few forms and shapes of this, but they are either going to have no body to the candlestick or at least a really small body. When you see that there is a Doji in the chart, it means that there is a fight that is going on between the bulls and the bears and no one is winning yet.

There are some times when the Doji will have a bottom and top wick that are unequal. If the top of the wick ends up being longer, it means that the buyer tried to get the price higher, but they were unsuccessful. They may show that the buyers are starting to lose power and it is possible that the sellers may start to take over. On the other hand, if the bottom wick is longer, this means that the sellers tried to push the price down and they were not successful. This may mean that there will be a takeover of the price action by the bulls.

You can definitely use this to help you see what trends are going on. If one of these candlesticks shows up during a bullish trend, it means that the bulls are wearing out and now the bears are trying to take over control of the price. If this candlestick forms when there is a bearish downward trend, it suggests that now the bears are tired and now the buyers or the bulls will take over the price. This can help you to see when a trend is about to occur in the market and can help you to make some smart decisions.

The candlestick pattern is a great way to predict how the market is going. When the market is going up based on these candlesticks, you will want to purchase and then sell before they go down. When the market is going down based on these candlesticks, you will either want to stay out of the market if you are not already in, or you will want to sell before the price goes down and you lose too much money. Take some time to learn how to make these charts, and you will find that they are a fantastic way for you to monitor the way that the market is going.

Candlesticks patterns

The "candlestick" pattern is best suited for people who would like to adopt a technical approach and trade based on patterns and predictions. The "candlestick" pattern involves the creation of patterns for particular stocks based on its "LOD" or lowest of the day and "HOD" or highest of the day prices. Depending on these statistics, the graph is plotted. There is a technique known as the doji reversal pattern that helps in establishing proper "candlesticks". Once the "candlesticks" have been established, the trader will be able to identify the pattern that the stock will follow. Once it has been established, he will predict whether the price will rise or plummet. Depending on the prediction the trader will decide to either hold on to the stock or sell it off. This technique is easy to follow if you understand the technique properly and for that.

CHAPTER 13:

Day Trading Strategies

ABCD Pattern

The ABCD trading pattern is a relative of the Elliot Waves in the sense that it is based on the fact that the market moves in an organized manner. In addition, it is one of the most profitable day trading strategies that you can find out there. Since the pattern is based on pure price action and follows market structure, it is a powerful leading indicator.

Structure

The pattern uses impulse and corrective waves to predict the future of the market. The points named A, B, C, and D represent significant highs and lows in the market.

When points A and B are joined, they form a wave known as a "leg." As such, the pattern is made up of legs AB, BC, and CD, where AB and CD are impulse waves, and BC is a corrective wave. AB and CD should be parallel to each other.

We predict the future of the market by placing trades at the end of leg CD and in the direction of BC.

- Leg AB is equal to Leg CD in the "classic ABCD" pattern.

- Leg CD can extend by 127.2% or 161.8% in the "ABCD extension" pattern.

- The time it takes to form AB is the same it should take to form CD in the "Classic ABCD" pattern.

- Leg BC is the corrective wave and gives the direction of reversal after the completion of the leg CD.

Before we go any further into this pattern, we need to discuss an important tool that should be used alongside the pattern for better analysis. It is called the Fibonacci sequence tool.

Classic ABCD Pattern

- The length of AB is equal to the length of the leg CD

- The time it takes to form AB is the same it takes to form CD

- Point C should not go near point A. Similarly, point D should not be near point C. In short, you should have clear swing points indicating a good trend.

- The leg BC should retrace to 127.2% or 161.8% of BC. To plot this, since we have an uptrend, the Fibonacci would be drawn from point B (swing high) up to point A (swing low). Then as the market unfolded, it would bounce off C (retracement level) and continue to create leg CD. Once the trader is sure that the classic ABCD has completed, they can enter a sell trade at point D (reversal into a downtrend).

Extended ABCD Pattern

An extended ABCD pattern is different from the classic ABCD pattern in that the leg CD can be longer than leg AB by between 127.2% and 161.8%. Also, the time that it takes to form CD can extend by the same percentages.

Trading With the ABCD Pattern

You can add some of the other tools like support & resistance to your ABCD pattern trading style to improve the accuracy of the turning points. The stronger a zone is, the more likely that your leg is accurate. Fibonacci levels also work well when combined with support & resistance zones. Confluence at turning points or entry points can be increased by utilizing the knowledge of candlestick formations or a few indicators. However, be careful not to have too many tools in your charts as this can lead to analysis paralysis.

It is very important that you always keep in mind that no trading strategy is foolproof. You might have the best analysis and find the most promising trade signals, but still, the market might ignore and oppose you. Therefore, to be safe from excess losses, make sure to always have a protective stop-loss order immediately after you place a trade. The ABCD pattern makes stop-loss placement very easy. You need to identify a zone below or above point D and place it there. The First Take-Profit Level can be placed at the level of C. You can have a Second Take-Profit Level at point A or where your Fibonacci extension level coincides with strong support or resistance level.

Bull Flag Momentum

A bull flag is a strong upward trend in the stock. However, after shooting upward, the stock enters a phase of consolidation, when people slow down or stop buying, but before a new rise may begin. The "flag pole" is a steep rise in the price of the stock over a very short time period. The "flag" is a time period when the price is high but stays about the same. A bull flag is a symbol of a buying opportunity for a stock that has already shown a significant increase. You should set your desired profit, buy and then sell when it begins increasing again up to the point where you have set to take your profit. You should always include a stop-loss, a bull flag is no guarantee and the price might actually start dropping.

When there is a bull flag, it is bordered along the bottom by a level below which the stock is not dropping, known as the support. On the top, there is a level above which the stock is not rising. This is called resistance. Eventually, the stock is going to break out of the resistance so you want to buy before this happens, as the stock may see a rapid rise again. A bull flag may occur multiple times during the day as the stock trends upward.

Reversal Trading

A reversal is a major change in the direction of the price of the stock. So, the trend completely shifts and moves in the opposite direction. In order to look for reversals, look at the candlesticks on a stock market chart. The body of the candlesticks and its size relative to the previous (to the left) candlesticks is what is important. First, let's consider a signal for a reversal where a declining stock price is going to be going up in the future. If the candlestick of the most recent time is larger and fully engulfs or covers the candlestick to the left, and it's the opposite color, i.e. a green candlestick following red candlesticks, this indicates a reversal of a downtrend into an increasing stock price. This is a good time to go long or buy calls.

On the other hand, let's now consider the case where the stock price is going up, with multiple green candlesticks in a row. Then it is followed by an engulfing red candlestick. This indicates a reversal so we will expect the stock price to begin going down. That is, this is a point where we should short the stock, or if trading options invest in puts.

The larger the engulfing candlestick, the stronger the reversal signal is. That indicates that the change in direction has a significant conviction behind the reversal, which is the confidence of investors, larger volume and the price will change in larger amounts over short time periods. If the wicks engulf the wicks of the previous period that is an even stronger signal that a reversal is underway.

When using reversals as a trading strategy, you need a minimum of five candlesticks in a five-minute chart. Then look at the relative strength index, which helps you evaluate overbought or oversold stocks. The RSI ranges from 0-100. At the top of an uptrend, if the RSI is above 90 that indicates that the stock is overbought and is probably going to be heading into a downturn. On the other hand, if you are looking at the bottom of a downturn, if the RSI is 10 or below, this indicates that the stock is oversold. That could be a signal that is about to see a price increase.

An indecision candlestick indicates neither an upturn nor a downturn. That is if you see a downturn followed by several indecision candlesticks, that could mean that the stock is about to turn upward again. Or vice versa – if an upturn is followed by several indecision candlesticks, that can indicate a reversal resulting in a downward trending stock price.

Looking at the wicks can be important as well. When the lower wick of the candlestick is longer, that may indicate that the price dropped over the period of the candlestick, but the stock turned and was bought up. On the other hand, if the candlestick has a long wick at the top that may indicate that the stock was bid up too much over the period. Traders lost interest and began selling off the stock.

At any time, there appears to be a reversal, a trend of indecision candles or stagnation represents a buying opportunity no matter which direction the stock may be trending. That is if you are in the midst of a downturn and the stock is moving sideways, then it may be a good time to go long on it or buy calls. The opposite is true if the stock is at the top of a potential reversal. If it's moving sideways, it may be a good time to invest in puts. Keep in mind that this does not always work. The best indicator is whether or not a green (red) candlestick following a red (green) candlestick which engulfs the candlestick to the left is the best indicator of a coming reversal.

Support or Resistance Trading

In order to understand the meaning of support and resistance levels, one needs a clear background check on what day trading entails. Day trading is the process of having a forecast in securities. This involves the purchase and sale of financial instruments within the same day of trading. The closure of business here is dependent on the end of the business day. Trading in this kind of manner is based on speculation. The probability of profit and loss is not defined. Owing to this, you may experience losses and profit in any instance. For one to engage in this type of trade and survive, one needs a well-structured strategy that will ensure you are speculating the right way. In a nutshell, day trading can be referred to as the acquisition or disposal of securities within a single trading day. The background of day traders is one that is full of funding and well-conversant with the business field. Their game is fixed on short-term strategies that have a high value of leverage. In this sense, they tend to capitalize on shifts in prices no matter how remote it may seem.

Day traders thrive on events that cause shifts in price. This is usually in the short term. The news is their biggest asset. Trading in the news will ensure that they have information concerning market psychology. This includes the announcement on various interest rates, statistics, market expectations, and corporate earnings. Day traders employ numerous strategies in their day to day activities.

These strategies include but are not limited to High-frequency trading, range trading, scalping and news based trading. The idea of day trading is fixed behind the misconception of getting rich quickly. Thus within a short period of time. This is often what attracts people to engage in this kind of trading. People who engage in this kind of trading without sufficient knowledge often end up in losses. Despite the risky nature in the manner of speculation that characterizes day trade, it is a lucrative business that puts food on the table for many lads. Its risky nature is what makes it so lucrative.

Behind every success story, there is a significant struggle story. People who engage in day trading have a view of making a profit. However, this is not always the case as some people result in irreparable loss. Before engaging in this particular type of trade, one needs an inner understanding of the factors at hand. The probability of making a profit is often lower.

CHAPTER 14:

How To Do Day Trading With Option

The simplistic meaning of an underlying financial derivative is an alternative. A civil arrangement gives you the right to buy or sell an item on or during a specified date the date of exercise. If you are the vendor, you are obliged to agree with the terms of the contract. It will be either selling or purchasing if the customer wants to exercise the right before the expiry date. Day trading options cover multiple markets. You will get equity options, options for the ETF, options for futures, and more. Also named vanilla options are such conventional alternatives. The simplistic meaning of an underlying financial derivative is an alternative. A civil arrangement gives you the right to buy or sell an item on or during a specified date the date of exercise.

They can be practiced from the date of acquisition before expiry at any point. However, European options can only be exercised after the expiry date. Options vs Futures There are many differences between day trading options and futures that many people quickly know. They are normally both based on the same instrument that underlies them. There are also several parallels to the structure of the real contracts. The distinction is how the trade takes place. You get a wider range of options with the packages.

There are various reasons you might make serious trading opportunities for capital. For some enticing factors, including placing financial remuneration on the side, day trading of options appeals. Greater Advantages You can benefit even more from an option as the stock moves. But a call option going from $1 per contract to a $5 contract will offer you a benefit of 500 percent. And with an alternative, you will earn more and with less time. Options can be successful when other markets struggle. Although other business segments struggle, options can be successful. Partly because you don't have to use the right to make the best of it. Besides, uncertainty can be positive for itself. Mutually beneficial – while stock options are often built on, add both and can offer you more benefits. That is because you can sell the income-generating right on stocks you already own. The trading of intraday options is multifaceted and carries tremendous opportunities for benefit with it. Perhaps the best aspect-usability. You can continue day-trading from anywhere in the world with options. What you need is to connect to the internet. Day trading and long-term investing are also feasible ways of stock trading and many traders are preferring to do so. Day trading means making trades that last for seconds or minutes, profiting from short-term swings in the price of an asset. Both accounts are opened and closed for day trading on the same day.

Understanding Margin

Day trading usually uses leverage margin during the day of trade. The margin rates and conditions differ according to the financial instrument of the Stock Margin and the broker. Day trading buying power for stocks and options has a lending ratio of 4 to 1 or four times the account's investment margin excess. In a simplistic way, that means that with the extra cash in the portfolio, you can buy stocks and options at just 25 percent of the market. Profit surplus is the norm to have client equity below debt. The overnight margin is between 2 and 1 or 50 percent of the value of the position.

Day traders can fall into traps if they don't know the profit is solely at the broker's discretion. Brokers will reduce the portfolio leverage ratio to 2 to 1, allowing 50 percent instead of 25 percent surplus equity for highly volatile stocks. This is a big consideration when initiating an intraday margin call. The broker is entitled to unwind a stake, frequently at the lowest times, when a margin call has to be reached. Stockbrokers can encourage traders to manipulate their cash and maximize their purchasing power intraday.

CHAPTER 15:

How To Do Day Trading With Swing Trading

Swing trading comes with different opportunities and also frequent scares. These trades are made in shaky markets, and any time the market can crash with all those dollars invested in it.

Its advantage is that it uses longer time frames to track; therefore, one can manage a full-time job as opposed to the shorter time frames on day trading. So to avoid any pitfalls, one is advised to try it on a demo account first while learning the ropes. While swing trading, do not need to keep worrying about the trades that you made. The long time frame allows you to easily pursue other things as you wait to conduct your trade. Such a trade is very convenient since it gives room for flexibility. You would like a trade that gives you freedom. You find that you do not need to keep worrying about the moves that you make since you feel secure in your deals. As a trader, you would like to engage in a deal that grants you your freedom. You want to be at a point where you can carry out your other activities as you keep trading. In this case, swing trading will act as a side job that earns you an income. You get to do other things as you conduct swing trading. It is more like killing two birds with one stone.

Swing trading is also best experienced once one has mastered the art of money management so that you can project your profits wisely. This advanced time on the market will help you identify the patterns in the stocks, and this will improve your decision-making ability. In any business investment, the management of money matters a lot. We have had some businesses start out really well and ended up failing. You will be amused that they do not fail due to the lack of a good strategy.

Instead, they fail due to poor management of finances. Any business that looks forward to making more profits, as the years advance, needs to look at how they manage their finances keenly. We have heard of cases where businesses started out well only to end up failing before making bigger strides. Money laundering has affected many businesses to the point of closure. Once you know how to engage in swing trading, ensure that you manage your finances. This will ensure that you make better decisions while carrying out various trades. With a good money management strategy, it gets easier to make progress in swing trading. You find that you will easily double your profits with this strategy.

Due to the longer time frames, have a reliable mode of communication as one is bound to forget to make moves on the market, thus ending up with huge losses. Timing is important in all the business deals that you engage in. The interesting thing about most motivational talks is how they insist on proper time management. You have probably come across some people that would prefer you to waste their money but not their time. The importance of time lies in the impact that it has on an individual. The time factor is also necessary while conducting various trades. Ensure that you are keen on the decisions that you make.

For instance, with the long durations in which the trades are carried out, you may forget the time you were required to trade. You find that you have a lot going on and keeping certain dates becomes a challenge. To avoid this, you can set a reminder on when you need to trade. At times, this will require that you are disciplined in carrying out your various activities. The decisions that you make, no matter how small, hold a big impact in your possibility of succeeding. Utilizing this strategy will help you a lot while trading options. It ensures that you are disciplined in keeping time and you trade in moments when you can get a big profit.

Observe the trends in the market and steer clear of trading with the trend. This is because its longevity might be questionable and therefore having a stock that fazed out while you were not tracking it is detrimental. Avoid trading against the most appealing trend and exercise caution by withholding yourself. As a trader, you need to be keen on how the market moves. You cannot achieve success in a certain area unless you fully understand what it entails. As an individual intending to engage in swing trading, one of the best strategies that you can utilize is knowing how the market operates. You will be surprised by the power of having information. In the world that we currently live in, ignorance will cost you a lot. Nowadays, information is readily available to us that one has no excuse not to learn.

In this era, the internet has done more good than harm to us. You can easily get any information that you want by conducting a simple search. We also have numerous resources within our reach that help us in acquiring the information that we would like. With the many resources, we certainly do not have any excuse for not having the knowledge that we need. Additionally, while learning, we can never completely finish learning everything. Each day comes with its own new things, and we need to embrace that. Have a positive attitude towards learning and see the impact it will have on conducting swing trades.

Swing trading allows for different skill sets in the trading as it takes a while for the stocks to exit the market. During this time, the beginner can go over whatever steps he would have forgotten in order to fortify his trading process. Asides from knowledge, we need to gain skills that help us in conducting different trades. These skills make the trading process easier. The difference between the people who succeed at certain things, and those that fail lies in the extra mile that they are willing to take. How hungry are you for success? What extra miles are you willing to make to get to a place that you would like to be? Your response to these questions can tell a lot about the kind of individual that you are. You find that successful people tend to be driven by their ambitions.

This does not only apply in other aspects of life, but it is also applicable in swing trading. There are many decisions that you will make, that will influence your general outcome. To become a good trader, you will have to come up with some tactics and strategies that make the trades manageable. Some people tend to view it as a complex thing, yet it is very easy to come up with tactics and strategies. The only thing that you will need is having adequate knowledge of how swing trading operates. Once you have the information, it is easy to come up with the strategies.

Know what stocks you are trading by keeping up with the latest using newspapers, financial markets and trade events. Use reliable sources to keep you up to tabs with the general markets and the high flying financial players. As the market expands, there is more to learn. We need to constantly keep up with the changing terms and factors influencing the market. It is a good thing that there are plenty of resources that we can utilize to have the information that you need. When you utilize this strategy, it allows you to be well informed. You find that you will even find it possible to make better decisions.

Be mentally prepared to make losses as much as you are prepared to make profits. This is an inevitable step in the trading process. Day trading is unpredictable as a stock can crash at any time during the day. This strategy has been a challenge for most people. You find that you are not open to the possibility of incurring a loss. Asides from the fact that the main purpose of investing is earning a profit, you have to be open to the challenges that come with investments. At times trades go contrary to what we expected. A single mistake can cause you to encounter a loss. At times, we have no control over some factors, and once we encounter a loss. While you engage in day trading, know that you can either win or lose at the end of the day. This will protect you from stress and other challenges that result from being stressed. You get to appreciate your efforts despite failing since you understand that failure is part of the success journey. Not every person can do this, but we need to encourage ourselves.

The time invested must be more than any other investment. The individual must set aside enough time to track and chart the stocks in order to see their performance and enable him to exit at the opportune time.

Use the percent rule in terms of funds. You must be willing to lose a bit so as to gain a lot in the financial markets. Some stocks are liable to burn while others are clear wins. At times we are advised that we need to part with money to make money. As we aspire to get rich, there are some major decisions that we will need to make. At times it will involve making sacrifices to get to the levels and positions that we aspire to be in. the path to success is not an easy journey, but we have to be fully committed to the process.

Learn how to time your trades. Even after getting on the market, allow some time to pass so as to see the stocks that are going to remain so as to avoid the volatile trends. During this time, you will have enough time to observe the patterns and allow for a window to make profits.

Avoid being enticed by buying so many stocks at once. Start small and get a maximum of two stocks that are easily managed within the small time frame that day trading provides. You are also likely to get more opportunities with these few stocks on the market. At times we have a misguided belief that the more stock one has, the more money they are likely to have. Contrary to this belief, one can make a loss while using such a strategy. Buying multiple stocks results in overtrading, and you may end up having overleveraged accounts. As a beginner, start with manageable stocks that you can handle. This allows you to evaluate the various stocks before purchasing them easily. You get to know the stocks that can earn you a profit as you avoid the stocks that will not help you in generating an income. Some expert traders are also unable to conduct multiple trades since they know the challenges that come with trading. This should show you how risky it is and help you avoid engaging in such. Ensure that you only engage in trades that you can manage so that you make wise decisions.

Be realistic about your profits and stick to the percentage rule so as to maximize your profits in the trade. Plan your exit strategy based on the profits you make and then leave. The high expectations that one has at the beginning makes them think that they can make money quickly. Sadly, day trading is not a plan to quickly earn an income. With this attitude, you will have major frustrations and disappointments. In the beginning, be patient enough to start small. You will grow as you proceed. The same way a child develops from childhood to adulthood in the same way that you can experience growth while day trading. It will take some time until you have the adequate skills to carry out trades successfully.

CHAPTER 16:

Essential Tool For Day Trading

For you to carry out day trading successfully there are several tools that you need. Some of these tools are freely available, while others must be purchased. Modern trading is not like the traditional version. This means that you need to get online to access day trading opportunities.

Therefore, the number one tool you need is a laptop or computer with an internet connection. The computer you use must have enough memory for it to process your requests fast enough. If your computer keeps crashing or stalling all the time, you will miss out on some lucrative opportunities. There are trading platforms that need a lot of memory to work, and you must always put this into consideration.

Your internet connection must also be fast enough. This will ensure that your trading platform loads in real-time. Ensure that you get an internet speed that processes data instantaneously to avoid experiencing any data lag. Due to some outages that occur with most internet providers, you may also need to invest in a backup internet device such as a smartphone hotspot or modem. Other essential tools and services that you need include:

Brokerage

To succeed in day trading, you need the services of a brokerage firm. The work of the firm is to conduct your trades. Some brokers are experienced in day trading than others. You must ensure that you get the right day trading broker who can help you make more profit from your transactions. Since day trading entails several trades per day, you need a broker that offers lower commission rates. You also need one that provides the best software for your transactions. If you prefer using specific trading software for your deals, then look for a broker that allows you to use this software.

Real-time Market Information

Market news and data are essential when it comes to day trading. They provide you with the latest updates on current and anticipated price changes on the market. This information allows you to customize your strategies accordingly. Professional day traders always spend a lot of money seeking this kind of information on news platforms, in online forums or through any other reliable channels.

Financial data is often generated from price movements of specific stocks and commodities. Most brokers have this information. However, you will need to specify the kind of data you need for your trades. The type of data to get depends on the type of stocks you wish to trade.

Monitors

Most computers have a capability that enables them to connect to more than one monitor. Due to the nature of the day trading business, you need to track market trends, study indicators, follow financial news items, and monitor price performance at the same time. For this to be possible, you need to have more than one processor so that the above tasks can run concurrently.

Classes

Although you can engage in day trading without attending any school, you must get trained on some of the strategies you need to succeed in the business. For instance, you may decide to enroll for an online course to acquire the necessary knowledge in the business. You may have all the essential tools in your possession, but if you do not have the right experience, all your efforts may go to waste.

CHAPTER 17:

Huge Mistakes That Beginners Make

A side from doing the right things, you'll also need to refrain from certain things to succeed as a day trader. Here are some of the most common day trading mistakes you should avoid committing.

Excessive Day Trading

By excessive, I mean executing too many day trades. One of the most common mistakes many newbie day traders make is assuming that they can become day trading ninjas in just a couple of weeks if they trade often enough to get it right. But while more practice can eventually translate into day trading mastery later on, it doesn't mean you can cram all that practice in a very short period of time via very frequent day trading. The adage "the more, the merrier" doesn't necessarily apply to day trading.

Remember, timing is crucial for day trading success. And timing is dependent on how the market is doing during the day. There will be days when day trading opportunities are few and far between and there'll be days when day trading opportunities abound. Don't force trades for the sake of getting enough day trades under your belt.

Even in the midst of a plethora of profitable day trading opportunities, the more the merrier still doesn't apply. Why? If you're a newbie trader, your best bet at becoming a day trading ninja at the soonest possible time is to concentrate on one or two day trades per day only. By limiting your day trades, to just one or two, you have the opportunity to closely monitor and learn from your trades.

Can you imagine executing 5 or more trades daily as a newbie and monitor all those positions simultaneously? You'll only get confused and overwhelmed and worse, you may even miss day trading triggers and signals and fail to profitably close your positions.

Winging It

If you want to succeed as a day trader, you need to hold each trading day in reverence and high esteem. How do you do that? By planning your day trading strategies for the day and executing those strategies instead of just winging it.

As cliché as it may sound, failing to plan really is planning to fail. And considering the financial stakes involved in day trading, you shouldn't go through your trading days without any plan on hand. Luck favors those who are prepared and planning can convince lady luck that you are prepared.

Expecting Too Much Too Soon

This much is true about day trading: it's one of the most exciting and exhilarating jobs in the world! And stories many day traders tell of riches accumulated through this economic activity add more excitement, desire, and urgency for many to get into it.

However, too much excitement and desire resulting from many day trading success stories can be very detrimental to newbie day traders. Let me correct myself: it is detrimental to newbie day traders. Why?

Such stories, many of which are probably urban legends, give newbies unrealistic expectations of quick and easy day trading riches. Many beginner day traders get the impression that day trading is a get-rich-quick scheme!

It's not. What many day traders hardly brag about are the times they also lost money and how long it took them to master the craft enough to quit their jobs and do it full time. And even rarer are stories of the myriad number of people who've attempted day trading and failed. It's the dearth of such stories that tend to make day trading neophytes have unrealistic expectations about day trading.

What's the problem with lofty day trading expectations? Here's the problem: if you have very unrealistic expectations, it's almost certain that you'll fail. It's because unrealistic expectations can't be met and therefore, there's zero chances for success.

One of the most unrealistic expectations surrounding day trading is being able to double one's initial trading capital in a couple of months, at most. Similar to such expectations is that of being able to quit one's day job and live an abundant life in just a few months via day trading. Successful day traders went through numerous failures, too, before they succeeded at day trading and were able to do it for a living.

Changing Strategies Frequently

Do you know how to ride a bike? If not, do you know someone who does? Whether it's you or somebody you know, learning how to ride a bike wasn't instant. It took time and a couple of falls and bruises along the way.

But despite falls, scratches and bruises, you or that person you know stuck to learning how to ride a bike and with enough time and practice, succeeded in doing so. It was because you or the other person knew that initial failures mean that riding a bike was impossible. It's just challenging at first.

It's the same with learning how to day trade profitably. You'll need to give yourself enough time and practice to master it. Just because you suffered trading losses in the beginning doesn't mean it's not working or it's not for you. It probably means you haven't really mastered it yet.

But if you quit and shift to a new trading strategy or plan quickly, you'll have to start again from scratch, extend your learning time, and possibly lose more money than you would've if you stuck around to your initial strategy long enough to give yourself a shot at day trading successfully or concluding with certainty that it's not working for you.

If you frequently change your day trading strategies, i.e., you don't give yourself enough time to learn day trading strategies, your chances of mastering them become much lower. In which case, your chances of succeeding in day trading becomes much lower, too.

Not Analyzing Past Trades

Those who don't learn history are doomed to repeat it, said writer and philosopher George Santayana. We can paraphrase it to apply to day traders, too: Those who don't learn from their day trading mistakes will be doomed to repeat them.

If you don't keep a day trading journal containing records of all your trades and more importantly, analyze them, you'll be doomed to repeat your losing day trades. It's because by not doing so, you won't be able to determine what you're doing wrong and what you should be doing instead in order to have more profitable day trades than losing ones.

Ditching Correlations

We can define correlations as a relationship where one thing influences the outcome or behavior of another. A positive correlation means that both tend to move in the same direction or exhibit similar behaviors, i.e., when one goes up, the other goes up, too, and vice versa.

Correlations abound in the stock market. For example, returns on the stock market are usually negatively correlated with the Federal Reserve's interest rates, i.e., when the Feds increase interest rates, returns on stock market investments go down and vice versa.

Correlations exist across industries in the stock market, too. For example, property development stocks are positively correlated to steel and cement manufacturing stocks. This is because when the property development's booming, it buys more steel and cement from manufacturing companies, which in turn also increase their income.

Ignoring correlations during day trading increase your risks for erroneous position taking and exiting. You may take a short position on a steel manufacturer's stock while taking a long position on a property development company's stock and if they have a positive correlation, one of those two positions will most likely end up in a loss.

But caution must be exercised with using correlations in your day trades. Don't establish correlations where there's none. Your job is to simply identify if there are observable correlations, what those correlations are, and how strong they are.

Being Greedy

Sadly for the owner, there were no golden eggs inside the goose because it only created and laid one golden egg every day. His greed caused him to destroy his only wealth-generating asset.

When it comes to day trading, greed can have the same negative financial impact. Greed can make a day trader hold on to an already profitable position longer than needed and result in smaller profits later on or worse, trading losses.

If you remember my story, that was greed in action. Had I been content with the very good returns I already had and closed my position, my paper gains could've become actual gains. I let my greed control my trading and chose to hold on to that stock much longer than I needed to. That trade turned into a losing one eventually.

That's why you must be disciplined enough to stick to your day trading stop-loss and profit-taking limits. And that's why you should program those limits on your platform, too. Doing so minimizes the risks of greed hijacking your otherwise profitable day trades.

CHAPTER 18:

Trading Mindset And Psychology

To succeed in day trading, day traders require many skills, including the ability to analyze a technical chart. But none of the technical skills can replace the importance of a traders' mindset. Discipline, quick thinking, and emotional control; all these are collectively called the trading psychology and are important factors for succeeding in the day trading business.

On the surface, day trading is an easy activity; markets go up and down and traders buy and sell with the price. Then how come 90% of traders make losses in day trading? The answer lies in trading psychology where most of the day traders fail. You will see many online courses advertising to teach day trading or technical analysis, but It is unheard of any course that teaching trading psychology to traders.

It is a well-known fact that controlling emotions of fear and greed are two of the most difficult decisions a day trader can take. Even those who prepare a trading plan, create trading rules; find it hard to stick to those rules and plans while trading in the stock markets. It is like dieting. When you are not supposed to think of ice cream, all you can do is think of ice cream.

Nobody is born with a successful trader's mindset. it is a skill developed with practice and self-discipline. Humans are emotional beings, so it is difficult to take emotions completely out of day trading. But traders can try to remain neutral and take the help of technology to trade, so their decisions are based on facts.

It is so easy to look at a chart and point, what was a good buying point and how much profit one could have made by trading in a certain way. But once markets open and the stock price starts changing its tracks, it sorts of hypnotizes traders in making wrong decisions. Emotions like greed and fear take over and traders keep making mistakes, accumulating losses instead of what should have been easy profits.

In stock markets, the simplest thing is the stock price's movement. It keeps going up or down rhythmically. Any child can tell when the price is going down, or when the price is going up. Still, day traders make the mistake of buying when the price is falling and selling when the price is rising. At any given time, half of the day traders believe that markets are at a good point to buy stocks, and the other half of day traders firmly believe that it is the right time to sell. Some of these traders are right half of the time, and some of these traders are wrong half of the time. Overall, none of them are right all the time. They get confused, not by the price movement; but by their own psychological reactions.

Understanding Trading Mindset and Psychology

For example, if a person is given two things to choose from, and given a time limit of 3 hours, he will do it in a relaxed way. However, if he is asked to decide within 3 seconds, he will panic. In other words, he will get into an emotional state.

Trading psychology involves two aspects; risk-taking and self-discipline. Traders know that emotions like greed and fear should not influence them, but they allow these emotions to affect their trading. Two other emotions are equally destructive; namely, hope and regret. Anger is an emotion that causes considerable loss to traders when they get frustrated by failure and indulge in revenge trading; which leads to more losses.

In greed, traders take more risk than is safe for them. In fear, traders avoid risk and generate very small profits.

Greed can encourage traders to indulge in over-trading. At times, it can cloud their rational thinking and judgment. It can lead to behavior that cannot be explained rationally. Traders may try to place big trades in a hurry to earn profits. If their trades are profitable, they may refuse to exit these trades even if the exit point has come and continue holding positions hoping for bigger profits. This behavior ultimately ends with loss because markets do not keep trending in one direction. Eventually, the market trend changes, and the profitable position turn into a loss-making one.

Fear has the opposite effect but the same result for traders. In the grip of fear, traders may close their position prematurely, then trade again to earn profits. It becomes a vicious cycle of fear and greed, where the trader is afraid to keep the position open longer but keeps trading again in greed.

Fear and Day Trading

The technical progress has made it possible for news to travel quick and reach far-flung places. This has created a unique situation for stock markets, where the positive news has a quick and positive reaction in the stock markets; but negative news causes sudden and a steep drop in stock prices as traders become gripped by fear and panic.

In situations leading to greed, traders still pause and think, if they are being greedy. But under the influence of fear, traders usually overreact and exit their position quickly. This has a chain-reaction effect on markets. Prices fall, traders sell in fear; prices fall further, traders sell more in fear. This emotion creates bigger ripples in stock markets than greed. Traders exit from their positions fearing that they will lose their profits or make losses. The fear of loss paralyzes novice traders when their positions turn into loss-making. They refuse to exit such positions, hoping for a bounce back in markets, hoping to turn their losses into profits. What should have been a small loss, eventually turns into a big one for them, sometimes even wiping out their all trading capital. A rationally thinking person will quickly exit from such a position. But fear is such strong emotion in day trading, that it stops even rational people from taking correct decisions.

Technology can help traders make the right decision in such situations. Automated trading is one aspect of trading that eliminates emotional content from day trading. But automated trading software is expensive and not every trader can afford those. Based on your trading plan, decide what will be your trade entry, exit, stop loss and profit booking levels. To stop yourself from trading before the trade entry point has arrived, put a limit order for that level. It will free you from watching the price constantly. And, if you are not watching markets constantly, the chance of wrong trading is also removed.

You cannot remove emotions from life. Therefore, it will remain a part of your day trading business. But you can control it by self- discipline and proper trade management techniques. Patience is also one such technique, where you stay away from trading until the right trade entry level arrives.

Why Trading Psychology is Important

Most of the people fail in day trading because they start at the wrong end. They start by learning trading skills first, then move on to money and risk management techniques, and the last stop is to learn, superficially, about trading psychology.

In fact, the right sequence of learning day trading should be learning the trading psychology first, then money and risk management techniques and the last part should constitute learning the trading skills. It is very easy to learn technical analysis and how to use technical indicators. But it is very difficult to control one's emotions like fear and greed while trading, or astutely manage money while day trading.

If you look at people in different fields, you will find the mind-set is the main difference between those who reach the pinnacle of their chosen career and those who remain mediocre. Be it business, science, technology, sports, or any other creative pursuit, people who train their minds for success are the ones who win the race. In intraday trading also, hundreds and thousands of day traders use the same methods of technical analysis, however, only a few of them succeed in making profitable trade and others go home with losses. it is the trading psychology, that makes the difference between successful traders and those who failed.

Every trader, who tries to learn day trading, knows that there are certain rules to be followed and still the majority of them fail to do so find therefore if you want to succeed in day trading, you must pay attention to how you react to markets. stock trading is nothing but watching the price rise and fall and trading off with the trend. But still, traders fail to follow this simple method of trading. Day trading happens 90% in the mind of a day trader, and only 10% in what happens in markets. A day trader takes decision based on what he or she thinks is going to happen in stock markets, and not on what is happening. This is the biggest mistake of day traders do and the reason is their emotions.

To overcome this psychological hurdle, day traders must learn how to manage their trades without emotions. They can do so only with the help of technology, and self-discipline. If they do not have self-control or do not follow a disciplined trading plan, they cannot make profits in stock markets.

CHAPTER 19:

Account Risk Management Entry Exit And Stop Loss

With any trade, risk management is an essential component despite the fact that it is often overlooked. It is crucial that day; traders learn about risk management if they are to successfully trade and remain profitable in the long term. The good news is that there are some simple strategies that can be adopted to ensure that trades are protected and risks management appropriately. Basically, risk management is one of the most important aspects of the life of any serious day trader. The reason is that a trader can actually see 90% of their trades make money, but the 10% losing money may result in a net loss if there is no proper risk management. Therefore, it is important to plan all trades carefully and to take measures to protect all trades against any losses.

Trades should be Planned Appropriately

It is a well-known fact that a good strategy will win the war rather than the battle. A good day trader needs to plan and come up with a winning strategy as the first step. A lot of traders often live by the mantra, "Plan the trade and trade the plan." This is also very similar to war planning because those who plan properly are likely to win.

Take Profit and Stop Loss Points

Traders need to come up with two very important points. These points represent two major keys that enable traders to plan ahead or in advance. A good day trader ideally knows their entry point as well as their exit points. These important points will guide the trades and will indicate at what point the trader should buy stocks and at what point the stocks should be sold off.

When a trader determines the price they wish to pay for a stock and the price they wish to sell, then it is possible to find out the likelihood of the stock performing as desired. If this can be measured and confirmed, then the trader should enter and execute the trade.

Also, traders who enter a trade without making these kinds of determinations are likely to suffer loss and will in effect cease trading and instead gamble with his resources.

Whenever traders start to make losses, they believe that they can always recover their money if they invest more. This is often a lack of discipline, and the trader is likely to lose even more money.

A stop-loss is defined as the actual price where a trader will choose to sell a stock and incur a loss on the particular trade. This is a situation that happens when trades do not proceed according to the trader's plans.

These points are ideally designed in order to limit losses before they get out of hand. It is always tempting for a trader who is losing money to hang in there in the hope that the losing trend will end and profitability will resume once again.

Converse to this is the take-profit point. It is important to set the take-profit, which is really the price at which a trader exits a trade by selling the security and then takes a profit from the sale. The take point is often the point at which any additional upside will become limited beyond this point. Let us assume the trade approaches a key resistance level after a large upward movement then traders can choose to exit the trade at this point.

Improving the Risk Management Process

1. Setting the Risk: Reward Ratio

When an entry signal is sighted, work out the most appropriate place to locate the stop loss than first take the profit order. Now should the outcome not be satisfactory, then it is advisable to quit the trade. Traders should generally not attempt to reduce the stop loss or widen the profit order. Discipline, at this point, is very important.

Rewards in trade are never certain and are the only potential. It is the risk that traders have control over so it should be seriously considered. A lot of the time, inexperienced traders will take the opposite approach and later suffer the consequences.

2. Traders should Avoid Break-even Stops

Creating a no-risk trade by locating the stop loss close to the entry point is something that should be avoided at all costs. The reason is that this is a dangerous move and most often not profitable. While seeking some protection is advisable, these kinds of moves cause more harm than good and should always be avoided.

3. Fixed Stop Distances should not be used

Sometimes a trader may wish to make use of a fixed number of points on the stop loss then place profit orders on markets and varied instruments. These are essentially shortcuts and should not be used under any circumstances. The reason is that they often neglect price movements and the general operation of the markets.

Also, things such as momentum and volatility are never static but always changing depending on various factors. These will also have an effect on the price movement and will affect fluctuations over time. When volatility is high, profit order points and stop loss points need to be wider to maximize profits during price swings and to prevent any premature stop runs.

4. Risk-Reward and Win-Rate Ratios should be compared together

There are traders who do not believe in the win-rate ratio and consider it irrelevant. This is actually not a wise thought because it is a very important metric. Win-rate on its own is not a very useful metric, but when pitted against the risk vs. reward ratio, then it provides important insights.

Traders should Work Out their expected Returns

Traders need to be able to work out any expected returns from their trades. Now both take-profit and stop-loss points are essential to work out this figure. Expected returns provide an important figure that cannot be underestimated. This figure that results from the calculations causes a trader to think and rationalize their trades. It also ensures that only the most profitable trades are chosen.

How to Set the Stop-Loss Points

It is the technical analysis that mostly helps to determine the take-profit and stop-loss points. However, fundamental analysis of the stocks in question does play a crucial role, especially with the timing. For instance, if a trader is holding stock and the earnings report is around the corner, then such a trader will have to dispose of those shares before the news affects the markets. This is necessary regardless of whether the stock has hit the profit margin or not.

One of the most popular ways of setting up these points is to use the well-known Moving Average. Moving averages are pretty simple to work out and are tracked closely by market players. Some of the important Moving Averages include the 9, 20, 50, 100, and 200-day averages. These should typically be applied to any stock in question and then making a determination as to whether they have had an effect on its price or not.

Also, the support and resistance trend lines can be used to place the take-profit and stop-loss levels. First, the trader needs to draw these lines simply by connecting all the past lows or highs that appeared on the above average and significant volumes. The main aim here is to effectively determine the levels where the stock price is affected by the trend lines when volumes are significantly high.

Traders need to be able to determine at what points they enter and exit any traders that they wish to participate in. This determination needs to be made before the trade is actually entered. When indicators such as the stop-loss are effectively used, then the trader will be able to minimize their losses and also reduce the frequency with which trades are excited unnecessarily. The bottom line here is to prepare early, well ahead of time so as to be sure of success in all trades.

CHAPTER 20:

Trading Business Plan

Aside from carefully evaluated day trading plans and strategies, here are other tips that can help optimize your day trading success.

Practice with a Trading Simulator First

These days, pilot trainees learn to fly airplanes on a simulator first before flying a real one. Why? By practicing with a flight simulator first, the risk of a pilot trainee crashing the plane becomes much lower. It's because flight simulators allow pilot trainees to experience how it is to fly a plane and how planes respond to controls without having to actually leave the ground. In case they commit major and potentially catastrophic mistakes during flight training, there will be no serious consequences other than low grades.

Day trading with real money on real stock or securities exchanges without first experiencing how it is to day trade is akin to learning how to fly a plane in a real plane in the sky! The risks of losing money are simply too high for a beginner to handle. By using your trading platform's trading simulator before day trading real money, you can afford to lose money as part of your learning process without actually losing money!

Stick to Your Daily Limits

While knowing how much capital you're willing to risk in day trading as a whole, you'll also need to have sub limits, i.e., daily limits. If you don't have such limits, it can be much easier to wipe out your entire trading capital in a day or two. A sensible guideline for your daily limit is to cut your losses when your daily trading position registers a maximum loss of 10%.

Avoid Becoming Attached to Your Stocks

As a newbie trader, your chances of becoming emotionally attached to your chosen SIPs are high. That's why a big chunk of the trading strategies enumerated earlier involve using numbers as triggers for entering and exiting positions in SIPs. Numbers are objective and if you stick to them, you can prevent your emotions from hijacking your trades.

Feel the Mood of the Market

Technical analysis, via candlestick charts and technical indicators, are very good ways to gauge the market's mood. However, they're not perfect and you may need to validate their readings by interacting with actual traders.

Trade Patiently

Only fools rush in, as the saying goes. However, it can be very easy to rush into trades, especially for newbies, when a significant amount of time has passed without any trades. It's because it can seem that one is wasting time by not trading.

The truth is, time will be wasted, as well as trading capital, by rushing into trades for the sake of making them. Remember, the point of day trading is to make money and not to simply trade. If no good opportunities are available, there's no need to force a day trade. Be patient and wait for trading signals to appear before taking positions.

Befriend Your Losing Trades

Nobody's perfect. That includes day traders. Even the very best still get into losing day trades, albeit their total trading profits significantly exceed their total trading losses.

Knowing that even the best of the best still have their share of losing trades should make you feel much better about losing trades. Even better, why not look at them from a different perspective just like how Thomas Edison looked at his "failed" experiments.

When asked about the first 1,000 failed experiments on the working light bulb, Edison corrected his interviewer by saying those weren't failed experiments. They were successful experiments because each of those first 1,000 light bulb experiments showed him how not to make the light bulb and in so doing, brought him a step closer to making a working version of the bulb.

Choose Your Broker Wisely

Many newbie day traders choose their brokers without really giving it much thought. Probably it's because they're overwhelmed with so many new things to learn that they fail to pay attention to the brokers they choose. Don't make the same mistake because remember, you'll be entrusting your precious day trading capital, which in the United States is a minimum of $25,000. And that's a lot of money to entrust, which means choosing a trustworthy and excellent day trading broker is a must.

With so many new online brokers popping up on the Internet these days, it can be quite challenging to sift through the reputable and not-so-reputable ones. Fortunately, there are many online resources and forums on which you can glean information on online brokers' reputations and quality of service.

Part of choosing the right broker is platform or order execution speed. Remember, day trading success is very dependent on how fast you can execute your orders in the market. So, choose a broker that's not just reputable but has a fast order-executing platform.

Don't Scrimp on Technology

I can't emphasize enough the importance of speed when it comes to day trading, where a mere few seconds can spell the difference between profitable and losing trades. For this, you can't afford to settle for the cheapest hardware and software, which most likely be too slow for consistent day trading success.

Now, I'm not saying you should get the most expensive, top-of-the-line computers for your day trading activities. It'll be like trying to kill a fly with a shotgun. However, your primary consideration for buying a computer and choosing an Internet service providers should be technical specifications. Price should only be the secondary factor and fortunately, you don't need to buy an iMac or a MacBook Pro just to day trade with sufficient speed.

Also, make sure that you have either a landline or a cellular phone line to reach your broker in the event that your Internet connection acts up for one reason or another. Better to err on the side of caution than on the side of negligence, don't you think?

Focus on Price Movements and News Triggers or Catalysts

Day trading relies on technical analysis and very little on fundamental analysis, except for news catalysts or triggers. And by nature of its reliance on technical analysis, it doesn't bother itself with a company's financial data and the like.

Why am I reminding you of this? One way you can sabotage your day trading success is by overanalyzing your stocks or securities. When you extend your research and analysis on a company's balance sheet and income statement items, as well as industry and economic trends, you'll spend too much time on things that aren't really important to day trading. Fundamental analysis is crucial for swing trading and long-term investing but with day trading, all you need to focus on is price movement and significant news announcements.

Stick to those two only so you can make the most out of your day trading time and so that you can enter and exit positions on a timely basis.

Conclusion

Thank you for making it through to the end of Day Trading, let's hope it was educative and able to provide you with all of the tools you need to achieve your goals whatever they may be.

You may have in mind the market that would interest you to trade. You should be in a position to find a repeating pattern that would be quite convenient to exploit and make profits from. As earlier indicated, no market is better than the other. What differentiates it is your capital investment and what exactly you want to trade. You realize that some markets may vary depending on the time of operation, e.g., for forex, it runs 24/7. In others, they do not charge any commissions. Other markets have high volatility; hence, the traders enjoy huge trade swings. This may work both as an advantage or a disadvantage since theses swing also mean enormous risks of huge losses. Do not take the risk to try to master all the markets that come your way. You just need to focus on one so as to avoid having divided attention. The moment you learn to make profits from one of the markets, it becomes easier to master the rest. If the wins are many and give high returns, then setting your stop loss a bit high would only work better for you as that would translate to higher profits. The idea of managing your risks is to make your losses quite small such that one single day of winning can compensate for the accrued losses.

The next step is to get started with some of the work that we are able to do when it comes to day trading. There are a lot of investment styles that are out there, and some of them are going to be simple to work with, and some are a bit harder to handle along the way. Being able to put them together and learn how to utilize day trading and the fast world that it belongs to could be the key that you need to see a lot of success.

This guidebook took some time to talk and explore all of the different parts that we need to know when it comes to day trading. There are a lot of people who are skeptical about working with day trading because they think it will fail at it, or they think that it is too risky. But with some of the methods and strategies that we have talked about in this guidebook ready to go, even someone who has not had a chance to do any investing at all in the past will be able to see some results.

DAY TRADING OPTIONS

A Crash Course For Beginners On How To Invest In The Stock Market, Including Technical Analysis, Trading Psychology, And Useful Strategies.

Matthew Swing

Introduction

A n option is simply a contract between two parties which is based on an underlying asset. You can create an options contract for any type of asset, but our focus is on options contracts for stocks.

They are called options because one party of the contract will have the option to buy or sell stocks depending on whether or not certain conditions are met.

Learning the lingo

- **Put Option:** A put option is an option contract to sell a particular stock under the terms of the put option contract. With a put option, you are 'putting it into the ownership' of the option buyer.

- **Call Option:** A call option is a contract to buy a stock according to the terms of the call option contract. A call option means you are calling upon the seller to sell you the stock, at the contract terms.

- **Long and Short:** Call options have two subsets; long and short. When you buy a call option to open a trade, you are said to be buying a long call. When you sell a call option to close a trade, you are selling a long call. When you sell a call to open a trade, you are said to be selling a short call. When you act to close that trade, you are buying a short call. As the price of the stock rises, your call option also rises in value.

- **American Option:** An American option is an option, whether a put or a call, that can be exercised at any time before the expiration date. American options are usually sold on the stock market.

- **European Option:** A European option can only be exercised on the expiration date, not before. However, it can be sold before the expiration date. European options are generally sold on the "Over the Counter" or OTC market.

- **Buyer and Seller:** For every purchase or sale there must be a sale or purchase that corresponds with it. The table below describes that correspondence for the buyer and seller. Notice that the buyer has the option but not the obligation to act, whereas the seller has the obligation to act if the buyer chooses to execute the option. Here, we refer in the most general sense to an investment 'instrument' which could be common stock or, for example, an ETF.

- **Execute:** This means that the buyer decides to act on the contract, to buy or sell; that is to execute the contract. It is also referred to as Exercising the Option.

- **Expiration Date:** When the contract is agreed upon, it runs for some finite period of time. After the expiration date, the contract expires; that is, it's no longer valid. After the expiration date, the value of the option is zero.

- **Market Price:** Market price is the current price of that stock today. Market prices vary minute by minute on the stock exchange.

- **Option Premium:** There is a cost for buying an options contract, either put or call. That charge, collected by the seller, depends on the length of the contract and the practice of the broker. Premiums can range from a few cents per contract to closer to $20. Option premiums are paid in cash; the cash you have in your brokerage account.

- **Intrinsic Value:** Value of the premium derived from the value of the underlying stock.

- **Extrinsic Value:** Portion of the premium related to volatility and time.

Types of Options

There are primarily, only two types of options, namely the Call options and Put Options. All others are basically a combination of strategies based on the former two.

Call Option

It is an option where the underlying stock can be purchased on or before its expiration date. While purchasing a Call Option, a certain amount of premium is paid to the selling party, which gives you the right to purchase the underlying stock at a predetermined price, which is referred to as the strike price.

Put Option

It is an option where the underlying stock can be sold on or before its expiration date. It implies that you are bearish about the market and thus wishing for the underlying stock price to drop to a level which is below the strike price of the put option at which it was purchased either before or at the time of expiration.

Options Contracts

The price of the contract an individual is participating in is often determined by the type of asset being traded. The contract of an options trade is supposed to have two parties who are either buying or selling the underlying assets. Let's expound on the stock options as the underlying asset. If an individual has the potential of purchasing one hundred shares of a certain company for one hundred American dollars, this will be the determinant of the value possessed by the option contract. An underlying asset can be a market index.

The contract agreed by option trading parties is supposed to have a clear indication of which type of option is being traded. The types of options that are known in the current world tend to categorize and named depending on the varied features they pose. People across the globe are familiar with two types of options. Calls and puts options are popular in the financial markets.

Strike Price

The presence of a strike price is a common phenomenon in the trade of options. It can be described as a major component when it narrows down to penning down of an option contract. Options such as calls, and puts are heavily dependent on this factor. Its critical nature can be shown by an option trader who needs the call options. It is important because it determines the value possessed by the option. Several people have familiarized strike prices with a different name which is known as the exercise price.

Premium Price

The premium can be described as the price an option buyer in a contract pays the seller of the option. Terms of an option contract state that the amount is always paid upfront. It is always important for a trader to always remember that this component of a contract is not refundable. The rule extends itself to the side that one cannot be refunded his or her money even if the contract has been exercised.

The premium quotation in a contract is always done in a certain way for efficiency. The most common way across the globe entails the quotation of option in the foundation of shares which is termed per share basis. The amount of premium is always affected by several variables before it is agreed on.

Expiration Date

One can easily understand the term expiration date of a contract as the last day he or she has the right to exercise either buying or selling the underlying financial instruments. A contract is termed worthless in moments the expiration date has passed. The expiration date tends to differ depending on the type of contract an individual has entered this despite the general principle of the contract being worthless after the last days.

Settlement Option

The settlement of options can be described as the process by which the holder and writer of an options contract resolve and exercise the terms stated. The process entails the participation of two parties in the trade of options and it differs depending on the options one has decided to trade.

Differences among Options, Forex, and Stocks

When it comes to forex trading, the entire system is totally different. Before you can trade using leverage, you need to have opened the forex trading account. That's the only requirement that is out there, nothing else. When you open a forex account, you can easily use the leverage feature. When you decide to trade stocks, you end up purchasing the companies' shares that have a cost from a few dollars down to even hundreds of dollars. Usually, the price in the market tends to share with demand and supply.

Paired trades

When you trade with forex, you are facing another world, unseen in the stock market. Though the currency of a country tends to change, there will always be a great supply of currency that you can trade. What this means is that the main currencies in the world tend to be very liquid. When you are in forex trading, you will see that the currencies are normally quoted in pairs. They are not quoted alone. This means that you should be interested in the country's economic health that you have decided to trade in. The economic health of the country tends to affect the worth of the currency.

The basic considerations change from one forex market to another. If you decide to purchase the Intel shares, the main aim is to see if the stock's value will improve. You aren't interested in how the prices of other stocks are.

Price sensitivity to trade activities

When we look at both markets, we have no choice but to notice that there is varying price sensitivity when it comes to trade activities done.

If a small company that has fewer shares has about ten thousand shares bought from it, it could go a long way to impact the price of the stock. For a big company such as Apple, such n number of shares when bought from it won't affect the stock price. When you look at forex trades, you will realize that trades of a few hundreds of millions of dollars won't affect the major currency at all. If it affects, it would be minute.

Market accessibility

It is easy to access the currency market, unlike its counterpart, the stock market. Though you may be able to trade stocks every second of the day, five days weekly in the twenty-first century, it is not easy.

CHAPTER 1:

The Opportunity of Options Trading

Many novice traders have visions of making millions of dollars buying and selling individual call options. It is possible to make money trading individual call and put options, however very few professional traders make a career doing so. The fact is that straight trading of individual options is not likely to bring consistent and long-term success. It is just too difficult to consistently predict which way a stock price is going to move over short time periods.

That said, everyone has to start as a level 2 trader, and you can look at the period of time that you spend trading call and put options as a chance to gain some experience. At first, start with single options contracts until you get used to the mentality and experience of options trading.

As you train yourself, although many will be tempted to stick with call options because they are the way people think (you make money when the stock rises in price), you should also look for opportunities to make money from put options, and trade them. This will help your skills as an options trader broaden and improve, and you will start learning how to recognize trends in the markets that move in both directions.

Adopt a Trading Type

We haven't gotten into all the trading strategies yet. But by the time you finish this reading, you will understand all the main ways that you can trade options and the main strategies that are used by professional options traders. As you are learning, you can try your hand at all of them and find out which ones you enjoy the most and which ones you are best at trading.

However, you should winnow out your trading methods. The best professional traders are those that focus on using only one or two trading strategies. Options traders that become sellers of options premium typically only sell options premium. Of course, some people are able to multi-task more than others, and so they may have a more diversified strategy. The traders on Tasty Trade are often using many different strategies. That said, when you are a new options trader, it is good to find one or two strategies and then master them. If you can work up a solid profit over the course of a year, then at that time you might want to expand your trading repertoire.

As another example, many traders like using iron condors to generate income. A large number of traders only trade iron condors. They have become experts at using this one technique, and so they spend their time looking for opportunities to apply the strategy and earning regular income.

Equipment and Location

Most options traders don't need a large amount of equipment. If you start saying the word "trader," you are probably approaching this issue thinking of day traders with banks of computer screens displaying lots of charts and tables. This is not necessary for the vast majority of options traders. You certainly should have a good desktop computer that you have access to, and optionally you should also have a smartphone or tablet you have access to as well. If you are using a trading platform that does not have a lot of analysis tools and you have to use a second website for that purpose, you might want to have a second desktop computer or use a second device like an iPad to be following stock charts and so forth. Most traders can get by with a good desktop computer, iPad, and smartphone. And of course, you will need a good internet and Wi-Fi connection. The last thing you want to do is get in a situation where you are needing to get out of a trade and your internet connection goes down. This is one reason why having a smartphone so that you can still access the trading platform when your internet is down being a good idea, rather than relying exclusively on a desktop computer.

You can trade at home and then use a smartphone to keep tabs of your trading when not at home. It is recommended that you set aside a space for your trading activities. This is a part of viewing your options trading as a business. If you were to start an at-home business, you would probably set aside some home office space for it. Do the same when it comes to your options trading.

Trading as a Business

Options trading is flexible. You don't have to dive into options trading full time if you don't want to. You can do it very part-time, and set a goal of only making a few hundred dollars a month, or you can go full-fledged into options trading and try and build a million dollar a year business.

Trading as a business can, but doesn't necessarily have to, mean setting up an actual business for your trading activities. Depending on the laws of your location, you can setup a corporate entity and use that for your trading activities. Approaching it in that way will require satisfying all of the legal requirements, including tax forms, and setting up separate bank accounts.

Of course, it is not necessary to setup a business for options trading. You can certainly do it and just treat it as an individual income. Keep in mind that options trading – for the most part – is going to involve short term capital gains. In the United States short term capital gains are treated as regular income for tax purposes. If you do invest in LEAPs and hold some assets for a year or longer, you may be able to treat your gains as long-term capital gains and get preferential tax treatment.

You are unlikely to run into any legal trouble with the one exception being opening a margin account. If you open a margin account and are unable to meet your debt obligations, then you could get into some trouble. That might be something to consider when thinking about whether or not you start your trading activities as an official business to separate it from your personal activities. But for most people, it shouldn't be necessary to go through all the trouble of setting up a business when it comes to options trading.

Risk Management

One of the most important things to get a handle on when you begin trading options is a plan for risk management. On the losing side, this means having a "stop loss." That is a value you use to determine when to exit a trade. So, if the options price were to drop say $50, you can setup your trading platform to automatically sell any options that fit this description. Alternatively, you can also setup trades to automatically sell when you reach a certain level of profit. This is called "take profit." Check to see if your trading platform allows you to enter automatic stop loss and take profit orders.

If you can, this will greatly simplify your trading activities, and keep you from making impulsive and emotional mistakes. Instead, you will be able to cap your losses on any given trade, and ensure that if stock prices are rising, you get out with profits without waiting too long because you get excited and greedy. Remember, that can lead to losses. It is better to put caps, which of course means that you are going to miss out on some gains from time to time. But more often than not, it means that you are going to avoid making large mistakes. It is better to consistently make $50 profits, rather than holding on too long all the time hoping to score big and ending up with small profits or even losses.

If your system does not allow you to enter automatic stop loss and take profit orders, you are going to have to develop some personal discipline and manage those manually. That means that you would have to pay attention to your gains and losses, and be ready to exit trades when the rule you have decided upon is realized. There are no hard rules to follow, you will have to pick something that works for you. But in my opinion, on a per option basis, a maximum loss of $25 is reasonable. So, if you enter into a trade and you are losing $25 per options contract, you should go ahead and sell your options. This is a matter of cutting losses without letting them get out of control while you hope that things get better. Also, it will keep you from panicking too easily, by setting a fairly significant loss level, you will keep yourself from jumping out too early when the stock is going to reverse and make profits for your options.

On the other side, for take profit, take a 2-to-1 to 4-to-1 ratio. So, if you are going to have a $25 stop loss limit, then set your take profit to $50, or possibly $100, per options contract or trade. These rules are not going to guarantee profits. Sometimes they are going to work to provide winning trades, and sometimes this is not going to appear to help you. What you are looking for is a systematic approach that will help you to earn profits on average. The specific values you pick are less important than simply having some kind of risk management system. Of course, you don't want to be too conservative, because then you will be missing out on a lot of profits and getting out of many trades too early. And don't stop here. Remember that we said you should be aiming to continually educate yourself as an options trader. So, get online and find out what other options traders are doing, and settle on the type of risk management system that fits you the best. Remember that different traders are going to have different levels of risk tolerance.

CHAPTER 2:

Who Is This Book for?

This guide is perfect if you are interested or are actually beginning your journey into Options Trading.

When trading options for beginners, we deal with the basics, the foundation of a strong foundation in learning stock trading. With the right knowledge, you can make a huge profit with stock options. For beginners in options trading, it can be difficult to tell the exact difference between stock market trading and stock option trading.

Due to the deadlines set for each trade, many beginners of options trading have a common misconception that stock options carry high risks. The period is often perceived as a loss of assets. Options trading has proven to be advantageous because traders approach it with a plan and knowledge of effective leverage techniques. Options are usually selected for a level of leverage with limited risk.

Just as successful entrepreneurs must create a business plan, beginners in options trading should have a plan when joining a trading company. Exploring a topic is always a good idea; you can create a strategy around the knowledge gained by merely searching the internet! Coaching programs are also a great way to find free seminars or websites that allow guests free online courses.

Through these programs, called "Webinars," you can find free websites and many online forums to help beginners in options trading build a basic set of skills and find the opportunities you have available for further education, all within a monetary commitment.

As a beginner in options trading, your top priority when setting up a plan is to ask yourself what you hope to gain from trading options. Where is your risk tolerance? What does your portfolio look like? How big do you want to start with a collection? As a newbie, you can't expect the worst too soon. It's not about getting rich quick; trading takes time, patience, and a lot of perseverance if you hope to see a profit. You may have to go through various strategies and suffer some losses before you find a strategy that suits you, but you can minimize losses with the right set of skills.

When I started, I traded in stock options with virtually no knowledge, so I can help beginners avoid the same mistakes I made. In the beginning, I had very unrealistic expectations. I had experienced in the stock market, but when I switched to stock options, I had four reasons:

1.) Options can be bought and sold for a fraction of the base price of the shares.

2.) Without ownership of the underlying shares, you can still manage them using the share option.

3.) You can always use this option no matter how the stocks move.

4.) You can manage risks by securing a trading position.

I've had some grim experience, but perhaps I can help you understand why many beginners fail in the end. The biggest mistake I made when I first started was not properly researching coaching programs. I wanted to become an expert quickly, so I enrolled in a program that far exceeded my abilities. In the end, I had to learn again, because these were not options for beginners.

The basics are essential for a better understanding; I can't stress this enough; the key is to become a successful trader. Option trading always carries risk like any other investment, but based on the basics, you can minimize your risk and find success!

Options are treated as derivatives because these financial transactions are based on the value of assets or underlying securities. Unlike stocks, options expire on specific dates and do not have a fixed number specified for availability. Most people may not understand how options work, but some have used them in their business. Beginners should know that there are two types of options they can work on. The first of these is, for example, the possibility of calling them. You can buy stocks at a specific price before a certain date. This can be compared to buying deposits.

Merchants pay a premium for the purchase of calling options. This payment gives them the right to purchase the underlying asset in the future at a predetermined exercise price. For example, traders are not allowed to buy shares because they are not obliged but lost money in the form of an option premium during the process if they are waiting to expire. Another type of option they can trade is called a put option. Traders can sell the underlying asset at an agreed price and on a specific day. Options, in this case, are comparable to insurance.

Traders can exercise their put options and sell assets at the insurance price. If the amount of the underlying asset increases, it does not have to exercise its put option, and the only cost incurred is the premium. Call and put settings are used by traders to reduce the risk of receiving them. Those who buy options have the right to exercise. Traders wishing to exercise their call option may purchase the underlying asset at a given exercise price, and those wishing to use their put option may sell it at an agreed price.

Although call and put sellers have the right to buy or sell, they are not obliged to do so. They may decide to exercise their rights, depending on their market analysis. There are several ways traders can set off their options, in addition to using their powers. They can dispose of it by buying or selling, or they can give it up. Traders may choose to give up their options if the remaining premium is lower than the cost of liquidation.

CHAPTER 3:

Why to Trade Options

There are several people who have found it appealing to trade in stocks because of its popularity. This is because several people fear trading other financial instruments. This is not supposed to be the case since other financial instruments such as options have a myriad advantage in the financial markets. Despite several people trading stocks, the numbers of people who are trading options have increased tremendously over the years. The major trigger of this increase is the advantages possessed by options. These advantages include;

Capital Outlay and Cost Efficiency

There is one of the major reasons that is owned by the trading of options. The talked about reason is the potential of making huge amounts of profits. It is more advantageous because an individual does not need to have huge capital investment in the trade. This phenomenon has made it ideal for an investor to focus on options trading because they can be able to start small as they invest more as time goes by. It is an attraction to even investors who have huge budgets as well because it proves to be cost-effective. In simple terms, one can be able to use leverage to acquire more trading power.

It is an occurrence that has been proved to be true in the financial market. It is in the sense that an option trader can be able to purchase options of similar stock. This will give him or her the power to purchase the stock by using a call option. Buying options and then buy shares, in the event he or she sells the shares in the present market situation, one can be in a position to make a huge amount of profits. The trade of options has certain positions an individual can take to make sure that he or she save his or her capita investment depending on the underlying asset.

Risk and Reward

The risk to reward advantage is often linked to the first advantage illustrated above. It is all narrows down to profits an individual is able to create in the options market. Traders and investors in the options markets can make proportionate gains with regards to the amount they have invested in the trade. A good depiction can be made from the potential an individual has to gunner from small investment which also has the potential of multiplying. The advantaged risk to reward ratio is achieved to its maximum potentials in the event that an individual uses the right strategies. It is important for an individual to constantly note that there will always be risks involved in options trading. This is because it is a characteristic of any form of investment or business done by any person. There are trading strategies that can be very risky when it comes to using them to base critical decisions such as those that are speculative. The general rule in options trading is that speculation with high potential returns tends to have high-risk involvement in it. On the other hand, options that have low-risk levels tend to have fewer amounts of gains. Options trading involves various types of options contracts. This makes it easy for an individual to limit risks in option trading depending on the contract he or she has settled on.

Flexibility and Versatility

Flexibility is one of the most appealing elements that options trading poses. It is often in contract to several forms that are resented as a passive investment while some are inactive forms. The common characterization here is that an individual is limited to making money or using other strategies. A good depiction can be used by an individual who buys stocks for the thought of building his or her portfolio so as to serve long term gains. Such an individual can be able to use two kinds of strategies. The first strategy will involve a trader focusing on the long term gains and purchasing a stock that has the potential to increase in value in the future. The second strategy will involve an options trader can choose to invest in stocks that give regular returns. Buy and hold is a strategy that has several techniques involved to help it to be a success.

However, the flexibility and versatility offered by the trading of options mean that an option trader has the potential of opening more opportunities. This means that a trader or investor of options has the ability to make profits in any kind of market condition. One is able to speculate price movements of foreign currencies, indices, and commodities. What this means is that a range of option trading strategies plays higher roles to a trader in the identification of other profitable ventures and being successful in them.

CHAPTER 4:

Options the Basics

For you to succeed, you need the basic knowledge of what you want to do for it will help you on how to do things the right way with less trouble. To fit in the options trading game, you need to know the basic knowledge about this type of trading to be on the safer side. We shall take a look at the strategies you can use, the types of options, how it works, and its drawbacks.

Strategies Used in Options Trading

Strategies are the set of guidelines you need to follow to achieve amazing results in what you are doing, and options trading has its strategies, too. Let us now dig deeper into a number of the strategies that you need to implement.

Covered call strategy. It is a market transaction where an individual, mostly an investor who is offering call options for sale, owns the same size as the market trade. It is executed when the individual with the long term asset writes the call options on the asset. Covered call strategy is a popular strategy because of its capability to minimize risks and promote income generation.

It is mostly applied when you, as an investor, have an asset with a short term and short position, wanting to hold it for long for you to receive the options premiums. A seller who has amazing knowledge on covered call strategy gets higher profits as compared to other strategies. The drawback of this strategy is that an individual does not receive full options premium when the stock rises above the strike price.

Long straddle strategy. This is an options strategy where a trader purchases an asset that has both the long standard options and put-call. Also, the agreed price plus the time of expiry are normally similar. This strategy generates massive profits by having long put and call options. The long call practice in the market happens when long put expires, and there is a rise in the price of the instrument. Moreover, the long put is practiced only in the fall of the stock's price scenario. You are advised to use this strategy when you think the volatility of the stock will be significant through the trade term. You suffer losses if your underlying stock comes in between the upper and lower breakeven point.

Short straddle strategy. It is a risky strategy that is the vice versa of the long straddle options strategy. As an investor, you are advised to apply this strategy when there are chances of low volatility in the market. You are likely to suffer from significant losses when the stock behaves significantly in the market. The investor generates income and holds on the premium when the stock behavior in the market does not have much change in either direction.

Long strangle strategy. How does long strangle strategy work? Here is the answer to it. An investor normally purchases out of money standard options and puts calls simultaneously on the instrument with a similar time of expiry. Out of the money call option is a call option with a lower market price than the price agreed on an asset. Conversely, out of the money put option is a market situation in the case that an asset has a price above the strike price.

Most of the investors who apply this strategy have the belief that the asset will have a huge change in its behavior but are not sure in which direction. It is a cheaper strategy with limited losses compared to straddle because of the options which are purchased out of the money.

Iron butterfly strategy. Iron butterfly strategy involves selling and purchasing an at the money put and also at the money call. All of the options normally have the same expiration dates on the asset. It is named after a creature because the short put and call are offered for sale at the middle strike price forming the body part of a butterfly, while the wings come into formation when the put and call options are purchased either above or below the middle strike price.

Most traders use this strategy when they believe there will be no changes in the stock's price within the time of expiry. You have a higher likelihood of getting huge profits when you are near the strike price in the middle.

Iron condor strategy. It is an options strategy that involves the sale of out of the money call and put spread on a similar instrument (preferably asset) with a similar date of expiration. It is created when the trader offers the out of the money put for sale and purchases another one of a lower strike price. Also, created by offering one out of the money call for sale and purchases another one of a higher strike price. The call and put spreads are normally of the same width. Many traders prefer this strategy because of the capability of generating huge credit on the same risk as compared to other options strategies.

Long call butterfly spread. In this type of strategy, a trader normally utilizes both bull and bear call spread strategies with three different strike prices on similar instruments and time of expiry. A trader normally purchases two contracts for options where one is of a greater agreed price than the other contract. Also, there is a sale of two other contract options at a price in the middle. The price agreed should be equivalent to the amount you get when you distinguish the top strike price and the lowest one.

Protective collar strategy. This strategy is exercised when you purchase a put and conversely write a call with the situation of out of the money in the market. It takes place on a similar stock with a similar time of expiry. Combining long put and the short call forms the collar of the stock, which is normally established by the agreed prices of the options. Its protective feature, moreover, comes up from the capability of the put option to offer protection on the stock until on the expiration of the option. Bear put spread trading strategy. A trader on this strategy buys put options at an agreed price then offers a similar amount of put for sale at a lower price. A similar type of option is on the same stock with the same date of expiration. Most bearish traders use this strategy with the expectations that the price of the stock will drop. The advantage of this strategy is its ability to offer minimal losses though it also offers minimal profits, which is a turn off for most traders.

Bull call strategy. You, as an investor, purchase calls at an agreed price and simultaneously offer the calls for sale at a greater agreed price. Normally happens in similar instruments having a similar time of expiration. Most bullish traders use this strategy expecting there will be an average increase in the price of the stock to gain profits.

Long put trading strategy. It is a bearish options trading strategy. An investor who uses this strategy expects the stock will move become lower before the time of expiration. Risks involved here are minimal to the amount of premium paid. The downside of this strategy is that the price of the asset must drop before the date of expiration, or else you lose all the option money. Short put trading strategy. Unlike the long put options strategy, a short put strategy is utilized mostly when the trader is bullish about the stock, that is, expects a rise in the stock's price. In any case, the agreed price becomes lower than that of the asset; then, the trader makes massive profits. The losses incurred here are unlimited.

Why Use Options?

Why should you use options? Here are a few reasons why you should utilize options as your tool for trading.

- You only need minimum initial cash outlay to purchase options as compared when buying stock in trading.

- Options such as call options enable investors to enter the market at a cheaper cost.

- Options also help investors to generate more income. It is seen mostly by using the covered call options trading strategy. The investor holds on to the stock believing the price will have few changes. As in, either to remain stable or increase a little.

• Purchasing calls and put options enable traders to invest with minimal risks since the major thing they can lose is premium.

• Using options will offer you more investment alternatives since it is a flexible trading tool.

How Options Work

After knowing the strategies and the reasons why to use options, let us now know how this type of trading works. Below are some of the details I have for you:

• Options have a time frame. They always have their date of expiration. You should be able to know their time frame to make profits. After they expire, you do not have the right to purchase or offer stock for sale at a specified price. The shorter the time it has till expiry, the lower the value of the option.

• Options have different strike prices, which normally indicate the price of the stock.

• Options offer you the right to purchase or offer stock for sale.

• Purchasing an option gives you the honor to purchase or offer the stock for sale.

• Selling an option gives you the honor of delivering the stock at an agreed price. The stock's current price is not under consideration.

CHAPTER 5:

What Is an Options Contract?

An options contract sounds fancy but it's a pretty simple concept.

- It's a contract. That means it's a legal agreement between a buyer and a seller.

- It gives the owner of the contract the opportunity to purchase or dispose of an asset with a fixed amount.

- The purchase is optional – so the buyer of the contract does not have to buy or sell the asset.

- The contract has an expiration date, so the purchaser – if they choose to exercise their right – must make the trade on or before the expiration date.

- The purchaser of the contract pays a non-refundable fee for the contract.

There are options contracts that take place in all aspects of daily life including real estate and speculation. A simple example illustrates the concept of an options contract.

Suppose you are itching to buy a BMW and you've decided the model you want must be silver. You drop by a local dealer and it turns out they don't have a silver model in stock. The dealer claims he can get you one by the end of the month. You say you'll take the car if the dealer can get it by the last day of the month and he'll sell it to you for $67,500. He agrees and requires you to put a $3,000 deposit on the car.

If the last day of the month arrives and the dealer hasn't produced the car, then you're freed from the contract and get your money back. In the event he does produce the car at any date before the end of the month, you have the option to buy it or not. If you really wanted the car you can buy it, but of course, you can't be forced to buy the car, and maybe you've changed your mind in the interim.

The right is there but not the obligation to purchase, in short, no pressure if you decided not to push through with the purchase of the car. If you decide to let the opportunity pass, however, since the dealer met his end of the bargain and produced the car, you lose the $3,000 deposit.

In this case, the dealer, who plays the role of the writer of the contract, has the obligation to follow through with the sale based upon the agreed-upon price.

Suppose that when the car arrives at the dealership, BMW announces it will no longer make silver cars. As a result, prices of new silver BMWs that were the last ones to roll off the assembly line, skyrocket. Other dealers are selling their silver BMWs for $100,000. However, since this dealer entered into an options contract with you, he must sell the car to you for the pre-agreed price of $67,500. You decide to get the car and drive away smiling, knowing that you saved $32,500 and that you could sell it at a profit if you wanted to.

The situation here is capturing the essence of options contracts, even if you've never thought of haggling with a car dealer in those terms.

An option is in a sense a kind of bet. In the example of the car, the bet is that the dealer can produce the exact car you want within the specified time period and at the agreed-upon price. The dealer is betting too. His bet is that the pre-agreed to price is a good one for him. Of course, if BMW stops making silver cars, then he's made the wrong bet.

It can work the other way too. Let's say that instead of BMW deciding not to make silver cars anymore when your car is being driven onto the lot, another car crashes into it. Now your silver BMW has a small dent on the rear bumper with some scratches. As a result, the car has immediately declined in value. But if you want the car, since you've agreed to the options contract, you must pay $67,500, even though with the dent it's only really worth $55,000. You can walk away and lose your $3,000 or pay what is now a premium price on a damaged car.

Another example that is commonly used to explain options contracts is the purchase of a home to be built by a developer under the agreement that certain conditions are met. The buyer will be required to put a non-refundable down payment or deposit on the home. Let's say that the developer agrees to build them the home for $300,000 provided that a new school is built within 5 miles of the development within one year. So, the contract expires within a year.

At any time during the year, the buyer has the option to go forward with the construction of the home for $300,000 if the school is built. The developer has agreed to the price no matter what. So if the housing market in general and the construction of the school, in particular, drive up demand for housing in the area, and the developer is selling new homes that are now priced at $500,000, he has to sell this home for $300,000 because that was the price agreed to when the contract was signed. The home buyer got what they wanted, being within 5 miles of the new school with the home price fixed at $300,000. The developer was assured of the sale but missed out on the unknown, which was the skyrocketing price that occurred as a result of increased demand. On the other hand, if the school isn't built and the buyers don't exercise their option to buy the house before the contract expires at one year, the developer can pocket the $20,000 cash.

What Is an Options Contract on the Stock Market?

On the stock market, we are betting on the future price itself, and the shares of stock will be bought or sold at a profit if things work out. The key point is the buyer of the options contract is not hoping to acquire the shares and hold them for a long time period like a traditional investor. Instead, you're hoping to make a bet on the price of the stock, secure that price, and then be able to trade the shares on that price no matter what happens on the actual markets. We will illustrate this with an example.

1. Call Options

A call is a type of options contract that provides the option to purchase an asset at the agreed-upon amount at the designated time or deadline. The reason you would do this is if you felt that the price of a given stock would increase in price over the specified time period. Let's illustrate with an example.

Suppose that Acme Communications makes cutting edge smartphones. The rumors are that they will announce a new smartphone in the following three weeks that is going to take the market by storm, with customers lined out the door to make preorders.

The current price that Acme Communications is trading at is $44.25 a share. The current pricing of an asset is termed as the spot price. Put another way, the spot price is the actual amount that you would be paying for the shares as you would buy it from the stock market right now.

Nobody really knows if the stock price will go up when the announcement is made, or if the announcement will even be made. But you've done your research and are reasonably confident these events will take place. You also have to estimate how much the shares will go up and based on your research you think it's going to shoot up to $65 a share by the end of the month. You enter into an options contract for 100 shares at $1 per share. You pay this fee to the brokerage that is writing the options contract. In total, for 100 shares you pay $100.

The price that is paid for an options contract is $100. This price is called the premium. You don't get the premium back. It's a fee that you pay no matter what. If you make a profit, then it's all good. But if your bet is wrong, then you'll lose the premium. For the buyer of an options contract, the premium is their risk.

You'll want to set a price that you think is going to be lower than the level to which the price per share will rise. The price that you agree to is called the strike price. For this contract, you set your strike price at $50.

Remember, exercising your right to buy the shares is optional. You'll only buy the shares if the price goes high enough that you'll make a profit on the trade. If the shares never go above $50, say they reach $48, you are not obligated to buy them. And why would you? As part of the contract deal, you'd be required to buy them at $50.

We'll say that the contract is entered on the 1st of August, and the deadline is the third Friday in August. If the price goes higher than your strike price during that time, you can exercise your option.

Let's say that as the deadline approaches, things go basically as you planned. Acme Communications announces its new phone, and the stock starts climbing. The stock price on the actual market (the spot price) goes up to $60.

Now the seller is required to sell you the shares at $50 a share. You buy the shares, and then you can immediately dispose of these at a quality or optimal amount, or $60 a share. You make a profit of $10 a share, not taking into account any commissions or fees.

2. The Call Seller

The call seller who enters into the options contract with the buyer is obligated to sell the shares to the buyer of the options contract at the strike price. If the contract sets the strike price at $50 a share for 100 shares, the seller must sell the stock at that price even if the market price goes up to any higher price, such as $70 a share. The call seller keeps the premium. So, if the buyer doesn't exercise their option, the call seller still gets the money from the premium.

CHAPTER 6:

Call and Put Options

Put and call options are referred to as a derivative investment. The movements of their prices depend on the movements of prices of a different financial product, also referred to as the underlying.

So, what is an option? It is defined as the right to sell or buy a certain stock with a set price given a specific time frame. With options, you won't have outright ownership of the shares, but you make calculated bets on a stock's price and what its value will be in the future, given the specified expiration of the option. What makes options attractive is that you are to choose whether you want to exercise them or not. If your bet is wrong, you can let the options expire. Although the options' original cost is lost, it still wouldn't compare had you paid for the stock's full price.

Call options are purchased when the trader is expecting the underlying's price to go up within a particular time frame.

Put options are purchased when the trader is expecting the underlying's price to go down within a particular time frame.

There's an option for puts and calls to be written or sold. This will still generate income, but certain rights have to be given up to the option's buyer.

For options defined for the US, a call is defined as an options contract giving the buyer rights to buy an underlying asset at a set price any time until the expiration date. For options defined for the EU, buyers can choose to exercise the option to purchase the underlying but only on the set expiration date.

The strike price is defined as a determined beforehand at which the call buyer has the choice to purchase the underlying asset. For example, a buyer of a certain stock call option with a 10$ strike price may opt to purchase that stock at the same price before the expiration date of the option.

The expiration of options may vary. It can also be short or long term. It can be worth the while for call buyers to exercise the option, which is to require the writer or seller of the call to sell the stocks at the set strike price., but only if the underlying's current price is more than the strike price. For example, if a stock trades at $10 at the stock market, it is not profitable for the buyer of the call option to exercise the choice to purchase that stock at $11 since they could get the same on the market at a lower price.

Put buyers reserve the right to sell stocks at strike price during a set time range.

The highs and lows the stock market goes through can be both exciting and nerve-wracking for newbie or veteran investors. Risking hard-earned money can make anyone anxious. But played right with sound and well-planned strategies, you can be successful in this field

If you are looking for a way to invest in the stock market but you are trying to avoid the risk of directly selling stocks or buying them, options trading might be perfect for you. Options are typically traded at significantly lower prices compared to the underlying prices of the actual shares. This makes trading them a less risky way to control a large stock position, although you don't own the shares. Using options strategically allows risk mitigation while maintaining huge profit potentials, and you will be playing in the field even if you're investing just a fraction of the stock's price.

All of these benefits of options trading got you excited, right? After all, options have a lower risk and they're a lot cheaper. There are two major disadvantages, however – the limited-time aspect and the reality that you don't own the stock until you choose to exercise your options.

Call Options

With call options, what you pay for is just 'rights to buy' certain shares at a set price and covered by a specific time frame. Let's say that stock ABC is selling for $90 per share in May. If you believe that the stock's price will go up over a few months, you'd purchase a three-month option to buy 100 shares of ABC by August 31 for $100. For this sample call option, you would be paying around $200 if the option cost per share is $2. In options, you are only allowed to buy in increments of 100 shares. This gives you the choice to purchase 100 shares of ABC anytime within the three-month timeframe. The $200 investment is significantly lower than the $9,000 you would have had to shell out if you bought 1000 shares outright.

If you bet right and on July 15, if the ABC shares hit the market at $115, you may exercise the call option and you would have gained $1,300 (that's 100 shares multiplied by the $15 profit you gained per share and deducted by your original investment of $200). If you don't have the resources to buy the shares, you can also make a profit if you re-sell the option to another investor or via the open market. The gain will be pretty much similar to this option.

If you bet wrong, and the price of ABC's shares fell to $80 never to reach $100 within the three-month timeframe, you can let the option reach its expiration, which saves you money (if you bought the shares outright, your original investment of $9,000 is now down to a value of only $8,000, so you lost $1000). This means you only lost $200, which was your investment for the call option.

Risks Involved in Call Options

Like any other form of investment, options have their share of potential risks. Taking the second scenario where you bet wrong as an example and stock ABC never got to $100 during the option's timeframe of three months, you would have lost the entire $200 of your investment, right? In terms of loss percentage, that's %100. Anyone who's been playing the stock market would tell you that it's extremely rare for an investor to suffer a 100% loss. This scenario can only happen if ABC suddenly went bankrupt, causing the price of their stocks to plummet down to zero value.

Therefore, if you look at it from a point of view of percentages, options can cause you huge losses. Let's elaborate on this point. If the price of ABC's share went up to $99 and it's the last day for you to exercise the option, choosing to purchase the shares will mean losing a dollar for each share. What if you invested $9,000 for the stock and you owned 100 stock shares? In three months, which is the option's expiration date if you took it, you would have gained 10% from your original investment ($99 from $90). Comparing both, you would have gained 10% if you purchased the shares outright and lost %100 if you chose the option but did not exercise it. This example shows how risky options can be.

However, the opposite can happen if stock ABC reached a price higher than $100. If you purchased the option, your gain percentage would have been substantially higher compared to buying the stocks outright. If the stock reached $110, you would have gained 400% ($10 gain versus the $2 per share investment) if you went for the option and only gained 22% ($20 gain versus the $90 per share investment) if you purchased the shares.

Lastly, when you own the stock, nothing can force you to sell. That means if after three months, and stock ABC's price goes down, you can hang on to it if you believe it still has the potential to recover and even increase in value compared to the original. If the price goes up dramatically, you'll make significant gains and you didn't incur losses.

However, if you chose options as your investment method, the expiration would have forced you to suffer a 100% loss after the set timeframe. There will be no option to hold on to the stock even if you believe it will go up in value soon.

Options have major pros and also major cons. You need to be aware of these before you step into the arena of options trading.

Put Options

On the other side of the options investment is the put option. Whereas call is the right to purchase, 'put' gives you the option to sell a certain security at a set price within a specific time frame. Investors usually purchase put options to protect the price of a stock in case it suddenly drops down, or even the market itself. With put options, you can sell the shares and your investment portfolio is protected from unexpected market swings. Put options are, therefore, a way to hedge your portfolio or lower its risk.

For example, you have invested in stock ABC for 100 shares, which you bought for $50 per share. As of May 31, the price per share has reached a market high $70. Of course, you'd want to maintain this position in your stock, and at the same time protect your gained profits in case the price of this stock goes down. To fit your requirements, you may purchase a put option with a three-month expiration and $70 per share strike price.

If ABC's stock price goes down drastically over the coming couple of months, reaching a low per-share price of only $60, you will still be protected. By exercising your put option, you will still be able to sell the shares at $70 each even if stock ABC is now trading at a lower value. If you are feeling confident that ABC can still recover in the future, you can hold on to the stock and just resell the put option. The price of this put option will have gone up because of the diving stock ABC took.

On the other hand, if stock ABC's value kept climbing, just let the put option expire and you would still profit from the increased price of the shares. Even though you lost what you have invested in the put option, you still have the underlying stock with you. Therefore, you can view the put option as a kind of insurance policy for your investment, which may or may not use. Another thing to remember is that you can purchase put options even if you don't own the underlying stock, just like you would in a call option. You are not required to own the stock itself.

Risks Involved in Put Options

Just as with call options, put options carry the same risks. There is also a 100% loss potential when the underlying stock price goes up, and a huge gain when the price dives because you can resell the option for a higher price.

CHAPTER 7:

Derivative Contracts

O ptions are a group of conditional derivative contracts, which means that they are derivative financial instruments. The main role of derivatives in the financial market is the transfer of risk. Therefore, there is a commodity or a financial instrument, or any assets that have marketability, and from whose price depends on the price of derivatives that are traded on the derivatives market or futures market. Many derivatives are used to reduce risk. For example, a farmer who is not sure what will be the price of corn at harvest and sales. To remove this uncertainty, it is protected by derivatives of corn futures prices fall, thus avoiding the high losses. The basic role of the derivatives is the transfer of risk to participants who are willing to accept that risk and achieve huge profits/losses, as their forecasts of future price movements opposing those who want to protect themselves from risk. Participants who want to protect themselves from the risk are called hedgers, and those who accept that risk, and by realized profits/losses, are called traders (traders) which are popularly called speculators. Exchange-traded options include the right to buy or sell an asset, and the ability to withdraw from this right are the basic elements that make a difference between the options and futures.

The futures market or the market of derivatives would not be able to function, without a large number of speculators who are always willing to "gamble." Some financial institutions tend to use derivatives as a source of income. This is a general reason of famous incident involving the collapse of Barings Bank in February 1995. But not just Barrings Bank dealt with difficulties. Great financial difficulties also had Procter

& Gamble, Orange Country, Hammersmith, and Fulham Local Authority. In the case of Barings Bank, Nick Leeson was obviously trying to take advantage of small differences in the prices of financial instruments which he bought on the stock markets of the Far East and sell them in other markets, trying to use a process known as arbitrage. In January and February 1995, he bet on Japanese stocks by buying a significant amount of futures contracts on the Nikkei 225 index on the stock exchanges in Osaka and Tokyo. There was a difficult period on the Japanese stock market which resulted in the disaster of the Barings Bank.

Options are the right to buy or sell a particular subject, such as stocks or government bonds at a predetermined price within a specified time limit.

the right to buy or sell an asset, and the ability to withdraw from this right are the basic elements that make a difference between the options and futures. Futures involve the need to sell an asset, on a certain day, at a specified price, if it did not "come out" of the contract. An option is considered to be a contract between the seller and the buyer in which he holds the right to buy or sell a financial instrument at a certain period of time or on a specified date in the future at a price specified at the moment of conclusion of the contract. The subject of the contract contained an option is called the basic investment (underlying asset). The subject of the contract can be:

• Goods (commodities) — agricultural products such as wheat, oil, wood, various metals, etc.

• Currency (currency)

• Action (stock, equities)

• Futures contracts (futures contracts)

• Stock indices (indexes) the price of the contract which is determined at the time of conclusion of the contract or the price at which the assets, which is the subject of an optional contract, may be bought or sold, is called the exercise price (strike price, exercise price). The strike price or exercise price of those options is usually very close to the current price of assets and it is subject to an optional contract, except in cases of exceptional growth or falling prices.

It is because the stock market is determining the strike price based on various analyses of the current market. Options are available in several amounts above or below the current price (current price, spot price) of the underlying investments. For example, stock prices that are below $ 25 per share usually have strike prices in the range 2½. The strike price of shares above $ 50 is generally in the range of $ 5. As for the share option, they are not available in every action. There are about 2,200 shares on which options are traded. Options are traded on stock exchanges around the world: LIFFE (London International Financial Futures and Options Exchange) -London, CBOE-Chicago, EUA-European stock market option, MONEY-France, and Deutsche Boerse and Eurex (German-Swiss international derivatives market) have opened a segment dedicated to the American actions. The opening of new markets in the segment of the Deutsche Boerse is intended to the best American actions-Xetra US Stars. Here we can find all the US stocks from the Dow 3ones Industrial Average, the S & P 100, Dow and NasdaqlOO 3ones Global Titans 50. On the same day, Eurex introduced options trading on stocks on denominated in the euro at 10 US stocks. These US stocks on which options can be found are AOL Time Warner, Cisco Systems, Citigroup, EMC, General Electric, IBM, Intel, Microsoft, Oracle and Sun Microsystems. The introduction of options on the most liquid US stocks, helped the Eurex to develop an even greater extent in its segment of options trading. Derivatives based on stocks are offering a significant increase in value and have great potential for growth. Investors are expecting from the leading stock markets to offer intelligent products for derivatives based on stocks, as well as for the American risk management instruments. London International Stock Exchange of futures and options-LIFFE announced that the total turnover of non-financial products traded in October

2001, was 16% higher than the same period last year. They traded with 395,103 contracts, compared to 341,249 in October 2000. The traffic increased in September when it was traded 369,464 contracts. The largest percentage of growth was recorded at the trade agreements with the ground in barley and coffee. Vendor of the options, or actually the side of the contract which must implement its obligation, in the case that the buyer (purchaser/ holder) of the option wishes that the contract to be implemented, is called the issuer. The date in the contract that represents a term in which the option matures and after which no longer applies is called the expiration date, and it is usually the third Friday of the month when the option expires. Expiration dates can vary from one month to three years in the case of LEAPS (Long-term Equity Anticipation Securities) options. If a customer wants to use the rights that the option provides, he has to pay an appropriate price, which is called the premium (premium). The premium is the price of an option and it is determined by many factors such as type of the basic investment, the current price, the rate of price volatility of the underlying investments in the prior year, current interest rate, the strike price of the option, and the time remaining until the expiration of the option. In a case of share options, the premium is calculated by the per-share method. Each option correspondent with the number 100. So, in case the premium is $2, the total premium for an option would be $200 ($ 2 x 100= 200$).

CHAPTER 8:

The Options Are a Flexible Tool

I f you were to first open your contract by selling, we say that you are "short." If you buy to open a position, we say that you are "long." The simplest way to trade options is to take a long position on a call or a put. Although when buying and selling stocks we say that someone "shorts" the stock when they are hoping to profit off a decline in share price, you can be hoping to profit from a decline in share price, but you are "long" with regard to the put option.

The strategy for profiting from going long on a call or put option is simple. You are hoping the price of the stock would move in your favor so that you will earn a profit. The industry is full of naysayers that downplay this basic strategy, however, the reality is you can definitely earn profits in this way. That is buying or selling individual options, be they the call or put variety. The key to success when doing this type of trading is to stay on top of it and don't buy options on a whim. You need a good reason to buy a call or a put option by itself, and that means paying attention to the financial news surrounding the company, earnings reports, and looking at simple market trends to determine when you have a reasonable probability of earning a profit.

Reading the Charts

As an options trader, you are going to have to learn how to read charts. The first thing to do is look up candlestick patterns so that you can recognize when a trend reversal might be coming. Candlestick patterns are not absolute rules or truth-tellers; they are an indicator. So you take the candlestick charts into consideration and use the entirety of the information that you have available to make your decisions.

As we said earlier, a candlestick can be divided into different timeframes. If you are looking to ride a trend over a single day, a five-minute timeframe is good to use. In this case, each candlestick is going to tell you what the price action was over the five-minutes period.

The candlesticks are going to be colored green or red. If a candlestick is green, it's a "bullish" candlestick. That means that over the period of interest, the closing price had risen to a larger higher than the opening price. By itself, it does not tell you where the price is headed. For a bullish candlestick, the top of the candle is the price at the end of the trading session, and the bottom of the body is the price at the start.

Each candlestick has "wicks" that come out of the top and bottom of the candlestick. The top wick gives you the high price for the time interval. The bottom candlestick gives you the low price of the time interval.

If a candlestick is red, that is a "bearish" candlestick. In that case, this means that the closing price was lower than the opening price. So, the top of the body is the opening price in this case, and the bottom of the body is the closing price (the price closed lower than it opened at). The meaning of wicks is the same.

A complete investigation of candlesticks is beyond the scope of this reading, so please see online resources or readings specifically addressing the topic, or day trading, to learn the patterns that you need to be looking for.

That said, here are the general rules for entering and exiting trades.

In the event of big news that you know is going to cause a massive move in the share price, you want to just get in early in the trading day.

If you are looking at a stock under normal conditions, that is no earnings report or other huge news, you want to wait for a downtrend in the share price so that you can enter a position at a relative minimum. So you buy the option at the lowest possible price given current market conditions. Then you wait until the price rises and the trend peaks out, and you close your position.

For beginners, I have to say get ready for the ride. If you are thin-skinned, this kind of trading is going to put you on pins and needles. As you know, stock prices do not follow a steady curve, they move up and down a lot. And as we have mentioned several times, a small move in share price which really isn't all that significant can have a big impact on options prices. It's not uncommon to get into a trade and see your option lose $75 or $100 over the course of a couple of hours, and then see it rise to a $50 or $100 profit in a few hours. So, this is not something for the faint of heart to get involved with.

But to avoid panic, you should rely on the indicators to help you make your decisions rather than relying on emotion.

The second big tool you need to use in your trading is the moving average. I like to use a 9-period case. This will be for an exponential moving average. Then for the long one, I will use twenty periods. Again, it will be an exponential moving average on the same chart. Moving averages average out the stock prices to give you smooth curves that show the overall price trend. Using two moving averages allows you to get signals when a trend is going to reverse. This actually works quite well in practice. The signal for a reversal is when the moving averages cross.

If a short period moving average crosses above a long period moving average, this is taken to be a signal of a coming uptrend. So in my case, I look for the 9-period moving average to cross above the 20-period moving average. This can be used to either reinforce your conviction that you should say in the trade or to enter a trade if you are looking to take advantage of a coming price movement (for call options).

If the short period moving average crosses below the long period moving average, that means that a downward trend is coming. So, if you have been riding a trend with a call option, that might be an indicator to sell to close your position.

You can also add a tool called the RSI to your charts, which is the relative strength indicator. This tells you if a stock is overbought or oversold. If the RSI is 70 or above, then the stock is considered to be overbought, and that can be a good time to exit a long call position. If the RSI is 30 or below, this is "oversold," and so it can be a good time to enter a long position for call options. I take the RSI with a grain of salt because I've seen it indicate overbought conditions which were then followed by continually rising prices, all too often. But it's one thing that you can consider looking at.

Finally, there are the Bollinger bands. These give you a moving average along with the standard deviation both above and below the moving average. If you are going to use this, the main reason would be to establish levels of support and resistance. A level of support is a low price level that the stock is unlikely to break below over a short time period. A level of resistance is the maximum price you are likely to see for the stock over a short time period. These are guidelines, a stock might suddenly break out of a range at any time.

Another reason to use Bollinger bands is for a guideline when selling to open a position. In this case, you could use one or two standard deviations to give you a boundary above and below which it's extremely unlikely the stock price is going to move. We will talk more about that in a few.

Having a Trading Plan

Having a trading plan in place is going to be important no matter what you do in the stock market. A trading plan should include the following:

- Your overall goal. This can include your reasons for investing as well as your goal for annual profits or ROI (return on investment).

- How much you are willing to put at risk. It should go without saying that you shouldn't bet the family farm on your trades. Set aside a fixed amount of money that you are willing to lose. If you are smart about your trading, you are unlikely to lose all of it, and hopefully, you don't have a string of losing trades. With options, you can start small and learn the ropes without risking large amounts of money. So start with something like $500. If you lose $500, it's not going to be the end of the world. If that happens, you can replenish it, and it's probably not going to put you in a position where you can't eat.

- Have a take profit level for the trade. This is done on a per-contract basis. The level I like to use is $50. It's true that you are going to miss out on some big gains some of the time, but having a fixed level ensures that overall you have a string of profitable trades. Remember that it is per contract, so you can trade five contracts on the same option and if you reach the $50 profit level, that is $250 in overall profit.

- Have an exit strategy. This is a personal tolerance level of risk. For me, it's a $100 loss on one contract, provided there are no signs of a turnaround coming. This is harder to quantify because options move up and down by large amounts over short time periods. So, if you are not somewhat flexible, getting out on a price move that is too small is going to cause you to lose out on a lot of trades. Remember that a $100 loss on a trade is only a price movement of $1-$2 on the underlying stock. It goes without saying that a stock that drops by $1 is just as likely to reverse course and go up by $1.

- Always watch time decay. You can profit on options at any time, but if you buy an option that you intend to hold for a period of several days, potential losses from time decay must be taken into account. One mistake that beginners make is not paying attention to time decay.

- Never let options expire. Another beginner's mistake is to buy options and just hold onto them waiting to see what's going to happen. Never hold onto an out of the money option. Even if you are going to sell it for a large loss, get out of it if the expiration date is approaching. When it comes to in the money options, you might sell the day before expiration. You are probably not going to want to keep an in the money option past that unless you want it exercised.

CHAPTER 9:

Make Profit from the Call

The goal when purchasing options contracts is to buy a stock at a price that is lower than its current market value. In other words, you want the stock price to be significantly higher than the strike price so that you're enjoying significant savings in purchasing the stock. When evaluating your options, you'll need to take into account the added costs of the premium paid plus commissions. In some cases, commissions can be substantial so make sure you know what they are ahead of time so that you choose a good strike price and exercise your options at the right time.

You're a trader, not an investor

You may be mentally conditioned to think in terms of investing. An investor wants to build a diversified portfolio over a long time period that they believe will increase in value over the long term. A trader operates in the same universe but has different goals. You are after short term profits – not investments. You are not going to hold this stock. If you were interested in holding the stock, you would simply buy it at the lower price that is currently on offer. Your goal is to be able to buy at the strike price when the stock has increased significantly in price and then sell it immediately so that you can pocket the profits.

Let's take an example. Suppose that XYZ corporation is currently selling at $30 a share. People are expecting the stock to rise, and some people are really bullish about their short-term prospects. If you are an investor, your goal is to get the stock at the lowest possible price and then hold it long term. If you are using strategies like dollar-cost averaging, you might be buying a few shares every month without paying too much attention to what the price is specifically on the day you purchase. In any case, as an investor, you'll simply buy the shares at $30.

As a trader, you're hoping to cash in on the moves of XYZ over the coming couple of months. You'll buy an options contract, let's say its premium is $0.90 and the strike price is $35. Your cost for the 100 shares is $90.

Then the stock price shoots up to $45. Since it passed the strike price, you can exercise your option to buy the shares at the strike price. You can buy them at $35 for a total price of $3,500. But remember — you're not an investor in for the long haul. You'll immediately unload the shares. You sell the shares for $4,500 and make a $1,000 profit. After considering your premium, your profit is $910. It will go a little bit lower after considering commissions, but you get the idea. The purpose of buying call options is to make fast profits on stocks you think are going to spike.

It's hard to guess when the best time is to really buy call options. Obviously, you don't want to do it when a major recession hit. The optimal time is during a bull market, or when a specific company is expected to hit on something big, that will suddenly increase its value in the markets. A good time to look is also when a recession hits, but it passes the bottom out period.

Benefits of Buying Call Options

Call options have many benefits that we've already touched on earlier. In Particular:

- Call options allow you to control 100 shares of stock without actually investing in the 100 shares — unless they reach a price where you get the profit that you want.

- Call options allow you to sit and wait, patiently watching the market before making your move.

- If your bet doesn't work out, you're only going to lose a small amount of money on the contract. In our example, if XYZ loses value, and ends up at $28 per share instead of moving past your strike price of $35, then you're only out the $90 you paid for the premium.

- Call buying provides a way to leverage expensive stock.

What to Look for When Buying Call Options

Now let's take a look at some factors that you'll be on the lookout for when buying call options. You're going to want to be able to purchase shares of the stock you're interested in at a price that is less than the price you think it will go up to. You need to do this in order to ensure that the stock price surpasses the strike price. Of course, it's impossible to know what the future holds so this will involve a bit of speculation. You'll have to do a lot of reading and research to make educated guesses on where you expect the stock to go in the coming weeks or months.

Second, you'll need to take into account the cost of the premium when making your estimates. For the sake of simplicity, suppose that you find a call option with a premium of $1 per share. You're going to need a strike price that is high enough to take that into account. If you go for a stock that is $40 a share with a $1 premium and a strike price of $41, obviously you're not going to make anything unless the stock price goes higher than $41. Remember that exercising your rights on the options contract is not a path toward immediate money. You're going to have to turn around and sell it ASAP in order to profit. Of course, when you sell is a judgment call as is when you exercise your right to buy. You're going to want to wait until the right moment to buy, but it's impossible to really know what that right moment is. This is where trading experience helps and even then, the most skilled experts can make mistakes. For a beginner, the best thing to do is exercise your right to buy the shares and then sell them as soon as they've gone far enough past the strike price for you to make a profit and cover the premium. If you wait too long, there is always the chance that the stock price will start declining again, and it will go below your strike price and never exceed it again before the contract expires.

Open Interest

If you get online to check stocks you're interested in, one of the measures you will see is "Open Interest." This tells you the number of open or outstanding derivative contracts there are for that particular stock. Every time that a buyer and seller enter into an options contract, this value increases by one. What you want to do with open interest as a trader looking to make real cash from call options is to look for stocks that show big movement in the number of open trades. You're going to want to look for increasing numbers. This means that other traders have an interest in buying call options on this stock and that they're expecting it to go up in value in the near future.

Of course, you're going to want to take an educated approach to this. Simply getting online and going through random stocks will be a waste of time, it might take you weeks to find something.

You're going to want to prepare ahead of time by keeping an eye on the financial news. Watch Fox Business, read the Wall Street Journal, and watch CNBC and read any other financial publications that are to your liking. Find out what stocks the experts are talking about and which ones they expect to make significant moves over the coming weeks and months.

Keep in mind these people and experts often make mistakes, so you're only using it as a guideline. You also don't want to focus solely on looking for stocks that are going to make moves; you want to keep up with company news. You need to keep your ears open for news such as the development of a new drug or the latest electronic gadget. Sometimes you might find out news about that before the stock begins attracting a lot of interest in the markets.

Tips for Buying Call Options

- Don't buy a call option with a strike price that you don't think the stock can beat.

- Always include the premium price in your analysis.

- Look for calls that are just in the money. These are likely to bring a modest profit.

- Call options that are out of the money might give you an option for a cheaper premium.

- However, the premium shouldn't be your primary consideration when looking to buy a call option. Compared to the money required to buy the shares and the potential profits if the stock goes past the strike price, the premium is going to be a trivial cost in most cases – provided of course the strike price is high enough to take the premium into account.

- Look at the time value. If you're looking for larger profits, it's better to aim for longer contracts. Remember, that with any call option you have the option to buy the stock at the strike price at any time between today's date and the deadline when the stock market price exceeds the strike price. Longer time frames mean you increase the chances of that happening. Even if the price goes a little above the strike price and dips down, with a longer window of time before the deadline, you can wait and see if it rebounds. Remember if it never does, you're only out the premium.

- Start small. Beginning traders shouldn't bet the farm on options. You'll end up broke if you do that. The better approach is to start by investing in one contract at a time and gaining experience as you go.

CHAPTER 10:

Strike Price

The strike price is one of the most important if not the most important thing to understand when it comes to option contracts. The strike price will determine whether the underlying stock is actually bought or sold at or before the expiration date. When evaluating any options contract, the strike price is the first thing that you should look at. It's worth investigating the concept and how it's utilized in the actual marketplace.

The strike price will let you home in on the profits that can be made on an options contract. It's the break-even point but also gives you an idea as to your profits and losses. Of course, the seller always gets the premium no matter what.

For a call contract, the strike price is the price that must be exceeded by the current market price of the underlying equity. For example, if the strike price is $100 on a call contract, and the current market price goes to any price above $100, then the purchaser of the call can exercise their right at any time to buy the stock. Then the stock can be disposed of with a profit. Suppose that the current price rises to $130. Then you can exercise your option to buy the stock at $100 a share, and then turn around and sell it on the market for $130 a share, making a $30 profit per share before taking into account the premium and other fees that might accrue with your trades. While as the buyer of the contract you have no obligations other than paying the premium, the seller is obligated no matter what, and they must sell you the shares at $100 per share no matter how much it pains them to see the $130 per share price. Of course, there are reasons behind the curtain that will explain why they would bother entering this kind of arrangement that we will explore when an opportunity arises.

For a put contract, the strike price likewise plays a central role, but the value of the stock relative to the strike price works in the opposite fashion. A put is a bet that the underlying equity will decrease in value by a certain amount. Hence if the stock price drops below the strike price, then the buyer can exercise their right to sell the shares at the strike price even though the market price is lower. So, if your price is $100, if the current price of the equity drops to $80, the seller obligated to buy the 100 shares per contract from you at $100 a share even though the market price is $80 per share. In this case, you've made a gross profit of $20 a share.

The value of the strike price will not only tell you profitability but give you an indication of how much the stock must move before you are able to exercise your rights. Often when the amount is smaller, you might be better off.

When you know the strike price of different options contracts, then you can evaluate which one is better for you to buy. Suppose that a stock is currently trading at $80 and you find two options put contracts. One has a strike price of $75 and the other has a strike price of $60. Further, let's suppose that both contracts expire at the same time. In the first case, the stock price in the market will need to drop just $5 before the contract becomes profitable. For the second contract, it will have to drop $20.

The potential worth of each contract per share is the difference. For the contract with the $75 strike price, that is only $5. For the second contract with the strike price of $60, the potential worth is $20, four times as much.

Determining which contract is better is a matter of analysis and taking some risk. You can't just go by face value, but you must take into consideration the expiration date together with an analysis of what the stock will actually do over that time period. It may be that it's going to be impossible for the stock to drop $20 in order to make the second contract valuable. If the expiration date comes before the stock drops that much in price, the contract will be worthless. In other words, you'd never be able to exercise your option of selling shares at strike amount. On the other hand, even though there is not much discrepancy between the strike and the market amount for the first contract, and the market price might only drop to say $70 per share, the chances of this happening before the expiration date is more likely.

Your analysis might be different if the contract with the lower strike price has a longer expiration date.

The lesson to take to heart is that a stock is more likely to move by smaller amounts over short time periods. But the higher the risk, the more the potential profits.

CHAPTER 11:

How to Close an Options Contract

The entry point in a trade is the point at which you want to buy an asset. It's the starting bid in your trade. Whether you are trading stocks or options, you will always have to have an entry point. Having a good plan for when you will enter into a trade is really beneficial because it means that you won't have to drive yourself mad. It also means that you won't be making an emotional choice regarding when to enter.

Choosing a good entry point means analyzing the chart for support, resistance, and trend. Look at the past movement of the chart and find the support and resistance. Then, look at the trend. Has the chart been moving in a specific trend line? Or has it been in a stage of consolidation? Or a period where the market has remained fairly steady? With a stock that has a trend line, you can choose a point right after a rebound. For example, let's say stock ABC was trading at $60 in November before dropping to $58. As the number starts to rise again, you can see if the chart seems like it's going to return to trend. If yes, then you can place your entry point at $60 and wait to see if the trend will continue upward.

In the case of a stock that is at a stage of neutral movement, then your support and resistance lines will be horizontal, and the chart will remain between those two lines. In this case, follow the pattern of the prior movement and again place your entry point at the price where a rebound is likely to happen. This should be close to the support line. There's a good chance that the stock value will rise again towards the resistance in this case.

Let's put this into action. Chose two different practice charts. One should have a stock that is trending upwards, and one should have stock that is steady and isn't trending in a particular direction. Taking the one that is trending upward, draw the trend line in the support line position. From there, choose a position that offers you a small swing up. At what point would you enter the swing? At what price point? How long would you remain in the swing? Do the same for the chart that is remaining steady. What point above the support line would you enter into the trade? It's easy to do this with past charts because everything is already lined up. But take the time to analyze the chart. What makes specific swings more successful and what makes them unsuccessful?

Now try with a practice future trade. Again, find a chart from a stock that you would be interested in purchasing. Map out your lines, find the zone you'll trade in, and then choose an entry point either in the present or the future. After that, watch the stock for the upcoming several days. Would your trade have panned out? If yes, why? And if no, why not? All of this practice gives you the opportunity to try out trades before investing any capital into it. Once you feel a bit more confident about entry points, move on to learn about exit points.

When you enter into the trade, you need to make sure that your risk/reward ratio makes the trade worth it. Once you calculate the ratio, you can determine at what point you can exit the trade in order to make the reward worth it.

Now we're going to learn how to exit a trade. It is very important to have an exit strategy. Without an exit strategy, you will choose to leave a trade whenever you feel like it, which can cause you some losses. You may exit too early or too late. It is better to have a strategy in place so that you know exactly when you'll exit. For example, if you determine that you would like to make a specific amount of profit, that's your exit point. Don't go past that.

As you throw it, momentum keeps it going higher but at a slower pace until it reaches its peak. At this point, momentum is zero and the ball falls back to your hands. In a swing trade, you want to exit the trade before the momentum reaches zero. Not at the peak, but before the peak. This is because most traders will be looking to sell at the peak of the trade, which will cause a drop in the market. Selling early before the estimated peak is a risk. It might mean that you lose out if the ball continues to go much higher than you anticipated. However, you will still have made a gain before any reversal happens and you can always buy back into the trend if you want to.

When looking at the charts for a stock, you should keep in mind your entry position and where you would like to exit. If the stock has stayed steady over the last bit of time and remains in its range, then looking at the support and resistance can give you a good idea of where to exit. If you entered near the support, then you can determine at what point you would like to exit. This depends on a lot of factors like your tolerance for risk and how long you want to stay in the trade. Generally speaking, if the stock value keeps increasing, you want to exit before it hits the resistance. Remember, in swing trading, it's all about small gains, not large ones so it's better to leave with some profit rather than no profit.

With your support and resistance marked on a chart, you can also look for key indicators that show you that it's time to sell. One of these indicators is either if the stock value exceeds its resistance, or if it drops below its support numbers. This can mean that it's starting to trend in one specific direction, but it could also mean that these little breakouts will backtrack into the range it was sitting at before. If the stock value exceeds its resistance and you haven't sold yet, then you can choose to wait until it returns to its range or see if it will be the start of a new trend. This decision, again, depends on how much risk you're willing to take.

There are a couple of things you can do to make sure that you are not staying in a trade too long. The first one is to set a stop-loss. A stop-loss is a tool that will sell your shares in the event that the stock price goes too low. The other option is to set a limit order. A limit order will sell your trades once they've reached your set peak value. Let's say that the current stock price for ABC is $20 per share when you enter. You can choose to set your limit order at $25 a share. You can also set it at a certain percentage point for profit. This means that at the $25 mark, your broker will sell your shares. This can be good because it can limit your losses, but it can also prevent you from taking advantage of a possible trend. So once again, make a decision based on your tolerance for risk.

As you make your exit strategy, you should ask yourself a few questions. You should know how long you are willing to stay in a trade, how much risk you can tolerate and at what point you want to get out. These three things will help you make a good exit strategy. For example, when asking yourself how long you want to stay in a trade, you can think about how long you want your capital to be tied up, what indicators you're looking for that will cause you to sell, etc.

When considering how much risk you're willing to take, try a few different scenarios. Also, consider what a profit is to you. Is it a $1 per share a decent profit or do you want to make more? Finally, consider when you want to leave the trade. You should have this written down clearly. Are you going to leave the trade once you've made a certain profit, once you hit the resistance level, or once you see another indication that it's time to go? When you've made your plan, it's important you stick to it. This will help you remain emotionally objective when trading.

Once you've made your exit plan, it's time again to practice. Look at some past charts and analyze where you would have entered and exited the trade, based on the indicators like support and resistance, or based on the moving average. Analyze every piece of a move. Why would a certain exit point have worked or failed? Afterward, try this again with a future chart. You can either do this in a simulation or using your own chart website of choice. Pick a stock you want to follow and find an entry point you think will work for you. Then, using your exit strategy, determine when you will exit the chart. Spend a few days looking at your plan as the chart moves forward. Did your plan work? Are there other ways you could have executed it? Keep practicing, don't just do this with one chart and think you're ready to start trading.

Where to place your stop-loss and why

We've talked a little about stop-losses, but let's look at them in more detail and explore the different types you can use. A stop-loss is very similar to a fire alarm. The fire alarm in your house starts to go off the moment that it senses smoke. It doesn't have to be a literal fire for it to sound the alarm. This can be kind of irritating, but it is also a very close analogy of what a stop-loss is. And yes, on occasion a stop-loss can also be irritating if it's not set correctly. A stop-loss can help you sell your trades when the market turns in an unexpected direction. It's your warning system and safety net in one. It makes sure that if the market is going to drop, you aren't going to lose a massive amount of money. However, sometimes a stop-loss is placed too tight which results in it being triggered during regular market volatility. This is that annoying accidental fire alarm. Even though it can be annoying, a stop-loss can save you considerable grief. As a swing trader, your trades will cover some days and weekends, which can result in precarious nights where the market shifts unexpectedly. A stop-loss can help you ensure your losses aren't too steep.

CHAPTER 12:

How Purchase of Option Works

To begin options trading, the following are some things to get started with:

1. Initial Preparation

2. Choosing an online broker

3. Finding your options trading niche

4. Finding option trades opportunities

5. Planning individual trades

6. Risk and money management

7. Monitoring your trades

Initial Preparation

It all starts with your mindset. Before you begin options trading, you have to make sure that you have the right mindset of successful options traders. Are you afraid of risk or you are risk lover? What is your attitude towards winning and losing? What is your approach to trading in the financial market? Analyze yourself and see if options trading for you, looking at your deep-seated values.

You also need to develop a trading plan. You've got to develop a trading plan that outlines your entry and exit strategy. If you don't have a long-term plan for options trading, chances are that you will give up in the first three or six months. Have profits targets and income ceiling to hit for options trading.

You also need to develop an action plan to get you doing. You have to make a to-do list for your options trading. How many hours will you be dedicated to the craft and focusing to increase your gains in options trading? How many minutes per day will you dedicate to studying the market and learning about options trading?

Choosing an Online Options Trader

To buy and sell options, you need a verified, licensed, and approved online broker. There is a lot of options broker out there catering for different needs and goals of people. The key is to be clear about your options trading plan and then decided on the type of options broker that will help you to get there. You need to check whether the broker has been approved. You also want to look at the customer service levels of the broker. If you can, call them to ask about brokerage fees, commissions, and service levels. Be clear about what you need so that it makes it easy for you to make your inquiry and find the best online broker that can meet your needs.

The best online brokers are focused on serving their customers. They have the best interest of their customers at heart. Therefore, their services are well-structured to meet their needs and help them to achieve their goals. They also have a high-quality trading platform with tools, analysis, and guides to help make your options trading fun and exciting. Finding Your Options Trading Niche

What is your options trading niche? Which kind of trade do you want to focus on? The type of options you choose can be based on your trading plan. Everything flows and revolves around your trading plan. This is why you must invest a considerable amount of time to develop a good trading plan that helps to define your options trading niche. Even if you choose to be a stock options trader, you have to clarify your position. Do you want to be a long-term investor, swing trader, day trader, value investor, or a technical analyst? Would you want to be a net buyer of options or a net seller of options? Usually, a net buyer of options focused on using strategies such as long calls, long straddles, long puts, long strangles and many more.

As a net buyer of options, you play at the debit side of the game, reducing the amount of risk in each trade and increasing your gains. A net seller of options is rather focused on using strategies such as short put, short calls, short straddles, short strangles and much more. In this game, you focus on receiving premiums for placing a trade and capping your risk every trade to maximize gains. You have to choose how to play the options trading and then become an expert in one particular area.

Finding Options Trading Opportunities

Once you have defined your niche, another step is to begin to find opportunities that fit your area of expertise. Finding opportunities have to do with working with your options broker. The main job of your options broker is to know your trading plan and then help you spot opportunities that are in align with your trading plan.

You might also choose to trade in companies that you are comfortable or understand what there are doing. That depends on your trading plan. But to find good options trading opportunities you have to make good use of your trading account and then also dedicate a certain amount of time to study the trade.

CHAPTER 13:

Covered Call Strategies

N
ow that you have your mindset down pat, it is time for you to start understanding the basic strategies of trading options. We will get more into the details of how to trade options using the day trading strategies eventually. For now, let's focus on what it looks like to trade options, including what types of contracts there are and how these contracts are bought and sold.

The first type of option we are going to look at is known as a "covered call." Covered calls are a type of call option that enables you to sell the right to purchase stock to another trader.

You will learn all about what a call option is, in detail, and how it can be sold to others.

What Are Covered Calls?

Call options are a type of options contract that has a buyer whose outlook is bullish and a seller whose outlook is bearish. This means that the individual buying the option believes that the underlying asset is going to increase in value, and the seller believes that the underlying asset is going to decrease in value. Based on this nature, a call option buyer will earn a profit when the underlying asset experiences an increase in price value.

Covered calls are a popular form of call option strategy that is made when the investor only expects a small increase or decrease in the cost of the underlying asset. These particular calls generate income through premiums, which are the prices that people pay in order to purchase the options.

The benefit of a covered call is that the investor gets into the option with the intention of holding a long position with the underlying asset. This way, they experience downside protection while also being able to generate passive income for the individual invested in this particular stock.

The big difference here is that a regular call option is taken for the short term position whereas a covered call option is taken for the long term position. In the end, the covered call provides higher risk protection and greater earning potential.

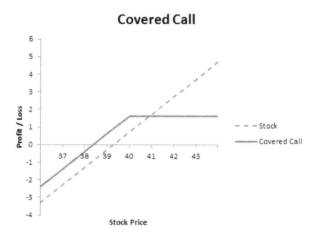

Covered Call Example

Selling covered calls mean that you get paid in exchange for giving up a portion of your future upside. You generally do this as a way to guarantee an increase in your prices, while also creating passive income right away through selling the call option itself.

You engage in covered calls when you think that stock you have already purchased is going to increase in value over a longer period of time. For example, let's say you buy ABC stock for $100 per share, and you believe that it will rise to $120 per share within 12 months. You might create a covered call option that allows people to buy the right to purchase that stock at $110 per share in six months, thus earning you the income from the cost of the contract, known as the premium, right away.

Then, if the buyers of your contract choose to purchase the stock in six months, you also gain the profits from that sale. Although the profits may not be as large had you held the position for the entire six months, they are more guaranteed and reliable than profits in the regular open market.

Writing your covered call takes some practice, but it can earn you a massive amount of profit in the long run. The first thing you need to do is start with identifying what stock you already own in your portfolio that has been performing well and that you are prepared to sell if the call option is assigned to a buyer who wishes to exercise their right to buy.

If you are bullish on a certain stock in the long term, or you believe it is going to increase exponentially, avoid choosing that stock as you may not earn as much profit through the covered call option. Instead, you want to choose a stock that you think is going to increase steadily, but not too incredibly high values so that you do not feel too heartbroken when it is time for you to part with that stock.

After you have chosen your stock you are going to need to choose your strike price, and your expiration date, which will, in turn, create your premium. These are the three elements of the contract that are going to outline how the buying and selling of your stock will work, what level of profit you will gain, and when that particular trade must be executed by in order for it to be valid.

Your strike price is the price that you feel you would be comfortable selling your stock at. When you are writing a covered call, you want to write a strike price that is out of the money or one that is lower than the current value of the stock. This way, should your buyer choose to enact their right to buy your stocks you are earning profits. You want the stock value to increase before you have to sell it to ensure that you are set up to receive profits, otherwise, you may not receive any profits from your trade deal.

The best way to pick your strike price is to look at how the stock has been performing so far, and look at how it is expected to perform going forward. You will want to conduct a technical analysis to ensure that you are following a trend that offers the most likely increase value for your stock prices. This way, when you set the strike price you are remaining reasonable while also creating a profitable price point for yourself.

After you have picked your strike price you need to decide when the option is going to expire. Generally, call options expire within 30-45 days of the call option being created, however, you can certainly increase or decrease that length of time. You are going to want to pick an expiration date that enables you to close out the trade quickly while also having an acceptable premium that people will be willing to pay. If your expiration date turns the premium into too high of a number you will have a difficult time selling your option, or you may never sell it at all.

After you have created your strike price and expiry date, your premium will be automatically determined for your covered call option. Generally, investors will favor premiums that are about 2% of the total stock value as this ensures that they also have the opportunity to make the most off the trade while incurring the least amount of losses.

This means that if you set your expiry date too far out in the future you might increase the cost of your premium too high, preventing investors from wanting to purchase it.

With that being said, always make sure that you are researching what has gone into creating your premium. Sometimes, premiums will seem abnormally high which can occur if there is something going on in the economy that might directly impact the value of the stock that you are trading. If this happens, you might need to adjust your covered call option or choose a different underlying asset to trade. Generally, if something seems too good to be true in the stock market, it is, so beware of premiums that seem too high.

Risks and Benefits of a Covered Call

There are three possible outcomes that you could experience if you were to engage in a covered call sell. The first one would occur if the stock price went down, the second would occur if the stock price stayed the same or slightly increased without reaching the strike price, and the third would occur if the stock rises past the strike price. Each of these outcomes will have different results for you, and you need to be aware of what might happen in each scenario.

Outcome One: The Stock Price Goes Down

If the stock price was to go down at the time of the option expiring, the option would likely expire worthlessly. If the buyer were to exercise their right to buy they would be paying higher than the value of the stock which would not make sense on their behalf. In this case, you would keep the entire premium for selling the contract. The stock price would be down, which may be unfortunate for the rest of your portfolio, but it would be positive that you had profited from the price of the premium.

If this happens, it is important to remember that you are not locked into the position of your contract. The value of the call option you sold will also be decreasing in value, which means that you can buy back the contract for less money than you sold it for so that you are not required to make the sale. Then, you can create a strategy for how you are going to manage the stock you have in your portfolio.

If you think it is going to start moving out of favor you can always dump it, or you can keep it and maintain your position if you think it is still going to behave as you anticipated it would when you bought it in the first place.

Outcome Two: The Stock Stays the Same or Slightly Increases without Reaching the Strike Price

The second scenario is that the stock price barely fluctuates and never reaches the strike price. In this case, there is no bad news. The call option will simply expire worthlessly and you will profit the entire premium from selling it. You may also see some increase in the value of your stock overall, adding a little more profits into your portfolio.

Outcome Three: The Stock Rises past the Strike Price

The third scene occurs when the stock price rises above the strike price, which means the call option is assigned and you will be required to sell 100 stock shares to the buyer.

In this case, you could experience frustration for setting the strike price lower and not receiving the full value of the stock at the point of selling it. While you will still receive profits, they will not be as massive as they could have been which can be frustrating.

Still, you have made profits so there is no reason to fret. You have earned more funds that you can place into your future trades, allowing you to increase your profitability with trading options.

CHAPTER 14:

Buy a Call

What to Look for to Buy Call Options

When you buy stock, you get what is known as a long position. When you buy a call option you get into a potential long position based on the underlying stock. On the other hand, when you sell a stock short, then you are short selling.

This essentially gives you a short position. Short selling means that you sell at a loss while long selling implies a profit. When you sell a naked call or an uncovered call, you will enter a potentially short position based on the underlying stock.

You enter a potential short position based on the underlying stock when you purchase a put option. Should you sell a naked put, you will enter a potential long position relative to the underlying stock.

If you can understand these four positions and keep them in mind, then you will easily understand the intricacies of selling and buying options. Ideally, you can buy call options and put options as well as sell call options and put options.

Holders: Anyone who buys options is generally referred to as the holder of an option

Writers: A person who sells an option is generally referred to as an options writer

Call and put holders are also known as buyers. They have the right to buy options but are not obligated to do so. They can exercise this right but only within the stipulated time and under the agreed conditions. This way, call and put holders only suffer losses equivalent to the premium charged for the options contract.

Call and put writers are sellers. They have an obligation to sell options or buy should the option expire, and the contract makes money. Therefore, sellers are always expected to oblige to the buyer's wishes. This exposes them to more risks. Therefore, writers stand to lose a lot more than just the cost of writing the options contract.

Example

Think about this company that you really like such that you would like to become a shareholder. According to your predictions, the stock price is going to rise. For instance, the current stock price of this company is $25 but you believe the price will be $35 in a year's time. You can purchase a call option that will grant you the rights to purchase the stock. On the contract, you can agree to a price of approximately $27 within the succeeding year. This contract will most likely cost you close to $1 per 100 shares. Now if the price does get to $35 as predicted, then you can exercise your right to buy the shares at $27. However, if the price remains constant or falls, you will not be obliged to buy and the only loss you will incur is the options fee.

Basic Put and Call Options Chain

This is a specific chain that is among the most popular options chains used by investors and traders, especially beginners. It is an excellent choice for those seeking to learn more about options. This chain presents a splittable with put options to the right and call options to the left. The different strike prices relevant to the options run to fight down the center of the table. This way, investors and traders can easily track put and call options of various strike prices. This is demonstrated via the image presented below.

If we closely examine the options chain above, we note that the strike prices run through the middle from top to bottom. We also note that the put options are located on the right side while the call options are on the left-hand side. Other parameters such as bid price, last price, ask price, volumes, price change from the preceding trading day, and open interested are displayed for both put and call options. When it comes to trading or investing this chain is the most widely used. It is popular with traders basically because it presents a lot of the information, they consider crucial. Important information necessary to execute trades is presented in a simple manner that is easy to read and understand. Using this chain, a trader can easily trace and identify the available call and put options as well as other parameters affiliated to each option. However, this chain is most suitable for traders interested in simple options trading strategies. There are other chains suitable for more complex strategies.

The Call and Put Options Price

The put and call price is a chain that presents the necessary data relating to basic call and put options. It also projects each option with five option Greeks. This way, an investor or trader who needs to use delta neutral options trading strategies and arbitrage strategies. The trader will be able to effectively make exact calculations regarding size and position to take. Looking at a relevant chain, you will easily note that all the five Greek symbols that include Vega, Rho, Theta, Gamma, and Delta are used. They are visible in the call and put options price. However, due to challenges in full-screen presentations, options prices usually present as either put options or call options only.

Options Strategies Chains

Specific options strategies chains are ideal for options traders or investors who prefer standardized options strategies like the covered call or the long straddle. The reason is that these chains drastically reduce the amount of work necessary to work out and calculate the options outlay as well as other specifics that relate to the specific strategy.

Options chains like this one generally present only the essential aspects of an options trading strategy across the various expiration dates and strike prices. This way, it can easily calculate and work out the net effect of a position and plenty of other useful detail. This way, a trader can make quick decisions on the spread to choose fast without spending time doing calculations and working out arithmetic.

Call and Put Options Matrix

This chain is the least used by investors and traders, especially beginners and retail options traders. This chain aims to present information on many options including their bid and ask prices over numerous expiration dates all on one page.

This options matrix generally presents only the ask and bid prices for all options listed on the chain but without additional information. This makes it a less useful table especially for beginners, amateurs, and retail traders who basically need a lot more information. However, it is considered by many traders to be the least useful chain out there.

Learn about Options Pricing

Another useful aspect of options trading that you need to be familiar with is the aspect of pricing options. The option price is also known as the option premium and consists of two distinct components. These are the intrinsic value and extrinsic value. Both are governed by the Put-Call Parity principle.

Tips and Tricks When Buying Call Options

• Don't buy a call option with a strike price that you do not think the stock can beat.

• Always include the premium price in your analysis.

• Look for calls that are just in the money. These are likely to bring a modest profit.

• Call options that are out of the money might give you an option for a cheaper premium.

However, the premium should not be your primary consideration when looking to buy a call option. Compared to the money required to buy the shares and the potential profits if the stock goes past the strike price, the premium is going to be a trivial cost in most cases — provided of course the strike price is high enough to take the premium into account.

Look at the time value. If you are looking for larger profits, it is better to aim for longer contracts. Remember, that with any call option you have the option to buy the stock at the strike price at any time between today's date and the deadline when the stock market price exceeds the strike price. Longer time frames mean you increase the chances of that happening. Even if the price goes a little above the strike price and dips down, with a longer window of time before the deadline, you can wait and see if it rebounds. Remember if it never does, you are only out the premium.

Start small. Beginning traders should not bet the farm on options. You will end up broke if you do that. The better approach is to start by investing in one contract at a time and gaining experience as you go.

The best-case scenario for you, as the buyer, is that the stock suddenly starts rising at a high speed before the deadline arrives. You want it to go beyond the strike price so that, when it comes time to exercise your right, you are purchasing your stock at a lower rate than it is now worth. Obviously, you then have the option to instantly list that stock as a covered sell, which would allow you to realize that profit in real money.

That final piece of the puzzle is the important one. As an options trader, you are not in the business of building a stock portfolio. You do not really want to own those shares – you want to make a profit on them as they pass through your hands. You want to buy them for less than they are worth and then sell them on, perhaps even for more than they are worth if you are lucky. It is within that transaction your money will be made.

Buying calls has several advantages for you as an options trader:

It does not cost much to get involved in the movement of a stock. You only need fork out the amount for the premium, after which you can sit back and wait to see what the stock does before making your purchase decision based on actual information, rather than on speculating what the market will do.

It allows you to make use of the kinds of "tips" that market experts have a bad habit of swearing by. You read the news, you are watching the markets and you have information that makes you think a certain stock is about to rise fast and hard. You want to take advantage of that, obviously, and options trading allows you to do so much more safely than simply buying the stock. If you are wrong, you will only lose your premium and you may even make a small profit. If you were wrong and purchased the stock and then it plummeted rather than rose, you stand to lose a whole lot more cash.

CHAPTER 15:

Buy and Sell Puts

How a Put Option Works?

I f you expect the price of a stock to drop, you can profit from this by investing in put options. Put options work in many ways in the same manner as call options. They have an expiration date, they have 100 shares of underlying stock, and their price depends on the price of the underlying stock. Meanwhile, they also suffer from time decay as the expiration date of the option approaches. However, put options actually gain value when the stock price drops, and they lose value when the stock price rises.

This means that put options can be used to "short" the stock. Shorting the stock is just jargon for earning a profit when the stock price declines. Normally, shorting a stock works like this. If you think that a stock is going to drop in value, you borrow shares from your broker — and you immediately sell them on the market at the current stock price. Then, assuming that your bet was the correct one, you buy the shares back when the price drops. Suppose for the sake of example that when you initially borrowed the shares, you sold them at $100 a share. Then the price drops to $80 a share — maybe the company had some bad earnings call, for example. When the price drops, you buy the shares back at $80 a share, and you return them to the broker (remember, you started the process by borrowing shares from the broker). This exercise leaves you with a $20 per share profit.

Of course, most small investors don't have $10,000 or more to chance on schemes like this, but put options enable you to earn profits if the price of a stock declines, using much smaller investments. The idea is basically the same, but when you suspect that the price of a stock is going to drop in the near future, you can buy put options on the stock. A put option has a strike price just like a call option, and when the share price is below the strike price, the put option is in the money. That's because you would be able to buy shares of stock at the market price, and then sell them at the strike price — earning a profit in the process.

Using the same example, we considered before, you could buy a put option with a $100 strike price. Then when the price of the shares dropped to $80, you could buy them on the market, and then sell them to the originator of the put option contract at the strike price - $100 a share. Buying a put option is something that doesn't require a large margin account to do.

When a put option is exercised, that is you sell the stock at the strike price, they say that the stock was "put to" the originator of the option contract. Of course, most options traders are not looking to exercise individual put options. If the stock price were really to drop $20 a share on a stock where you bought put options with a $100 strike price, the value of the put options would go up substantially, because you could exercise them and make solid profits. Since there are other traders who would be interested in selling the stock, you will be able to sell your put option to another trader for a profit. Remember that if you buy to open an options contract, you are not obligated to anything and are free and clear once you sell it to someone else.

Think of put options in the same way as call options, but with the price going up to $100 every time the stock drops by $1. Like call options, the pricing of put options is impacted by many factors, and so this is an ideal relationship that we are thinking about here. But it gives you a rule of thumb to understand how put options works (the more in the money they are, the closer they are going to get to the ideal case). Likewise, if the price of the stock rises by $1, the value of a put option would move down by $100. So, with put options, it's an inverse relationship.

A Put as an Insurance Instrument

You buy put options when you believe the value of a stock is going to decline. If a company has some bad earnings call, this can be a good time to buy a put option. Typically, the price of the stock will drop a lot, possibly over a day or two, and then stabilize at a new, lower level. Any bad news of any kind provides an opportunity to profit from put options. This is a kind of flexibility that doesn't exist for most stock traders and investors, being able to earn money when stocks are declining. The fact that you can open your eyes to the potential that options have in expanding your ability to make profits from the stock market. An options trader has the ability to profit under all possible scenarios of stock market movements.

CHAPTER 16:

In and Out of the Money

The terms "in the money" and "out of the money" are slang used by options traders to indicate whether an option is really worth something or not. It turns out that even out of the money options are worth something, but before we get to that let's learn what these terms mean and how different call options fit in with the definitions.

The first definition you need to know about is "in the money." A call option is in the money when the strike price of the call option is lower than the current share price. In other words, a call option is in the money when you can buy the shares at a discount price relative to the market price.

To really be worth it, however, you need to understand how the breakeven price fits in. If the stock is trading at $101 a share, technically speaking a call option with a strike price of $100 a share is in the money. However, if you paid $2 per share for that option, then it is not really in the money, because you'd lose $1 a share exercising the option.

So from a practical standpoint, an option has to be positioned such that the market share price has risen enough to account not only for the strike price, but also the price paid to buy the call option. So you need to pay more attention to the breakeven price rather than the in the money price – if you are interested in buying the shares of stock.

Call Options: Out of the Money

So to summarize, a call option is in the money if the share price rises above the strike price. On the other hand, if the strike price is above the share price for a call option, then that option is said to be "out of the money." Out of the money options are less desirable than in the money options, and so they are priced at lower levels. The more in the money a call option, the more the option is worth. However, you should not neglect out of the money options. If an option is a little bit out of the money, but the pricing trend is in its direction, the value of the option can still rise. So you can make profits from out of the money options, although it's a little bit trickier. Holding them overnight can also cause problems because options lose value due to time decay. The key thing to remember about out of the money options is that they expire worthless. That is, if you hold an out of the money option through expiration, once the option expires it has zero value. That means your investment in the option is completely lost. If you are going to trade out of the money options, then you should be sure to get rid of them as soon as possible. This is a good reason to be trading liquid options.

When is an option liquid?

Liquidity is one of the most important concepts in finance and trading. Simply put, liquidity is a measure (vague, but real) of how quickly you can convert something into cash. A cashier's check is very liquid. Cash is 100% liquid. A bar of gold is pretty liquid because you can take it to a gold or coin dealer and sell it immediately for cash. Stocks are liquid, but less liquid than these items because you can't immediately access the cash you get from selling stocks (most brokers will make you wait a few days). You can compare liquidity between different types of assets. To explain what we mean, let's focus only on options. Some options are going to be more liquid than others. No matter what, your broker is going to have rules on being able to get the cash out, but that isn't our concern when talking about the liquidity of options. Those rules are going to apply to all options.

Our concern here is how easy it is to buy and sell a particular option.

Options trading can move fast. In my own experience, I have seen options that I've purchased lose and gain $100 or more over a matter of 30-90 minutes. The rapid price movements of options coupled with the fact that they lose value through time decay every single day that passes means that when the time is right to get in and out of an options contract, you want to be able to do it right away.

So the concept of liquidity when it comes to trading options comes down to being able to buy and sell an option instantly. The market provides two important pieces of information that you can use in order to determine how liquid an option is.

CHAPTER 17:

Market Strategies: 5 Strategies Explained for the Reader

Long Straddle

Astraddle is an options trading system that allows traders to have a position in both a put option and a call option with the same exercise price and expiration date. This means that traders have the right to buy and sell a given currency pair at the same exchange rate and for the same period. Traders usually use this system if they do not have a clear view of the future direction of the currency pair in a certain period. However, they are convinced that the currency pair will move significantly.

Long straddle: As the name suggests, a long straddle is simply a strategy in the Forex options trading system, where the trader goes a long (buys) call option and an extended option for the same currency pair at the same exercise price and expiration date.

Rolling Out Options

A rollout is a strategy that is used to extend the lifetime of an option that hasn't quite worked out. This is going to be a strategy used by options sellers. A rollout might be something you would consider doing when you've sold a naked call, and the share price is closing in on your strike price, creating a risk that the option will be exercised. By doing a rollout you can keep the trade going longer, and possibly make some changes to give the trade better odds of being profitable. Typically, you will choose to do a rollout when it is close to the expiration date.

Definition of the Rollout Strategy

A rollout strategy works in the following way. You will close your current option contract by buying it back, and simultaneously open a new contract of the same type, with changes. One way to change is by altering the strike price. Another method that is more common is to move up the expiration date. A common practice is to open the new contract with an expiration date that is further out in the future. For example, you could close a naked put option that is expiring in two days by buying it back and opening a new contract by selling a new naked put option. You would use the same stock and the same strike price, but with an expiration date that is three weeks into the future. This is a standard strategy where we say that the option contract was rolled out.

You can also follow the same strategy choosing either a higher strike price or a lower strike price. For example, if we have an Apple naked put with a strike price of $205, we could roll up the option by closing this position and selling a new naked put on Apple with a strike price of $206. Alternatively, you could choose a lower strike price. Using the same example, instead of going with a $206 strike price, we could go with a $203 strike price. Maybe, in that case, the Apple share prices are dropping and it got a little too close for comfort. When you select a lower strike price, they say that you have rolled down the trade. It's also possible to roll out and roll up or down. In other words, you can close your current contract and open a new one that has a further expiration date, but you also change the strike price.

Types of Options Where Rolling Strategies Are Used

You can use a rollout, roll up, or roll down strategy on any type of option, including options that you buy to open (long calls and puts). However, the vast majority of options contracts that are rolled are short (buy to open) options. You can use rolling techniques on any of the major strategies covered here, such as put credit spreads, strangles, or iron condors.

Why Roll an Options Contract

The main reason that options traders roll an option contract is that they are in the money and there is an assignment risk. By rolling it out, you can keep the trade going but avoid assignment. Sometimes just moving the expiration date is good enough to accomplish this. An option can be assigned at any time, but in most cases, it has to reach expiration in order to be assigned. By using a rollout, the trader can avoid this situation. Of course, rolling up or rolling down can also help avoid assignment, since changing the strike price might allow you to move from an in the money situation to an out of the money situation.

There are other reasons that are sometimes used to justify rolling an option. For example, when you are selling for income, you can roll the trade to keep generating more money. Changing market conditions might also be a reason to roll a trade. When rolling a spread, strangle, or iron condor, there are many possibilities that exist for altering the trade. Suppose you have a put credit spread with strikes of $207 and $204. We could change one or both of the strike prices, and we could also change the expiration date. Maybe we want to tighten or widen the spread, so we could roll out and also roll down the lower strike price, and have a new spread with strike prices of $207 and $202, for example.

A Rollout is a Single Trade

It's important to note that a rollout is one trade, and not two. You are simultaneously closing one option (possibly with multiple legs) and opening a new contract in its place.

Strangle

A strangle is similar to a straddle, but in this case, the strike prices are different. In this case, you will buy a just barely out of the money call option, while simultaneously buying a slightly out of the money put option. The two options will have the same expiry date. The breakeven points for a strangle will be calculated in the same way as the breakeven prices for a straddle, but you will use the individual strike prices for a call and put it because they are different. You calculate the total premium paid, which is the total amount paid for the call option plus the premium paid for the put option. Then the breakeven points are given by the following formulas:

- To the upside, the breakeven point is the strike price of the call plus the total premium paid.

- On the downside, the breakeven point is the strike price of the put minus the total premium paid.

Similar to a long straddle, the maximum loss is going to occur when the share price ends up in between the two strike prices. Therefore, you might want to choose strike prices that are relatively close to minimize the range over which the loss can occur. There is a tradeoff here. The closer in range the strike prices are, the more expensive it is going to be in order to enter the position. But, it's going to increase your probability of profit because if the strike prices are tight about the current share price. There is a higher probability that the share prices are going to exceed the call strike plus the premium paid, or decrease below the put strike price less the price paid to enter the contract (the premium).

Married Puts

Usually, the married puts approach is used when an optional trader is abundant on a stock, wants the benefits of stock ownership (dividends, voting rights, etc.) but wary of short-term uncertainty.

Cash-secured Puts

The term cash-secured put relates to the approach of selling the contract to purchase the security if it is traded at a price below its current market price. Cash-secured putting involves both writing the option and depositing cash into a sweep account to purchase the underlying security.

CHAPTER 18:

To Become a Successful Trader:
Mindset and Study

No one can guarantee your commercial success. This is a problematic adventure right from the start, and you are up against the brightest. From my own experience as well as from many successful traders, here are five main steps that, if followed earnestly, will put you on the right track for successful trading.

1. Learn How to Read the Chart for Good Trading

Many are looking to sell you the new predictor or device in the trading industry. The statements are always high: not so much of the results, unless proved. You will end up finding it unwise to rely solely on systems and indicators. You get a buying signal that last week was good, but this week, it's not. It occurs very frequently. Why that failed is unclear.

The best thing you can do is learn how to read an uncluttered chart for your trade consisting of price candles and volume. Quantity reveals behind-the-market fuel; the result is the price of that fuel. For instance, if the amount rises after a long rally but the price doesn't rise, it may mean the market has reached a peak. At the very least it shows you that profits are going into the rally. None of the metrics will tell you. Different price and volume trends and trade setups occur in all phases of a business cycle. First, you want to know some time-proven trading metrics of primaries, because they work together when modified and don't conflict with each other. I'm using MACD and RSI as they stood test time and didn't clutter results.

It is important to note that all systems/disciplines need to operate with an excellent trading experience; if you have access to or have established that expertise, then you are off to the races. If not, the ability to disseminate good knowledge from the poor is most important. Understanding these trends will provide you with a real advantage in trade.

2. Practice Sound Money Management Trading

No trading system is 100%. Trades would still lose out. Money management lets you decide how much to lose on each deal, and even with a series of losses, keep you in the game. This will help to identify role sizing and notify the degree of stoppage. Trading success would be elusive without sound money-management practices.

Money management is more than just finding out how much you need to gamble on some specific trade. It also involves items such as when to step upscale. For example, if you are in a trend, you know that this market has a high chance of closing at its peak. This is when sound money management suggests you put the full size of your place on. These times can make a big difference for the week or month in which you profit.

3. Create a Trading Strategy

There's no trading for skilled traders without planning. A trading strategy includes decisions that you will make ahead of time. These include trading markets, trading schedules, timeframes, position sizing, risk parameters, how to make money, how to increase the size of the position, what to do in case of a significant drawdown, when to take advantage of the account and so on.

4. Consider Trading Mental Game

A lot is going on 'between the ears' which affects your trade. Few traders put a great deal of energy into the psychological side of trade before they lose out or find their psychology working against them. They cannot pull the trigger on a sound commercial system, for example. Many professional athletes focus on their game's mental side, as it gives them a competitive advantage. There are two aspects of psychology: one helps you minimize and remove unforced trading errors; the other enables you to improve your trading skills and abilities.

5. Practice Well

This creates unique competences. How can you develop ability without putting it into practice? Simulation and paper-trading for the aspiring trader are highly useful practices. Even traders with experience will always learn new trading concepts. You will learn what trade of preference looks like, the market conditions under which it operates best, the best reasons for entry, and the fair benefit targets from practice trades.

Most of the new traders begin by studying other traders 'trading strategies. Nonetheless, it is easy to build the first trading strategy, but it is hard to develop a sustainable trading strategy.

It's difficult to find an objective trading edge. You'll see the company goes beyond your trading plan successfully. So why should you still be shaping your trading strategy, and why not use a good trader's trading strategy? Traders may be exchanging their resources and approaches, but no trader can guarantee your income or will do so. Every single trader is different. Therefore, you can only benefit from a unique and personal combination of trading instruments. Developing your Trading strategy is the easiest and most sustainable solution.

You will need access to charts to construct a plan that represents the timeframe to be exchanged, an inquisitive and analytical mind, and a pad of paper to list your ideas. You then formalize these concepts into a plan, and on other maps, "visually backtest" them. We are going over the process from start to finish in this article and providing crucial questions to ask along the way. Once you have achieved this, you will be ready to start developing your plans in any market and in any timeframe.

Time & Location

You need to narrow down the chart options before you can build a plan. Are you a day trader, an investor, or a swing businessman? Are you going to trade on a one-minute or monthly timeframe?

Then you want to focus on which market you're going to trade: stocks, options, futures, forex, or commodities? If you have chosen a timeline and a market, determine what type of trading you want to do. As an example, let's assume that you want to search for stocks on a one-minute timeline for day-to-day trading purposes, and that you want to focus on stocks that move within a range. You can now run a stock screen for stocks that trade within a range and meet certain conditions, such as minimum volume and price criteria.

Assets, of course, change over time, so when appropriate, run new screens to find assets that suit your trading criteria until the former stocks are no longer trading in a manner that suits your strategy.

Creating and Implementing Plans

Having a workable strategy makes it much easier to stick to your business plan because the work is the strategy. Suppose a day trader wants to look at the stocks over five minutes, she has a stock selected for certain requirements from the stock list created by the stock screen she ran. She'll look for money-making opportunities on this 5-minute map.

The investor is going to look at the ups and downs and see if anything has precipitated such movements. All measurements are analyzed, such as time of day, patterns of candlesticks, patterns of charts, mini-cycles, length, and other trends. After a new approach has been discovered, it helps to go back to see if the same thing has happened with other moves on the map. Could this approach have made a profit on the last day, week, or month? If you're trading for more than five minutes, keep looking at just five-minute timeframes, but look back in time and at other stocks that have similar requirements to see if they've done the same.

After you've established a set of rules that would allow you to enter the market and make a profit, look at the same examples and see what the risk will be. To gain income without being interrupted, decide what your stops would need to be on future trades. Analyze price change after entry, and see where a stop should be put on your charts.

You should look for techniques that work over succinct times, depending on how much you choose to look for strategies. Short-term anomalies often occur, which allow you to extract consistent income.

Such tactics may not last longer than several days but are likely to be used again in the future as well.

Keep track of all the tactics you use in a report and include them in a business plan. If circumstances for a specific approach turn undesirable, you can prevent it. You will rely on that in the market when circumstances support a strategy.

Strategies fall in and out of fashion over various periods; changes will sometimes be needed to accommodate the current market and our situation. Build your plan or use somebody else's strategy and check it for a time that suits your choice. You can give yourself some high starting points by looking back to make more money and avoid losses as you get more experience. Track all the techniques you use to be able to use those strategies again when circumstances support them.

CHAPTER 19:

Trading Psychology

W e associate trading psychology to some behaviors and emotions that are often the triggers for catalysts for decisions. The most common emotions that every trader will come across are fear and greed.

Fear

At any given time, fear represents one of the worst kinds of emotions that you can have. Check-in your newspaper one day, and you read about a steep selloff, and the following thing is trying to rack your brain about what to do following even if it isn't the right action at that time.

Many investors think that they know what will happen in the following few days, which makes them have a lot of confidence in the outcome of the trade. This leads to investors getting into the trade at a level that is too high or too low, which in turn makes them react emotionally.

As the trader puts a lot of hope on the single trade, the level of fear tends to increase, and hesitation and caution kick in.

Fear is part of every trader, but skilled traders have the capacity to manage the fear. There are various types of fears that you will experience, let us look at a few of them:

The Fear to Lose

Have you ever entered a trade and all you could think about is losing? The fear of losing makes it hard for you to execute the perfect strategy or enter or exit a strategy at the right time.

As a trader, you know that you need to make timely decisions when the strategy signals you to take one. When you be afraid guiding you, the level of confidence drops, and you don't have the ability to execute the strategy the right way, at the right time. When a strategy fails, you lose trust in your abilities as well as strategy.

When you lose trust in many of the strategies, you end up with analysis paralysis, whereby you don't have the capacity to pull the trigger on any decision that you make. Making a move becomes a huge challenge.

When you cannot pull the trigger, all you can think about is staying away from the pain of losing, while you need to move towards gains.

No trader likes to lose, but it is a fact that even the best traders will make losses once in a while. The key is for them to make more profitable trades that allow them to stay in the game.

The Fear of a Positive Trend Going Negative (and Vice Versa)

Many traders choose to go for quick profits and then leave the losses to run down. Many traders want to convince themselves that they have made some money for the day, so they tend to go for a quick profit so that they have the winning feeling.

So, what should you do instead? You need to stick with the trend. When you notice a trend is starting, it is good to stay with the trend until you have a signal that the trend is about to reverse. It is only then that you exit this position. To understand this concept, you need to consider the history of the market. History is good at pointing out that times change, and trends can go either way. Remember that no one knows the exact time the trend will start or end; all you need to do is wait upon the signal.

The Fear of Missing Out

For every trade, you have people that doubt the capacity of the trade to go through. After you place the trade, you will be faced with many skeptics that will doubt the whole procedure and leave you wondering whether to exit the strategy or not.

This fear is also characterized by greed — because you aren't working on the premise of making a successful trade rather the fact that the security is rising without you having a piece of the pie.

This fear is usually based on information that there is a trend that you missed that you would have capitalized on.

This fear has a downside — you will forget about any potential risk associated with the trade and instead think that you have the capacity to make a profit because other people benefited from the action.

Fear of Being Wrong

Many traders put too much emphasis on being right that they forget that this is a business they should run the right way. They also forget that being successful is all about knowing the trend and how it affects their engagement. When you follow the best timing strategy, you create many positive results over a certain time.

The uncanny desire to focus on always being right instead of focusing on making money is a great part of your ego, and to stay on the right path; you need to trade without your ego for once.

If you accommodate a perfectionist mentality when you get into trades, you will be after failure because you will experience a lot of losses as well. Perfectionists don't take losses the right way, and this translates into fear.

Ways to Overcome Fear in Trading

As you can see, it is obvious that fear can lead to losses. So, how can you avoid this fear and become successful?

- Learn

You need to find a way to get knowledge so that you have the basis for making decisions. When you know all there is to know about options, you know what to buy and when to sell, and learn which ones to watch. You are then more comfortable making the right decisions.

- Have Goals

What are your short term and long-term goals? Setting the right goals helps you to overcome fear. When you have goals, you have rules that dictate how you behave, even in times of fear. You also have a timeline for your journey.

- Envision the Bigger Picture

You always need to evaluate your choices at all times and see what you have gained or lost so far for taking some steps. Understanding the mistakes, you made gives you guidance to make better decisions in the future.

- Start Small

Many traders that subscribe to fear have lost a lot before. They put a lot of funds on the line and ended up losing, which in turn made them fear to place other trades. Begin with small sums so that you don't risk too much to put fear in you. Once you get more confident, you can invest larger sums so that you enjoy more profit.

- Use the Right Strategy

Having the right trading strategy makes it easy to execute your trades successfully. Make sure you look at various options trading strategies so that you know which one is ideal for your situation and skills. Many strategies can help you succeed, but others might leave you confused. If you have a strategy that doesn't give you the returns you desire, then adjust it to suit your needs over time. Refine it till you are comfortable with its performance.

- Go Simple

When you have a strategy that is simple and straightforward, you will be less likely to lose confidence along the way because you know what to expect. Additionally, the easier the strategy, the faster it will be to spot any issues.

- Don't Hesitate

At times you have to jump into the fray even if you aren't so comfortable with the way it works. Once you begin taking steps, you will learn more about the trade.

However, you need always to be prepared when taking any trade. The more prepared you are, the easier it will be for you to run successful trades.

- Don't Give Up

Things might not always go as you expect them to do. Remember that mistakes are there to give you lessons that will make you a better trader. When you lose, take time to identify the mistake you made and then correct it, then try again.

Greed

This refers to a selfish desire to get more money than you need from a trade. When the desire to get more than you can usually make takes over your decision-making process, you are looking at failure.

Greed is seen to be more detrimental than fear. Yes, fear can make you lose trades, but the good thing is that you get to preserve your capital. On the other hand, greed places you in a situation where you spend your capital faster than you return it. It pushes you to act when you shouldn't be acting at all.

The Danger of Being Greedy

When you are greedy, you end up acting irrationally. Irrational trading behavior can be overtrading, overleveraging, holding onto trades for too long, or chasing different markets.

The more greed you have, the more foolish you act. If you reach a point at which greed takes over from common sense, then you are overdoing it.

When you are greedy, you also end up risking way much more than you can handle and you end up with a loss. You also have unrealistic expectations from the market, which makes it seem as if you are after just money and nothing else.

When you are greedy, you also start trading prematurely without any knowledge of the options trading market.

When you are too greedy, your judgment is clouded, and you won't think about any negative consequences that might result when you make certain decisions.

Many traders that were too greedy ended up giving up after making this mistake in the initial trading phase.

How to Overcome Greed

Like any other endeavor in trading, you need a lot of effort to overcome greed. It might not be easy because we are talking about human emotions here, but it is possible.

First, you have to know that every call you make won't be the right one at all times. There are times when you won't make the right move, and you will end up losing money. At times you will miss the perfect strategy altogether, and you won't move a step ahead.

Secondly, you have to agree that the market is way bigger than you. When you do this, you will accept and make mistakes in the process.

Hope

Hope is what keeps a trading expectation alive when it has reached reversal. Hope is usually factored in the mind of a trader that has placed a huge amount on a trade. Many traders also go for hope when they wish to recoup past losses. These traders are always hopeful that the following trade will be the best, and they end up placing more than they should on the trade. This type of emotion is dangerous because the market doesn't care at all about your hopes and will take your money.

Regret

This is the feeling of disappointment or sadness over a trade that has been done, especially when it has resulted in a loss.

Focusing too much on missing trade makes the trader not to move forward. After you learn the lessons after such a loss, you need to understand the mistakes you made then move ahead.

When you decide to let regret to rule your thinking, you start chasing markets with the hopes that you will end up making money on a position by doubling the entrance price.

CHAPTER 20:

Tools and Platforms

You will need to accept the help of some outside 'forces' to succeed in day trading business. Apart from your efforts, three things will decide if you can succeed or not at earning profits from day trading. These are trading platforms, charting software, and brokerage services.

Day trading was made popular by the electronic trading systems, also known as online trading platforms. These are computer software programs, for placing buy and sell orders for different financial products. On online trading platforms, the speed of data feeds and fast execution of orders have made them very popular with day traders. This is one of the reasons why many people now prefer to become individual day traders and conduct their business from any place, especially from their homes.

This is in stark contrast to traditional trading which usually happens on stock exchange floors where brokers yell on telephones and clients find it hard to get their desired trades executed immediately.

Electronic trading platforms also have another advantage. These relay live market prices to the clients' computer screen, which traders can use to decide whether they want to buy, or sell, or hold their positions.

Apart from an online trading platform, day traders also need to have sophisticated trading tools; such as charting software; account management tools; and newsfeed. In today's technology-driven age, one cannot imagine indulging in day trading with no charting software.

This software helps in technical analysis of stock prices, based on which, traders take to buy and sell decisions. Automatic or algorithmic trading is rapidly expanding. Big traders use automatic charting software to generate trading signals that are automatically executed on their behalf.

According to their trading styles, traders have different requirements. Trading software is also based on various trading styles. For day traders, the speed of execution and tools for chart analysis are very important. Brokerage houses provide trading platforms that fulfill these requirements and attract many day traders as their customers. Some other companies have nothing to do with brokerage services but provide standalone charting software of excellent quality.

The third essential requirement for day trading is selecting a good broker, who provides competitive brokerage rates. With every trade, day traders have to pay some fees to the broker, which is called brokerage or commission. Since day traders usually trade in every session and mostly execute more than one trade every day, they need a brokerage plan where the trading commission is at a minimum. Take it this way; as the trading commission, traders incur a financial loss as soon as they place a trade, with every trade. Every trade has two legs; one buys and one sell. The brokerage is charged on both legs. To keep this money-outflow to a minimum, traders need a broker, who provides them necessary day trading facilities but does not charge hefty fees for this.

All these things; online trading platform, charting software, and broker's commission; will also constitute parts of your investment in day trading business. You will need to research and compare various services and tools, before taking a final decision. Once you invest money in these "parts" of the business, it will not be easy to change.

Trading Platforms

Trading platforms are technical tools created with computer software. These platforms are used for trade execution and managing open positions in the stock markets. Online platforms range from a basic screen to sophisticated and complex systems. The simple and basic trading platforms usually provide only order entry facilities, not much beyond that. Advanced trading terminals have many other facilities, such as streaming quotes, newsfeed, and charting facilities.

Day traders should consider their needs while selecting a trading platform. For example, are they at a beginner's level or professional? No need to spend money on highly sophisticated platforms, when you are just beginning your day trading career. Different trading platforms are tailored to suit different markets: such as stocks, forex, commodities, options, and futures.

Based on their features, trading platforms can be divided into categories of commercial platforms and crop platforms. For day traders and retail investors, commercial platforms are more useful. These are easy to use and have many valuable features. On these platforms, day traders will find the news feed and technical charts good for day trading. Investors can use research and education related tools. Prop trading platforms are more sophisticated and are customized for large brokerage houses, who wish to provide a unique trading experience to their clients.

For beginners, it is advisable to go for some basic online trading platform that provides a simple and easy-to-understand interface. In the beginning of the day trading career, it will be difficult to adjust to the market volatility and learn new things with every trade. On top of that, any complicated trading program may confuse a novice day trader and cause losses instead of providing ease of business.

Day traders should consider two factors before choosing a trading platform; its price and available features. A live data feed is a must for any good platform. At the same time, it should not cost the moon and some more. Therefore, the day trader will have to balance between the price and trading features. Going for a cheap platform may help cut costs, but it could provide delayed data which will destroy your day trading business. On the other hand, a fancy trading platform will put a hole in your pocket and confuse you during trading by its overwhelming range of features.

Those, who day trade in options, will need different charting features than those who trade in stocks. Similarly; day traders in forex markets will need different types of trading platforms. Carefully consider what tools are available on any online platform. If that suits your requirements and budget, make a final decision to purchase it.

Some trading platforms are available only for those, who have an account with a broker. Some may have high deposit rates before allowing traders to use it. It is also possible that some online trading platforms will easily give margin facility to their customers; while others may not provide it. All these things should be considered before investing in any trading platform.

Before making a choice, it will be better if you make a list of your requirements, then check that list against the features of any platform. Purchase the one that fulfills all or most of your requirements.

Day Trading Software

Many day traders use computer software for automated trading. This takes away their headache of spotting the trend and deciding the trade entry and exit points. Also, they need not spend hours on chart analysis and reading economic news to understand what will happen in stock markets. Day trading software takes care of all their time consuming and decision-making problems.

These days, trading software automatically analyzes chart signals, decide trade entry and exit points, profit booking and stop-loss levels, and execute the trade on behalf of the trader. The biggest advantage of automated trading is; it takes away the hazards of emotional trading. Not everyone can control their emotions, especially in stock markets, where fear and greed overcome day traders. Under the influence of emotions, they do not spot the right trend and make trading mistakes. This is one of the very common mistakes in day trading, and most of the day traders who suffer losses, do so because they cannot control their emotions.

Different types of automated trading programs are available nowadays. The simplest type of such program is standalone websites that provide trade signals for time-based subscriptions. These websites display trading charts, where real-time prices run through the session and generate intraday buy and sell signals. Day traders have to watch these signals and manually trade on their own trading platform. Such programs cost little, and day traders can continue their subscription, or discontinuous it, based on how much profit they make from it.

Some brokerage firms also provide automated trading programs to their clients. These programs run only on that company's trading platform, and day traders can directly place buy and sell orders from the program.

Choosing a Suitable Broker

In the day trading business, a brokerage service will be like your business partner, which will link you with the stock exchanges and give you a platform to execute your trade. Also, this service will demand a fee from you for every executed trade. Therefore, you will have to consider many points before you choose a broker for day trading.

A high brokerage can create setbacks in your profit-making efforts, and a low brokerage may hide some low-quality features of the trading platform. Since this brokerage service will be the medium through which you will execute your day trading business; compare different services before making your choice.

The first thing to consider will be; does the broker fit your needs? If you are going to focus only on day trading, then you must choose a service where the brokerage will be affordable for you. Check its features whether they are suitable for intraday trading or not. Choosing the right broker will be the first step in investing in your trading business. Investing in the right tools and services will provide a solid foundation for trading.

Different brokers cater to different trading and investing needs. Their tools and features are also tailored according to their customers' needs. A brokerage service, which is focused on long-term investors, may not be a good fit for day traders. In day trading also, there are various services that are tailor-made for day traders of forex markets, some other target day traders in commodities markets. For day trading in stocks, you will have to focus on brokers that have the most comprehensive features for stock traders.

The second most important step in finalizing a broker will be its trading fees and facilities. As a day trader, you will be placing more trades every day. Therefore, a low brokerage will suit your needs. Also, look for margin facilities for intraday traders, which will help you at a fraction of the original cost of trading.

Check out the broker's trading platform. Does it provide a live data feed of markets; or, is there any delay in its price feed? For a day trader, going for a trading platform with a delayed price feed will be like committing hara-kiri. Getting the right price at the right time is a must for making correct trade decisions. Also, the broker's trading platform should have good speed and should not face connectivity problems. Check out social media forums to know what other customers of the broker say about its services.

As a beginner, it will be better to go with a simple brokerage plan that fulfills your basic day trading needs. In the initial stages, you will have to focus on learning how stock markets function, and how to trade correctly. Once you have successfully established your day trading business, and feel confident about various trading tricks, you can think of upgrading your system and go for more advanced trading platforms and charting software.

Remember, tools and services can help you only up to a limit. Your biggest trading accessory will be your knowledge and skills that will help you establish a good day trading business.

Conclusion

Congratulations on reaching the end of this book. It shows real dedication on your part to exploring options day trading as a career for you. In closing, let us quickly recap. An option is a financial contract that facilitates the right to buy or sell an asset by a certain date at a specific price called the expiration date for a certain price called a strike price.

The contract is named an option because the holder of the contract is under no obligation to exercise this right by the date specified. Options are not to be confused with stocks, which are a representation of ownership in an individual company. Stocks are an example of an asset that can be associated with an option.

Options day traders open option positions at the beginning of the day and close them by the end of the day. This is a full-time, challenging career that can be highly lucrative when done right. Benefits of day trading options include:

- Affordability as trading options is significantly lower priced than other major forms of investment like buying stock.
- Having no obligation to buy or sell anything unless it is beneficial to do so.
- Having the ability to build a diverse portfolio.
- Having the ability to gain profit from assets owned.
- Being sustainable.

Call options and put options – these are the two fundamental types of options. Call options give the trader the right to purchase the associated asset on or before the expiry date. Put options gives the trader the right to sell the asset attached to the contract at the strike price on or before the expiry date. These two types of options can further be divided into whether or not the seller owns the associated asset.

How a day trader options chooses to pursue an option position depends on its trading style, and how it performs technical analyzes, refers to price charts and other reference instruments. Trading strategies for the popular options include:

- Covered call strategy
- Credit spreads
- Debit spreads
- Iron condor
- Rolling out options
- Straddle strategy
- Strangle strategy

No matter what strategy or combination of strategies that an options day trader chooses to pursue, it all starts with:

- Practicing proper money management and risk management.
- Ensuring that risks and rewards are balanced.
- Having an effective trading strategy.
- Working with the right brokerage firm for you.
- Having realistic expectations.
- Growing your career over time with practical steps rather than big, moves that are not thought out.
- Ensuring that exits are automated.
- Doing your homework and doing pre-market preparation daily.
- Being flexible, patient, hard-working, and dedicated.

As an options day trader who has found massive success, I recommend this career to anyone who wants a challenge and a job that has no limits.

Don't take on this career out of greed. Love of options trading is necessary for success. You have to love performing trades. You have to love learning techniques and strategies. You have to love keeping abreast as to what is going on, in the financial markets and on the news globally. You have to love technical analysis and reading charts. You have to love applying the power principles. There is much to love about day trading options as long as you are in this for the right reasons.

I wrote this to reach out to the person who has an analytical mind, who has big dreams and is willing to put in the work to make those dreams come true. The knowledge imparted here is a great jump point for your new career. Don't stop here, learn more, read more, watch videos, listen to podcasts, find a mentor, and most importantly; do the work strategically to reap the rewards. Good luck!

Bonus Strategy (Credit Spreads)

Put Credit Spread Basic Setup

The idea of a put credit spread starts with a similar idea that we saw in the case of a debit spread. That is, we are going to be buying and selling two options simultaneously. They are both going to be the same type (in this case put options) and they are going to have the same expiration date. However, they are going to have different strike prices.

The difference between a credit and a debit spread is that this time we are looking to sell an option that has a higher strike price, and hence more valuable. In the case of a debit spread, the goal is to earn money from the stock price declining. In the case of a put credit spread, we are only hoping that the stock price remains above the higher strike price in our spread. We are not going to earn money from the price movement of the stock, this is an income-generating situation. So we don't really care what the stock does other than hoping that it is going to remain above the higher strike price of the two options. So although some people talk about this as being a "bull" credit spread, or a "bet" that the stock price is going to rise, it really isn't either of those things. If the stock price drops some, but it stays above our strike price, we are still going to make money. In fact, all we really care about is that it stays above the breakeven price.

The risk that is associated with a put credit spread is that the stock will drop by a large amount, that turns out to be big enough so that it drops below the upper strike price in the spread. We will look at the risks involved in detail below.

When NOT to sell a put credit spread

There are certain situations that you want to avoid selling a put credit spread. Under normal conditions, selling put credit spreads is a low-risk activity. However, if you are in a situation where the stock is moving by a large amount, with a lot of selloffs, then it is higher risk.

For that reason, you don't want to sell put credit spreads that are going to be active after some earnings call. As we noted on straddles and strangles, an earnings call is one of those times when stock can move by huge amounts. If the stock moves up by a large amount, your put credit spread would be unaffected. If the stock stays about the same or only moves by a small amount, your put credit spread would also be unaffected. But, if the earnings call was negative earnings call that really disappointed investor, the stock price may fall by large amounts — and put your higher strike price put in the money. With that in mind, you want to be conscious of when the earnings call dates are for the companies that you are investing in. And avoid selling put credit spreads during those weeks. Earnings calls are staggered, so when you are on the sidelines with one stock you can be investing in a different stock by selling put credit spreads.

There are other events that can cause your put credit spread to be at risk. A major downturn in the overall market can certainly do so. When the market starts dropping, most stocks are going with it (otherwise the market would not be dropping), and nobody really knows when the stock is going to bottom out. So if this is an ongoing process it might be better to wait on the sidelines or even switch to selling some call credit spreads, which we will discuss below.

However, even in bad markets selling put credit spreads can work. Many very successful traders earned good money continuing to sell put credit spreads (or naked puts as well) during the 2008 financial crisis. The problem with this is you have to be very smart about what you use for your strike prices. Most people will find it easier to switch to selling call credit spreads during these types of situations, including mere "corrections."

Often bad news is hard to predict. At the time of writing, there has been a parade of bad news (as far as the markets are concerned) in the form of what can be described as extrinsic events. That is, these are events that are outside the stock market itself. For example, Trump is involved in his trade war with China. That may or may not be a positive thing, but the markets aren't very happy about it and would like to see a deal worked out. So every time that Trump tweets about raising tariffs, the market goes through a major drop. That could put your positions at risk if you are selling put options. But again, choosing carefully can help avoid too much risk. Also, you can always get out of a position, something that we will be discussing.

CPSIA information can be obtained
at www.ICGtesting.com
Printed in the USA
LVHW080816120221
678844LV00051B/55